LAND OF THREE RIVERS

NEIL ASTLEY founded Bloodaxe Books in 1978, and was given a D.Litt by Newcastle University for his pioneering work. As well as *Staying Alive*, *Being Alive* and *Being Human* – and *Essential Poems from the Staying Alive Trilogy* – he has edited over 1000 poetry books, and has published over 20 other anthologies, including *Passionfood*, *Earth Shattering*, *The Hundred Years' War*, *Land of Three River*, *Soul Food* [with Pamela Robertson-Pearce]; the DVD-books *In Person: 30 Poets* and *In Person: World Poets* [filmed by Pamela Robertson-Pearce]; two poetry collections, *Darwin Survivor* and *Biting My Tongue*; and two novels, *The End of My Tether* (shortlisted for the Whitbread First Novel Award), and *The Sheep Who Changed the World*. He has lived in the North East since 1975, latterly in Northumberland's Tarset valley.

LAND OF
THREE RIVERS

THE POETRY OF
NORTH-EAST ENGLAND

EDITED BY
NEIL ASTLEY

WITH HISTORICAL NOTES BY
ALAN MYERS

BLOODAXE BOOKS

Introductory essays by Neil Astley copyright © 2017, Rodney Pybus
copyright © 1966, 2017 and Andy Croft copyright © 2010, 2017.
Historical notes by Alan Myers [AM] copyright © Zarina Parastaeva 2017.

Copyright of poems rests with authors and other rights holders
as cited in the publication acknowledgements on pages 518-22,
which constitute an extension of this copyright page.

ISBN: 978 1 78037 376 8

First published 2017 by
Bloodaxe Books Ltd,
Eastburn,
South Park,
Hexham,
Northumberland NE46 1BS.

www.bloodaxebooks.com
For further information about Bloodaxe titles
please visit our website or write to
the above address for a catalogue.

Supported by
ARTS COUNCIL
ENGLAND

LEGAL NOTICE

All rights reserved. No part of this book may be reproduced,
stored in a retrieval system, or transmitted in any form, or
by any means, electronic, mechanical, photocopying,
recording or otherwise, without prior written permission
from the copyright holders listed on pages 518-22.

Bloodaxe Books Ltd only controls publication rights to
poems from its own publications and does *not* control
rights to most of the poems published in this anthology.

Cover design: Neil Astley & Pamela Robertson-Pearce.

Printed in Great Britain by Bell & Bain Limited, Glasgow, Scotland, on
acid-free paper sourced from mills with FSC chain of custody certification.

CONTENTS

Vin Garbutt	14	John North
Neil Astley	15	Land of Three Rivers: 1
Rodney Pybus	18	The Poetry of North-East England (1966)
Andy Croft	30	Writing on Teesside: 1 (2010)
Neil Astley	33	Land of Three Rivers: 2
Basil Bunting	38	What the Chairman Told Tom
Andy Croft	40	Writing on Teesside: 2 (2010)

LAND OF THREE RIVERS

W.H. Auden	45	*from* New Year Letter
Lilian Bowes Lyon	47	The Glittering North
Mark Akenside	47	*from* The Pleasures of the Imagination
A.C. Swinburne	49	Northumberland
Basil Bunting	52	*from* Briggflatts
Fred Reed	62	Springan

HADRIAN'S WALL

W.H. Auden	64	Roman Wall Blues
Rudyard Kipling	65	The Roman Centurion's Song
Wilfrid Gibson	66	On Cawfields Crag
Wilfrid Gibson	67	Chesterholm
Wilfrid Gibson	67	The Watch on the Wall
Frances Horovitz	69	Poem found at Chester's Museum, Hadrian's Wall
Frances Horovitz	70	Rain – Birdoswald
Frances Horovitz	71	Vindolanda – January
Frances Horovitz	72	Brigomaglos, a Christian speaks…
Frances Horovitz	73	The Crooked Glen
Roger Garfitt	74	The Hooded Gods
Gareth Reeves	75	Stone Relief Housesteads
Esther Jansma	76	AD 128
Katrina Porteous	77	This Far and No Further
Alistair Elliot	89	After Heavenfield
Peter Armstrong	89	Between Greenhead and Sewingshields

JARROW

Bede	91	On Caedmon
U.A. Fanthorpe	93	Caedmon's Song
Norman Nicholson	94	Caedmon
Kathleen Raine	95	Northumbrian Sequence
Anne Stevenson	104	Jarrow

Carol Rumens	105	Jarrow
Alistair Elliot	106	Talking to Bede
W.N. Herbert	111	Bede's World
Jake Campbell	113	On Not Finding Bede
Tom Kelly	114	Monument
Tom Kelly	115	The Time Office, 1965
Tom Kelly	116	The Wrong Jarrow

BORDERERS

Traditional	117	The Battle of Otterbourne
Fleur Adcock	121	Hotspur
Peter Armstrong	127	Borderers
Pippa Little	128	*from* Foray: Border Reiver Women 1500-1600
	129	*The Cheviots*
	129	*Alicia Unthank's Ark*
	130	*The Robsons Gone*
	131	*Truce Day*
Linda France	132	The Spur in the Dish
Robyn Bolam	132	Raiding the Borders
Katrina Porteous	134	Borderers
Fred Reed	138	Northumborland (2)
A.C. Swinburne	138	A Reiver's Neck-Verse
A.C. Swinburne	139	A Jacobite's Exile (1764)

NORTH TO SOUTH NORTHUMBERLAND

Traditional	142	Old Border Rhyme
Wilfrid Gibson	142	The Cheviot
Traditional	143	Dunnie's Song
John Mackay Wilson	143	The Tweed Near Berwick
Katrina Porteous	145	*from* Tweed
Vincenza Holland	147	The Harbourmaster's Daughter
Anne Ryland	148	Midsummer Night, Berwick
Peter Bennet	149	Duddo Stones
Rodney Pybus	149	Routing Linn, Northumberland
Linda France	151	Acknowledged Land
Paul Summers	158	acknowledged land
Tony Harrison	159	Stately Home
Sir Walter Scott	159	*from* Marmion
Wilfrid Gibson	162	Lindisfarne
Katrina Porteous	163	Holy Island Arch
Matthew Hollis	164	Causeway
Cynthia Fuller	164	St Cuthbert on Inner Farne
Andrew Waterhouse	165	Making the Book

Katrina Porteous	167	A Short History of Bamburgh
Fred Reed	168	Bamburgh Wind
A.C. Swinburne	169	Grace Darling
Michael Longley	172	Grace Darling
Katrina Porteous	172	Charlie Douglas
Katrina Porteous	174	The Marks t' Gan By
Katrina Porteous	175	Stinky
Wilfrid Gibson	176	Dunstanborough
Katrina Porteous	177	*from* Dunstanburgh
Alistair Elliot	181	Deposition
Katrina Porteous	182	Alnmouth
Gillian Allnutt	184	At the Friary in Alnmouth
R.V. Bailey	184	Druridge Bay
Traditional	185	Felton Lonnen
Basil Bunting	185	The Complaint of the Morpethshire Farmer
Paul Batchelor	187	Butterwell
Fred Reed	188	The Pit Heap
Pippa Little	190	Seacoaling
Tony Harrison	191	The Earthen Lot
Traditional	192	The Blackleg Miner
James Henry	193	'Two hundred men and eighteen killed...'
Joseph Skipsey	195	The Hartley Calamity
Joseph Skipsey	198	The Collier Lad
Joseph Skipsey	200	Get Up!

NORTH TYNE, REDESDALE, COQUETDALE

Robert Roxby	202	*from* The Lay of the Reedwater Minstrel
Billy Bell	205	Winter on the Carter Fell
James Armstrong	207	Wild Hills O' Wannys
Tom Pickard	209	The Raw
Robert Hunter	212	Epitaph for Ned Allan
Fred Reed	212	Northumborland (1)
Basil Bunting	213	'Stones trip Coquetburn'
Colin Simms	214	*from* Hen Harrier Poems
Colin Simms	214	'There are, were, four couples south of Cheviot...'
Colin Simms	214	'Formerly on traditionally-managed haughland...'
Colin Simms	215	Katharine Macgregor – of The Sneep, Tarset
Colin Simms	215	'The cadence of a Strathspey, played slow...'
Peter Armstrong	216	Between Lord's Shaw and Pit Houses
Wilfrid Gibson	217	Sundaysight
Wilfrid Gibson	218	Hareshaw
Wilfrid Gibson	218	Hareshaw Linn
Peter Bennet	219	Hareshaw Linn

Billy Bell	220	An Old Shepherd's Adventure at Bellingham
Philip Larkin	223	Show Saturday
Peter Armstrong	226	Bellingham
James Armstrong	227	The Kielder Hunt
Christy Ducker	228	How Mackie Did the Drowning, Plashetts
Colin Simms	229	'Out, Northumberland, Out!'
Traditional	230	The Water of Tyne

TYNEDALE, SOUTH TYNE, NORTH PENNINES

Wilfrid Gibson	231	In Hexham Abbey
Wilfrid Gibson	232	The Abbey Tower
Wilfrid Gibson	233	Devilswater
Wilfrid Gibson	234	Mother and Maid
Terry Conway	235	Fareweel Regality
Wilfrid Gibson	236	Fallowfield Fell
Lauris Edmond	236	At Bywell
Lilian Bowes Lyon	237	Allendale Dog
W.H. Auden	238	Allendale
Lilian Bowes Lyon	239	A Rough Walk Home
W.H. Auden	241	The Old Lead-mine
W.H. Auden	242	Rookhope (Weardale, Summer 1922)
W.H. Auden	242	The Pumping Engine, Cashwell
W.H. Auden	242	The Engine House
W.H. Auden	243	Lead's the Best
W.H. Auden	245	The Watershed
Jon Silkin	247	Killhope Wheel, 1860, Co. Durham
Jon Silkin	248	Strike
Jon Silkin	249	Spade
Pru Kitching	250	Killhope
Pru Kitching	251	What's It Like Up There?
Dorothy Long	252	Road
Barry MacSweeney	253	No Buses to Damascus
Barry MacSweeney	253	Cushy Number
Colin Simms	254	High Fells, April 2011
Colin Simms	255	Where Rise Watters of Tyne, Tees, Wear

NEWCASTLE

John Cleveland	256	News from Newcastle
Tony Harrison	260	Newcastle Is Peru
Brendan Cleary	265	Newcastle Is Benidorm
Ellen Phethean	266	Bacchantes
Julia Darling	266	Newcastle Is Lesbos
W.N. Herbert	268	The Entry of Don Quixote into Newcastle upon Tyne

W.N. Herbert	270	Song of the Longboat Boys
John Cunningham	271	Newcastle Beer
Rodney Pybus	273	'Our Friends in the North'
George Charlton	275	A Return to Newcastle
Robyn Bolam	275	Hyem
Robyn Bolam	276	Moving On
Julia Darling	277	Satsumas
Julia Darling	278	A Short Manifesto to My City
Julia Darling	278	Old Jezzy
Anna Adams	279	The Wild Life on Newcastle Town Moor
Michael Roberts	280	Temperance Festival, Town Moor, Newcastle
W.H. Auden	281	*from* Twelve Songs
Richard Kell	281	Traditions
W.N. Herbert	284	The Hoppings
Tony Harrison	284	Divisions
Fred Reed	286	Brazen Faces
Kathleen Kenny	286	Grainger Market
John Challis	288	Gift of the Gab
Fleur Adcock	289	Street Song
Anonymous	290	A riddle on the steeple of St Nicholas's Cathedral, Newcastle
Peter Hebden	290	Thin Riddle
Joan Johnston	292	On Falling Up Dog Leap Stairs
Rodney Pybus	292	Salvaging
Rodney Pybus	294	The Side
Mark Knopfler	294	Down to the Waterline
Bernardette McAloon	295	Mistress of the Crown
Traditional	296	The Keel Row
Traditional	297	Do-li-a
Alan Hull	297	Fog on the Tyne
Jimmy Nail	298	Big River
James Kirkup	300	Tyneside, 1936
Rodney Pybus	301	Bridging Loans
Rodney Pybus	307	Passed By
Rodney Pybus	308	Down the Town
Robyn Bolam	309	Where Home Started
Tom Pickard	310	The Devil's Destroying Angel Exploded
Barry MacSweeney	312	I Looked Down on a Child Today
Kayo Chingonyi	314	Baltic Mill
Jen Campbell	314	Treading Water
Ellen Phethean	315	The West End
Stevie Ronnie	316	Rebuilding the West
Edward Chicken	317	*from* The Collier's Wedding

Gillian Allnutt	322	About Benwell
Gillian Allnutt	323	After the Blaydon Races
Geordie Ridley	324	The Blaydon Races
W.N. Herbert	325	The Blazing Grater, *or*, The Olympic Torch Passes Through Tyneside
Andy Croft	326	*from* Great North
Richard Kell	328	Cutty Sark Race, 1986
W.N. Herbert	330	Zamyatin in Heaton
Sean O'Brien	331	Fantasia on a Theme of James Wright

GATESHEAD

Thomas Wilson	332	*from* The Pitman's Pay
Joe Wilson	335	Maw Bonny Gyetside Lass
Tom Pickard	336	Gateshead
George Charlton	337	Gateshead Grammar
Mark Robinson	338	Angel of the North
Jen Campbell	339	The Angel
Jen Campbell	340	Angel Metal

NORTH TYNESIDE

Michael Roberts	341	H.M.S. *Hero*
James Kirkup	341	Tyne Ferry: Night
Francis Scarfe	342	Night Fishing
Francis Scarfe	343	Trawlers
William Watson	343	When the Boat Comes In
Sting	344	Island of Souls
A.C. Swinburne	346	The Tyneside Widow
Traditional	348	Bobby Shafto
William Lisle Bowles	349	Written at Tynemouth, Northumberland…
Wilfrid Gibson	349	The Coast-Watch
James Kirkup	350	Balloons in Sunrise
James Kirkup	351	The Harbour: Tynemouth
Michael Blackburn	352	The North Sea at Tynemouth
Helen Tookey	352	At Tynemouth
Peter Mortimer	353	View
Mike Wilkin	354	Cullercoats
Fred D'Aguiar	355	Whitley Bay Sonnets
U.A. Fanthorpe	359	Tyneside in Winter
R.V. Bailey	360	Whitley Bay
Mark Knopfler	361	Tunnel of Love

SOUTH SHIELDS

James Kirkup	363	The Town Where I Was Born
James Kirkup	364	View from the North East

Francis Scarfe	365	Miners
Francis Scarfe	366	Tyne Dock
Francis Scarfe	367	Tyne Dock Revisited
Francis Scarfe	368	In Memoriam
Francis Scarfe	369	The grotto
James Kirkup	370	Marsden Rock
Francis Scarfe	372	The Knocker-up
James Kirkup	372	The Knocker-up
James Kirkup	373	View from the Town Hall, South Shields
James Kirkup	374	Spring in the Public Gardens
James Kirkup	375	The Old Clothes Stall, South Shields Market
James Kirkup	376	South Shields Town Hall in Snow
James Kirkup	378	The Old Library, Ocean Road, South Shields
Jen Campbell	379	Cross-hatch

WEARSIDE

Traditional	380	The Lambton Worm
Lewis Carroll	382	The Walrus and the Carpenter
William Martin	386	His Bright Silver
William Martin	389	Song of the Cotia Lass
William Martin	391	Wiramutha Helix
William Martin	407	Song
James Kirkup	408	Penshaw Pastoral
Johnny Handle	409	Jack Crawford
Ron Knowles	411	Where in This Wind
Tom Pickard	411	Ship 1431
Tom Pickard	412	What Maks Makems
William Martin	414	A19 Hymn
Jake Campbell	418	A184 Hymn

DURHAM

Anonymous	419	Durham
Gillian Allnutt	420	Arvo Pärt in Concert, Durham Cathedral, November 1998
William Martin	422	Durham Beatitude
Tony Harrison	423	Durham
James Kirkup	425	Durham Seen from the Train
Katrina Porteous	426	Durham Cathedral
Mark Robinson	426	Durham Cathedral
S.J. Litherland	428	Durham in February
Heidi Williamson	428	River Wear, Durham
David Constantine	429	'But with a history of ECT'
David Constantine	430	The Pitman's Garden

CO. DURHAM

Traditional	431	Rap 'Er te Bank
Tommy Armstrong	432	The South Medomsley Strike
Tommy Armstrong	433	The Durham Lock-out
Wilfrid Gibson	435	The Ponies
John Seed	436	*from* Brandon Pithouse
Anne Stevenson	443	Forgotten of the Foot
Anne Stevenson	445	Salter's Gate
Dora Greenwell	446	To a Remembered Stream, and a Never-Forgotten Friend
Dora Greenwell	447	Lilies
J.C. Grant	449	A Camp in Chopwell Woods
James Kirkup	451	Chester-le-Street from the Train
James Kirkup	451	View of Ferryhill
Richard Dawson	451	The Ghost of a Tree
Peter Armstrong	453	A695 Hymn
Peter Armstrong	454	Among the Villages
Gillian Allnutt	454	The Singing Pylons
Cynthia Fuller	455	Esh Winning
Cynthia Fuller	456	Lost Landscape
Cynthia Fuller	457	Deerness Valley
J.S. Cunningham	458	North
George Charlton	460	Sea Coal
Bill Griffiths	461	The Box-Eggs
Bill Griffiths	463	The Strike
Anna Woodford	464	Two Up Two Down
Mark Robinson	465	Dalton Park/Murton
Jock Purdon	466	The Easington Explosion
Katrina Porteous	467	The Pigeon Men
Eddie Gibbons	468	Early Morning, West Hartlepool, 1963

TEESDALE

Sir Walter Scott	469	*from* Rokeby
Thomas Babington Macaulay	474	A Jacobite's Epigraph
Richard Watson	475	*from* My Journey to Work
W.H. Auden	479	The Engine House
Andrew Young	479	In Teesdale
Lindsay Balderson	480	High Force to Low Force
Anne Hine	481	Low Force
Pat Maycroft	481	Cockfield Fell in Winter
Pauline Plummer	482	Whorlton Lido
Anonymous	483	A Darlington rhyme

John Horsley	483	Darlington Fifty Years Ago
Marilyn Longstaff	485	Darlington
Gordon Hodgeon	486	North Tees Epiphany
Mark Robinson	487	Teesdale, Thornaby

MIDDLESBROUGH

Angus Macpherson	489	*from* Cleveland Thoughts; *or*, The Poetry of Toil
A.E. Tomlinson	492	Furnaces
Wilfrid Gibson	493	Cleveland Night
Wilfrid Gibson	494	Fire
Andy Croft	495	Sunlight and Heat
Andy Willoughby	500	The Cold Steel
Keith Porritt	500	Smelter
Maureen Almond	503	The Works
Mark Robinson	504	Dockside Road, South Bank
Mark Robinson	505	Teesport, Redcar
Jo Colley	506	Peg Powler
Bob Beagrie	506	Cook, The Bridge and the Big Man
Bob Beagrie	507	Occasion for Keeping Shtum
Angela Readman	508	Acklam Rainbow
Angela Readman	509	Easterside '59
Angela Readman	509	Easterside '89
Maureen Almond	510	Boro Babe
Jo Colley	511	Boro Girl

CLEVELAND

Andy Willoughby	512	*from* Between Stations
Pauline Plummer	513	On the Gare at Night
Andy Croft	514	Redcar Sands
Gordon Hodgeon	514	Potato Sellers – Cleveland
Pauline Plummer	515	Saltburn

FAREWELL

Sean O'Brien	516	*from* Never Can Say Goodbye
Traditional	517	Bonny at Morn

518	*Acknowledgements*
523	*Index of writers*
525	*Index of places*

NOTE ON TEXT:

The source cited at the end of a poem indicates where and when that poem was first published; the second entry indicates where it is currently or was most recently available. For full source information on work still in copyright, see Acknowledgements on pages 518-22.

John North
(lyrics)

Ah my name is John North from the South of the Forth,
In the Land of Three Rivers I dwell.
In the steelworks and pits I've worked with me mates,
Not a bad word against them I'll tell.
They're the best bunch of lads and I'll tell you for why,
If they thought it would help you they'd jump in the Tyne.

    CHORUS:
In the Land of Three Rivers
I'm longing to be,
Where the Tyne, Wear and Tees
Meet the North's rolling sea.

From Carlisle to Dover, from Bristol to Hull
And every town in between
I'm known in them all by my accent and gall
And friendship to pauper and queen.
I've got lots of friends, aye, but still not enough
I'm a means to their end when the going get rough.

In centuries gone our ancestral homes
Were prey to the Romans and Danes.
But Hadrian knew and Odin did too
The North East was no place for games.
They tried to enslave us but all efforts failed
While the strength of Saint Hilda and Aidan prevailed.

I work hard, I play hard, as hard as I toil
And I drink the best ale in the land.
My roots nestle deep in Northumbrian soil,
The branches akin outstretched hands.
When loneliness takes you and dampens your song
If you meet up with John North you'll not go far wrong.

CHORUS (TWICE)

VIN GARBUTT
Eston California, 1977

NEIL ASTLEY
Land of Three Rivers: 1

Land of Three Rivers is a celebration of North-East England in poetry, featuring its places and people, culture, history, language and stories in poems and songs with both rural and urban settings. Taking its bearings from the Tyne, Wear and Tees of the title (from Vin Garbutt's song 'John North'), the book maps the region in poems relating to past and present, depicting life from Roman times through medieval Northumbria and the industrial era of mining and shipbuilding up to the present day.

It is also the first historical anthology of the poetry of North-East England, starting in the 8th century with Caedmon, the first English poet, and continuing through the centuries to poets writing now. There are classic North-East songs from the oral tradition of balladeers, pitmen poets and rural chroniclers alongside the work of literary figures like Mark Akenside from the 18th century, followed by evocations of Northumberland by decadent gentry poet Algernon Charles Swinburne contrasting with grim tales of life down the pit by Tommy Armstrong and Joseph Skipsey in the 19th century.

The anthology also has modern perspectives on historical subjects, such as W.H. Auden's 'Roman Wall Blues' and Alistair Elliot on the aftermath of the Battle of Heavenfield in the 7th century. Poems written by poets such as Angus Macpherson and A.E. Tomlinson when the furnaces of Teesside were belching flames like volcanoes in the night sky in the late 19th and early 20th century are followed by evocations of today's post-industrial communities. Richard Watson gives a first-hand account of a lead miner's life in Teesdale in the mid-19th century. Less than 50 years later, the abandoned mines of neighbouring Weardale are gripping Auden's imagination, marking a seminal moment in his creative life.

For much of this historical background, I am greatly indebted to two past chroniclers, the late Alan Myers (1933–2010) and the poet Rodney Pybus. Born in South Shields, Alan moved south during the 1950s, becoming a distinguished scholar and translator of Russian poetry and prose, but kept returning to the North East over the years to research its largely unsung literary heritage. He published his wonderful *Myers' Literary Guide: The North East* with MidNAG/Carcanet Press in 1995, a compendium filled with fascinating accounts of the lives of the region's writers highlighting their connections to particular localities. After the book went out of print, Alan moved its entire contents to his Myersnorth website (published by the Centre for Northern Studies) and continued to expand and add to the entries. He also wrote an invaluable guidebook, *W.H. Auden: Pennine Poet*, with Robert Forsythe (North Pennines Heritage Trust, 1999), which includes much original research on the influence of the landscape and industrial remains of the North Pennines on the young Auden. Alan's account of how these experiences were to become a recurrent source of reference throughout the poet's life established this theme in the mainstream of Auden criticism; Robert Forsythe's research identified the exact locations featured in many of Auden's poems, some of which Auden scholars had thought to be fictional or had placed elsewhere.

It seemed a great shame to me that with Alan's passing, this unique resource built up by him over many years was no longer available to readers, once his website had also expired. I am enormously grateful to his niece, Zarina Parastaeva, for allowing me to draw upon all of Alan's pen portraits of poets in this anthology. These are identified with his initials; where his notes have been updated or expanded, this is also indicated.

I didn't think it necessary to have notes on the numerous contemporary poets included in the book, except where significant details relating to places or history needed to be glossed. Most are poets either from the North East or who live here now. There are also some poets who lived in the region for a number of years, such as Fleur Adcock, David Constantine, Fred D'Aguiar, U.A. Fanthorpe, Roger Garfitt, Frances Horovitz and Carol Rumens, as well as frequent visitors like Philip Larkin and Michael Longley. I've only included work by poets who've written highly memorable poems in response to the place, its people and history, and so was unable to represent other excellent poets who've not written work relating directly to the North East, notably Richard Caddel (1949-2003), a key figure whose meditations on the minutiae of the natural world could (and often did) relate to other places where he'd lived.

I've tried to show the continuity of the North East's oral tradition from earlier centuries by including some later folksongs along with classic modern songs by Alan Hull, Mark Knopfler, Jimmy Nail and Sting. The second British folk revival achieved prominence in the North East around the same time as the modernist-inspired 'British Poetry Revival', with the High Level Ranters being formed in 1964, the same year as the founding of Morden Tower readings, and there has long been a crossover between poets and musicians in the region involving many collaborations, including individual artists working together (e.g. poet Katrina Porteous with musicians Alistair Anderson and Chris Ormston) as well as funded commissions supported by Folkworks, BBC Radio, Newcastle Poetry Festival and other organisations. This anthology is being launched by Magnetic North East (see note below), and I am especially grateful to Kathryn Tickell for her encouragement and support. Kathryn was aware that I had been wanting to produce this book for many, many years, but other projects kept taking precedence. Her generous offer of a Magnetic North East launch for the book at Sage Gateshead has helped to make it happen.

I am also most grateful for help of various kinds (including recommendations of poems and songs) from Linda Anderson, Rosie Bailey, Bob Beagrie, Liz Conway, Andy Croft, Dorothy Fleet, Michael Fraser, Catrin Galt, Dorothy Fleet, Judy Greenway, Marilyn Longstaff and Vane Women, Rodney Pybus, Prof. Andrew D. Roberts, Mark Robinson, Bruno Scarfe, Mike Tickell, Sheila Wakefield and Andy Willoughby; to all the writers who have agreed to the inclusion of their work; and to the late Vin Garbutt for his song 'John North', aka 'Land of Three Rivers' (which he had looked forward to singing at the book's launch).

The historical introduction by Rodney Pybus which follows this preface reprints most of an essay published in *Stand* magazine in 1966. This is followed by an excerpt from an essay by Andy Croft on the history of writing from Teesside, and by a second introduction in which I've attempted to give a summary of developments in poetry in the North East in the fifty years since Pybus's survey, with additional input from Andy Croft on what's been happening on Teesside.

MAGNETIC NORTH EAST

Magnetic North East is a Community Interest Company set up in 2015 by Northumbrian pipers Kathryn Tickell and Andrew Davison to promote, support and develop the music, arts and culture of the North East of England and its borders (the area covered by the ancient kingdom of Northumbria). It includes an entertainment agency, record label, webshop, a commissioning service and also runs events, training courses and traditional music tuition as well as its own youth folk ensemble Superfolkus.

Magnetic North East is part of a community which takes great pride and pleasure in the cultural and natural heritage of the region: its arts, culture, heritage, places and people; its long history of creativity; its strong sense of identity coupled with its adaptability and receptiveness to change. MNE aims to help maintain and develop an energised and vibrant community, where increasing numbers of people enjoy, experience and share the unique culture of the North East of England.

www.magneticnortheast.com

RODNEY PYBUS

The Poetry of North-East England (1966)

Given that there are more important writers in or from the North East than there ever have been before, why is it that the region appears to have an atmosphere and climate traditionally antipathetic to literature? Looked at from a historical and social point of view, the main reasons for this comparatively thin vein of literary talent are not too difficult to establish: there is simply no tradition of written, as opposed to oral literature in the region.

The North East until very recently has tended to isolate itself from other parts of the country with a dialect which is near-impenetrable to the outsider. With few exceptions, the energies of the people of the North East have been consumed in making a living from the land, or from coal-mining and the industries that came with it (even in the 19th century the region's writers were more concerned with trying to improve social and educational conditions, than writing novels or poetry).[1] There has never been in the North East any tradition of vernacular, written literature as there has been in, for instance, southern Scotland more or less from the time of Barbour's *Bruce* at the end of the 14th century.

The dialect of the North East is not merely a convenient geographical division – it is also social and occupational, like the mining terms in Fred Reed's poem 'Springan' [62-63]. Because the region has tended to be isolated geographically and historically, the dialect became almost a separate language from the mainstream of standard English. Because of that isolation, the degree of linguistic change evident in the rest of the country from, say, the 11th century onwards was much less in the North East. While it is true that up to about Chaucer's time English writers tended to use the dialect of their own region quite naturally, the North East did not keep pace in adopting what was broadly the dialect of the East Midlands (Oxford, Cambridge and the Court) as the standard form of English: from the glossary to 'Springan' it is clear how many dialect words in the North East have altered little since the periods of Old and Middle English. It is interesting, however, in view of the much-publicised cultural imbalance between the North and the South today, to remember that up to the 11th century Northumbrian was one of the four main English dialects; and that the late 7th century to early 9th century was the great period of Northumbrian civilisation and history, when the region could fairly have claimed to be the most cultured part of the country. The Venerable Bede, Cuthbert, Caedmon, and the

Lindisfarne Gospels, for example, all fall into this period.[2]

But with the invasions from Scandinavia there followed 500 years of almost total silence (though Duns Scotus seems to have lived in Newcastle as a young man). The Old English Northumbrian dialect broadly subdivided into Scots and North-Eastern, and an increasing number of Scandinavian words appeared. In the late 13th century there was a Northumbrian dialect version of the Psalms.[3] There is even a 12th-century poem about Durham City in a classical, rhetorical metre [419-20], but very little else. John of Trevisa, the 14th-century Cornishman, commented on the differing dialects of his time, and pointed out that people in the Midlands had the advantage of knowing a bit of most dialects (a further reason why it became the basis of standard English).

For the dialect of the North was already a subject of comment in 1387: 'All the language of the Northumbrians, and especially at York, is so sharp, slitting and frotting, and unshape, that we southern men may that language unnethe [*hardly*] understand.' (This may well be a translation by Trevisa of a quotation from William of Malmesbury's *Gesta Pontificum*, written about 1125, in which case it is even more remarkable.)[4] And Chaucer, almost certainly with humorous intent, has his two clerks John and Aleyn in *The Reeve's Tale* talk in a northern dialect. The North East at this time was barbarous, under-populated, and a backward region even by the standards of the 14th century – the Newcastle Mystery Play Cycle (of which only a Noah's Ark text survives) is one of the few cracks in the darkness. Minstrel poetry, however, had a longer life in the North East than elsewhere (though wandering minstrels were banned in 1597 by Elizabeth I as no better than 'rogues, vagabonds, and sturdy beggars'). Percy, in his *Reliques of Ancient English Poetry* (first published in 1765), says that most of the minstrels of the 15th and 16th century belonged to the North, and mentions that Giraldus Cambrensis in Henry II's time commented on the 'propensity' north of the Humber for 'symphonious harmony'. Typical of Percy's ancient ballads are 'Chevy Chase' and 'The Battle of Otterbourne' [117], both of them probably written in the 16th century, but referring to the 14th century.

But up to the 18th century the North East (which until then had been a kind of bloody no-man's-land between England and Scotland) produced virtually no writers of any significance. In the 16th century Northumberland was still virtually impenetrable to carriages,[5] and there were reputedly only 21 schoolmasters in the whole county, 11 of whom were in Newcastle, which then had a population of about 10,000. Alone in the 17th century appears the

Puritan pamphleteer John Lilburne (1615–77). The son of a Co. Durham squire, he became leader of the Levellers, a radical reform group with a strong streak of Calvinism. In the 1640s Lilburne was a serious rival to Cromwell as a popular leader. He seems to have led his stormy political career in the South, however, and it is difficult to say whether his background had any direct effect on, say, his campaigns for fairer distribution of Parliamentary seats or the protection of the rights of the people; except that he was extremely proud of being the son of a 'gentleman' rather than a 'yeoman' – he even had the wording of an indictment against him changed to this effect.

In the 18th century there are signs of life, not all of it civilised. John Wesley visited Newcastle in 1742 and was highly shocked by it: '... so much drunkenness, cursing and swearing (even from the mouths of little children) do I never remember to have seen and heard before, in so small a compass of time...' He preached to a large audience near Sandgate, and afterwards observed 'the people when I had done to stand gaping and staring upon me, with the most profound astonishment...' Some of his audience, however, were not quite so astonished: they assured him that they were 'members of a religious society, which had subsisted for many years... They likewise informed me what a fine library they had, and that the Steward read a sermon every Sunday...'[6] He was there again in 1745 when the city was preparing its defences against the Pretender: '...Those within the walls were almost equally busy in carrying away their money and goods; and more and more of the gentry every hour rode southward as fast as they could...'[7] Dr Johnson in Scotland in 1773 produced one of his innumerable snide remarks about the country, and added '(you go) then to Newcastle, to be polished by colliers...' Certainly the industrial and social character of the North East had been firmly moulded by coal-mining by the middle of the 18th century, though it is interesting, in view of the career of the poet Mark Akenside, that Newcastle should have had a highly organised medical profession by the same time. Shipbuilding, iron-, rope-, and glass-works grew up in the second half of the century, followed in the 19th century by the proliferation of engineering and chemical trades.[8]

Mark Akenside (1721–70) [47-48] was a very important figure of his time, however minor he may seem today. He was born in Newcastle, the son of a prosperous butcher, but apparently became ashamed of his background (the fact that he nearly cut his foot off as a child with a cleaver may have had something to do with this...) He had some verse published in the *Gentleman's Magazine*, in the style of Spenser, as early as 1737. The magazine's principal contributor, Dr Johnson, joined it in 1738, the year Akenside went to Edinburgh to study divinity, which he quickly abandoned in favour of medicine. In 1743 he completed what was to remain his major work, *The Pleasures of the Imagination* [47-48]. This brought him fame among his contemporaries, and praise from Pope. He spent little time in Newcastle after he finished his studies, and in 1748 he settled in London, where he eventually became the Queen's Physician. He was a dour man who did not make friends easily – he was caricatured as 'the Doctor' in Smollett's *Peregrine Pickle*.

His 'Hymn to the Naiads' was considered, up to the time of Keats' 'Hyperion' and 'Endymion', to be one of the best attempts of that period to reproduce the classical spirit. But *The Pleasures of the Imagination* undoubtedly holds the best of Akenside. Discounting the fact that he wrote it in his early 20s, it is still an interesting and partially successful attempt at a didactic poem expressing Plato's philosophy in blank verse, though the blend of philosophy and rhetoric does tend to coagulate into obscurity. It incidentally included an early expression of the idea that 'beauty is in the eye of the beholder':

> Mind, mind alone (bear witness earth and heaven!)
> The living fountains in itself contains
> Of beauteous and sublime...'

His verse is densely packed with classical allusions, the language and style is highly mannered. It seems that only in his very rare references to his native background does a, for him, surprising vigour come into his verse.

But these are isolated references in the work of a man who appears to have mentally suppressed his regional identity almost entirely in favour of a more conventional 18th-century outlook. Dr Johnson made some typically pertinent comments on Akenside in his 'Life': of *The Pleasures of the Imagination*, he said, '...To his versification justice requires that praise should not be denied. In the general fabrication of his lines he is perhaps superior to any other writer of blank verse... but the concatenation of his verses is commonly too long continued, and the full close does not recur with sufficient frequency. The sense is carried on through a long intertexture of complicated clauses, and as nothing is distinguished, nothing is remembered... His diction is certainly poetical as it is not prosaick, and elegant as it is not vulgar...' He then dismisses the odes and lyrics with 'short consideration', and concludes, '... for to what use can the work be criticised that will not be read?' Dr Johnson was harsh, but proved to be accurate.

The 'mad poet' Christopher Smart (1722–71) may or may not have been actually born in Co. Durham, but he did attend Durham

School as a boy; though it seems to have made even less impression on his work than Akenside's Newcastle and Northumberland.

During the same period a very minor poet of his time, John Cunningham (1729–73) [272], spent half his life in Newcastle. He was a Dublin-born actor who played the North of England, and probably his only slender claim to fame now is that he was portrayed by the engraver Thomas Bewick. He was a dull, uninspired pastoral poet – the only poem that comes to life, invigorated by a genuine feel for its subject, is his eulogy 'Newcastle Beer' [271] (the North-East tradition of strong ale appears to be nearly as old as the history of coal-mining in the area). Despite a reference to Edward Chicken's 'The Collier's Wedding' [317] by the 19th-century Gateshead poet Thomas Wilson [334], little dialect literature seems to have been *written* in the region in the 18th century. Nothing, at any rate, like the work of the Cumberland schoolmaster Josiah Relph (1712–43)[9] whose pastoral verse was strongly vernacular, and full not only of deliberate archaisms like 'ondergang' for 'undergo', but of dialect expressions like 'sweels of laughter'.

Though Thomas Bewick (1753–1828) is not strictly relevant here, his importance to the cultural life of the region is undeniable. His perception of natural life, in his different medium, was in some ways keener than Gilbert White's, and his memoir gives the feel of town and country life at the end of the 18th century with vivid immediacy. Born on Tyneside, he tried London but couldn't endure it: he spent most of his time talking with Novocastrians and reading the Newcastle newspapers in the 'Hole-in-the-Wall' in Fleet Street. It's worth noting that the first edition of Bewick's famous *Quadrupeds* was elegantly published in Newcastle, not London. Later in life he did illustrations for the poems of Thomson and Burns, but nothing after his *Birds* of 1804 was as successful artistically.

Though the social and industrial conditions in the North East at the beginning of the 19th century were incredibly horrifying in their viciousness and squalor, there was a fast-growing middle class with pretensions to culture and a civilised way of life. Newcastle aped the fashions of London and the Continent,[10] and the foundation of the Literary and Philosophical Society in Newcastle in 1793 is evidence of educated interests. An important but neglected figure is James Losh (1763–1833), a Carlisle barrister who was based in Newcastle for 35 years. He was a close friend of Wordsworth, who linked him with Coleridge and Lamb in bemoaning the loss of three close friends within a year.[11] He was 'editor of the *Areopagitica*, dedicated and fearless campaigner for Parliamentary reform, leader in all humanitarian movements for the northern counties'.[12] But his talents were social and practical rather than literary, and with two important exceptions, the North East's contributions to literature in the 19th century are almost as sparse as in preceding periods.

There was certainly a strong oral tradition of folk ballads and street-songs (which survive even today), the majority either rural-historical or intimately connected with mining; and a great deal more prose and verse were written and published than previously. But from a literary point of view, the quality remained significantly mundane: vigour and artistic skill seemed to be the prerogative of the oral-dialect tradition.

Fairly typical printed productions seemed to have been similar to *The Northern Minstrel: or, Gateshead Songster* published in Gateshead in 1806. This collection of approved 'modern songs' certainly scored for quantity. Nor was it a rare item: the editor-publisher apologised – 'Publications of a kind similar to this are already so numerous, some apology may perhaps be expected for increasing their number...' Many of the items were pro-Scots, like 'Donald MacDonald', or fervently patriotic, like 'Brave Admiral Nelson', 'Bonaparte's Character', or 'The Heroes of Britain'. The outstanding item in the collection is 'Donocht-Head' by George Pickering of Newcastle. The idiom is distinctly Burnsian – the last verse is

> 'Nae hame have I, the minstrel said,
>   'Sad party-strife o'erturned my ha';
> 'And, weeping at the eve of life,
>   'I wander thro' a wreath o' snow.'

It might well have been inspired by the poetry of Burns, for the latter recommended Pickering's poem, and said in a letter to his friend Thompson in October 1794: '"Donocht-Head" is not mine – I would give ten pounds it were. It appeared first in the *Edinburgh Herald*, and came to the editor of that paper with the Newcastle post mark on it.' And Dr James Currie considered it was 'worthy of Burns or Macneill'. It was certainly much superior to other work by Pickering in the vein of 'Sweet Anna', which begins

> Sweet Anna to the sea-beach came,
> And softly sigh'd her Edwin's name;
> And as the lab'ring surges rose,
> The pensive maiden sung her woes...

Another production of that period was 'The Lay of the Reedwater Minstrel' by 'A Son of Reed' [Robert Roxby, 205], published in Newcastle in 1809. There is very little dialect in this long survey in verse of the history and place-names of Northumberland, and its interest must have been largely restricted to the Newcastle Topographical Society. Robert White, a Scotsman who came to live in Newcastle in 1825, wrote a great deal of eminently forgettable verse: *Three Poems* ('The Tynemouth Nun', 'The Wind' and 'England'; Newcastle, 1858), and *Poems, including Tales, Ballads, and Songs* (Kelso, 1867) all reveal an educated sensibility but little or no poetic skill and imagination. He appears to have been quite a prominent citizen of mid-19th century Newcastle, but this comment from his introduction to *Three Poems* may not wholly be due to arrogance on his part: 'Of "The Wind", both the subject and treatment are essentially poetical, and as few possess the power of judging accurately on this species of composition, the poem can only engage the attention of a limited number of readers...'

One wonders whether he knew the work of one of the two main exceptions to the generally dull level of literary writing in the North East at that time – the poetry of Thomas Wilson (1773–1858), whose classic *The Pitman's Pay* [332] was published in Gateshead in 1826-30. Wilson; had been in the mines as a youngster but managed to leave, acquire an education, and eventually became an alderman, spending his life trying to improve social conditions.

Wilson regarded the 1840s as an enlightened age – as it was, relative to the 18th century – as far as the conditions of the miners were concerned. Referring to the 'bad old days' of the 18th century, he mentions that the miners, particularly those on Wearside, were in the habit of striking: '... a practice that would not be even thought of in the present day.'! He argued that the establishment of Sunday Schools in the early 19th century, the increase in cheap publications, and the introduction of Savings Banks all combined to raise the level of existence of the miners and their families. He was extremely sympathetic towards the miners, having been one himself, but not wholly accurate. There *were* strikes in his time, and the conditions that existed made them virtually inevitable. In *A Voice from the Coal Mines* (a pamphlet published by the Northumberland miners in 1825) it was said, for instance, that some miners were granted an extra 6d. a day for working in temperatures of up to 130 degrees. Up to 1815 inquests were not held after men had been killed in mining accidents in Northumberland and Durham, where the miners had become almost indifferent to danger. The practice of putting women and girls down the pits still existed when Wilson was a boy, and in the early 19th century boys' hours were 18 to 20.[13] In viciously undermanning boats, the shipowners were no better than the mine-owners: troops were brought in in 1815 to break up a seamen's strike in the North East.

Wilson's *The Pitman's Pay* is a long poem which first appeared between 1826 and 1830. In it he tries to paint a faithful picture of the lives of miners at the end of the 18th century. Most of it is in dialect, put in quotation into the mouths of his miner characters: every line sings its authenticity, and the rich vitality of the language, and the use of the dialect by an obviously educated man, are extraordinarily successful:

> The crowdy is wor daily dish,
> But varry different is their Minny's;
> For she gets a' her heart can wish,
> In strang-lyeced tea and singin' hinnies.
> [...]
>
> Maw canny bairns luik pale and wan,
> Their bits and brats are varry scant:
> The mother's feasts rob them o' scran,
> For wilfu' wyest myeks woefu' want.

His eye for the telling details, however repulsive, is deadly accurate:

> She peels the taties wiv her teeth,
> And spreads the butter wiv her thoom:
> She blaws the kyel wi' stinkin' breath,
> Where mawks and caterpillars soom!

Wilson himself, when not speaking through the mouth of one of his miners, is more immediately comprehensible but less effective:

> The remnant left's a motley crew –
> The din they make a perfect Babel –
> Contending who the most can hew,
> With thump for thump upon the table...

He wrote a large number of other very successful dialect poems, like 'On the Intended New Line of Road from Potticar Lane to Leyburn Hole', and another classic of the genre, 'The Oiling of Dicky's Wig': this remarkably comprehensive study of the best pubs in Gateshead memorably ends with

> Here DICKY'S tongue wad de ne mair,
> His *wig* was oiled completely;
> And iv'ry *drouthy* crony there
> Was dished and duin up neatly.'

crowdy: oatmeal mixed with hot water; *strang-lyeced tea:* tea with 'grog' in it; *singin' hinnies:* currant griddle cakes or scones; *bits and brats:* food and clothes; *scran:* food; *kyel:* coal; *mawks:* maggots; *soom:* swim; *drouthy:* thirsty.

The remainder of Wilson's poetic output were mainly folksy, pseudo-philosophical verses, like 'The Happy Home', which were apparently popular when they were written but now seem as forgettable as last year's Christmas card jingles. The fact that he appears to have little or no recognition outside the North East is, I would suggest, a loss to the rest of the country – though here again his very successful use of the local dialect, which gives his verse most of its passion and emotive power, would only serve to isolate him further from his potential public: even the Gateshead edition of his poems has a very extensive glossary of dialect words and phrases for the benefit of a presumably local audience. Nevertheless, much of Wilson's work is regional literature in the best sense, drawing its vitality from North-East life and traditions, and, once the dialect has been penetrated, by no means restricted by geographical, historical or social limitations.

The second exception to the uninspired level of literature in the region in the 19th century is the work of a self-educated miner, Joseph Skipsey (1832–1903) [201]. He was the youngest of eight children; his father was shot by a special constable in a mine strike, and at the age of seven he was working shifts of up to 14 hours in the pits. Few poets of any importance can have started their lives with disadvantages so abysmal. He nevertheless educated himself to a point where he could read freely in English literature, and even translations of Goethe and Heine. He produced several volumes of poetry during the second half of the 19th century, including *Poems* (published in 1871 – in Blyth!) and *Carols of the Coal-fields* (1886). He was much admired by Rossetti and Burne-Jones, and there are signs of Rossetti's influence right from the start of what he thought was one of Skipsey's best poems, 'Bereaved':

> One day as I came down by Jarrow
>   Engirt by a crowd on a stone
> A woman sat moaning, and sorrow
>   Seized all who gave heed to her moan.
>
> 'Nay, blame not my sad lamentation,
>   But, oh let,' she said, 'my tears flow,
> Nay offer me no consolation –
>   I know they are dead down below.'

I would agree entirely with Ifor Evans[14] that '…it is remarkable verse for a miner entirely self-educated to have written, but it is not remarkable, absolutely, as poetry'. This applies, too, to poems like 'The Hartley Calamity' (about a big mining disaster during his own lifetime) [195], and the pieces of fancy like 'The Violet and the Rose'. But I cannot agree with Evans when he argues that Skipsey's 'masterly use...of simple vocabulary and syntax for the suggestion of deep emotion' in 'Mother Wept' is 'reminiscent of Blake'. If this is a qualitative judgement, I think it is certainly arguable. Skipsey was severely limited, as well as nourished, by his background, for when he was away from the mining milieu – as, for instance, when he held the curatorship of Shakespeare's house at Stratford – he shut himself off from 'the centres of suggestion which made his poetry possible' (Evans). But whether or not, in the last analysis, one makes allowances for Skipsey's environmental disadvantages, he remains a minor poet with a distinctive place in the late 19th century.

There are a few other more significant writers with more tenuous links with the North East: Algernon Charles Swinburne [50-52], for instance, spent some of his childhood at Capheaton in the Tyne Valley, where his French grandfather lived; Lewis Carroll (Charles Lutwidge Dodgson) [385] spent part of his childhood at Croft-on-Tees near Darlington, returning there on family visits in later years; Elizabeth Barrett Browning was born at Coxhoe Hall, Co. Durham, but was taken south while very young. Wilfrid Gibson (1878-1962) [232-33], the prolific Hexham-born poet, figured in Georgian poetry circles earlier this century. He moved to London in 1912 and achieved wide recognition as a poet of the First World War but never actually served abroad. He remains a minor poet despite the production of more than 20 volumes of verse.

At the end of the 19th century there must have been a much larger and more appreciative audience for literature in the North East, due to the general rise in social and educational conditions. Newcastle was certainly no cultural desert at that time, if one can judge from visiting guests who addressed the Tyneside Sunday Lecture Society in the 1880s and 90s: among them Oscar Wilde, William Morris, Kropotkin, Stanley, Edmund Gosse, Conan Doyle and Keir Hardie (though it is evident from these names that there was a strong emphasis on social and political subjects).

Now, nearly a century later, it seems at last that the worst effects of the hangover of the Industrial Revolution are beginning to recede. And it may be that a country, or a region, needs a period of recuperation in which to settle down and re-establish its priorities, after a period of intense industrial and social development. In the North East, for instance, it is possible that the second half of the 19th century and the early part of the 20th century formed just such a period of establishment, after the pressurised development of the previous hundred years. (We are, of course, still too close to this period to do more than speculate.) As I have pointed out, much of the writing, and much of the interest in writing, in the North East in the 19th century was directed, on a practical level, at improving social conditions, and in a more general way, in politics and social affairs – men like Losh and Wilson show the beginning of this trend. A broad parallel may be drawn with countries which have experienced Communist-Marxist revolutions in the past 50 years: after the revolutions most of the traditional bourgeois art, of whatever standard, has been suppressed, and literary talents forced into the service of didacticism and social expediency. Only when the country has settled down and to some extent acclimatised itself to its new structure, have the arts started to flourish more freely: what chance would Yevtushenko and Voznesensky have had in the Russia of 30 years ago? The difference between these two patterns is not so much that in Eastern Europe the process has been largely involuntary on the part of the writers, but that where the pressures have been social and economic rather than directly political the process of re-adjustment seems to take much longer, as in the North East.

But I would suggest that this period of acclimatisation in the North East has now more or less passed: the poets Gibson, Basil Bunting [60-61] and Francis Scarfe [367], and novelists Sid Chaplin, Herbert Sutherland and Catherine Cookson, among others of the older generation have shown over the last 30 years that from a variety of backgrounds and in spite of antithetical social pressures it is possible for the North East to produce writers of importance. What is more concerning is the apparent failure of the following generation to consolidate this advance, despite the achievement of writers like James Kirkup [371] and playwright Ann Jellicoe. I am not arguing that we should necessarily expect some kind of literary arithmetic progression from generation to generation. But there are apparently very few promising writers under 40 in the region, a generalisation seemingly confirmed by the results of *Stand*'s survey – and this at a time of more widespread education than ever before, and a range of cultural facilities scarcely dreamed of 20 years ago.

The traditional antipathy towards literature seems to be waning (though library and bookshop facilities are still half a century behind the times), and one can only hope that henceforth the region will be able to produce writers, in terms of quality and quantity, on a par with its musicians and visual artists. Dialect as a living medium for verse or prose is less likely to play any part in regionally produced literature for the very reasons that have made the North East less isolated than it used to be: wider and quicker travel, more education, more vigorous mass media, and more money. It could well be, however, that some of today's writers still feel hampered by the lack of strong literary traditions in the region. I do not pretend that I have managed to include in this article every single writer who has contributed to such traditions as do exist; but I hope I have established the general lines of the development of literature in what was once 'the backyard of England', and the conditions which have militated against it for a thousand years.

1. In this respect I think it's significant that the North East has had a high reputation for a long time as a breeding-ground for journalists.
2. And possibly the Anglo-Saxon poet Cynewulf – *if* he was Northumbrian.
3. G.L. Brook, *English Dialects* (1963).
4. *Cambridge History of English Literature*, vol. i.
5. Tomlinson, *History of Northumberland*.
6. *The Rev. John Wesley's Journal*, Everyman, vol. I, pp. 374-5.
7. *ibid*, p. 525.
8. Edward Hughes, *North Country Life in the 18th Century*, vol. I.
9. Raynor Unwin, *The Rural Muse* (1954).
10. Edward Hughes, *op. cit.*
11. Paul Kaufman, 'Wordsworth's Candid and Enlightened Friend', *Notes & Queries*, 207 (1962), pp. 403-8.
12. *ibid*.
13. J.L. Hammond and Barbara Hammond, *The Town Labourer, 1760-1832* (1917).
14. Ifor Evans, *English Poetry in the Late 19th Century* (1933), pp. 322-25.

A longer version of Rodney Pybus's essay, published in *Stand* in 1966 (Vol. 8 No. 2), also covered fiction writers and an initiative to attract new regional writers to submit work to the magazine. However, his historical survey did not include writing from Teesside, covered in this anthology with two extracts from an essay by Andy Croft.

ANDY CROFT

Writing on Teesside: 1 (2010)[1]

Most of Teesside's most famous writers have not written about Teesside; only Pat Barker, Jane Gardam and Mark Adlard may be said to have made the area their subject. Writing this kind of literary history might be interesting as a narrative of exile, part of a larger story in which – traditionally – becoming a writer meant leaving home and the loyalties of landscape and social identity. But it would be largely the story of a cultural absence, a way of saying that Teesside has had no native literary history.[2]

In these circumstances, it is hard to write about the area without being defensive. And it's even harder to write a history of writing about Teesside without deferring to pre-existing definitions of the area in the national imagination. This essay is therefore a sketch towards an internal, local literary history, a look at three moments when writers living and working on Teesside have sought to negotiate the oppositions of the local and the national, of historical experience and imagined futures.

The first was in the second half of the 19th century, when a group of poets, journalists, anthologists and publishers emerged in what was then South Durham and the North Riding – principally Thomas Cleaver, William Hall Burnett, Henry Heavisides, Angus Macpherson [492], James Milligan, Elizabeth Tweddell ('Florence Cleveland'), George Tweddell, Tom White and John Wright. Connected by geography, friendship, patronage and sometimes marriage, they spoke for and to the new industrial conurbations on the banks of the Tees; William Hall Burnett was editor of Middlesbrough's first daily newspaper, George Tweddell edited a weekly newspaper in Stokesley.

Tweddell was also the author of *The Bards and Authors of Cleveland and South Durham* (1872), an introduction to the work of almost 40 writers associated with the region, from Caedmon and Gower[3] to the late 19th-century poets of industrial Teesside:

> My object in the present volume is to bring under the notice of the people of Cleveland and South Durham, the Bards and other authors, who by birth or residence, have been connected with the district... I have long cherished the idea of a work similar to Chambers's excellent *Cyclopaedia of English Literature*, to be confined to the Poets and Prose Writers of the North of England... Every intelligent man and woman will desire to possess some knowledge of the writers which their own part of the country has produced: and in Authors neither South Durham nor Cleveland has been barren, – as the following pages will show...

It was a bold attempt to assert an alternative, even rival cultural narrative to the English literary canon then emerging in the new universities. At one stage Tweddell was planning a two-volume sequel which was to include another hundred writers. 'I could,' he wrote, echoing Leigh Hunt, 'name a local writer for every tick of my watch.' It was also a politically radical project. Tweddell, for example (who often wrote under the pseudonym 'Peter Proletarius') was a Chartist, a supporter of the Cleveland Ironstone miners' union, author of *The People's History of Cleveland* (1872) and a friend of the radical Sheffield poet, Ebenezer Elliot. Above all, these writers employed poetry to interrogate the Victorian narratives of empire, science, commerce, industry and progress, and to negotiate a place for Teesside within them. When Gladstone compared Middlesbrough to an 'infant Hercules', he was drawing on the language and iconography of heavy industry already established by the region's poets, as is clear from Angus Macpherson's 'Cleveland Thoughts, or The Poetry of Toil' [489].

The second moment was in the late 1930s and 1940s, when Ormesby Hall – the home of Ruth Pennyman, a poet and playwright sometimes known as the Red Duchess – became the meeting place for a remarkable group of amateur and professional artists and writers. Michael Tippett wrote his first opera, *Robin Hood* (with a radical libretto by Ruth Pennyman) while staying at Ormesby Hall. It was performed by unemployed Ironstone miners in Boosbeck. Ruth Pennyman wrote plays for local WI drama groups and staged performances of Shakespeare plays at Ormesby Hall in which working-class amateurs appeared with professionals like Mary Casson and Martin Brown. In 1937, one of her plays, *Happy Families*, was performed in venues across Teesside to raise money for Quaker Relief in Spain. (During the Spanish Civil War, the Pennymans arranged for Basque refugee children to stay at nearby Hutton Hall.)[4]

During the Second World War, much of this cultural energy was channelled into the Teesside Guild of the Arts. The Guild ran drama, writing, photography, film and gramophone groups, a regular series of concerts and published a monthly newsletter. They worked with the British Drama League and CEMA (later the Arts Council) to organise an annual drama festival in Middlesbrough. CEMA brought touring art exhibitions to Teesside. The Adelphi Players and the Pilgrim Players visited the town. The Century Players and the Compass Players were based at Ormesby Hall; immediately after the Second World War, Theatre Workshop – run by Communists Joan Littlewood and Ewan MacColl – was based at Ormesby Hall. Teesside Youth Theatre was later based there.

Ruth Pennyman was also involved in a radical amateur drama group called Teesside Unity Theatre; writing their own material, they staged plays and poetry readings at the YCL premises in Middlesbrough and took satirical sketches around working men's clubs. Through Bill and Betty Farrell – then living at Ormesby Hall – Teesside Unity Theatre was connected to the Middlesbrough and Spennymoor Settlements (whose classes were attended by the young Norman Cornish and Sid Chaplin). *Gabriel*, a play written by Ruth Pennyman and Bill Farrell about Gabriel Peri (a French Communist writer executed by the Nazis for his part in the Resistance), was first performed in 1944 at the Everyman Theatre in Spennymoor. Another member of Teesside Unity Theatre, Dave Marshall, fought with the International Brigades; on his return he published a poem in the bestselling anthology *Poems for Spain*, connecting Middlesbrough and Spain, conflict and comradeship:

> Go back –
> Six-feet of snow on the Aragon front;
> While here
> Kids slide in the roadways
> Steadied feet thudding in the gutters:
> Ice blurs
> The red orange blue of neon lights –
> The harlot shops invite.
> But there
> The café lights blink and blacken
> Ribs tighten, skin grows ware –
> After the momentary adjustment
> A fumbling for the tasteless glass –
> A startled touch of warm-whorled fingers
> A greedy intake of smoke
> – the lung-shock battens the nerves –
> Strange faces glow intimate
> Red-arc'd by the fitful cigarette.[5]

1. This essay is the first of two excerpts from 'A Writer for Every Tick of My Watch: A History of Writing on Teesside' by Andy Croft, from *Fix This Moment: Writers respond to North-East literary history*, ed. Stevie Ronnie & Claire Malcolm (New Writing North, 2010).

2. See Andy Croft, 'A Hole Like That: the Literary Representation of Cleveland' in *The Cleveland and Teesside Local History Society Bulletin*, no. 58 Spring 1990.

3. George Tweddell claimed that John Gower was born at Stittenham, Sheriff Hutton, Cleveland. Later scholars assert that he was from Kent.

4. For Ruth Pennyman, see Mark Whyman, *The Last Pennymans of Ormesby Hall* (2008) and Malcolm Chase and Mark Whyman, *Heartbreak Hill* (1991).

5. Dave Marshall, 'Retrospect', in John Lehmann and Stephen Spender (eds) *Poems for Spain* (1939); for Marshall see his *The Tilting Planet* (2005).

NEIL ASTLEY
Land of Three Rivers: 2

In 1966, shortly after Jon Silkin had moved the magazine from Leeds to Newcastle, *Stand* published a survey of contemporary writing in North-East England. The editors' conclusions, given by Rodney Pybus (in a part of his essay not included here), were that most of the work by new writers submitted for the 'regional writing' issue was 'worse than third rate...abysmal'; the exceptions were two young Newcastle poets, Tom Pickard and Barry MacSweeney, and Fred Reed, a 66-year-old dialect poet from Ashington.

Yet the mid-1960s can now be seen as a pivotal period of renewal for poetry in the North East. Basil Bunting's *Briggflatts* had been published earlier in 1966, and that issue of *Stand* also included an essay by Dr Robert Woof on Bunting's poetry which provided the first authoritative critical introduction to a work which had baffled many of its first readers.

Tom and Connie Pickard started Morden Tower poetry readings in 1964 in a turret room on Newcastle's medieval city walls. After their first reading – by poet and songwriter Pete Brown – Tom Pickard tracked down Bunting, then living in obscurity in Northumberland, and soon the enthusiastic young Morden Tower audiences were encouraging him to start writing again. In 1965 he gave the first public reading of *Briggflatts* at Morden Tower. Other early Tower readings featured a number of America's Beats and Black Mountain poets, including Allen Ginsberg, Lawrence Ferlinghetti, Gregory Corso, Anne Waldman, Ed Dorn and Jonathan Williams, along with leading figures from the modernist and radical wings of British poetry, such as Hugh MacDiarmid, Roy Fisher, Tom Raworth, Gael Turnbull, Lee Harwood, J.H. Prynne and Adrian Mitchell. These poets, amongst others, inspired many of the young writers present, including Barry MacSweeney and Richard Caddel as well as Pickard himself. For the next 40 years, Morden Tower provided a stimulating international focus for poetry in Newcastle, aligned initially with the poets of the so-called 'British Poetry Revival', a modernist-inspired reaction to the Movement's more conservative strand in British poetry, and later broadening the range of its programming as British poetry became more diverse and pluralistic.

In 1967 Tony Harrison became the first writer to move to the region to take up the Northern Arts Literary Fellowship (later renamed North Eastern Literary Fellowship) based at the universities of Newcastle and Durham. In common with several later holders of the post, Harrison chose to settle here. Others who stayed and became part of the North East's community of poets included W.N. Herbert, Sean O'Brien and Anne Stevenson, all of whom have written work inspired by the region, as did others who moved away but maintained their links with the North East, including Fleur Adcock, Fred D'Aguiar, U.A. Fanthorpe and Carol Rumens. Another residency at Sunderland Polytechnic later brought Roger Garfitt (with Frances Horovitz) to the North East for a period during which he was able to help poets such as Peter Armstrong and William Martin.

By the 1970s, a number of influential new imprints, poetry reading venues and community arts projects were being set up across the North East. Opened in Newcastle in 1968, the Northern Arts Poetry Library had the biggest public collection of modern poetry outside London or Edinburgh; it was later re-housed by Northumberland County Council in Morpeth and re-named the Northern Poetry Library. As well as reviving interest in the town's pitmen painters and bringing live concerts and RSC plays to Ashington, George Stephenson's Mid Northumberland Arts Group, or MidNAG (1971–2005), produced poetry posters for schools and published books by writers including Sid Chaplin, John Clare, Alistair Elliot, Ivor Gurney and James Kirkup as well as *Myers' Literary Guide*. Chris Carrell set up the Ceolfrith Press imprint (1969–1985) at Sunderland Arts Centre, showcasing new poetry alongside the work of visual artists, and publishing a number of significant titles by poets from the North East, including William Martin's first pamphlet, *Easthope* (1970), Basil Bunting's edition of 19th-century pitman-poet Joseph Skipsey (1976), and Alistair Elliot's first collection, *Contentions* (1977).

Richard Caddel founded Pig Press in Durham with Ann Caddel in 1972, and in 1975 co-founded Colpitts Poetry, hosting readings in Durham with David Burnett and Diana Collecott (then Surman); in 1988 he co-founded the Basil Bunting Poetry Centre at Durham University with Diana Collecott. In 1973 Peter Mortimer published the first issue of *Iron* magazine, providing a national platform for many North-East writers for the next 26 years, most of that time from his house in Cullercoats. Its last issue appeared in 1997, but Iron Press, founded in 1975, initially to publish the plays of C.P. Taylor, Tom Hadaway and Leonard Barras, has continued, and was the first publisher of David Almond's fiction. The Tyneside Poets were organising group readings in pubs and publishing their magazine *Poetry North-East*. Keith Armstrong's *Ostrich* magazine was followed by his Strong Words socialist publishing imprint, and later by his Northern Voices Community Projects, giving a platform to working-class writers from the North East and championing the work of earlier figures such as Thomas Spence and Jack Common. Brian Marley ran his Laundering Room Press and Colin Simms' his Genera Editions from Newcastle, while Peter Hodgkiss moved his magazine *Poetry Information* (replaced by *Not Poetry*) and Galloping Dog Press from Swansea to Newcastle.

By the time I arrived in Newcastle, in 1975, it had become one of the liveliest centres for poetry in Britain, and there was even more activity in poetry and literature starting to take off across the North East. In those days Jon Silkin used to sell copies of *Stand* to people waiting in theatre queues. With his dishevelled hair, white beard and earnest manner, he looked every bit the impoverished poet, and sold hundreds of copies of the magazine hand-to-hand by playing this part. In the course of relieving me of 50p for the latest issue, he learned that I was an ex-journalist with experience of newspaper production work. A week later I had a part-time job as production editor for the magazine. When I started an English degree at Newcastle University later that year, I was already working on *Stand* and becoming acquainted with the kinds of work it favoured, which included American poetry, translations of Eastern Bloc poets, and what Silkin characterised as poetry of social conscience – as well as attending Friday nights at Morden Tower, where I heard and met all kinds of writers, from agitprop, avant-garde and pop poets to lively new poets and highly respected literary elders. Gordon Brown's *High on the Walls: A Morden Tower Anthology* (1990) gives a flavour of the vibrant mix of poets reading at the Tower in its first 25 years.

I also came into contact with editors of other magazines and presses active in the North East at that time, each with its own distinctive editorial style and particular areas of interest. It wasn't long before I was designing and producing pamphlets myself, both for *Stand*'s own pamphlet imprint, Northern House (the prototype of Bloodaxe's early pamphlets), and for Morden Tower. Bloodaxe's eclectic, democratic style of publishing was inspired by Newcastle's energetic, internationally-minded poetry culture.

Stand and Morden Tower introduced me to the work of many poets I would later publish at Bloodaxe. When I founded the imprint in 1978, I wanted to showcase the work of northern writers largely ignored by the literary establishment alongside new and established British poets. The early titles included pamphlets by Ken Smith, Fleur Adcock and John Cassidy; a debut pamphlet by a young poet from Sunderland, Vincent Morrison; first books by David Constantine (then living in Durham) and Helen Dunmore; an LP record of Basil Bunting reading *Briggflatts*; and anthologies of new poets from the North East and Hull introducing the work of poets such as Peter Armstrong, George Charlton, Sean O'Brien and Peter Didsbury. Over the course of the next decade I broadened the list to include Irish, European and American poets as well as providing a much-needed publishing platform for women poets.

Other initiatives to promote the work of women writers took off during the 1980s and 90s. Linda Anderson, Sheila Whitaker, Eileen Aird and Gay Clifford (later joined by Cynthia Fuller) started publishing the magazine *Writing Women* in 1981, which ran until 1998. Julia Darling founded the Poetry Virgins women's performance group of poets and actors in 1988, and formed Diamond Twig Press with Ellen Phethean in 1992. Gillian Allnutt and Margaret Wilkinson started their Writing from the Inside Out course at Newcastle University's Centre for Lifelong Learning in 1989, helping to nurture the work of many women writers for the next 20 years. The women writers collective Vane Women came together in 1990 at Darlington Arts Centre (in Vane Terrace), and have since organised many readings and workshops as well as running a press publishing anthologies and collections of their work. In 1999 Debbie Taylor launched *Mslexia* in Newcastle, 'the magazine for women who write'.

Over the same period other writers set up yet more presses and magazines. Former Morden Tower organiser Paul Summers founded and co-edited the magazines *Billy Liar* and *Liar Republic* and was part of Liar Inc Ltd, facilitating many community and educational projects. Ex-*Stand* editors and Tower organisers Brendan Cleary and Michael Blackburn started their imprints in Newcastle, Cleary later moving his Echo Room Press and magazine to Brighton, and Blackburn taking Jackson's Arm to Lincoln, while Michael Farley ran Taxus Press from the North East for part of its life (1983–1998), publishing books by poets including William Martin and Evangeline Paterson. Michael O'Neill and Gareth Reeves ran *Poetry Durham* for 35 issues from 1982 to 1994. Evangeline Paterson revived *Other Poetry* (co-founded with Anne Stevenson 20 years earlier and previously run from Oxford and Leicester) in Newcastle in 1995, editing the magazine for several more years with Peter Bennet, Michael Standen and Richard Kell. Another source of encouragement for poets during the late 1980s and early 90s was Graeme Rigby's *The Page*, a literary supplement given away free with *The Northern Echo*, which gave North-East poets a massive readership for new work, some of this commissioned by the paper.

Peter and Margaret Lewis ran Flambard Press from Newcastle and later Fourstones, from 1990 to 2013, with substantial poetry and fiction lists, providing a national platform for many leading poets from the North East and elsewhere, but had to fold when they lost their Arts Council funding. (Morden Tower readings were discontinued some years earlier after suffering a similar fate.)

In the meantime, four other new presses had been set up: Arrowhead Press in Darlington by Vane Women's Joanna Boulter in 2001, followed by Smokestack Books by Andy Croft in Middlesbrough in 2004 ('to hold open a space for what is left of the English radical poetic tradition in the 21st century'), and then Red Squirrel Press in 2006 at Stannington near Morpeth by Sheila Wakefield, who has since published many collections by North-East poets. And Brian Lister ran Biscuit Publishing in Washington from 2000 to 2013, organising poetry competitions and publishing poets including Maureen Almond, Bob Beagrie, Pippa Little and Angela Readman.

The Newcastle/Bloodaxe Poetry Lectures series was established in 2001 at Newcastle University, with leading contemporary poets invited to speak about the craft and practice of poetry to audiences drawn from both the city and the university, with the lectures later published in book form by Bloodaxe. Then in 2009 Linda Anderson founded Newcastle Centre for the Literary Arts (NCLA) at Newcastle University, running events, creative writing courses and other projects including publications; the first Newcastle Poetry Festival followed in 2015, hosting readings and talks by nationally and internationally renowned poets, and launching its *Steps in Time* poetry app at the 2017 festival. Also in 2009, Inpress, the sales agency for independent presses, moved from London to Newcastle, and in 2016 took over the beleaguered Poetry Book Society and has since revived and reinvigorated this poetry-only book club founded by T.S. Eliot in London in 1953.

In 2012 the first issue of the magazine *Butcher's Dog* appeared, commissioned by Durham Book Festival and founded by seven poets who had each won New Writing North's Northern Promise Award with mentoring from Clare Pollard.

There are now more published poets, poetry imprints and organisations promoting poetry in the North East than in any region of comparable size in Britain. The range and nature of the support given to writers in the North East has been instrumental in bringing about this cultural shift. Where once poets were given short shrift (see pages 38-39 below), now they are given awards for their writing; they are helped to run imprints and encouraged to develop or be involved with community arts projects, assisted by agencies and initiatives supported by government or university funding. Much of this work was supported initially by Northern Arts and then continued under Arts Council England through funding for agencies like New Writing North (with Northumbria University supporting its Northern Writers' Awards), and later through ground-breaking initiatives organised by NCLA. Many poets now earn their living through teaching literature or creative writing at universities or through residencies, public art commissions, and community projects in schools, prisons and libraries.

Andy Croft described how 'historically, the region's native writers …had to leave the region in order to be writers. These days, however, published writers move to the region because of the support that exists here for writing and for the sense of a community to which writers can belong.'[1] Fewer than a quarter of the poets included in the anthology *North by North-East* were born in the North East. Most moved here for work, or for education, and stayed: 'This is consistent with the immigrant history of the region. But it is a wholly new feature of the region's cultural life.'

The driving force behind much of what's happened in poetry over the past three decades on Teesside has been Andy Croft, who gives his own account of these developments in the following essay but without acknowledging his own role. After initially working in community writing projects through what was then called the Extra Mural Department of the University of Leeds based in Middlesbrough, he directed the Writearound Festival (1989–2000), organised monthly Poetry Live!/The Buzz/Crossing the Tees poetry readings (1989–2008), helped organise the Teesside Musha'ara (1990-99), and was editor of Mudfog Books (1993–2003) before founding Smokestack Books in 2004. He is also founder-director of T-junction, Teesside's biannual international poetry festival, which he has run with Bob Beagrie, Andy Willoughby and Mark Robinson since 2014.

1. *North by North-East: the region's contemporary poetry*, ed. *Andy Croft & Cynthia Fuller* (Iron Press, 2006).

* * *

What the Chairman Told Tom

Poetry? It's a hobby.
I run model trains.
Mr Shaw there breeds pigeons.

It's not work. You dont sweat.
Nobody pays for it.
You *could* advertise soap.

Art, that's opera; or repertory –
The Desert Song.
Nancy was in the chorus.

But to ask for twelve pounds a week –
married, aren't you? –
you've got a nerve.

How could I look a bus conductor
in the face
if I paid you twelve pounds?

Who says it's poetry, anyhow?
My ten year old
can do it *and* rhyme.

I get three thousand and expenses,
a car, vouchers,
but I'm an accountant.

They do what I tell them,
my company.
What do *you* do?

Nasty little words, nasty long words,
it's unhealthy.
I want to wash when I meet a poet.

They're Reds, addicts,
all delinquents.
What you write is rot.

Mr Hines says so, and he's a schoolteacher,
he ought to know.
Go and find *work*.

BASIL BUNTING

New poets living in the North now might well apply for a Northern Writers' Award for help with time to write. The situation 50 years ago was rather different. Basil Bunting wrote this poem in 1965 about Tom Pickard's attempt to gain financial support. It may have been written in jest, as Bunting asserted, but Pickard has said that the speaker was based on the Lord Mayor of Newcastle City Council and Chairman of the Cultural Activities Committee, Mrs Gladys Robson, 'magistrate, leader of the council' (*Chicago Review*, Spring 2000).

ANDY CROFT
Writing on Teesside: 2 (2010)[1]

The emergence of new cultural forms and technologies over the past 20 years has begun to flatten cultural hierarchies and to devolve cultural power away from the metropolis. The result has been the development on Teesside of an independent and increasingly self-confident native literary culture that does not defer to either Newcastle or London. A quarter of the poets in the 2006 Iron Press anthology *North by North East: the Region's Contemporary Poetry* were from Teesside – including Maureen Almond, Bob Beagrie, Joanna Boulter, Bob Cooper, Gordon Hodgeon, Marilyn Longstaff, Norah Hill, John Longden, Pauline Plummer, Mark Robinson and Annie Wright.

One of the key figures in all this was Communist poet John Miles Longden (1921–1991). In the 1960s, Longden used to read his poems in the Purple Onion Café in Middlesbrough; in the 1970s he was involved with Pavilion poets in Thornaby; in the 1980s he was running his own 'University of Cleveland' in bars all over Teesside.[2]

Meanwhile, students at Teesside Polytechnic – notably Trevor Teasdel and Ann Wainwright (later Richard Briddon) set up the Multi Media Society. Out of this came *Poetic Licence* magazine and regular poetry readings at the Dovecot in Stockton. Briddon set up Paranoia Press. Longden, Teasdel, and Terry Lawson, a poet from Staithes, helped to set up Teesside Writers Workshop, a group of amateur writers with an interest in publishing as well as performance. Out of TWW came the magazine *Outlet*.

Since the 1970s, another poet – Gordon Hodgeon (1941–2016) – working for the local education services, was helping to pioneer some of the region's first writing residencies in Cleveland libraries, including Bob Pegg, Peter Morgan, Kath McCreery and Rukhsana Ahmad. Unlike the North Eastern Literary Fellowship (based in the universities of Durham and Newcastle), these residencies were based in libraries and in schools on housing estates.

At the end of the 1980s, Hodgeon, Teasdel, Briddon, Lawson and Longden helped to set up the annual Writearound festival [*with Andy Croft*]. Beginning as a week of readings, the festival soon expanded into a three-week programme of readings, performances, workshops and launches across the whole of Cleveland. As well as showcasing a new generation of local poets, novelists and playwrights, Writearound worked with some of the area's published writers like Gordon Steele, Eleanor Fairbairn, Tanya Jones, Barbara Gamble, Julian Atterton and Mark Adlard, and brought back to Teesside some of the area's most successful and distinguished literary exports like Jane Gardam, Theresa Tomlinson, Pat Barker, Robert Holman and Philippa Gregory. It published a magazine, *Writearound the Year*.[3]

Mark Robinson – then working at Cleveland Arts – brought the magazine *Scratch* to Teesside and set up the Bare Faced Cabaret. Meanwhile, Leeds University's Adult Education Centre in Middlesbrough was running Poetry Live! and an extensive programme of free creative writing courses across Teesside and North Yorkshire. It was from one of these courses that Derek Gregory launched *Tees Valley Writer*. The *Evening Gazette* began a regular column of readers' poems and a quarterly supplement of poetry from local schools [edited by Andy Croft]. Mark Robinson and Pauline Plummer helped me set up Mudfog Press (with money from the Communist Party). Out of Mudfog came Smokestack Books, Ek Zuban and *Kenaz* magazine. And in a comparable development in adult education in Darlington, Vane Women Press was established, soon followed by Arrowhead.[4]

Out of Writearound and Cleveland Arts' Literature Development unit emerged Buzzwords, a literature development programme of community writing projects and writing events in schools. And out of Buzzwords came a series of reading and performance spaces – the Buzz, Crossing the Tees, the Verb Garden and the Hydrogen Jukebox, led by poets Bob Beagrie, Jo Colley and Andy Willoughby.[5]

Like the 'Bards of Cleveland' and the Ormesby Hall radicals, this is an activist culture, run by writers for other writers and would-be writers, a collective, co-operative and democratic endeavour combining poetry and politics, amateurs and professionals, writers and audiences, publishing and performance and maintained by a combination of enthusiastic volunteers and public support (principally from Northern Arts – later the Arts Council – Cleveland County Council, the Teesside Development Corporation, Community Arts Middlesbrough, Leeds University and Cleveland Arts). And it has consistently sought to connect the local, the national and the international – or as John Longden once expressed it, 'Teesside Twinned with the Universe':

> WOW as we breast the lip a' the long rise
> > flanking the flatlands all along the Tees
> > league upon league a'yellow crocuses
> > embrace the dark flood-plain 'n fill our eyes

> This swarm outshines our sister galaxies
> > it fills the view the lungs the art the mind
> > burstin f'm the black country a' the blind
> > Here the entrenched osts a' Ironoplis
> spread rape-gold vistas in the frozen night
> > Gorse blooms invincible through all seasons
> > a blaze then a few sparks Come rhyme come reason
> > frost or flood drought or blizzard calm or riot
> Clevelands gold lamps light up their massed barrage
> Our twinned night sky's the Boro written large

1. This essay is the second of two excerpts from 'A Writer for Every Tick of My Watch: A History of Writing on Teesside' by Andy Croft, from *Fix This Moment: Writers respond to North-East literary history*, ed. Stevie Ronnie & Claire Malcolm (New Writing North, 2010).

2. For John Miles Longden, see his posthumously published *LPs and Singles* (1995).

3. Writearound was featured on a BBC2 Open Space programme, *Breaking the Ice*, 19 June 1990, and on *A Sense of Place*, broadcast on BBC Radio 4, 8 July 1991.

4. See Rebecca O'Rourke, 'Written on the Margins: Creative Writing and Adult Education in Cleveland' (1994) and Mark Robinson, 'Teesside: Building a Democratic Poetic Culture' in *Poetry Now: Contemporary British and Irish Poetry in the Making*, ed. Holger Klein, Sabine Coelsch-Foisner and Wolfgang Gortschacher (1999).

5. See Andy Croft, 'Magic, Mimesis and Middlesbrough', in *Words Out Loud*, ed. Mark Robinson (2002).

LAND OF THREE RIVERS

In memoriam
ALAN MYERS

LAND OF THREE RIVERS

from **New Year Letter**

No matter where, or whom I meet,
Shop-gazing in a Paris street,
Bumping through Iceland in a bus,
At teas when clubwomen discuss
The latest Federation Plan,
In Pullman washrooms, man to man,
Hearing how circumstance has vexed
A broker who is oversexed,
In houses where they do not drink,
Whenever I begin to think
About the human creature we
Must nurse to sense and decency,
An English area comes to mind,
I see the nature of my kind
As a locality I love,
Those limestone moors that stretch from BROUGH
To HEXHAM and the ROMAN WALL,
There is my symbol of us all.
There, where the EDEN leisures through
Its sandstone valley, is my view
Of green and civil life that dwells
Below a cliff of savage fells
From which original address
Man faulted into consciousness.
Along the line of lapse the fire
Of life's impersonal desire
Burst through his sedentary rock
And, as at DUFTON and at KNOCK,
Thrust up between his mind and heart
Enormous cones of myth and art.
Always my boy of wish returns
To those peat-stained deserted burns
That feed the WEAR and TYNE and TEES,
And, turning states to strata, sees
How basalt long oppressed broke out
In wild revolt at CAULDRON SNOUT,

And from the relics of old mines
Derives his algebraic signs
For all in man that mourns and seeks,
For all of his renounced techniques,
Their tramways overgrown with grass,
For lost belief, for all Alas,
The derelict lead-smelting mill,
Flued to its chimney up the hill,
That smokes no answer any more
But points, a landmark on BOLTS LAW,
The finger of all questions. There
In ROOKHOPE I was first aware
Of Self and Not-self, Death and Dread:
Adits were entrances which led
Down to the Outlawed, to the Others,
The Terrible, the Merciful, the Mothers;
Alone in the hot day I knelt
Upon the edge of shafts and felt
The deep *Urmutterfurcht* that drives
Us into knowledge all our lives,
The far interior of our fate
To civilise and to create,
Das Weibliche that bids us come
To find what we're escaping from.
There I dropped pebbles, listened, heard
The reservoir of darkness stirred;
'*O deine Mutter kehrt dir nicht
Wieder. Du selbst bin ich, dein' Pflicht
Und Liebe. Brach sie nun mein Bild.*'
And I was conscious of my guilt.

(1 January 1940)

W.H. AUDEN
The Double Man, 1941 | *New Year Letter*, 1941 | *Collected Poems*, 1976
➤ AUTHOR NOTE PAGES 64 & 246-47

'The German lines are loosely adapted from speeches in Wagner's *Siegfried*. The first two sentences may be translated roughly: "Your mother does not return to you: I am yourself, your duty and love"; Auden invented and added *Pflicht und Liebe* (duty and love). The third sentence is a subordinate clause that means, in its original context, "though it has shattered my image. Auden perhaps thought his sentence meant either "My image now is shattered" or "Now shatter my image".' – Edward Mendelson: *Early Auden, Later Auden: A Critical Biography* (2017).

The Glittering North

Wind falls, a fountain of stillness in the mind;
Takes toll of grief this tough and moorland grass.
Sky-wounded water, having caught infinity
Flying yet rooted in your reedy glass,
You draw their tenuous dole who wander blind.

From cloud-shed mistily shining, world moss-wet
The visiting glory fades, a foot-sore dream.
Melts into wrack my yonder of serenity:
Yet leaves me pondering every stone-bred stream
That braids the glittering North, a ghost in debt.

LILIAN BOWES LYON
Bright Feather Fading, 1936 | *Collected Poems*, 1948
➤ AUTHOR NOTE PAGE 241

from The Pleasures of the Imagination

from Book II

A solitary prospect, wide and wild,
Rushed on my senses. 'Twas a horrid pile
Of hills with many a shaggy forest mixed,
With many a sable cliff and glittering stream.
Aloft, recumbent o'er the hanging ridge,
The brown woods waved; while ever-trickling springs
Washed from the naked roots of oak and pine
The crumbling soil; and still at every fall
Down the steep windings of the channelled rock,
Remurmuring rushed the congregated floods
With hoarser inundation; till at last
They reached a grassy plain, which from the skirts
Of that high desert spread her verdant lap,
And drank the gushing moisture, where confined
In one smooth current, o'er the lilied vale
Clearer than glass it flowed.

from **Book IV**

Would I again were with you! – O ye dales
Of Tyne, and ye most ancient woodlands; where,
Oft as the giant flood obliquely strides,
And his banks open, and his lawns extend,
Stops short the pleased traveller to view
Presiding o'er the scene some rustic tower
Founded by Norman or by Saxon hands:
O ye Northumbrian shades, which overlook
The rocky pavement and the mossy falls
Of solitary Wensbeck's limpid stream;
How gladly I recall your well-known seats
Beloved of old, and that delightful time
When all alone, for many a summer's day,
I wandered through your calm recesses, led
In silence by some powerful hand unseen.

   Nor will I e'er forget you; nor shall e'er
The graver tasks of manhood, or the advice
Of vulgar wisdom, move me to disclaim
Those studies which possessed me in the dawn
Of life, and fixed the colour of my mind
For every future year.

MARK AKENSIDE
The Pleasures of the Imagination, 1744

The Newcastle poet-physician **Mark Akenside** (1721–1770) was born at 33 Butcher Bank (now Akenside Hill). The son of a butcher, he was rendered lame by an accident with his father's cleaver. Trained in Edinburgh and abroad, Akenside eventually rose to be physician to the queen at the accession of George III in 1763.

   Akenside was very touchy about his humble origins; possibly as a result, he gained the reputation of behaving roughly to the poor, especially to women. He was not an easy man to like, despite being ready to praise other poets; he had annoyed the testy Scottish novelist Tobias Smollett by disparaging Scotland, and was consequently satirised as the conceited and pedantic doctor in *Peregrine Pickle* (1751).

   In Newcastle, Akenside wrote a number of minor poems for *The Gentleman's Magazine*, including 'A Hymn to Science', but it was while visiting relations at Morpeth that he conceived the plan for *The Pleasures of Imagination* (1744), his most celebrated work. It is a long, erudite and complex poem, which takes on the difficult task of rendering a philosophical treatise in verse. Dr Johnson was not an admirer: 'The words are multiplied till the sense is hardly perceived.' There are occasional striking passages, but it has to be admitted that there is much leaden verse, stuffed with classical allusions. Recalling his youth by the 'dales of Tyne' and the Wansbeck however, Akenside finds more immediacy. [AM]

Northumberland

Between our eastward and our westward sea
    The narrowing strand
Clasps close the noblest shore fame holds in fee
Even here where English birth seals all men free –
    Northumberland.

The sea-mists meet across it when the snow
    Clothes moor and fell,
And bid their true-born hearts who love it glow
For joy that none less nobly born may know
    What love knows well.

The splendour and the strength of storm and fight
    Sustain the song
That filled our fathers' hearts with joy to smite,
To live, to love, to lay down life that right
    Might tread down wrong.

They warred, they sang, they triumphed, and they passed,
    And left us glad
Here to be born, their sons, whose hearts hold fast
The proud old love no change can overcast,
    No chance leave sad.

None save our northmen ever, none but we,
    Met, pledged, or fought
Such foes and friends as Scotland and the sea
With heart so high and equal, strong in glee
    And stern in thought.

Thought, fed from time's memorial springs with pride,
    Made strong as fire
Their hearts who hurled the foe down Flodden side,
And hers who rode the waves none else durst ride –
    None save her sire.

O land beloved, where nought of legend's dream
    Outshines the truth,
Where Joyous Gard, closed round with clouds that gleam
For them that know thee not, can scarce but seem
    Too sweet for sooth,

Thy sons forget not, nor shall fame forget,
    The deed there done
Before the walls whose fabled fame is yet
A light too sweet and strong to rise and set
    With moon and sun.

Song bright as flash of swords or oars that shine
    Through fight or foam
Stirs yet the blood thou hast given thy sons like wine
To hail in each bright ballad hailed as thine
    One heart, one home.

Our Collingwood, though Nelson be not ours,
    By him shall stand
Immortal, till those waifs of oldworld hours,
Forgotten, leave uncrowned with bays and flowers
    Northumberland.

ALGERNON CHARLES SWINBURNE
A Channel Passage and Other Poems, 1904

Algernon Charles Swinburne (1837–1909), though born in London, was early removed from it and disliked it throughout his life. The son of an admiral, he was brought up on the Isle of Wight, but spent a good deal of the year at Capheaton Hall, the house of his grandfather, Sir John Swinburne (1762–1860), who had a famous library and was President of the Literary and Philosophical Society in Newcastle until 1837. Swinburne considered Northumberland to be his native county, 'the crowning county of England – yes, the best!' He used to ride his pony over to Cambo, where the perpetual curate, John Wilkinson, prepared him somewhat desultorily for entry to Eton. 'He was too clever and would never study,' complained the curate.

    Despite Swinburne's later fame as a poet, it is in his novel *Lesbia Brandon* that we find the spell of the North at its strongest. The splendid landscape and seascape – what Swinburne called 'the joyful and fateful beauty of the seas off Bamburgh' – are certainly Northumbrian, while his character Herbert Seyton's exhilarating contact with the sea mirrors the pain which for Swinburne was notoriously inseparable from pleasure. Swinburne's abiding love for the region (his favourite word for the north is 'bright') is memorably reflected in poems like the intensely patriotic 'Northumberland', 'Grace Darling' [169], 'The Tyneside Widow' [346], 'Winter in Northumberland' and 'A Jacobite's Exile' [139], with its haunting echoes of the Till, the Wansbeck and the Tyne. Swinburne was fond of reciting as he rode across the moors (he was a daring horseman) 'through honeyed leagues of the northland border'. He never called it the Scottish border.

    William Bell Scott painted an extraordinary portrait of the red-haired Swinburne against the background of the Northumberland coast, the drawings for which were made on the trip the two made to Grace Darling's Longstone lighthouse in 1859. It now hangs in Balliol College, Oxford (from which Swinburne was rusticated).

In the years 1857-60, Swinburne became one of Lady Pauline Trevelyan's intellectual circle at Wallington Hall, which he recalls in a poem of 1882 to William Bell Scott as 'that bright household in our joyous north'. Indeed, the dominant old lady character in his novel *Love's Cross-Currents* is said to be based on Lady Pauline, who is supposed to have died with the poet's name on her lips. Ernest Radworth may well be based on Sir Walter Trevelyan. Somewhat eccentric, Sir Walter once found a Balzac novel Swinburne had left on the drawing-room table, and threw it on the fire in disgust. Swinburne was outraged and walked out of the house.

When his father was displeased at his failing to take a degree at Oxford, Swinburne withdrew again northwards to Capheaton. After his grandfather's death in 1860, he stayed with the Bell Scotts at 14, St Thomas' Crescent in Newcastle, lying before the fire, surrounded by piles of books resembling a ruined fortress. Scott recalls holding Swinburne's head while a Newcastle dentist removed a 'mighty grinder' bit by bit, noting that the poet was almost indifferent to the pain. In December 1862, Swinburne arrived hot foot from Wallington and proceeded to accompany Bell Scott and his guests, probably including Dante Gabriel Rossetti, on a trip to Tynemouth. Scott writes that as they walked by the sea, the poet declaimed the 'Hymn to Proserpine' and 'Laus Veneris' in his strange intonation. while the waves were 'running the whole length of the long level sands towards Cullercoats and sounding like far-off acclamations'.

In London, Rossetti was delighted with his 'little Northumbrian friend' whose controversial *Poems and Ballads* (1866) had made an impact of seismic proportions in the Victorian literary world. Swinburne was indeed small, though no weakling, and his head was disproportionately large, making him something of an odd figure. Henry Brooks Adams described Swinburne as 'a tropical bird, high-crested, long-beaked, quick-moving... a crimson macaw among owls'. His behaviour was certainly disconcerting; at 30, he knelt down before Giuseppe Mazzini to read a poem. Rossetti, dismayed that Swinburne was hiring flagellants to beat him, paid an actress £10 to bring him back to the sexual straight and narrow: the effort was a failure and she returned the money. Swinburne was not above writing about such things, however; his fantasy *La Soeur de la Reine* imagines what few others would – Wordsworth seducing Queen Victoria. By now his addiction to drink was wrecking his health and trying his friends' patience to breaking point. Eventually, his friend Theodore Watts-Dunton took him under strictly sober supervision at his house, 'The Pines', in Putney.

Swinburne's love for Northumberland lasted his whole life. Tennyson had included an altered version of Malory in his story of Balin and Balan in the *Idylls of the King*, but Swinburne gave full vent to his Northumbrian patriotism in his *Tale of Balen* (1896). He describes Balen riding down across the Tyne and Tees to Camelot, where the 'southern' knights are jealous and hostile. He meets his valiant brother:

> His brother Balan, hard at hand,
> Twin flower of bright Northumberland,
> Twin sea-bird of their loud sea-strand.
> Twin bird-song of their morn.

After many doughty deeds, Balen and Balan are tricked into slaying one another, and are buried in one tomb. A life well-lived is no cause for sorrow to Swinburne, however. As Balen lies dying, his thoughts echo Swinburne's own youth in Northumberland – and his love of the Border ballads:

> He drank the draught of life's first wine
> Again: he saw the moorlands shine,
> The rioting rapids of the Tyne,

> The woods, the cliffs, the sea.
> The joy of crags and scaurs he clomb,
> The rapture of the encountering foam
> Embraced and breasted of the boy,
> The first good steed his knees bestrode,
> The first wild sound of songs that flowed
> Through ears that thrilled and heart that glowed,
> Fulfilled his death with joy.

   Swinburne is out of fashion nowadays. T.S. Eliot's attack on his romantic vagueness was too devastating for most, while others are still disturbed by hymns to flagellation and necrophilia. Despite the occasional intoxicating brilliance of his technique, he never grew out of his romantic youth. It is poignant, all the same, to think of the former devotee of liberty, the lover of sea and moorland, under strict supervision at 'The Pines' for the last 30 years of his life. [AM]
   See also 'A Reiver's Neck-Verse' [138], 'A Jacobite's Exile (1764)' [139], 'Grace Darling' [169] and 'The Tyneside Widow' [346].

from Briggflatts
An Autobiography

For Peggy

> *Son los pasariellos del mal pelo exidos*
>
> The spuggies are fledged

I

Brag, sweet tenor bull,
descant on Rawthey's madrigal,
each pebble its part
for the fells' late spring.
Dance tiptoe, bull,
black against may.
Ridiculous and lovely
chase hurdling shadows
morning into noon.
May on the bull's hide
and through the dale
furrows fill with may,
paving the slowworm's way.

A mason times his mallet
to a lark's twitter,
listening while the marble rests,
lays his rule
at a letter's edge,
fingertips checking,
till the stone spells a name
naming none,
a man abolished.
Painful lark, labouring to rise!
The solemn mallet says:
In the grave's slot
he lies. We rot.

Decay thrusts the blade,
wheat stands in excrement
trembling. Rawthey trembles.
Tongue stumbles, ears err
for fear of spring.
Rub the stone with sand,
wet sandstone rending
roughness away. Fingers
ache on the rubbing stone.
The mason says: Rocks
happen by chance.
No one here bolts the door,
love is so sore.

Stone smooth as skin,
cold as the dead they load
on a low lorry by night.
The moon sits on the fell
but it will rain.
Under sacks on the stone
two children lie,
hear the horse stale,
the mason whistle,
harness mutter to shaft,
felloe to axle squeak,
rut thud the rim,
crushed grit.

Stocking to stocking, jersey to jersey,
head to a hard arm,
they kiss under the rain,
bruised by their marble bed.
In Garsdale, dawn;
at Hawes, tea from the can.
Rain stops, sacks
steam in the sun, they sit up.
Copper-wire moustache,
sea-reflecting eyes
and Baltic plainsong speech
declare: By such rocks
men killed Bloodaxe.

Fierce blood throbs in his tongue,
lean words.
Skulls cropped for steel caps
huddle round Stainmore.
Their becks ring on limestone,
whisper to peat.
The clogged cart pushes the horse downhill.
In such soft air
they trudge and sing,
laying the tune frankly on the air.
All sounds fall still,
fellside bleat,
hide-and-seek peewit.

Her pulse their pace,
palm countering palm,
till a trench is filled,
stone white as cheese
jeers at the dale.
Knotty wood, hard to rive,
smoulders to ash;
smell of October apples.
The road again,
at a trot.
Wetter, warmed, they watch
the mason meditate
on name and date.

Rain rinses the road,
the bull streams and laments.
Sour rye porridge from the hob
with cream and black tea,
meat, crust and crumb.
Her parents in bed
the children dry their clothes.
He has untied the tape
of her striped flannel drawers
before the range. Naked
on the pricked rag mat
his fingers comb
thatch of his manhood's home.

Gentle generous voices weave
over bare night
words to confirm and delight
till bird dawn.
Rainwater from the butt
she fetches and flannel
to wash him inch by inch,
kissing the pebbles.
Shining slowworm part of the marvel.
The mason stirs:
Words!
Pens are too light.
Take a chisel to write.

Every birth a crime,
every sentence life.
Wiped of mould and mites
would the ball run true?
No hope of going back.
Hounds falter and stray,
shame deflects the pen.
Love murdered neither bleeds nor stifles
but jogs the draftsman's elbow.
What can he, changed, tell
her, changed, perhaps dead?
Delight dwindles. Blame
stays the same.

Brief words are hard to find,
shapes to carve and discard:
Bloodaxe, king of York,
king of Dublin, king of Orkney.
Take no notice of tears;
letter the stone to stand
over love laid aside lest
insufferable happiness impede
flight to Stainmore,
to trace
lark, mallet,
becks, flocks
and axe knocks.

Dung will not soil the slowworm's
mosaic. Breathless lark
drops to nest in sodden trash;
Rawthey truculent, dingy.
Drudge at the mallet, the may is down,
fog on fells. Guilty of spring
and spring's ending
amputated years ache after
the bull is beef, love a convenience.
It is easier to die than to remember.
Name and date
split in soft slate
a few months obliterate.

[...]

   from **IV**

As the player's breath warms the fipple the tone clears.
It is time to consider how Domenico Scarlatti
condensed so much music into so few bars
with never a crabbed turn or congested cadence,
never a boast or a see-here; and stars and lakes
echo him and the copse drums out his measure,
snow peaks are lifted up in moonlight and twilight
and the sun rises on an acknowledged land.

My love is young but wise. Oak, applewood,
her fire is banked with ashes till day.
The fells reek of her hearth's scent,
her girdle is greased with lard;
hunger is stayed on her settle, lust in her bed.
Light as spider floss her hair on my cheek which a puff scatters,
light as a moth her fingers on my thigh.
We have eaten and loved and the sun is up,
we have only to sing before parting:
Goodbye, dear love.

Her scones are greased with fat of fried bacon,
her blanket comforts my belly like the south.
We have eaten and loved and the sun is up.
Goodbye.

Applewood, hard to rive,
its knots smoulder all day.
Cobweb hair on the morning,
a puff would blow it away.
Rime is crisp on the bent,
ruts stone-hard, frost spangles fleece.
What breeze will fill that sleeve limp on the line?
A boy's jet steams from the wall, time from the year,
care from deed and undoing.
Shamble, cold, content with beer and pickles,
towards a taciturn lodging amongst strangers.
[...]

from V

Shepherds follow the links,
sweet turf studded with thrift;
fell-born men of precise instep
leading demure dogs
from Tweed and Till and Teviotdale,
with hair combed back from the muzzle,
dogs from Redesdale and Coquetdale
taught by Wilson or Telfer.
Their teeth are white as birch,
slow under black fringe
of silent, accurate lips.
The ewes are heavy with lamb.

Snow lies bright on Hedgehope
and tacky mud about Till
where the fells have stepped aside
and the river praises itself,
silence by silence sits
and Then is diffused in Now.

Light lifts from the water.
Frost has put rowan down,
a russet blotch of bracken
tousled about the trunk.
Bleached sky. Cirrus
reflects sun that has left
nothing to badger eyes.

Young flutes, harps touched by a breeze,
drums and horns escort
Aldebaran, low in the clear east,
beckoning boats to the fishing.
Capella floats from the north
with shields hung on his gunwale.
That is no dinghy's lantern
occulted by the swell – Betelgeuse,
calling behind him to Rigel.
Starlight is almost flesh.

Great strings next the post of the harp
clang, the horn has majesty,
flutes flicker in the draft and flare.
Orion strides over Farne.
Seals shuffle and bark,
terns shift on their ledges,
watching Capella steer for the zenith,
and Procyon starts his climb.

Furthest, fairest things, stars, free of our humbug,
each his own, the longer known the more alone,
wrapt in emphatic fire roaring out to a black flue.
Each spark trills on a tone beyond chronological compass,
yet in a sextant's bubble present and firm
places a surveyor's stone or steadies a tiller.
Then is Now. The star you steer by is gone,
its tremulous thread spun in the hurricane

spider floss on my cheek; light from the zenith
spun when the slowworm lay in her lap
fifty years ago.

The sheets are gathered and bound,
the volume indexed and shelved,
dust on its marbled leaves.
Lofty, an empty combe,
silent but for bees.
Finger tips touched and were still
fifty years ago.
Sirius is too young to remember.

Sirius glows in the wind. Sparks on ripples
mark his line, lures for spent fish.

Fifty years a letter unanswered;
a visit postponed for fifty years.

She has been with me fifty years.

Starlight quivers. I had day enough.
For love uninterrupted night.

BASIL BUNTING
Briggflatts, 1966 | *Complete Poems*, 2000

from **Bunting's notes to *Briggflatts*:**

The Northumbrian tongue travel has not taken from me sometimes sounds strange to men used to the koine or to Americans who may not know how much Northumberland differs from the Saxon south of England. Southrons would maul the music of many lines in *Briggflatts*.

An autobiography, but not a record of fact. The first movement is no more a chronicle than the third. The truth of the poem is of another kind.

No notes are needed. A few may spare diligent readers the pains of research.

Spuggies: little sparrows.

May the flower, as haw is the fruit, of the thorn.

Northumbrians should know Eric *Bloodaxe* but seldom do, because all the school histories are written by or for Southrons. Piece his story together from the Anglo-Saxon Chronicle, the Orkneyinga Saga, and Heimskringla, as you fancy.

We have burns in the east, *becks* in the west, but no brooks or creeks.

Scone: rhyme it with 'on', not, for heaven's sake, 'own'.

Wilson was less known than *Telfer*, but not less skilful.

Sailors pronounce *Betelgeuse* 'Beetle juice' and so do I. His companion is 'Ridgel', not 'Rhy-ghel'.

Sirius is too young to remember because the light we call by his name left its star only eight years ago; but the light from *Capella,* now in the zenith, set out 45 years ago – as near fifty as makes no difference to a poet.

Basil Bunting (1900–1985) was born in Scotswood, Newcastle. His father, Thomas Lowe Bunting, originally from Derbyshire, was the pit doctor for Montagu Colliery as well as a Newcastle GP. His mother Annie, *née* Cheesman, came from Throckley, Northumberland, where her father was the colliery manager.

He spent his childhood in Newcastle – the early years at 27 Denton Road, Scotswood – but his strongest sense of locality and culture came from the Cheesmans and their circle in Throckley – where he later lived between long periods spent abroad. The family speech – like his own – was strongly Northumbrian in character, marked in particular by the Throckley dialect with its soft burr and rolling 'r's. His mother was related to several Border families, including the Charltons, and as a child he delighted in stories and songs of the Border reivers. In 1913 he spent the first of many holidays at the small Cumbrian Quaker hamlet of Brigflatts with the family of his school friend John Greenbank, whose sister Peggy was the adolescent sweetheart remembered in *Briggflatts* (which is dedicated to her), and began attending meetings at the 17th-century meeting house. His formative visits to Brigflatts in his teens were enormously important to him, both in terms of personal experience and his later remembrance and embodiment of that time in his poetry.

(It should be noted that Brigflatts the place has one *g*, but Bunting spells it *Briggflatts*. Also, while Brigflatts was then in Cumberland – east of the Eden valley, now part of Cumbria – Bunting was not alone in viewing that part of the northern Pennines as Northumbrian.) Writing in later life to Louis Zukofsky (16 December 1964), he acknowledged the debt he felt he owed to

> Peggy Greenbank, and her whole ambience, the Rawthey valley, the fells of Lunedale, the Viking inheritance all spent save the faint smell of it, the ancient Quaker life accepted without thought and without suspicion that it might seem eccentric: and what happens when one deliberately thrusts love aside, as I then did – it has its revenge. That must be a longish poem.

Profoundly affected by a Quaker boarding school education, Bunting stopped short of becoming a member of the Society of Friends, but as a pacifist, refused to fight in the First World War, and served time in various prisons from April 1918 until May 1919.

For the three decades he led a life of wandering and penury – in Italy, England, Berlin, Tenerife, America and Persia, returning to live with his mother in Throckley (at 242 Newburn Road, known locally as The Villas) when unable to make a living elsewhere. In 1923 he was living in Paris, working on the *Transatlantic Review*, later following Ezra Pound to Rapallo in Italy where Yeats knew him as 'one of Pound's more savage disciples'. 1928 saw him briefly back in England, writing reviews for London weeklies while living in a cottage at Coldside Farm in the Simonsides, where he absorbed many aspects of rural Northumberland life (including the training of sheepdogs) he later drew upon in his poetry.

After spending the first years of the War in balloon operations, and then as an aircraftsman in Iraq, he became an intelligence officer, and by 1945 had become Squadron-Leader

Bunting and Vice-Consul of Isfahan in Persia, where he had initially been posted as an interpreter, because of his knowledge of Persian, albeit the medieval variety (which he had learned in order to read the classical Persian poets). After the War, he served as chief of political intelligence in Tehran, and then as *Times* correspondent in Tehran, until his expulsion by the new Iranian leader Mossadeq. By 1954 he was living back in Throckley with his mother, second wife Sima and young family, eventually finding work as a nightshift sub-editor on the *Newcastle Daily Journal*. In 1957 they moved to Wylam, and he was able to transfer to the sister paper, the *Evening Chronicle*, for which he worked until his retirement in 1966. Also working on the *Chronicle* during the latter period was Barry MacSweeney, who had left school at 16 to become a cub reporter.

During these years he established a reputation in America as the most significant English poet of his generation, at the same time as his work was neglected in Britain, but it was not until the publication of *Briggflatts* in 1966 that his genius was finally recognised.

The cultural revolution of the 1960s saw poetry revivals centred in Newcastle, Liverpool and London. Its focus in Newcastle was the Morden Tower turret room on the city's medieval walls, where Tom and Connie Pickard started putting on poetry readings in June 1964. Pickard had written for advice to Jonathan Williams at Jargon Press in North Carolina, who suggested he get in touch with Basil Bunting, a writer none of Pickard's writer friends in Newcastle had heard of, let alone read. His meeting with Pickard was the catalyst which transformed Bunting's life and reputation. As well as giving him a highly receptive young audience of poetry enthusiasts, Morden Tower published *The Spoils* (rejected by T.S. Eliot at Faber after its US publication in *Poetry* in 1951). Many famous poets of the time came to Newcastle, not just to read at the Tower but to meet and talk to Bunting, from Allen Ginsberg and Robert Creeley to Hugh MacDiarmid and Lawrence Ferlinghetti. Stimulated by this contact with poets and poetry readers, and most importantly by his continuing correspondence with Louis Zukofsky, Bunting toiled over the next year on his master work, *Briggflatts*, buoyed up by Tom Pickard's enthusiasm and – as the myth has it – wanting to show the young poet how to write a long poem.

Bunting called *Briggflatts* his 'autobiography'. It is a complex work, drawing on many elements of his life, experience and knowledge. Cut from an alleged 2000 lines to around 700, its structural models include Scarlatti sonatas and the latticework of the Lindisfarne Gospels. After the first public reading of the poem at Morden Tower on 22 December 1965, *Briggflatts* was published in 1966 in Chicago in *Poetry* and then in London by Fulcrum Press, an imprint renowned in the 60s for contemporary, experimental poetry.

Briggflatts was immediately hailed as a major work, with Cyril Connolly calling it 'the finest long poem to have been published in England since T.S. Eliot's *Four Quartets*'. In 1968 Bunting was given a two-year appointment as Northern Arts Literary Fellow at the Universities of Durham and Newcastle, and his first *Collected Poems* was published by Fulcrum. Hugh MacDiarmid wrote that Bunting's poems were 'the most important which have appeared in any form of the English language since T.S. Eliot's *The Waste Land*'.

In 1977, the Buntings separated, and for four years the ageing poet had to live in a tiny box-like house in Washington New Town, far from his beloved Northumberland fells. In 1981, however, he was able to move into a cottage at Greystead, Tarset, in the North Tyne Valley, where he lived for three years until he had to move again in 1984, this time to Fox Cottage at Whitley Chapel in Hexhamshire. He died in 1985. A stone bearing his name and dates marks the place where his ashes were strewn in the burial ground at Briggflats.

Springan

Caa, caa, ye noisy craas!
Gobby a bord as ivvor waas.
Yon tree's se like a hoose o' lords.
Whaat's meant b' them donart words?
    Aa'm sure nebody knaas.

Abeun the hemmel, ower bye,
Wheelin' in the dappled sky,
Ye'll droon oot spuggies, lairks 'n' wrens,
An' set the laddies hoyin' styens
    Wi' yor feckless cry!

Like a kibble gyen amain,
Spring comes boondin' doon the lane,
An' buttercups 'n' pittlybeds
Lift thor bonny gowlden heids
    Aglistenin' wi' rain.

The lambs are lowpin' doon the neuk,
Or, dunchin' yows, they thrust 'n' suck.
Aa'll skelp yon tyke that's barkin' lood
An' chasin' coneys i' the wood
    Wi' neethor airt nor luck.

The born runs deep in yalla mud
And at the bend hes kirved a jud,
Then doon the swally lowps 'n' reels
An' blethors, froths, 'n' cowps hor creels
    Se rollickin' in flud.

Doon wheor the willas hev thor fling
Fornenst the footbridge, catkins hing,
An' heor the tits are aall agabbor,
The robin playin' hitchy-dabbor
    Afore he tyeks t' wing.

Belaa the knowe the slope's ablaze
Wi' saffron broom 'n' bluebell haze,
An' heor the stallion whustles oot
An' raises high his gyepin' snoot
    In statuesque amaze.

The peewit's cry aches ower the field
Aall furrowed for a bagey yield,
An' stottin' doon the lonnen's ditch
The dronin' bummlor powks his snitch
    In dusty gowld concealed.

Wi' musky yarbs the air smells fine,
The low shines softly 'n' benign,
The arth wears resurrection's smock
For chthonian dreams the noo hev brock
    Amang the eglantine.

FRED REED
Stand, 1966 | *The Sense On't*, 1973 | *The Northumborman*, 1999

craa: crow; *gobby:* vaunting, boastfully verbose; *donart:* foolish; *knaas:* knows; *abeun:* above, beyond; *hemmel:* open-fronted animal house; *spuggies:* sparrows; *hoyin' styens:* throwing stones; *feckless:* weak, helpless (not *fond* as in standard English); *kibble:* waggon; *gyen:* gone; *pittlybeds:* dandelions; *lowpin':* leaping; *neuk:* corner, sheltered place; *dunch:* bump; *yows:* ewes; *skelp:* hit, strike as a punishment; *coney:* rabbit; *airt:* sense, mood; *born:* burn, stream; *kirved a jud:* eroded a curve; *swally:* (mining) stratified depression; *lowp:* leap; *blethor:* chatter, talk without sense; *cowped hor creels:* did a somersault; *willas:* willows; *fornents:* opposite to; *agabbor:* vaunting, boastfully verbose; *hitchy-dabbor:* hopscotch; *knowe:* hill; *gyep:* gape; *snoot:* snout; *bagey:* turnip; *stottin':* bouncing; *lonnen:* lane; *bumler:* bumble bee; *powks:* pokes; *snitch:* nose; *yarbs:* herbs; *low* (rhymes with *now*): light; *the noo:* now; *brock:* broken;

Fred Reed (1901–1985) was Northumberland's best-known dialect poet of the 20th century, and drew on the Pitmatic variety of Northumbrian dialect particular to his native pit-town of Ashington (the former smell of which is immortalised in 'The Pit Heap', see page 188). Born 'several feet from an open midden and earth closet in the back yard', he received 'a very slight education and went to work the pit at 14'. In 1928, he 'escaped and became a clerk and educational lecturer'. He published a sonnet sequence, *An Undine Overture*, in 1929, and won the Sir Arthur Markham Memorial Poetry Prize, a competition for mine workers. In *Cumen and Gannin* (1977), he wrote: 'The dialect I have found to be highly expressive and of maximum desired impact, and dialect verse to be the music of rhythmical vocal sound, when the mind is suffused with feeling and it finds adequate expression.' All his poetry is collected in *The Northumborman: the dialect poetry of Fred Reed* (1999). His LP *Northumbrian Voice* (1978) was reissued on CD by the Northumbrian Language Society in 2002.

HADRIAN'S WALL

Roman Wall Blues

Over the heather the wet wind blows,
I've lice in my tunic, a cold in my nose.

The rain comes pattering out of the sky,
I'm a Wall soldier, I don't know why.

The mist creeps over the hard grey stone,
My girl's in Tungria; I sleep alone.

Aulus goes hanging around her place,
I don't like his manners, I don't like his face.

Piso's a Christian, he worships a fish;
There'd be be no kissing if he had his wish.

She gave me a ring but I diced it away;
I want my girl and I want my pay.

When I'm a veteran with only one eye
I shall do nothing but look at the sky.

(October 1937)

W.H. AUDEN
Another Time, 1940 | *Collected Poems*, 1976

On 25 November 1937, Auden and Benjamin Britten were present at the BBC studios in Newcastle, then in New Bridge Street, for the broadcast of their radio play *Hadrian's Wall*, about the history of the wall featuring a family's daytrip to Housesteads, which included 'Roman Wall Blues'. Britten's setting of the poem was lost until rediscovered in 2005 by filmmaker John Mapplebeck, thanks to a chance conversation with a 99-year-old former singer who'd been part of a choir brought in but not used for the 1937 recording. The play was restaged for the first time with Britten's music included at Sage Gateshead in 2007.

See other note on Auden and the North Pennines on pages 246-47.

The Roman Centurion's Song
(Roman Occupation of Britain, AD 300)

Legate, I had the news last night – my cohort ordered home
By ships to Portus Itius and thence by road to Rome.
I've marched the companies aboard, the arms are stowed below:
Now let another take my sword. Command me not to go!

I've served in Britain forty years, from Vectis to the Wall,
I have none other home than this, nor any life at all.
Last night I did not understand, but, now the hour draws near
That calls me to my native land, I feel that land is here.

Here where men say my name was made, here where my work was done;
Here where my dearest dead are laid – my wife – my wife and son;
Here where time, custom, grief and toil, age, memory, service, love,
Have rooted me in British soil. Ah, how can I remove?

For me this land, that sea, these airs, those folk and fields suffice.
What purple Southern pomp can match our changeful Northern skies,
Black with December snows unshed or pearled with August haze –
The clanging arch of steel-grey March, or June's long-lighted days?

You'll follow widening Rhodanus till vine and olive lean
Aslant before the sunny breeze that sweeps Nemausus clean
To Arelate's triple gate; but let me linger on,
Here where our stiff-necked British oaks confront Euroclydon!

You'll take the old Aurelian Road through shore-descending pines
Where, blue as any peacock's neck, the Tyrrhene Ocean shines.
You'll go where laurel crowns are won, but – will you e'er forget
The scent of hawthorn in the sun, or bracken in the wet?

Let me work here for Britain's sake – at any task you will –
A marsh to drain, a road to make or native troops to drill.
Some Western camp (I know the Pict) or granite Border keep,
Mid seas of heather derelict, where our old messmates sleep.

Legate, I come to you in tears – My cohort ordered home!
I've served in Britain forty years. What should I do in Rome?
Here is my heart, my soul, my mind – the only life I know.
I cannot leave it all behind. Command me not to go!

RUDYARD KIPLING
Three Poems, 1911 | *Rudyard Kipling's Verse: Definitive Edition*, 1940

Rudyard Kipling (1865–1936) knew the Northumberland Fusiliers best of all the British army regiments (he called them the 'Tyneside Tail-Twisters') in India in 1886-88. Bobby Wicks, the idealised young officer in the story 'Only a Subaltern' is drawn from the regiment. Kipling wrote: 'The man who has never heard the "Keel Row" rising high and shrill above the sound of the regiment...has something yet to hear and understand.'

In *Puck of Pook's Hill* (1906), there are three chapters devoted to a centurion of the XXX Legion, staunchly defending the Roman Wall in the days of imperial decline. The town Kipling mentions, 'Hunno', seems to be Corstopitum (Corbridge), then on the main road from York to Scotland.

He cannot have been to the fort in Wallsend, however, as he describes it as 'Segedunum on the cold eastern beach'! His 'Roman Centurion's Song' is a plea to work in Britain and not be recalled to Rome.

For Kipling, the *Mauretania* (launched from Wallsend in 1906) was a mighty symbol. In 'The Secret of the Machines' (1911), he writes:

> The boat-express is waiting your command!
> You will find the 'Mauretania' at the quay,
> Till her captain turns the lever 'neath his hand
> And the monstrous nine-decked city goes to sea.

Lady Noble records that Kipling visited the Armstrong works at Elswick in 1915, presumably in connection with his books *Fringes of the Fleet* and *The War at Sea* (1916). [AM]

On Cawfields Crag

So old the curlew seems,
Grey, lean and ancient, with his curving bill,
So rich and mellow his clear April call
From hill to hill,

That, listening to that voice
Whose very beauty moves my heart to tears –
The beauty only ripening wisdom brings
With the full years –

It almost seems to me
Believable the Roman sentry heard,
Standing on Cawfields Crag as I stand now,
That very bird.

WILFRID GIBSON
The Golden Room and Other Poems, 1928
➤ AUTHOR NOTE PAGES 232-33

Chesterholm

If a Roman ghost should come
To the haughs of Chesterholm
Where, turf-hid from human eyes.
Ruined Vindolanda lies,
Would he grieve to think how she
Lost her world-wide mastery,
Grieve to think how fallen Rome
Lost the world, and Chesterholm?

WILFRID GIBSON
The Golden Room and Other Poems, 1928

The Watch on the Wall

From his high station on the Great Whin Sill
In a milecastle of the Roman Wall
Watching the dim fells dreaming in the still
Tender Spring moonshine, now he hears the call
Of courting curlew from a nearby syke
Answered by crake of wild-duck and the scream
Of seagull nesting on far Hallypike.
And, as he listens, still alert to hear
The approach of enemy aircraft, in a half-dream
He gazes at the rippling shimmer and gleam
Of light on Broomlee Lough; and thinks of all
The fighting and the fury and the fear
These Northern wastes have known since time began –
Forgotten tribes of prehistoric man
Warring with wolves and their own wolf-like kind:
The ancient Picts, stemming the Northward sweep
Of Roman cohorts on this very steep,
Storming and harrying year after year,
Until at length the legions were withdrawn
Southward in panic, summoned in headlong haste
Back to the succour of their mother Rome,
Or, battleworn deserters, they strayed to find

And settle in some peaceful British home:
The coming of the Saxons; and the hordes
Of Vikings sallying inland from the coast
Time and again in many a bloody dawn
From their beached longboats, host on murderous host
With wide-winged helms and bitter-biting swords.
The Normans in baulked anger laying waste
The hills and dales of all Northumberland:
The longdrawn civil conflicts breaking out
Through the ensuing centuries till the last
Forlorn adventure of the Jacobites:
And, always, startling the dark Northern nights
With fiery forays, the Border reiving clans.
And, recollecting how these fells have been
Bloodsoaked so often and how these hills have seen
Defeat and victory and foes put to rout
Or vanquished in a last heroic stand
Times out of mind; and wondering at man's
Insatiable lust for killing, his heart is filled,
As in the haunted night he watches alone,
With dire despair, to think that now the whole
World seethes in insensate slaughter fiercer far
Than even these Border battlefields have known
Through their long history of futile strife;
And every instant under sun and star
Cities are stormed and men in thousands killed,
And all the hardwon ideals of man's soul
In shattering disaster overthrown;
While, caught in the blind frenzy, such men as he
Who only asked to lead a peaceful life
And be allowed to cultivate and build
For future generations now should be
Compelled, by total annihilation faced,
To join in the destruction, and lay waste
Their best years, waging war with their own kind.

And, even as he stares into the blind
And ominous future, he marks the hostile drone
Of Westward-flying planes from oversea.

WILFRID GIBSON
The Searchlights, 1943

Poem found at Chesters Museum, Hadrian's Wall

To Jove, best and greatest
and to the other immortal gods;
to Augustus, happy and unconquered
Victory, holding a palm branch;
to Hadrian
commemorating 343 paces of the Roman Wall

> *bill hook, holdfast, trivet*
> *latch lifter, nail lifter, snaffle bit*
> *sickle blade, terret ring, spear butt*
> *boat book, entrenching tool*
> *chisel, gouge, gimlet, punch*

To Longinus, trumpeter
and Milenus, standard bearer
1st Cohort of the Batavians;
to Cornelius Victor
served in the army 26 years
lived 55 years 11 days
erected by his wife;
to Brigomaglos, a Christian;
to my wife Aelia Comindus
who died aged 32

> *unguentaria*
> *balsamaria*
> *ivory comb*
> *pins of bronze and bone*
> *dress fastener*
> *strap fastener*
> *spinning whorls*
> *needles, spoons*
> *Millefiori beads*
> *ligula, earprobe*
> *tongs*

To the woodland god Cocidius;
to Coventina, water goddess
and attendant nymphs

– in her well
axe hammer
spiral ring, jet ring
dogbrooch, coins

To the Mother Goddesses
to the gods of this place
to the goddesses across the water
to the old gods
to a god...

dedication partly obliterated
with human figure in rude relief
text of doubtful meaning
dedication illegible

uninscribed

stone of...

FRANCES HOROVITZ
Wall, 1981 | *Snow Light, Water Light*, 1983 | *Collected Poems*, 1985

Rain – Birdoswald

    I stand under a leafless tree
more still, in this mouse-pattering
    thrum of rain,
than cattle shifting in the field.
    It is more dark than light.
A Chinese painter's brush of deepening grey
    moves in a subtle tide.

    The beasts are darker islands now.
Wet-stained and silvered by the rain
    they suffer night,
marooned as still as stone or tree.
    We sense each other's quiet.

    Almost, death could come
inevitable, unstrange
    as is this dusk and rain,
and I should be no more
    myself, than raindrops
glimmering in last light
    on black ash buds

or night beasts in a winter field.

FRANCES HOROVITZ
Snow Light, Water Light, 1983 | *Collected Poems*, 1985

Vindolanda – January

    winter light
a track through trees
leaning with frozen snow;
boy and dogs whoop ahead,
in a white flurry
vanish over the near horizon

    slush, mud underfoot
the sign-post obscured

    Vindolanda
a word warm on the tongue
– voices returning
bronze glint by firelight
smoke from the hill

    over the black burn
through stark trees
a stone tower
    white shrouded,
blue shadowed humps in the land

    birds hop, silent
a moon sharpens the yellow sky

    snow drives into the angled field

    on the map of the land
boy, dogs wheel and turn
perspectives away

FRANCES HOROVITZ
Wall, 1981 | *Snow Light, Water Light*, 1983 | *Collected Poems*, 1985

Brigomaglos, a Christian, Speaks…

    'Some say they saw the Bull,
stamping under the skyline
with the new sun rising between his horns.
They say the black blood flows like water …

    I don't believe them.
It was only the officers,
    never the men
(any god would do for us
    till the White Christ came).
They'd see anything, anyway,
stumbling out of their caves
dizzy with darkness and the stink of blood.

Strange how they thought they brought the light to birth.

    We pulled their temple down in the end,
opened it up to the proper light
– plenty of black birds flapping around
but never their Raven that flies to the sun.

    We have the Sun,
our Christ is the Son who is brought to birth.
He is a white Dove
    who walks in fields of light,
brighter than snow-light or water-light.

His light burns in us.
He has engraved our souls like glass
to hold his seeds of light.

   Those old gods should keep their place
under the dark of stones
or in the deep wood.

They should fade like the last wood-ember
or the last sputtering flame of the lamp,
be echoed only in children's songs.

   In sleep they crowd
riding the uneasy edge of dreams...'

FRANCES HOROVITZ
Wall, 1981 | *Snow Light, Water Light*, 1983 | *Collected Poems*, 1985

The Crooked Glen

I saw nothing but waves and winds

       ...the moon resting in a broken apple tree
  an ushering wind shake ash and alder
              by the puckered river.
Lightly, like boats, the thin leaves rock and spin.

Blood-dark berries stir; above my head the thorn trees lean.
In their black pools the moon fragments herself.

  Ghost dry the unquiet reeds ...

I saw nothing but the waters wap
            and waves wan

FRANCES HOROVITZ
Snow Light, Water Light, 1983 | *Collected Poems*, 1985

Frances Horovitz (1938–1983) was a teacher, broadcaster, actress and poet, and a friend of both Kathleen Raine and Winifred Nicholson. She spent two winters at a farmhouse at Kiln Hill, near Birdoswald Fort on the Roman Wall (1980–82). *Wall* (1981), an LYC Gallery collaboration on which she worked with poets Roger Garfitt, Richard Kell and Rodney Pybus alongside four visual artists, is a product of this period, as is *Snow Light, Water Light* (1983). The latter contains many moving and delicately precise lyrics, often compared to Oriental landscape poetry. Among these poems are 'Rain – Birdoswald', 'Vindolanda – January', and others referring to Chesters Fort and the Mithraic Temple at Carrawburgh, believed to have been pulled down by Christians in AD 297. Near Birdoswald is Camboglanna (the Crooked Glen), reputed site of Camlann, King Arthur's last battle. Horovitz's poem 'The Crooked Glen' alludes to this. [AM]

The Hooded Gods

> three male gods of healing, fertility, and the underworld, from
> a stone plaque in Housesteads Museum, Hadrian's Wall.

These are the odds and sods among the gods,
the other ranks, the omnipresences,
teamen, charmen, male midwives: the daily helps
from history's basement, the caretakers

who rarely come to light. They have become
their deliverances, their many hands
beneath notice and now beyond telling.
They surface from the sleep of history

whose care suffuses history like sleep,
powers of recovery and repair
who keep the middle watch, the graveyard shift,
the seamsters who knit up the ravelled sleeve.

Empire succeeds empire over their heads.
The paces centuries set in the Wall
have doubled under artillery wheels.
Now low-flying Phantoms ghost from the stones.

Their histories are the interleaves,
the pages happiness has written white.
They show as lapses in the chronicle,
or specks of dialect in letters home.

No stars in their eyes. No shrinking either.
These are the hard core. These are the heart's wood.
Three grey bottles still standing on the Wall.
Three pollards who can make a fist of green.

ROGER GARFITT
Wall, 1981 | *Selected Poems*, 2000

Stone Relief Housesteads

Mediterranean, alien,
stone-flesh chafed
and chastened, whipped
by wind, by hail,
dissolved in rain, till legs
shrank to spindles
and quiver hung
awkwardly from shy
shoulders – or did
the carver's bare hands
shiver, and the chisel
stop too soon?
However it was,
this meagre figure
is our knock-kneed Diana,
our uncomfortable, chill
madonna of the North.

GARETH REEVES
Real Stories, 1984 | *To Hell with Paradise*, 2012

AD 128

I come from the mud, with cohorts
up to my eyes in sublunary shite I've razed
forests, repaved and rerouted roads, rebuilt
the Imperial Border. The places I've seen,

pal, soft as porridge the soil there, you drown
in sludge, dine on swill, your billet's a one-arsed
village of sludge slapped into bricks and dried –
not that the bloody sun ever shines there,

it turns its misery-stricken face away,
hides in a slate-grey crying fit of mist
and more vicious, remorseless
pissing rain than you'd believe – but

the crack was good as well. Plenty of blondes,
Batavian whores. Who bleat or is it moo as you
screw them. As for their grasping hard-and-fast
fingers, fair enough, I had the cash.

After that the crossing and work on the wall,
hand of a god who keeps us safe and warm.
The job is done. I stayed on, I live in clover
here in the glow of this stone hand's palm

that reddens as I write. Sunset casts
the shape of old hills on these grasslands,
the clouds above are new, the shades
of night are closing in. I wait.

ESTHER JANSMA
Alles is nieuw, 2005 | *What It Is: Selected Poems*, 2008
translated from the Dutch by Francis R. Jones

Dutch poet Esther Jansma was one of several poets from countries that had once garrisoned Hadrian's Wall who took part in the Writing on the Wall project organised by Arts UK. Also an archaeologist, she was the obvious poet to invite as a latter-day representative of the Batavians. This is the Germanic tribe who lived in what are now the Dutch provinces of Utrecht and Gelderland, and who are self-deprecatingly satirised in 'AD 128'. [Tr.]

This Far and No Further

From Cawfield to Winshields,
From Thorny Doors and Bogle Hole,
From Peel Crags and Steel Rigg,
Aa' the way to Sooin' Shields.

Blow, wind,   *From Hoond Hill*
Splinter, crack,   *To High Shields,*
Snap the spine   *From Hotbank*
Of the rock.   *To Hoosesteeds,*
Bring rain,   *From Cuddy's Craig*
Drive snow,   *To Clew Hill,*
Ice, winter –   *Aa' the way*
Wind, blow.   *To Sooin' Shields.*

From Cowburn Rigg and Cawburnshield,
From Close-a-Burns and Crindledykes,
From Bonnyrigg and Beggar Bog,
Aa' the way to Sooin' Shields.

I am the King of all you see,
The sky-wide, the slant country.

Frozen breakers of bare rock
Bow before me, splinter, crack;

Black wounds where the earth bled
Intractable matter. Peat, mud,
Water closes upon its dead.

The Cow Burn,
The Knag Burn,
The Brackie Burn,
The Bean Burn,
Crag Lough,
Broomlee,
Greenlee
And Grindon.

The rush, the bent-grass and the seg,
The crippled hawthorn on the crag,

*The Lang Field, the Hen Field,
The Back Fell, Seat-Side…*

The hawk, the crow, the fox, the hare –
All my creatures prick with fear.

I drive the clouds, the light that picks
Shadows out among the rocks.

I heft the sheep upon the hill,
The days across the empty fell.

By night, a riveted shield of stars
Arches above my dark land, scarred
By sediments of hope and care,

Stony marks that human hands
Have written, lightly, on the land.
They go. I stay. I am the wind.

*From Cowburn Rigg and Cawburnshield,
From Close-a-Burns and Crindledykes,
From Bonnyrigg and Beggar Bog,
Aa' the way to Sooin' Shields.*

The quad-bike bumps
Over boulders, thumps;
Over fox-hole and cord-rig it tears,
The shepherd, a sack
Of feed on the back
And a thousand yowes in his care.

Through glaur and burn
The big tyres churn
As he flies across the fell.
Through the roar of gears
He scarcely hears
The story that each stone tells:

The tall stone of the wicket-post,
The blackened stone of the hearth,
The silent stones of the burial-place
With their secretive, circular marks,

Their meanings lost
Like a memory passed
In whispers down the days,
Round the dancing flames
When the strangers came,
In the ashes when they marched away.

> *From Hoond Hill*
> *To High Shields,*
> *From Hotbank to Hoosesteeds,*
> *From Cuddy's Craig*
> *To Clew Hill,*
> *Aa' the way to Sooin' Shields.*
>
> *The Lang Field,*
> *The Hen Field,*
> *The Back Fell,*
> *Seat-Sides,*
> *The Bull Park,*
> *The Lake Field,*
> *The White Bank,*
> *Brocky.*

There's many a place aboot the countryside
Where a farmer is master ower aal;
But here, the land decides what ye can dae wi' it:
The land's the boss alang the Waal.

For it's never gonna be barley land
And it's never gonna be bagie land.
There's nowt but yowes and galloway cows
And rashers alang the Waal.

Above Crag Lough the wild geese cry,
And scribble their signature over the sky.

A flock of lapwings flips like a tide,
Summer to winter, black to white.

Hidden in reeds, the water-rail
Screeches like a barrow with a stiff, dry wheel,

And the rook on the Wall is a soldier, bored;
His claws are wire, his beak a blade;

On the ruck of the wind he is blown awry.
The brown hare sneaks from the bracken. High

On bleak Queen's Crag, a tall stone stands,
Battle-scarred, scored by forgotten hands
From the unwritten histories of the land:

Four-thousand tuppings and four-thousand lambings,   *The Cow Burn, the Knag Burn,*
A million nights of the stars' reckonings.   *The Brackie Burn, the Bean Burn,*
                                                Craig Lough, Broomlee,
Its finger stabs at the streaming sky.   *Greenlee and Grindon.*
Into the distance the wild geese fly,   *The Lang Field, the Hen Field,*
                                           The Back Fell, Seat-Side,
Scrawling inscriptions of summer passed   *The Bull Park, the Lake Field,*
While the grass goes over from green to rust   *The White Bank, Brocky.*

And the long wind keens, and the squat trees bow:

Who does the land belong to now?

I, the Wall,
Defend this place.
Across a dizziness
Of space
I am control:
A ruled line,
Mark of the safe,
The sure, the known.
I am the edge –
The frontier.
This is where the world ends:

Here.

Cliff-edge
Hawk-ledge
Fox-ladder
Adder-bed
Thorn-snag
Wind-rip
Rock-ruckle
Rook-castle
Sheep-slip
Stone-dip.
Deep drop.

Full stop.

Butter and eggs kept the house
And the wool paid the rent.
So we were warmed and fed
When pay was scant.

How many lambings passed
Since a bairn hungered?
Scarcely a living soul
Left who remembers.

And now the sheep worth nowt,
And the house to sell.
A hand that's never lambed a yowe
On Grindon Fell,

That's never once led muck from the byre
Or milked a cow,
Mouths from his soft armchair: 'Them things
Don't matter now.'

The King's Crag,
The Queen's Crag,
The Black Dyke,
The Fozy Moss,
The Cow Field,
The Pit Field,
The King's Wicket,
Caa'd Knuckles.

The jagged scrapyard of hawthorn,
A rush of wind in its hooks,
Berries ablaze like a lantern,
A robin among its roots:

The sons of ancient hedges
Bow to the east. Below,
Sky pools in the vallum.
The fields of the south glow,

Burnished copper. The north
Is verdigris and rust.
The wind harrows the silent
Lough. Violent, possessed,

Unpossessable country;
It stretches away
Into the distance, free-fall.
The rowan clings to the scree.

Neither England nor Scotland,
Itself alone:
Acres of secrets. Mouths
Stopped with a rubble of stones.

Twist and writhe   *The Cow Burn, the Knag Burn,*
And snake and stretch   *The Brackie Burn,*
Up rig and spine,   *The Bean Burn,*
Through slack and ditch;   *Craig Lough,*
The Wall goes under   *Broomlee, Greenlee*
Like a stitch.   *And Grindon.*

'Are ye dykin' it or capin' it, Davey?'
In the dip where the highroad falls
Into the vallum at Sewingshields
Two mend a wall;

Trying them this way, then that way, then this way,
Under a cold Northumbrian sky –
Dyke-stone, middle-stone, thruff-stone: drystone.
'Ye need a true eye,

Fatther used to say; and Aah can alwess mind it,
A good waaller never picks a stoene up twice.
Aye, an' there's a place for every stoene, if ye can find it.
Nivvor leave a space.'

Trying them this way, then that way, then this way,
A long time looking for the right stone. Bend
Your body to the rhythm of the wall and follow it;
Weight of the shoulder, eye, hand.

'The mowldie's a good hand at knockin' a dyke doon;
Soft, wet groond to the norrard, an' aal;
Frost in the joints; straight joints and watter.'
Time and forgetting will make them fall,

Trying them this way, then that way, then this way,
Brian and David, a stone at a time,
Bring a rough music to the jumble of boulders around them –
Make the stones rhyme.

Who says   *From Cawfield*
The world ends here?   *To Winshields,*
Who brings   *From Thorny Doors*
Peace and safety?   *And Bogle Hole,*
Who wields   *From Peel Crags*
The two-edged sword?   *And Steel Rigg,*
It's this far and no further now.   *Aa' the way to Sooin' Shields.*

Who owns the past?   *From Hoond Hill*
That spring,   *To High Shields,*
The stream that bears   *From Hotbank*
The money in.   *To Hoosesteeds,*
It's a fine line,   *From Cuddy's Craig*
It's a thin wall   *To Clew Hill,*
That says: This far   *Aa' the way*
And no further now.   *To Sooin' Shields.*

It's a Tourist Trail,   *From Cowburn Rigg*
It's a working farm,   *And Cawburnshield,*
It's a battleground,   *From Close-a-Burns*
It's a place to live,   *And Crindledykes,*
Where each man kills   *From Bonnyrigg*
The thing he loves   *And Beggar Bog,*
And Leisure's   *Aa' the way*
Where the money is.   *To Sooin' Shields.*

And it's this far and no further.
It's a balancing act for the future.
It's the Park and the Trust and the farmer
Who keep things just the way they are.

And it's more sheep and fewer men,
And it's more paperwork to plough through;
And it's more moor and it's fewer farms,
And it's more authorities to bow to.

It's a wet night, it's a foul night,
When the wind cracks and the rain rattles
The stones of the Wall and the sores of the heart,
It's a night for the fire and the whisky-bottle…

In the Milecastle Inn they are talking prices:
'Fower poond-twenty a yowe, and a poond expenses!'
'When mine went to mart, Aah come away wi' a bill!
Ye can guess where the next lot ended up – In a hole
Wi' a bullet between the ears. D' ye think Aah'm daft?
Whae, Aah ha' t' be, t' be farmin' alang the Waal…'

It's a black-dark back-end night. There are lights on the hill.
Out there, young Willie's cutting silage still
Over the bones of a dead Roman, in the rain.
Snug in the firelight, Willie of Edge's Green,
Rowley, Davey, Graham, Nick – the same
Fire-red faces, gutturals and names
As when Haltwhistle burned, a sheet of flames.

The Romans came
Like a bunch of thieves,
Boned our land
Like a side of beef,
Built their camps
Where our steadings lay:
It's the Romans get the plenty and the farmer pays.

They split our shielings
As ye'd paunch a hare;
When ye cross at the wicket
They grab their share.
They hammer out rules
And we obey:
It's the Romans get the plenty and the farmer pays.

Now regulations
Grow thick as weeds
And nobody asked us
And nobody agrees;

But when in Rome
It's the Roman way –
It's the Romans get the plenty and the farmer pays.

And it's more paper and less sense,   *From Cowburn Rigg and Cawburnshield,*
And it's more bureaucracy to plough through; *From Close-a-Burns and Crindledykes,*
And it's more moor and it's fewer farms,   *From Bonnyrigg and Beggar Bog,*
And it's more authorities to bow to.   *Aa' the way to Sooin' Shields.*

> *Once Brewed,*
> *Twice Brewed,*
> *Stell Green*
> *And Bradley's;*
> *Hawkside,*
> *Crow Crag,*
> *Milking Gap*
> *And Ridley's.*

Out in the dark, backs to the rain,
On Ridley Common, Bradley Green,

At Cawfields, Winshields, in the slack
Of Melkridge Common, Milking Gap,

The sheep lie down. Between them strides
The unnegotiable divide.

The same rain blows on either side.

It was the Powers-That-Be decided it:
The subsidies. Dependency. The sheep an' cows
Went on the same as ever, but control had shifted.
Aye, hinny. It's a different country now.

Aah rode a pony to the school at Hindley Steel.
Bairns waalked there from Scotchcoulthard through the benty groond.
Aah wadn't want them days a hunger back again.
Aye, hinny. But they're comin' tae us now.

Aah still can smell the hay-pikes, hear the horses'
Slow hooves doon the lonnen. Then the tractors came.
Wha wad a thowt the world wad shrink sae quickly?
Aye, hinny, but Aah've seen a deal a change.

Ye can churn an' churn aal day, an' the butter's no comin'.
Ye can try an' change, but this land winna bend nor bow.
Ye can watch the fell we fought for gan tae wilderness.
Aye, hinny. An' that's what's comin' now.

Who won this land and carved it?
Loved it, cursed it, marked it?
Who's reached the end of the safe and the known?
Whose powers do we fear to harm it?
We cared for the fell. The fell kept us.
Now they're paying us not to farm it.

And the wind bowls out of the darkness,   *From Cawfield to Winshields,*
And it sings of change and sameness;   *From Thorny Doors and Bogle Hole,*
From Cawfield Rig to Sewingshields Crag   *From Peel Crags and Steel Rigg,*
It can find no rest, no stillness,   *Aa' the way to Sooin' Shields.*

For the laws of the dark are the ways of the heart,
Of the crow, of the claws   *From Cowburn Rigg and*
    on the fox and the hawk –   *Cawburnshield,*
It's the line of the tide   *From Close-a-Burns and*
    in the sand we're writing –   *Crindledykes,*
It's the slant of the land,   *From Bonnyrigg and*
    it's the slope of the age,   *Beggar Bog,*
It's the rain and the cold   *Aa' the way*
    and the wind we're fighting.   *to Sooin' Shields.*

And it's no the stone but the waal,   *The Cow Burn, the Knag Burn,*
And it's no the day but the life   *The Brackie Burn, the Bean Burn,*
And it's no the word but the tale that ye tell: *Craig Lough, Broomlee,*
Go ask the farmer's wife.   *Greenlee and Grindon;*

For it's no the stone but the waal,   *The Lang Field, the Hen Field,*
And it's no the rain but the burn;   *The Back Fell, Seat-Side,*
Marry the farmer, ye marry the farm,   *The Bull Park, the Lake Field,*
And ye make your bed for life.   *The White Bank, Brocky;*

And it's no the word but the tale,   *The King's Crag, the Queen's Crag,*
And it's no the day but the life,   *The Black Dyke, the Fozy Moss,*
And it's no the stone but the strength of the waal: *The Cow Field, the Pit Field,*
Go ask the farmer's wife.   *The King's Wicket, Caa'd Knuckles.*

The Wall's fine line divides our land.
It cuts across it like a knife,
A stony scar that will not mend.
Aah cannot say much good about it.

Aah cannot say much good about it.
Memory's short and regulations
Tie our hands and test our patience –
It's a fine line between staying and leaving.

It's a fine line between staying and leaving
When a beast sickens on a dark morning.
On the sweet fell at the spring calving
It's a fine line between hate and loving.

It's a fine line between hate and loving.
Aah cannot say much good about it.
When he's out at the yowes with the snaa' blawin'
It's a fine line, living, dying.

It's a fine line, dying, living.
From the stone on the fell to the stone in the steading,
It's a fine line between staying and leaving.
It's a fine line between hate and loving.

From Cawfield to Winshields,
From Thorny Doors and Bogle Hole,
From Peel Crags and Steel Rigg,
Aa' the way to Sooin' Shields.

High on its crag, the Wall glares down
On moss and moor, on track and stone;

On lintel, hearth and cairn; all marks
Invisible beneath the dark.

The last light burning on the hill
At Hotbank Farm snaps out. The fell

And miles of scarp stretch black and blind,
And there is no voice but the wind:

I wear men down like stones. They pass
Into the dark, no more, no less
Than wave on wave through the long grass.

Once Brewed,
Twice Brewed,
Stell Green
And Bradley's;
Hawkside,
Crow Crag,
Milking Gap
And Ridley's;

From Cawfield
To Winshields,
From Thorny Doors
And Bogle Hole,
From Peel Crags
And Steel Rigg,
Aa' the way
To Sooin' Shields.

The King's Crag,
The Queen's Crag,
The Black Dyke,
The Fozy Moss,
The Cow Field,
The Pit Field,
The King's Wicket,
Caa'd Knuckles.

From Cawfield to Winshields,
From Thorny Doors and Bogle Hole,
From Peel Crags and Steel Rigg,
Aa' the way to Sooin' Shields;

From Hoond Hill to High Shields,
From Hotbank to Hoosesteeds,
From Cuddy's Craig to Clew Hill,
Aa' the way to Sooin' Shields.

Blow, wind,
Splinter, crack,
Snap the spine
Of the rock.
Bring rain,
Drive snow,
Ice, winter –
Wind, blow.

From Cowburn Rigg
And Cawburnshield,
From Close-a-Burns
And Crindledykes,
From Bonnyrigg
And Beggar Bog,
Aa' the way
To Sooin' Shields.

KATRINA PORTEOUS
BBC Radio 3, 2001 | *Two Countries*, 2014

After Heavenfield

Trailing our battle-perfumes, we fall down
to the undusted stream, and stick our blades
into the muscling water. The cold flow
bears off our weariness as well. We hear
the rush of elements, and look round again:
'God, what a cut!' 'There's something in your beard.'
And thinking of our families and the wives
of those we buried on the hill, we dip
our helmets for a drink, and throw the rest
at friends, liquid that sparkles in the air
and glows on backs. We shout: We won! We won!
and bare-arsed in the sun, we share the bread
on crumbling stones, and brush the flies away,
and eat in silence, as the morning goes.

ALISTAIR ELLIOT
Talking Back, 1982 | *My Country*, 1989

Following the death of the Northumbrian king Edwin at the hands of the invading Welsh and Mercians in 633, a Northumbrian army under Oswald of Bernicia defeated the Welsh under Cadwallon at a site just to the north of Hadrian's Wall, just east of Chollerford, which became known as Heavenfield, where St Oswald's Church was later established. [NA]

Between Greenhead and Sewingshields

You never meant to come to this
emblem of the distances,
nor understood how mind could lie
stripped of its contingency.
You know the kind of road I mean:
Zeno's proof embodied in
this tarmac and unbroken line
by which you near, though never reach,
the blind crest of the moon-drawn ridge.

You'll flick the headlights up to full
and give yourself to that parable
of the further edge, where for good or ill
the field of vision's infinite
as the nothing you illuminate.
The guide geography's written for your heart
has brought you to your heart's desire:
neither destination nor detour
but, friend, indubitably here.

Soon, you will pull over,
turn the lights and engine off,
and step without a thought onto the verge,
where, lacking name or face or age,
we'll leave you to, or not, or past, yourself,
the propositions night dissolves,
that sometime fellow-traveller, belief.
Goodnight. Good luck. God help you, friend,
world without (I mean it) end

PETER ARMSTRONG
The Book of Ogham, 2012

JARROW

On Caedmon

In this abbess's monastery was a certain brother especially made famous and honoured with a divine gift. Because he used to compose poetry inspired by religion and piety, so that whatever he learned from sacred literature through scholars, after a short interval, he brought it forth adorned with the greatest sweetness and inspiration in poetic language in well-fashioned English. And the minds of many men were often incited by his songs to contempt for the world and to association with the heavenly life. And also many others after him among the English people began to compose religious poetry; but none nevertheless could do it as well as he could. Because he didn't learn the art of poetry from men, nor through man, but was divinely helped and received the skill of poetry through the grace of God. And he therefore could never compose any fable nor empty song, but only those things alone relating to religion and befitting his pious tongue to sing.

He was a man set in secular life until well advanced in years, and he had never learned any songs. And therefore often at the feasting, when there was judged cause for happiness, and they all had to sing in turn to the harp, he would rise then for shame from the feast and go home to his house when he saw the harp approaching him. When he did that on one occasion, he left the house of feasting and went out to the cowshed of the beasts whose care had been entrusted to him that night, set his limbs to rest there and slept, whereupon someone appeared to him in his dream and saluted and greeted him, calling him by his name: 'Caedmon, sing me something.' Then he answered and said: 'I don't know how to sing; and that's why I left the feasting and came here, because I had no idea how to sing.' Again he who was speaking with him said: 'Nevertheless, you can sing.' Then he said: 'What must I sing?' 'Sing to me about the Creation,' he said.

When he received this answer, then he immediately began to sing verses and words he had never heard before in praise of God the Creator, in these words:

> Nu scylun hergan   hefaenricaes uard,
> *Now we must praise   the Guardian of the heavenly kingdom*
> metudæs maecti   end his modgidanc,
> *the might of the Creator   and His conception,*

        uerc uuldurfadur,   sue he uundra gihuaes,
        the work of the glorious Father   as He for each of the wonders,
        eci dryctin,   or astelidæ.
        the eternal Lord   established a beginning.
        He aerist scop   aelda barnum
        He first shaped   for the sons of the Earth
        heben til hrofe,   haleg scepen.
        heaven for a roof,   the Holy Judge.
        Tha middungeard   moncynnæs uard,
        Then the Middle World,   mankind's Guardian,
        eci dryctin,   æfter tiadæ
        the eternal Lord,   made afterwards,
        firum foldu,   frea allmectig.
        the Earth for men,   the almighty Lord.

Then he arose from sleep, with everything he had sung while asleep still fresh in his memory, and immediately added to those words many more worthy songs to God in the same metre.

    Then in the morning, he went to the reeve, who was his superior, and told him what gift he had received. And the reeve brought him immediately to the abbess and had him repeat everything to her. Then she ordered all the most learned men and the scholars to assemble, and ordered him to tell the dream to everyone present and sing the poem so that it might be decided by their judgement what it was and how it had come to him.

    Then it seemed to them all, just as it was, that he had been given heavenly grace from God himself. Then they related a certain holy story to him and told him words of divine teaching, and commanded him then, if he could, to turn that account into harmonious song. When he had taken this in, he went home to his house, and returned the next day, and sang what they had asked adorned in the best verse.

BEDE
FROM *An Ecclesiastical History of the English People,* Anglo-Saxon translation, *c.* 930
translated from the Anglo-Saxon by Neil Astley
(with Caedmon's hymn translated from the early Northumbrian version,
Cambridge University Library Kk.5.16, Ms origin Northumbria [Wearmouth-J.])

Bede (AD 673-735) was probably born at Monkton, near Jarrow, and was sent to be educated at the monastery at Monkwearmouth at the age of seven, transferring around 682 to its sister monastery at Jarrow, where he remained for the rest of his life. He wrote around 40 religious works at Jarrow, including his celebrated *History of the English Church and People* (731), the most valuable single source for the early history of Britain. Two of its passages are particularly notable in relation to English poetry.

His account of the poet Caedmon (*fl.* AD 670-680) tells of how this servant at Abbess Hild's monastery at Strenæshalc (now Whitby) received the gift of song in a dream vision. Caedmon is the earliest English Christian poet we know by name, just as Bede is the first prose writer in English. Caedmon's Hymn, like all Anglo-Saxon poetry, was composed to be sung, and is the first known poem in the Northumbrian dialect.

Caedmon's song

Forst ther wes nowt   nowt and neewhere
God felt the empty   space wi his finga
Let's hev sum   light sez God
Ootbye and inbye   so the light happened.

Up ower theer, thowt God, airy and open
We'll hev a sky   and a shavin' of cloud
Here's a bit watter   we'll caal this whale-road
Dolphin-drive, duck alley Davey Jones' locka.

Next orth appeared   a canny bit greenstuff
Rhubarb an raspberry   leafcome an leaf-faal.

God saw the heavens wes   handsome but homely
Made sun and moon   an the sharp stars their marrers.
Gannen to be good, sez God, else Ah'm a gowk.

Friday he thowt on   flatfish an flounders
Halibut, hake   an haddock an herrin
Likewise the cushat   chunterin an clockin
Seagull an skylark   an the shrewd spuggy.

Last cam the fowk, so   canny an careful
Hey, bonny lads, sez God, how will this suit yez?

U.A. FANTHORPE
Queuing for the Sun, 2003 | *New & Collected Poems,* 2010

The version of Caedmon's Hymn we are all familiar with is from Bede's Latin, usually rendered in a Whitby voice. There is also a rather longer and more detailed MS in Northumbrian Old English, here presented as the modern Tyneside idiom. (J.G. Collingwood, *The Harp Refused: Caedmon and his Hymn*) [UAF]

Caedmon

Above me the abbey, grey arches on the cliff,
The lights lit in the nave, pale prayers against the night,
For still the Blessed Hilda burns like a brand
Among the blackthorns, the thickets of darkness,
The ways and walls of a wild land,
Where the spade grates on stone, on the grappling gorse,
And the Norse gods clamber on the Christian crosses.
Below me the sea, the angry, the hungered,
Gnashing the grey chalk, grinding the cobbles.
The snow falls like feathers, the hail like quills,
The sun sets, and the night rises like a sea-mist,
And the fog is in the bones of the drowned. Here fare far out
Mariners and marauders, foragers and fishermen,
Tearing their treasure from the teeth of the waves, from the gullet of the
      gaping shores –
Over the heaped and heaving hills they return to the wistful harbours,
The freeman's blood and the sea's salt frozen on the gold.
Honour to warriors and wanderers, honour to the wise,
Honour to kings and kinsmen of kings, honour to councillors,
Honour to priests, honour to pilgrims,
Honour even to minstrels, the many-songed migrants.
But never have I ventured forth, neither on the northern tides,
Nor more than a shin's depth down the steep and staggering shore;
I have not roamed with the fighting men nor fired the Scotsmen's byres.
Yet I, even I, have heard the angels speak,
I, who never learned the liturgical tongue,
Who cannot read the written revelation,
Walking at night on the shingle, waking at dawn in the straw,
I have seen long spears of lightning lance at my eyes,
And felt the words, pricked out with fire,
Notched in my bones and burning in my body.
The angels crawled like gold lice through my dreams.
By the grey sea, under the grimacing clouds,
I hack and hammer at the handiwork of verse,
Feeling the sting of words, fearing the angels' threats,
Hoping that when the tide is full I may seek my unhaunted bed.

NORMAN NICHOLSON
Rock Face, 1948 | *Collected Poems*, 1994

In another passage from his *History of the English Church and People*, Bede quotes an elder's image for our earthly life which has inspired many poets, including Kathleen Raine (below), Anne Stevenson [104] and Carol Rumens [105]. Probably derived from the teachings of Plato or Plotinus, this was advice given to Edwin, king of Northumbria, who had proposed conversion to Christianity. Man's life on earth is symbolically depicted as a sparrow flying through a door into the feasting hall and pausing for some moments before flying back into the darkness.

Northumbrian Sequence

> So seems the life of man, O King, as a sparrow's flight through the hall when you are sitting at meat in winter-tide, the fire on the hearth, the icy rainstorm without.
>
> The sparrow flies in at one door and tarries for a moment in the light and heat of the hearth-fire, then flies forth into the darkness whence it came.
>
> *Words attributed to an ealdorman, in Bede's account of the conversion of Eadwine, King of Northumberland.*

1

Pure I was before the world began,
I was the violence of wind and wave,
I was the bird before bird ever sang.

I was never still,
I turned upon the axis of my joy,
I was the lonely dancer on the hill,

The rain upon the mountainside,
The rising mist,
I was the sea's unrest.

I wove the web of colour
Before the rainbow,
The intricacy of the flower
Before the leaf grew.

I was the buried ore,
The fossil forest,
I knew the roots of things:
Before death's kingdom
I passed through the grave.

Times out of mind my journey
Circles the universe
And I remain
Before the first day.

   2

Him I praise with my mute mouth of night
Uttering silences until the stars
Hang at the still nodes of my troubled waves –
Into my dark I have drawn down his light.

I weave upon the empty floor of space
The bridal dance, I dance the mysteries
That set the house of Pentheus ablaze –
His radiance shines into my darkest place.

He lays in my deep grave his deathless fires,
In me his flame springs fountain tree and heart,
Soars up from nature's bed in a bird's flight –
Into my dark I have drawn down his light.

My leaves draw down the sun with their green hands
And bind his rays into the world's wild rose.
I hold my mirroring seas before his face –
His radiance shines into my darkest place.

   3

See, the clear sky is threaded with a thousand rays,
The birds' unseen but certain ways
That draw the swallow and the homing dove
As eyebeams overleap distances between stars.

Whistle of wings heralds oncoming spirit –
Life-bearing birds follow the bright invisible trace
That draws the skein of grey geese flying north
Or hangs the hawk at one point, motionless.
Life's ways pass through us, over us, beyond us.

Birds home to the house of the world, to the islands,
To ledges of sheer cliff, to wind-tossed tree-tops
To the high moorland where the lapwing builds –
Nest and grave are where the quick joy fails.

Their great and certain impulses are spent
In snowdrift, salt wave, dashed against rock-face,
But strong wings buffeted by wind and blizzard
Still follow the way that leads through storm to rest.

Bird angels, heavenly vehicles,
They die and are reborn – the bird is dust
But the deathless winged delight pursues its way.

Shining travellers from another dimension
Whose heaven-sent flight homes to the green earth,
What gossamer desire floats out to guide
Spirit ascending and descending between grave and sky?

    4

Let in the wind
Let in the rain
Let in the moors tonight.

The storm beats on my window-pane,
Night stands at my bed-foot,
Let in the fear,
Let in the pain,
Let in the trees that toss and groan,
Let in the north tonight.

Let in the nameless formless power
That beats upon my door,
Let in the ice, let in the snow,
The banshee howling on the moor,
The bracken-bush on the bleak hillside,
Let in the dead tonight.

The whistling ghost behind the dyke,
The dead that rot in mire,
Let in the thronging ancestors
The unfulfilled desire,
Let in the wraith of the dead earl,
Let in the unborn tonight.

Let in the cold,
Let in the wet,

Let in the loneliness,
Let in the quick,
Let in the dead,
Let in the unpeopled skies.

Oh how can virgin fingers weave
A covering for the void,
How can my fearful heart conceive
Gigantic solitude?
How can a house so small contain
A company so great?
Let in the dark,
Let in the dead,
Let in your love tonight.

Let in the snow that numbs the grave,
Let in the acorn-tree,
The mountain stream and mountain stone,
Let in the bitter sea.

Fearful is my virgin heart
And frail my virgin form,
And must I then take pity on
The raging of the storm
That rose up from the great abyss
Before the earth was made,
That pours the stars in cataracts
And shakes this violent world?

Let in the fire,
Let in the power,
Let in the invading might.

Gentle must my fingers be
And pitiful my heart
Since I must bind in human form
A living power so great,
A living impulse great and wild
That cries about my house
With all the violence of desire
Desiring this my peace.

Pitiful my heart must hold
The lonely stars at rest,
Have pity on the raven's cry
The torrent and the eagle's wing,
The icy water of the tarn
And on the biting blast.

Let in the wound,
Let in the pain,
Let in your child tonight.

   5

The sleeper at the rowan's foot
Dreams the darkness at the root,
Dreams the flow that ascends the vein
And fills with world the dreamer's brain.

Wild tree filled with wind and rain
Day and night invade your dream,
Unseen brightness of the sun,
Waters flowing underground
Rise in bud and flower and shoot,
And the burden is so great
Of the dark flow from without,
Of sun streaming from the sky
And the dead rising from the root,
Of the earth's desire to be
In this dreaming incarnate
That world has overflowed the tree.

Oh do not wake, oh do not wake
The sleeper in the rowan's shade,
Mountains rest within his thought,
Clouds are drifting in his brain,
Snows upon his eyelids fall,
Winds are piping in his song,
Night is gathered at his root,
Stars are blossoming in his crown,
Storm without finds peace within,
World is resting in his dream.

Lonely dreamer on the hill
I have dreamed a thousand years,
I have dreamed returning spring,
Earth's delight and golden sun,
I have dreamed the pheasant's eye,
The heather and the flashing burn,
For the world has filled my dream:
Dream has overflowed the tree.

World without presses so sore
Upon the roots and branches fine
The dreamer can contain no more
And overflows in falling flowers,
Lets fall the bitter rowan fruit
Harsh as tears and bright as blood,
Berries that the wild birds eat
Till stripped of dream the sleeper lies,
Stripped of world the naked tree.
But on the hillside I have heard
The voice of the prophetic bird
That feeds upon the bitter fruit,
I have heard the blackbird sing
The wild music of the wind,
Utter the note the sun would cry,
Sing for the burn that flows away.

The sleeper of the rowan tree
As full of earth as dream can know,
As full of dream as tree can bear
Sends the bird singing in the air
As full of world as song can cry,
And yet the song is overflowed,
For pressing at the tree's deep root
Still underground, unformed, is world.

The invading world must break the dream
So heavy is the weight of sky,
So violent the water's flow
So vast the hills that would be born,
Beyond the utterance of bird
The mountain voice that would be sung,
The world of wild that would be man –
The dream has overflowed the tree.

6

The window-panes grow dark, the walls recede,
Grow infinitely remote, and the familiar room
No longer houses me, no longer encloses;
House insubstantial into nothing dwindles,
I and the earth must part – and who am I
That with this dark winged messenger must fly
Into the soul's dark night?

I – who am I, that enter death's dimension?
I and this swift-winged bird-form have grown one,
My thought is fused with his thought, will with his will,
And we are one in purposes unknown
To bird or soul, human or angel mind,
And yet we go – the destination draws us.

As sleeper wakes from sleep, I wake from waking.
World's image fails and founders, mountain forms,
Garden and trees, heel over into darkness,
Go down the night like ice in northern ocean,
Nothing withholds house from crumbling, hills from falling.
Only the bird-flight, and this travelling
Of the soul into its own night, are certain.

House that has sheltered me since I was born,
Flowers and trees and skies and running burn,
Body of death I lifelong have been building,
My face, hands, voice, language and cast of thought
No longer me, or mine – I dreamed them into being,
Being that is unmade again into the night,
Grows tenuous, and is gone.

In the round barrow on the moor, a king's sword rusts
Under the cropped turf, necklace and golden cup
Lie in the finer dust of a dead queen,
And when the ghosts come blowing on the north wind
They find again the treasures that once seemed
Inseparable from their own living, underground
In the earth circle, in the bone's mound.

I too have haunted memories,
Places once loved, travelled back thirty years
To where home was, to find the hills still standing

To find the old stone house, the trees cut down,
But water still flowing from the village well
Where once I dipped my bucket as a child.
Even such returning desecrates –
Do not disturb the barrow on the hill,
Leave buried there the treasure of past days.

Not in overlong continuance see
Of amulet or ghost, in wraith of what has been,
Evidence of soul's immortality.
The ghost that haunts, the haunting memory
Is the continuance only of the dead.
Such earth-bound spirits, into soul's night unborn
Miss the one way to that destination
From which the homing soul knows no return.

Yet with what infinite gentleness being flows
Into the forms of nature, and unfolds
Into the slowly ascending tree of life
That opens, bud by bud, into the sky.
World, with what unending patience, grows,
Ascends the roots from the dark well of night
From stone to plant, from blind sense into sight
Up to the highest branch, where the raven head grows white.

But body was imperfect from the first,
Heart, sense, and the fine mesh of word and thought
Will not contain the abundance of the world.
The god that in the ascending tree, bird, stone,
River and mountain, wind and rain
Has remained hidden since the world began,
The power that overflows and shatters every form,
Calls on death to come, to break the imperfect mould.

Spirit, freed from the form into which you flowed,
Prisoned merlin of the groaning tree,
The self you were in nature falls away
All at once into dust, as the bird-heart homes.
Dark into dark, spirit into spirit flies,
Home, with not one dear image in the heart.

KATHLEEN RAINE
The Year One, 1952 | *Collected Poems*, 2008

Kathleen Raine (1908–2003) was born in Ilford, Essex, the daughter of a Scots mother, who was a major influence on her daughter, and a Durham father (born in Wingate). Her paternal grandfather was a Durham miner, and Kathleen stayed at the village post office in Newfield on at least one occasion. Her parents met as students at Armstrong College in Newcastle.

She spent part of the First World War, 'a few short years', with her Aunty Peggy Black at the Manse in Great Bavington in Northumberland. For her this was an idyllic world and the declared foundation of all her poetry. The period is described in *Farewell Happy Fields* (1973): 'In Northumberland I knew myself in my own place; and I never "adjusted" myself to any other or forgot what I had so briefly but clearly seen and understood and experienced.' In an essay for Jeni Couzyn's *Bloodaxe Book of Contemporary Women Poets* (1985), she writes:

> The roots of my poetry go back for more generations than I can trace. I have written of my childhood in the first volume of my autobiography, *Farewell Happy Fields* – of the rich world of a country childhood in Northumberland during the First World War, and of the different inheritances I received from each of my parents. On my mother's side I inherited Scotland's songs and ballads – lowland Scotland, not the Gaelic Highlands, which has another culture altogether – sung or recited by my mother, aunts and grandmothers, who had learned them from their mothers and grandmothers before universal literacy destroyed an oral tradition and culture that scarcely any longer exists.

Her maternal grandfather worked as a teacher in Kielder, and after his retirement lived at 1 Percy Terrace, Bellingham. She had vivid and happy memories of the house and the fields around, with their flowers, mushrooms (often puffballs) as well as the flowers in her grandfather's garden and the fuchsias in his window. She also mentions outings to Newbiggin-by-the-Sea.

In 1939-41 Kathleen Raine and her children shared a house in Penrith with Janet Adam Smith and Michael Roberts and later lived in Martindale. She was a friend of Winifred Nicholson and remarked that she had failed to realise how near this area was to her beloved

> Inviolate sanctuaries of the heather and the bees,
> The hare's form, the lapwing's nest, the high places of joy.
>
> ('The Roman Wall Revisited')

Her unrequited love for Gavin Maxwell was an important event in her life. She recalls standing on the bridge at Kielder, as he had done – 'Gavin was native of my paradise' – and he used a beautiful line from one of her poems as the title of his famous otter book, *A Ring of Bright Water* (1960). The poem does not refer to Maxwell, it should be stressed. Love, even unrequited love, is the power that moves all things, and though when the relationship ended in 1956, she felt that her life was ended too; in fact it proved to be a rich beginning.

Raine published thirteen books of poetry. While she acknowledged the influence of her Northumberland childhood on her work and vocation, she was never a nature poet, but rather a philosophical poet – in the Platonic tradition of Plato, Blake, Coleridge, Yeats, Edwin Muir and Vernon Watkins – whose work embodies her belief in the sacred nature of all life, all true art and wisdom. Along with Iris Murdoch (novelist *and* philosopher), Raine is regarded as the leading modern creative exponent of Platonic philosophy, and her 'Northumbrian Sequence' represents and develops, section by section, nearly all of her philosophical ideas, elaborating on Bede's image of our earthly life as like the sparrow flying through the hall quoted in the epigraph, and culminating in the return of the bird of spirit to its eternal rest. For Raine, this place of childhood happiness was emblematic of a state of paradise experienced when 'outer and inner reality are one: when the world is in harmony with imagination'; her evocation of that time in the poem is 'a screen in and through which is projected a profound mystical vision' (Brian Keeble).

Raine was a distinguished scholar, the author of world-renowned studies of W.B. Yeats and William Blake in particular. She co-founded the magazine *Temenos* and for many years was involved with the Temenos project, aimed at bringing about a change of heart in society, and move it in an anti-materialist direction. She had what she called 'a sense of the sacred', an intense, mystical view of the natural world. This also informs her work on William Blake and the Neoplatonic tradition. [AM/NA]

Jarrow
(for Fr Aelred Stubbs)

Would want to paint them,
these town bright boys
at the dead end of the track
where it coils down away
from church and mound
leaving almost an island,
as it once must have been
when Bede set his *Lucem Vitae*
lightly on the pages of
these empty mudflats.

One thousand three hundred years
to set that orange apparatus
(for loading coal?) cleanly
in the mouth of the Tyne
and decide to abandon it
there, beneath that regiment
of scarred blue oil drums.
The scene looks set for
a study of bad times
in the lap of old times,

dead machinery teasing the live,
hooting youths who have
nothing to do here in their
circus clothes, their peaked pink
hair like traffic cones.
The more civilised the civilised,
the more barbarian the barbarians.
Such vivid colours, though,
like fresh paint on what
seems to be one more picture of

enough. A passing sparrow would
see it, flying from winter
into winter: the cracked black
skin of the tide between ripples of
couch grass, the blue sheet of river
rusty with ships, the cranes
against the monks' sky, crossed by high
pylons in their chains of power.
Lightbearers. *Lucifera*. Latin would have
named them, as the kneeling church

outlasts them in its green patch of
ruin. I would like to paint
the sparrow's view – the prefabs
(now the monks' cells), the heaps of
sweet timber by the sawmill's warehouse
fenced from an old blind horse
in a field, polished copper lamps
along the walks, a smudge of kids
in the distance. I would, in my painting,
be a brushstroke. *Talis vita in terris...*

ANNE STEVENSON
Winter Time, 1986 | *Poems 1955-2005*, 2005

Jarrow

Nothing is left to dig, little to make.
Night has engulfed both firelit hall and sparrow.
Wind and car-noise pour across the Slake.
Nothing is left to dig, little to make
A stream of rust where a great ship might grow.
And where a union-man was hung for show
Nothing is left to dig, little to make.
Night has engulfed both firelit hall and sparrow.

CAROL RUMENS
From Berlin to Heaven, 1989 | *Poems 1968-2004*, 2004

Talking to Bede

'You think historians must be keen to see
What followed their escape from history?
You think we can't find out? I'd rather hear
The earth described. Remind us of the Wear,
The creatures, plants and light where I began
To look around the domicile of man,
The home I only saw till I was seven.'

You miss the handiworks of God, in heaven?

'That's what we all must go without; so when
You die, bring news of nature, not of men.
None of us saw enough: we lived too much
In the small range of feelings, taste and touch.'

What, even you?

                    'You'd think not, but I still
Long for one walk across a field or hill.'

The Tunstall Hills, then, limestone – did you know
More than two hundred million years ago
They were a barrier reef, at the equator?

'I knew God made the world; I did think later –
As well as man's Last Judgement being soon.'

We still think that!... You've... heard about the moon?

'I know you... we... Man... Armstrong has been there,
Taking, as well as bait, a flask of air,
And whistled sweetly through the crystal spheres
We thought a solid mesh of ringing gears.
We got the moon wrong; but I told the tides
With some effect for sailors and their brides...'

Indeed you did. But how you told the tale
About the monks at sea without a sail!
Bringing down wood on rafts to Tynemouth, *they*
Were caught by wind and stream and borne away,
Till like a seabird swimming far from view
They hardly showed across the shifting blue.

Out rushed a squad of Brothers, with the Prior,
And knelt, and sent up prayers – like mortar fire!
I like your verse! – while the whole show was guyed
By local heathen from the South Shields side.
(For good men's fates give joy to reprobates!)
Among these Geordie rustics and their mates
Stood Cuthbert, still a boy, appalled to find
It isn't all that natural to be kind.
He tried to rouse Their Noble Savagery
To pray, and when they wouldn't, *bent his knee*
And pressed his face to earth. The wind backed east,
Or else turned turtle, for the future priest,
The rafts reached shore, and the embarrassed clods
Admitted Cuthbert's God outshone their gods.

    But surely the next tide, the evening breeze
Onshore, were not surprising prodigies
To you, but chance, coming out right for once.

'The eyes of sadness and of confidence
See the same world. You'll know whose eyes were sharp
Someday. Till then, keep looking, and don't carp.'

Forgive me, Bede. The old see more; the dead,
If anything, see more than can be said.
    Do you see Durham, where your leavings lie,
Translated from the Jarrow cemetery?
– 'Or rather, stolen, by a sacristan –
Aelfrid – a relic-crazy Westoe man –'
Who made you share a coffin – was that nice? –
With the shy saint whose *Life* you'd written twice.
    I went there from Pons Aelius upon Tyne
(Where Aelliots start to draw their family line?),
And saw, inside that one majestic room,
How blessed are the meek in Cuddy's tomb.
He's got two covers on his burial place:
One says, 'Ricardus Heswell', to his face;
The other, laid above it, back to back,
Is meant for us: CUTHBERTUS, gold on black.
They've left his pillow with him – Oswald's head –
But now you're honoured with a separate bed.
    I stood and thought of you, the Church's light,
Your only miracle that you could write
Here in the dark of Britain, stay-at-home

Doctor, Transhumbria's answer to Jerome,
Your undivided virtue ending on
The last notes of the Gospel of St John:
*'Even the world itself could not contain
The books that should be written.* Aah... Amen.'
A life of ivory, in and out of books,
Leaving no record of your wit or looks –
The little teacher's jokes in your short course
On Writing Latin Right were never yours:
'Melissus said buttocks is feminine,
But Verrius recommends the masculine...'
'Tibiae: human shin-bones; later, flutes...'
'Riches is always plural – so is toots
(Darling – but only in the vocative)...'
'Bellus (lovely) has no comparative...'
And so on, tags I guess as old as Latin,
That sent a groan round classes Virgil sat in.
They take our feelings back to someone young
Trying the tastes of grammar on his tongue,
But not to you, I think. We can't see you
Or those you name – you didn't mean us to? –
Except: you wore your hair cut Peter's way;
In memory of the crown of thorns, you say.
Other men show us Caesar pleased at winning
A laurel crown because his hair was thinning,
Or Cleopatra's smile as Marcus took
His only catch, her kipper, off his hook,
Or, burning cakes he was supposed to cook,
The first translator of your *History* book.
You never give such details. But may I,
A disappointed customer, ask why?
I brood on how your Brothers used to make
The illuminations down by Jarrow Slake:
They drew with templates, compass and a rule –
Like pattern lessons at an infant school –
Or copied Bibles, inch by inch. Next door
You cut up Commentaries, and made more,
Wrote Christian elegiacs for relief,
Collected folktales with a saint-motif,
Learned from the authors on the library shelf
And turned into a scholar by yourself.
You never left Northumbria. But, Bede hinnie,
How could you take your geography from Pliny?

'Pax. Skinchies, Elia-Aelle-What's-your-name:
Forbear to judge. It's blasphemy to blame
The inhabitants of heaven, or of earth:
I wrote, like you, for all that I was worth.'

Since Dante put you in his *Paradise*
You don't need praise; and who could criticise
The writer who rose earliest to walk
About our glittering language, still all talk?

'Pity my native stuff is lost. God knows
I worked on that despised vernacular prose...'

Strange to compose without a lexicon!

'And spell the passing words, before they're gone,
Like Adam's animals, never seen before –
And maybe soon extinct, or heard no more.
    'Tell me about some animals, in fact.
Forget the Wear: thanks for your silent tact
About my birthplace and my monastery,
Despoiled by bookless raiders from the sea
And then by the original filth of man.
    'Show a consoling wonder – if you can.'

Oh Bede! Your churches of St Paul's and Peter's
Are kindly kept, with services and heaters.
Through the same windows Jarrow light still falls
On surpliced cantors in their choir stalls.
There's a Musaeum: people come for miles
To see torn straps, smashed glass, nails, broken tiles,
And not to touch, relics not even yours,
For holy curiosity, not for cures.

'Yes, yes, the leavings: when they come, they see
The horrible marks of human territory
All round, where no one wants to live. What monk
Prays in these deserts of industrious junk?'

I saw a wonder on a summer's day, Bede:
I was walking on the landward way
To Lindisfarne, and found the sort of place
That puts agnostics in a state of grace,
Two rivers north of Tyne. A little breeze;

Bright ripples in the underskirts of trees;
Among the flowers on the sandy shore
Hovered an insect overlooked before
In years of scarcely looking. It was stout,
Furry and pear-shaped, with the stalk held out
To drink its nectar from a moving cup –
Two wings, so not a bee. I looked it up:
Bombylius major L. – Linnaeus too
Had seen a bee-fly in his day. Did you?
I bet, like me you'd never heard of it.
    Another first time, I watched cuckoo-spit
Nymphs blowing bubbles, and looked up at home
These things that lay their house in farts of foam:
Grown, they're the brown kind that shoot up like spray
From boots in heather or bare feet in hay:
Froghopper, typical homopteran.
    For you, Bede, dry and fresh as that dry man
Whose book connects the stages of a creature
As if there were no miracles in nature,
I hope these views from pleasant earth can cross
The barriers of years and bodily loss,
And –
        'Yes. They reach me; almost with the smell
Of seasons I excluded from my cell...
Enough for now. I'll ask for a repeat
When it's your heavenly birthday.'

                – If we meet.

'Benedictus benedicat!'

        And God bless
Your abbot Ceolfrith, patron of my Press,
And Benedict Biscop, your first abbot, who
Gathered the library that nourished you:
Tell them – they may be pleased – their fame's not large
Enough (like yours) to christen a garage,
But they're remembered where their scholar is:
You all gave names to Jarrow terraces.

ALISTAIR ELLIOT
Talking Back, 1982 | *My Country*, 1989

Bede's World

On the metro to the monastery I ping out
a filling whilst picking my teeth with a pen top,
pop it back into place and bite down hard.
It stays. I get off at Bede Station and make
pilgrimage through industrial estate;
by dual carriageway I walk me along.

Soon there is no pavement, just a track
around the timber yard and over a weak bridge:
'BUY AN OUNCE AND YOU'LL BE STONED ALL DAY'
grey spraypaint on its blue metal side advises.
Instead I visit Bede's World.

                        A longhair,
more gonk than monk, meditates with plastic bag
in the grounds of St Paul's, while I pass
an Asian couple in matching sky-blue grinding
gently together in the lane by the Don
where the kitchen garden would have sloped.

I have gone the long way round to get in
to the eighth century it seems, looking back
over the wall at cranes and drums and half-
empty car-parks hemmed in by a fence of pylons
and the lack of ships in Tyne Port.

The kids, who may not be all right, have kicked
in the floodlights, taking out portions
of fourteenth century with them. I check out
the interior for lumps of vinescrolling
and the Jarrow lectures: 'The Codex Amiatinus
and the Byzantine element in the Northumbrian
Renaissance', 'Early Christianity in Pictland'.

The women minding the church's shop have
an engrossing rosary of others' ailments
to recite, filling the site with a locality
its surroundings continue to deny.

The museum most of all – with its salmon-
pastel round of brick and paddle-pool blue

of fountain, more atrium than cloister,
more Roman than Catholic – is not here.

Inside you pick up telephones to hear
the Gododdin spoken in Old Welsh,
like cricket results or the weather,
and think how fleetingly theme parks catch
the attention of their visitors, like

a swallow flying into a hospital ward,
full of a terror shared by those in every bed,
battering itself off too much glass before
finding a way back out into the world.

Outside, withies and wattles prevail,
old breeds of hog and sheep and bull
from Ronaldsay and other outer zones
are clustered in the dark age hollow,
emmer, spelt and einkorn grow together in
the one authentic field, while a timber hall
and grubenhaus are being copied from
genuine remains.

   Only this incompletion
seems real: the workmen's radio tuned in
to a golden hour as None approaches is
as dependable as Bede's voice singing
'Ter hora trina uoluitur'; the photocopied
labels on the fences as trustworthy as
the copy of his *Historia* displayed
indoors as a superb example of Insular
miniscule script.

   Only our discrepancies
are real here; our marches in the face
of parliament, our writings in despite
of the vikings, even our theme parks
in the midst of recession, are bits
picked out from the sad mixture flowing
between black mud banks and made our own.

W.N. HERBERT
Cabaret McGonagall, 1996

On Not Finding Bede

At the throat of the Don
        where twin Tyne tunnels
undercut Crackwillow
        we searched for you.

We searched for you
        in Go-To-Bed-At-Noons,
by Pellitory-Of-The-Wall,
        through Lady's Bedstraw.

At Station Burn, Field Scabious
        could have been your glow;
Black Medic your remedy.
        We searched for you

the way Small Tortoiseshells
        and Meadow Browns
search Timothy and Tansy;
        how miners' caged Linnets

trace Bernician sky.
        We thought we traced
your coracle over Whitburn Steel;
        clouds scattering

for your arrival, but as we looked
        beyond Souter Point
we could only see waves –
        like praying hands of saints.

JAKE CAMPBELL
The Fat Damsel, 2016

Monument

    Jarrow's shipyard, Palmers, was closed by the cartel, National
    Shipbuilding Securities in 1933 which led to mass unemployment
    and the Jarrow Crusade of 1936.

Jarrow's MP, Ellen Wilkinson speaking in the House of Commons, 1936

    Today is mixed with yesterday,
    Pathé News becomes flesh and blood,
    men with Charlie Chaplin trousers
    return to where they once stood.

'In the Jarrow area there is 72 per cent unemployment, in Jarrow Town the percentage nearly 80. Jarrow must be made a special case. Jarrow is the victim of ruthless rationalisation which is being backed by the Government.'

    Uncle Johnny gave me his badge,
    I see him on the Edgware Road,
    marching in rain-soaked mackintosh
    and now tears stick in me throat.

    They presented their petition,
    Jarrow's Mayor dropped his heavy chain,
    Wasn't defiance, he told me,
    It was a slip I'd do again.

'Is the President of the Board of Trade aware that the government's complacency is regarded throughout the country as an affront to the national conscience?'

    Some shed bitter tears, railed,
    Ya knaa we've been sold down th' Thames.
    Has ti be more, can't be just this.
    Is this how our battle ends?

    On Guy Fawkes they came home by train,
    knowing their place, third-class single,
    handed them cheap suits and cheers
    still their pockets didn't jingle.

'*In St Paul's Cathedral there is a memorial to Sir Christopher Wren, which reads: "If you seek a monument look around".*'

'*If the Attorney General wants to see a monument to the capitalist system that he is so proud of, I will take him to Jarrow and show it to him.*'

TOM KELLY
Spelk, 2016

The Time Office, 1965

In the dock a boat straddles, a big man wearing a too small jacket;
my corduroy trousers run to Chelsea boots,
glowing with impossible dreams as the Tyne ruffles,
nudges nervously dock gates, a pulsing lung,
yet I can barely breathe with ignorance.

The tank cleaners' cigarette smoke crawls from clawed fingers,
they throw cruel jokes, cigarette butts and disappear into toxic;
wrapped in oil, painting everything.
It is all about money: the quicker they work,
the sooner they leave phlegm, rags and buckets of oil.
I calculate their wages, dry figures under ochre light.

At half-two in the morning, shipwrights, labourers, riggers,
embrace a boat, leaving after a refit,
heading out the Tyne without a backward glance to *Amsterdam*,
Limassol, badges rusted to their sterns:
a bad bruise after a rough night.

Workers' bikes creak in hold-your-breath early mornings,
night giving in inch-by-inch to light:
I still see them heading home,
as I whisper lives into a black ledger.

TOM KELLY
The Time Office, 2012

The Wrong Jarrow
(thanks to Andy Willoughby)

In the wrong Jarrow
there's no cobbled streets
no men hunched round corners
eyeing up the ground
there's no gas lamps and hobnailed boots
singing down Ellison Street
there's no one gathering around the Town Hall with banners
and the Bishop of Durham
isn't saying it's wrong.

It's the wrong Jarrow
the hunger should be more real
like in some African state
trousers should be shiny, threadbare
there should be more hate
policemen should use truncheons more
let's see more blood
broken bones.

This is the wrong Jarrow
poverty needs to be more visible
this is the wrong Jarrow
there's unemployment and deprivation
and no steelworks and shipyard and the clubs are dead
and there's problem estates and no go areas
and drugs on tap.
But it's the wrong Jarrow
It's not what I want
not what I want at all.
I'll come back when it's burning.

TOM KELLY
The Wrong Jarrow, 2007 | *The Time Office*, 2012

BORDERERS

The Battle of Otterbourne

It fell about the Lammas tide
   When the muir-men win their hay,
The doughty Douglas bound him to ride
   Into England, to drive a prey.

He chose the Gordons and the Graemes,
   With them the Lindesays light and gay;
But the Jardines wald not with him ride
   And they rue it to this day.

And he has burned the dales of Tyne
   And part of Bambrough shire;
And three good towers on Reidswire fells,
   He left them all on fire.

And he marched up to Newcastle
   And rode it round about:
'O wha's the lord of this castle,
   Or wha's the lady o't?'

But up spake proud Lord Percy then,
   And O but he spake hie!
'I am the lord of this castle,
   My wife's the lady gay.'

'If thou'rt the lord of this castle
   Sae weel it pleases me!
For ere I cross the Border fells
   The tane of us shall die.'

He took a lang spear in his hand,
   Shod with the metal free,
And for to meet the Douglas there
   He rode right furiouslie.

But O how pale his lady looked.
    Frae aff the castle wa',
When down before the Scottish spear
    She saw proud Percy fa'.

'Had we twa been upon the green,
    And never an eye to see,
I wad hae had you, flesh and fell;
    But your sword sail gae wi' me.'

'But gae ye up to Otterbourne
    And wait there dayis three,
And if I come not ere three dayis end
    A fause knight ca' ye me.'

'The Otterbourne's a bonnie burn,
    'Tis pleasant there to be;
But there is nought at Otterbourne
    To feed my men and me.'

'The deer rins wild on hill and dale,
    The birds fly wild from tree to tree,
But there is neither bread nor kale
    To fend my men and me.

'Yet I will stay at Otterbourne
    Where you shall welcome be,
And if ye come not at three dayis end
    A fause lord I'll ca' thee.

'Thither will I come,' proud Percy said,
    'By the might of our Ladie!' –
'There will I bide thee,' said the Douglas,
    'My trowth I plight to thee.'

They lighted high on Otterbourne
    Upon the bent sae brown;
They lighted high on Otterbourne
    And threw their pallions down.

And he that had a bonnie boy
    Sent out his horse to grass;
And he that had not a bonnie boy,
    His ain servant he was.

But up then spake a little page
   Before the peep of dawn:
'O waken ye, waken ye, my good lord,
   For Percy's hard at hand.'

'Ye lie, ye lie, ye liar loud!
   Sae loud I hear ye lie:
For Percy had not men yestreen
   To dight my men and me.

'But I hae dreamed a dreary dream
   Beyond the Isle of Sky;
I saw a dead man win a fight,
   And I think that man was I.'

He belted on his guid braid sword
   And to the field he ran;
But he forgot the helmet good
   That should have kept his brain.

When Percy wi' the Douglas met,
   I wat he was fu' fain!
They swakked their swords, till sair they swat,
   And the blood ran down like rain.

But Percy with his good broad sword
   That could so sharply wound
Has wounded Douglas on the brow,
   Till he fell to the ground.

Then he called on his little foot-page,
   And said – 'Run speedilie,
And fetch my ain dear sister's son,
   Sir Hugh Montgomery.

'My nephew good,' the Douglas said,
   What recks the death of ane!
Last night I dreamed a dreary dream,
   And I ken the day's thy ain.

'My wound is deep, I fain would sleep;
   Take thou the vanguard of the three,
And hide me by the braken bush
   That grows on yonder lilye lee.

'O bury me by the braken bush,
   Beneath the blooming brier;
Let never living mortal ken
   That ere a kindly Scot lies here.'

He lifted up that noble lord
   Wi' the saut tear in his e'e;
He hid him in the braken bush
   That his merrie men might not see.

The moon was clear, the day drew near,
   The spears in flinders flew,
But mony a gallant Englishman
   Ere day the Scotsmen slew.

The Gordons good, in English blood
   They steeped their hose and shoon;
The Lindsays flew like fire about
   Till all the fray was done.

The Percy and Montgomery met
   That either of other were fain;
They swapped swords, and they twa swat,
   And aye the blude ran down between.

'Now yield thee, yield thee, Percy!' he said,
   'Or else I vow I'll lay thee low!'
'To whom must I yield,' quoth Earl Percy,
   'Now that I see it must be so?'

'Thou shalt not yield to lord nor loun
   Nor shalt thou yield to me;
   But yield thee to the braken bush
That grows upon yon lilye lee.'

'I will not yield to a braken bush
   Nor yet will I yield to a brier;
But I would yield to Earl Douglas,
   Or Sir Hugh the Montgomery, if he were here.'

As soon as he knew it was Montgomery
   He struck his sword's point in the gronde;
The Montgomery was a courteous knight
   And quickly took him by the honde.

This deed was done at the Otterbourne
   About the breaking of the day;
Earl Douglas was buried at the braken bush
   And the Percy led captive away.

TRADITIONAL
Sir Walter Scott, *Minstrelsy of the Scottish Border*, 1802-3

Lammas tide: 1 August; *win:* take in; *bound him:* got ready; *Bambrough shire:* south of Berwick; *Reidswire:* Carter Bar on the border above Redesdale, site of an earlier battle in 1575, the subject of another Border ballad; *tane:* one: *free:* fine; *fell:* skin; *sail gae:* shall go; *kale:* borecole, green kale; *fend:* provide for; *lighted:* dismounted; *bent:* moor covered with bentgrass; *pallions:* pavilions, tents; *yestreen:* last evening; *dight:* chastise, beat; *kept:* protected; *wat:* know; *fu' fain:* overjoyed; *swakked:* brandished; *swat:* sweated; *Sir Hugh:* Percy was captured by Sir John Montgomery of Eglisham; *lilye:* lovely; *flinders:* smithereens; *fain:* eager; *swapped:* struck; *loun:* low-born, peasant.

'The Battle of Otterbourne' is a Scottish ballad which gives a more accurate account of the Scottish victory at Otterburn in 1388 than the English 'Ballad of Chevy Chase', of which there are two versions.

Hotspur
A ballad for music by Gillian Whitehead

I

There is no safety
there is no shelter
the dark dream
will drag us under.

*

I married a man of metal and fire,
quick as a cat, and wild:
Harry Percy the Hotspur,
the Earl of Northumberland's child.

He rode to battle at fourteen years.
He won his prickly name.
His talking is a halting spate,
his temper a trembling flame.

He has three castles to his use,
north of the Roman Wall:
Alnwick, Berwick, Warkworth –
and bowers for me in them all.

I may dance and carol and sing;
I may go sweetly dressed
in silks that suit the lady I am;
I may lie on his breast;

and peace may perch like a hawk on my wrist
but can never come tame to hand,
wed as I am to a warrior
in a wild warring land.

       *

High is his prowess
in works of chivalry,
noble his largesse,
franchyse and courtesy.

All this wilderness
owes him loyalty;
and deathly rashness
bears him company.

II

The Earl of Douglas clattered south
with Scottish lords and men at arms.
He smudged our tall Northumberland skies
black with the smoke of burning farms.

My Hotspur hurried to halt his course;
Newcastle was their meeting-place.
Douglas camped on the Castle Leazes;
they met in combat, face to face.

It was as fair as any fight,
but Douglas drew the lucky chance:
he hurled my husband from his saddle,
stunned on the earth, and snatched his lance.

I weep to think what Harry saw
as soon as he had strength to stand:
the silken pennon of the Percies
flaunted in a foreign hand.

'Sir, I shall bear this token off
and set it high on my castle gate.'
'Sir, you shall not pass the bounds
of the county till you meet your fate.'

The city held against the siege;
the Scots were tired and forced to turn.
They tramped away with all their gear
to wait my lord at Otterburn.

III

I sit with my ladies in the turret-room
late in the day, and watch them sewing.
Their fingers flicker over the linen;
mine lie idle with remembering.

Last night the moon travelled through cloud
growing and shrinking minute by minute,
one day from fullness, a pewter cup
of white milk with white froth on it.

These August days are long to pass.
I have watched the berries on the rowan
creeping from green towards vermilion,
slow as my own body to ripen.

I was eight years old when we married,
a child-bride for a boy warrior.
Eight more years dragged past before
they thought me fit for the bridal chamber.

Now I am a woman, and proved to be so:
I carry the tender crop of our future;
while he pursues what he cannot leave,
drawn to danger by his lion's nature.

Daylight fades in the turret-slit;
my ladies lay aside their needles.
They murmur and yawn and fold away
the fine-worked linen to dress a cradle.

And I should rest before the harvest moon
rises to dazzle me. But now
I stitch and cannot think of sleep.
What should I be sewing for tomorrow?

    IV

It fell about the Lammastide –
the people put it in a song –
the famous fray at Otterburn,
fought by moonlight, hard and long.

The Percies wore the silver crescent;
the moon was a full moon overhead.
Harry and his brother were taken,
but first they'd left the Douglas dead.

Who was the victor on that field
the Scots and the English won't agree;
but which force won as songs will tell it
matters little that I can see:

it surges on from year to year,
one more battle and still one more:
one in defence, one in aggression,
another to balance out the score.

        *

Crows flap
fretting for blood.
The field of battle
is a ravening flood.

There is no safety
there is no shelter
the fell tide
will suck him under.

V

He did not fall at Otterburn;
he did not fall at Humbledowne;
he fell on the field at Shrewsbury,
a rebel against the crown.

He might have been a king himself;
he put one king upon the throne,
then turned against him, and sought to make
a king of my brother's son.

Families undo families;
kings go up and kings go down.
My man fell; but they propped him up
dead in Shrewsbury Town.

They tied his corpse in the marketplace,
jammed for their jeers between two stones;
then hacked him apart: a heavy price
he paid for juggling with thrones.

Four fair cities received his limbs,
far apart as the four winds are,
and his head stared north from the walls of York
fixed on Micklegate Bar.

*

Now let forgetfulness wash over
his bones and the land's bones,
the long snaky spine of the wall,
earthworks and standing stones,
rock and castle and tower and all.

*

There is no safety
there is no shelter
the fell flood
has drawn him under.

FLEUR ADCOCK
Hotspur, 1986 | *Poems 1960-2000*, 2000

Henry Percy, known as Hotspur, eldest son of the first Earl of Northumberland, was born on 20 May 1364. The Percies were of Norman descent; they controlled the north of England with something like kingly power for several centuries, first as feudal lords and then as Barons of Alnwick and later Earls of Northumberland. They have been described as 'the hereditary guardians of the north and the scourge of Scotland'.

Accounts of Hotspur's life appear in the *Dictionary of National Biography* and the *Complete Peerage* and, in a fictionalised form, in Shakespeare's *Richard II* and *Henry IV, Part I*. He was a valiant and precocious warrior, and soon became a favourite with the people. He held such positions as were consistent with his rank and descent – Governor of Berwick and Warden of the Marches – but his chief pleasures were warfare (against the Scots or the French or anyone else) and, as an incidental sideline to this, political intrigue. It proved his undoing. He was killed at the Battle of Shrewsbury on 12 July 1403 in an unsuccessful rebellion against Henry IV, whom he had conspired to put on the throne.

His character was not entirely admirable, to modern eyes: he had a tendency to change sides and to choose his allies according to their usefulness, disregarding former loyalties; and he was as brutal as any of his opponents when he chose: his fate of being quartered after his death was one which he had himself ordered to be performed on a defeated enemy. However, his personal courage and his even then slightly anachronistic devotion to the ideals of chivalry made him a natural focus for the legends which have clung to his name.

The ballad is sung in the person of his wife Elizabeth Mortimer (not Kate, as Shakespeare calls her). She was born at Usk on 12 February 1371 and was the daughter of the Earl of March and the granddaughter, through her mother, of Edward III. She married Hotspur in 1379 and they had a daughter (whose date of birth is not recorded) and a son, born in 1393 and named after his father. [FA]

A halting spate: Hotspur was said to have some kind of impediment in his speech, which at times delayed his fiery utterances.

High is his prowess: This section quotes the traditional elements of the ideal of chivalry.

Castle Leazes: The pasturelands north of the city wall.

'Sir, I shall bear this token off...': The two speeches are taken from the version quoted by Froissart.

Otterburn: The battle was probably fought on the night of 19 August 1388, by moonlight.

Silver crescent: This was the cap-badge of the Percies; their coat of arms bore a blue lion rampant.

His brother: Ralph Percy.

Humbledowne (or Humbleton, or Homildon Hill): The battle fought here on 13 September 1402 was Hotspur's revenge for Otterburn. The English won, capturing the 3rd Earl of Douglas (Archibald, successor to James, the 2nd Earl, who fell at Otterburn) and many other Scots.

He might have been a king himself: Not by legal succession; but if Elizabeth's nephew, the young Earl of March, had been set on the throne, Hotspur would very probably have been regent. In any case his popularity was such that the people could well have seen him as a possible king.

Four fair cities: After his body had been displayed in the marketplace at Shrewsbury it was buried; but a rumour arose that he was still alive, and his corpse was therefore disinterred and dismembered, and the four limbs sent to London, Bristol, Chester and Newcastle to be shown as evidence of his death.

Borderers

Imagine land of lank grasses,
of acid soil fixed kingdoms gutter on
where the honed wind sounds
the wire's harmonic
                        and the mind opens
on long marches, a cadence of fells
beneath the mist's bled flank
and further back
in momentary focus, riders
close to ground.

They are moth against bark,
bracken's geometry,
lichen on stone crosses,
mind brooding on morphology.

Hedging bloodfeud, bordering
the dumb wound of moor
they are adrift among nations, a people
at the mind's turning
                      entering
on grey; the bearing of their voices lost
beneath the wind's sloughed locutions.

And if mist rises
see them here
between washed skies
and the rivers' absolution

hinged on nothing
– that filament of cirrus
light animates.

PETER ARMSTRONG
Risings, 1988

from Foray: Border Reiver Women 1500-1600

In the 16th century the lands surrounding the Scots/English border resembled a war zone. Though Borderers were descended from the same stock, spoke much the same language and had more in common with each other than with those living in London or Edinburgh, political interests instigated wars of aggression which kept them at each others' throats.

Violence created poverty and raiding became a means of survival. The words 'bereave' and 'blackmail' came into our language through the actions of the Elliotts, Armstrongs, Charltons, Kerrs, Scotts and many other riding names, including the Littles. Though Wardens were appointed to dispense the law across the Western, Eastern and Middle Marches, these men were often corrupt and justice was more likely to be found by the reivers taking matters into their own hands.

For women on either side of the Border life was extremely hard. Farms and smallholdings could not sustain families, but it fell to women to raise children, grow crops and keep animals. There would be continual raids or forays when their sheep or cattle would be stolen along with anything of value, even pots, pans and coats. Their own men folk would often be gone on raiding expeditions and either returning wounded or not returning at all. Rape, though seldom mentioned in contemporary accounts or subsequent studies, would have been a common reality. Feuding between families was also widespread, with bloody reprisals and counter-reprisals.

Alastair Moffat comments on a duality of opposites running through the long story of the Borders: that its extremes of landscape, from bleak, windswept hill country to douce green fields and 'knowes', echo the dour and taciturn, almost silenced, will to endure that co-exists with a love of words, a love of singing, of the voluble and imaginative, which came to a flowering in the Border Ballads.

Not much has been written about the women of the reiving communities in comparison with their men. Yet it's widely accepted that women were keepers of the Ballads, that through the very worst of times they kept them alive. These poems add their singing to that chorus.

PIPPA LITTLE
Foray: Border Reiver Women, 2009

The Cheviots

are a long, darkening room, unswept

as if men who came hungry
cleaved its hearthstone with their axes,
tore cloth from skin, skin from bone,
departed bloody-handed

but it was winters and a northern wind
rived down the roof beams, softened and rotted them,
and evening shadows over Alwin water
that kissed the lichens and tussocks
an ashy grey on dead beasts' backs:

home, with stones in it for potatoes, drove roads
a gleam of leavings: carcass bones, the dropped blade
from a hand that will not fist again.

And then in the dim, smudged mark that might be a window yet,
chairs are set so the dead might sit, lit by an ember
whispered into being by a woman's breath.

Alicia Unthank's Ark

They stuffed me in
like an old coat, not folded or bundled
but a bird, trussed,
a raven cut down from the sky,
neck snapped, wings broken back
all snarled and trampled,
made of me grave-goods:

blind and mute but not deaf
to their voices, footsteps
doing their foul work,
upside down I flew
to the well's dark end,
bottom of the world or its beginning:

while our door
cried its broken hinge
in the north wind,
and you came at last to drag me out
wailing the breath of a drowning soul,
a child new-cut from the caul.

In George MacDonald Fraser's book *The Steel Bonnets* there is an account of a raid on the Unthank family in their farm at Melkridge in Northumberland. Alicia was the only member of the family present and the reivers locked her in a large store chest or 'ark'.

The Robsons Gone

They went to keep the tryst
seven nights since and are not returned.

I watch the hills until my eyes itch shadows
that will not turn into human shapes.

Such quiet around us now they are gone,
and hunger stalking our skirts.

They were bound for the border
mustering Milburns on their journey

now their hoof beats' echo
is an ash beaten by the wind, or only

thudding of my heart.
Each day is a stone added to my back

as I sweep and mend and nurse the fire.
Come home, whisper the flames. *Come home*

come home call the birds, from farther
and farther away.

Truce Day

Hard-bitten, aye: by loss
and sorrow, those scavengers.
There's only sleep keeps a truce.
In men's dreams, spilled blood dries,
it's drink that runs over.

And yet –
foot follows foot along the path to where
flags leap, tethered ponies eager for the gallop,
footba' and races run for a silver bell,
kissing and punches and long-lost faces!
Just one day, fat as a trout tossed up from the burn
into our open hands, both buttered and salted,
even the spine-bones sweet.

And yet, and yet,
my mouth's sour
with its tin spoon taste of rain.
Trouble stumps along beside: they say
it's Sandy's Tom to hang,
some laying bets already on his neck.
The old unbridled fear, bitter
to the quick, comes up in me,
but how I love the dancing!

Shadows on the skyline; enemies surround us,
look out from our own eyes.
To babies heavy-headed, dandled on a shoulder,
someone's singing lullabies,
old songs of killing.
How many times
have I seen flesh mend until the scars
seemed trespass on it? *Safe*,
safe, I mutter it under my breath:
yet – someone is singing.

PIPPA LITTLE
Foray: Border Reiver Women, 2009

The Spur in the Dish

First, there is this: the fine softness
of my children's skin I stroke and stroke
to blunt the iron of their absence.
Then this: the spur in the dish, a spike
in the tender place at the root of my throat.

The border gaol is a beacon of stone
guiding my young warriors home
after days in the hills reiving. I count
each brick, crush lichens into dust, fretting
over nothing but a spur in the dish.

This hungry ache is what time does left
to its own devices: plucks the petals
from daisies; weaves a ribbon of horses' hooves.
Border warfare leaves a bruise; my heel, a blue
and gold fleur-de-lys when I remove my shoes.

LINDA FRANCE
The Gentleness of the Very Tall, 1994

The spur in the dish was a old Northumbrian custom: the lady of the house brings a platter to the table bearing not food but a single spur, indicating to the border chief and men of his household that it was time to 'ride and reive' if they wanted to eat. Such a scene is pictured in a painting with this title (1858–59) by William Bell Scott which hangs at Wallington Hall. [NA]

Raiding the Borders

Limmer thieves from robber towers,
the reivers rode after Lammas
when nights were longest, horses stronger.
Sometimes those they sought to plunder
saw the fires lit in warning,
heard the fray bell, were prepared.

Centuries later feuds were buried,
families allied to survive.
As my mother met my father,
back through the Bolams and the Halls,
Rutherfords, and Burnses further north –
marriages crossed over borders.

When they came down from the shires
the auld Halls settled by the Tyne
in a home the Percies gave them.
Walls a yard deep like a stronghold,
for the proud hill a proud cottage –
and we stayed two hundred years.

The line grew through generations:
six children, nine, then eleven.
Grandmother, the eldest daughter,
a widow at twenty-seven –
sixty years without her husband –
taught me how to live with borders.

When she crossed I could not follow,
but learnt how silent some raids were.
By twenty I knew treachery;
a friend, a sister was stolen
in the dark months of winter
then, after a long siege, my father.

We are never free from borders.
My mother died on an ocean,
shores at its reaches; no fixed limits,
just sea reclaiming then retreating.
The house was empty of all it guarded:
another raid had been unexpected.

We meet now on debatable land –
neither south nor north, but beyond both –
and in those moments everywhere
is full of her – the sky, the sun
as it falls by an open door –
she's before me throughout the house.

In the air I feel her pity
for the way we let rooms trap us;
the need we have to put up walls
and defend them; the fear we make
for each other by warring raids
which haste us to that last border.

When I surrendered their old home
I dreamt one night they all came back,
waved to me, walking down the path –
five generations who had striven
to keep the house their parents left them.
If we can't defend we are forgiven.

ROBYN BOLAM
Raiding the Borders, 1996 | *New Wings*, 2007

Borderers

(Whispered, menacing)
Are ye one of us?
Are ye for us or agin us?
Are ye one of us?
Are ye for us or agin us?
Are ye one of us?
Are ye for us or agin us?
Are ye for us or agin us?
Are ye one of us?

Are ye Armstrong, are ye Johnstone,   *Are ye one of us?*
Are ye Hall or Reed or Heron,   *Are ye for us or agin us?*
Are ye Henderson or Graham,   *Are ye one of us?*
Are ye Beattie, Bell or Potts,   *Are ye for us or agin us?*
Are ye Musgrave, are ye Dixon,   *Are ye one of us?*
Are ye Widderington or Nixon,   *Are ye for us or agin us?*
Are ye Charlton, are ye Robson,   *Are ye for us or agin us?*
Are ye wi' us, or ye not?   *Are ye one of us?*

Wool on the whin's barb marks the track.

The violence of molten rock
Stretches before you like the sea.

From Eildon's summit you look out
On frozen time. For miles, the black

Impenetrable, speechless hills
Of Liddesdale and Teviotdale,

Redesdale, Coquetdale, North Tyne –
Rucked and buckled, patched with pine,

Cold, embattled, acid-green
Moorland, blackland, carved between
Floes of ice and tides of men,

Fastnesses of bracken, slopes
And gullies – fold their secrets close,

While the searchlight of the sun
Sweeps across them, one by one.

> *Are ye one of us?*
> *Are ye for us or agin us?*
> *Are ye one of us?*
> *Are ye for us or agin us?*
> (Fade down)

Three things have no end:
Fear, hunger and the wind.

They blast the open heathland where
A single strand of wire runs.
Such a fine thread holds the peace.

Bold, defiant in the east,
At Sweethope Crag, a tower bursts
Out of bare rock, a brandished fist,

The only still, straight edge in sight.
While ragged flags of cloud and light

Tear like promises, it keeps
Its stony word upon the hill,

Unmoved, untouched, unblinking eye –
Outstares the armies of the sky,
Time its only enemy.

> *Are ye one of us?*
> *Are ye for us or agin us?*
> *Are ye for us or agin us?*
> *Are ye one of us?*
> *(Fade down)*

Yarrow Water, Ettrick, Tweed:
A ruckle of stones and a nettle-bed,

Grey-boned hawthorn, flecked with blood,
Almost turned itself to stone,

Lichened trunk and strangled root,
Braid their shadows by the burn

In the places they belong.
Stone and tree-root: make us strong

Where the wind blows on the fell,
Where the track runs up the hill.

Who cares where you came from now?
Every ditch and fold and knowe

And the white grass that swallows down
Arrow-head and carved stone,

Becomes a place to watch and hide.
The wide land bristles, sharp with eyes.

Are ye Elliott or Maxwell,   *Are ye one of us?*
Are ye Milburn, Tait or Turnbull,   *Are ye for us or agin us?*
Are ye Rutherford or Pringle,   *Are ye one of us?*
Are ye friend or are ye foe?   *Are ye for us or agin us?*
Are ye Kerr or Hume or Little,   *Are ye one of us?*

Are ye Laidler or Liddle,   *Are ye for us or agin us?*
Are ye Storey, are ye Ridley,   *Are ye for us or agin us?*
Are ye one of us or no?   *Are ye one of us?*

Are ye Dodd or are ye Trotter,   *Are ye one of us?*
Are ye Selby, Gray or Forster,   *Are ye for us or agin us?*
Are ye Davison or Pringle,   *Are ye one of us?*
Are ye Collingwood or Scott,   *Are ye for us or agin us?*
Are ye Douglas, are ye Dixon,   *Are ye one of us?*
Are ye Heatherington or Nixon,   *Are ye for us or agin us?*
Are ye Charlton, are ye Robson,   *Are ye for us or agin us?*
Are ye wi' us, or ye not?   *Are ye one of us?*

Where Tweed and Teviot's waters meet,
They carry all away: the gates,

The fences, signposts. Pine trees sway
Like ships at mooring on their slopes.

Tree-root, picket, branch, black loam –
The flood unfastens all; its broom

Sweeps the living and the dead
Towards a place that has no borders.

South and north, the colours drain
From drowned fields as night falls

On far, unfathomable hills
That sink their differences in sleep;

One ocean, darkening. Who knows
Where the fence runs on the fell?

The fading light, equivocal
As quicksilver, the cloud, the rain
The water singing in its veins,

Leave the earth to dark and wind.

KATRINA PORTEOUS
A Sense of Place (BBC Radio), 2002 | *Two Countries*, 2014

Northumborland (2)

Northumborland!
Aa think it is a wild majestic word!
Theor cum's a battle's thunnor when it's hord,
And ower the heathored moors of Otterborn
Aa see thi stalwaarts of an army horn
Scream inta battle, feyor in thor eyes –
A Fenwicke, A Fenwicke! A Hotspor-or-or! –
Heor on thi wind theor fierce hairt-lowpin' cries,
'Neath moonlit cloods abeun the gloomy heights,
An' bords affrighted high in wheelin' flights….
They spy at dawn thi wounded spreed afaar
Doon Elsdon's dip and up ti Carter Bar.
Aa knaa nex' day the heaps of bluddy slain
Alang the Elsdon chorch-waal will be lain,
Shorn o' thor claes, the pikes they'll waant ne mair,
Aye, rob the deid men nyeked; they'll not care!

FRED REED
Northumbrian Miscellany, 1978 | *The Northumborman*, 1999
➢ AUTHOR NOTE PAGE 63

feyor: fear; *lowpin'*: leaping; *claes*: clothes; *nyeked*: naked.

A Reiver's Neck-Verse

Some die singing, and some die swinging,
   And weel mot a' they be:
Some die playing, and some die praying,
   And I wot sae winna we, my dear,
   And I wot sae winna we.

Some die sailing, and some die wailing,
   And some die fair and free:
Some die flyting, and some die fighting,
   But I for a fause love's fee, my dear,
   But I for a fause love's fee.

Some die laughing, and some die quaffing,
    And some die high on tree:
Some die spinning, and some die sinning,
    But faggot and fire for ye, my dear,
    Faggot and fire for ye.

Some die weeping, and some die sleeping,
    And some die under sea:
Some die ganging, and some die hanging,
    And a twine of a tow for me, my dear,
    A twine of a tow for me.

ALGERNON CHARLES SWINBURNE
Poems and Ballads, third series, 1889
➤ AUTHOR NOTE PAGES 50-52

A Jacobite's Exile (1764)

The weary day rins down and dies,
    The weary night wears through:
And never an hour is fair wi' flower,
    And never a flower wi' dew.

I would the day were night for me,
    I would the night were day:
For then would I stand in my ain fair land,
    As now in dreams I may.

O lordly flow the Loire and Seine,
    And loud the dark Durance:
But bonnier shine the braes of Tyne
    Than a' the fields of France;
And the waves of Till that speak sae still
    Gleam goodlier where they glance.

O weel were they that fell fighting
    On dark Drumossie's day:
They keep their hame ayont the faem,
    And we die far away.

O sound they sleep, and saft, and deep,
   But night and day wake we;
And ever between the sea-banks green
   Sounds loud the sundering sea.

And ill we sleep, sae sair we weep,
   But sweet and fast sleep they;
And the mool that haps them roun' and laps them
   Is e'en their country's clay;
But the land we tread that are not dead
   Is strange as night by day.

Strange as night in a strange man's sight,
   Though fair as dawn it be:
For what is here that a stranger's cheer
   Should yet wax blithe to see?

The hills stand steep, the dells lie deep,
   The fields are green and gold:
The hill-streams sing, and the hill-sides ring,
   As ours at home of old.

But hills and flowers are nane of ours,
   And ours are oversea:
And the kind strange land whereon we stand,
   It wotsna what were we
Or ever we came, wi' scathe and shame,
   To try what end might be.

Scathe, and shame, and a waefu' name,
   And a weary time and strange,
Have they that seeing a weird for dreeing
   Can die, and cannot change.

Shame and scorn may we thole that mourn,
   Though sair be they to dree:
But ill may we bide the thoughts we hide,
   Mair keen than wind and sea.

Ill may we thole the night's watches,
   And ill the weary day:
And the dreams that keep the gates of sleep,
   A waefu' gift gie they;

For the sangs they sing us, the sights they bring us,
    The morn blaws all away.

On Aikenshaw the sun blinks braw,
    The burn rins blithe and fain:
There's nought wi' me I wadna gie
    To look thereon again.

On Keilder-side the wind blaws wide;
    There sounds nae hunting-horn
That rings sae sweet as the winds that beat
    Round banks where Tyne is born.

The Wansbeck sings with all her springs,
    The bents and braes give ear;
But the wood that rings wi' the sang she sings
    I may not see nor hear;
For far and far thae blithe burns are,
    And strange is a' thing near.

The light there lightens, the day there brightens,
    The loud wind there lives free:
Nae light comes nigh me or wind blaws by me
    That I wad hear or see.

But O gin I were there again,
    Afar ayont the faem,
Cauld and dead in the sweet saft bed
    That haps my sires at hame!

We'll see nae mair the sea-banks fair,
    And the sweet grey gleaming sky,
And the lordly strand of Northumberland,
    And the goodly towers thereby:
And none shall know but the winds that blow
    The graves wherein we lie.

ALGERNON CHARLES SWINBURNE
Poems and Ballads, third series, 1889
➤ AUTHOR NOTE PAGES 50-52

NORTHUMBERLAND

FROM NORTH TO SOUTH

Old Border Rhyme

Quoth Tweed to Till,
What gars ye rin sae still,
Quoth Till to Tweed,
Sae still's I rin and sae fast's ye gae,
Whar ye droon ae man I droon twae.

ANONYMOUS
James Christie, *Northumberland*, 1893

gars: makes; *rin:* run.

The Cheviot

Hedgehope Hill stands high,
The Cheviot higher still:
The Cheviot's wreathed with snow
When green is Hedgehope Hill.

But at break of day,
Or coming on of night,
Hedgehope Hill is dark
While Cheviot's wreathed with light.

WILFRID GIBSON
Whin, 1918 | *Collected Poems 1905-1925*, 1926
➤ AUTHOR NOTE PAGES 232-33

Dunnie's Song

Cuckenheugh there's gear enough,
Collierheugh there's mair,
For I've lost the key o' the Bounders,
An' I'm ruined for ever mair.
Ross for rabbits, and Elwick for kail,
Of a' the towns e'er I saw Howick for ale,
Howick for ale, and Kyloe for scrubbers,
Of a' the towns e'er I saw Lowick for robbers,
Lowick for robbers, Buckton for breed,
Of a' the towns e'er I saw Holy Island for need,
Holy Island for need, and Grindon for kye,
Of a' the towns e'er I saw Doddington for rye.
Doddington for rye, Bowisdon for rigs,
Of a' the towns e'er I saw Barmoor for whigs,
Barmoor for whigs, Tweedmouth for doors,
Of a' the towns e'er I saw Ancroft for whores,
Ancroft for whores, and Spittal for fishers,
Of a' the towns e'er I saw Berrington for dishes.

TRADITIONAL
Michael Denham, *Folk-lore, or, A collection of local rhymes, proverbs, sayings, prophecies, slogans, &c. relating to Northumberland, Newcastle-on-Tyne, and Berwick-on-Tweed*, 1858

bounders: or, 'I've lost the key o' the Bowden door'; *scrubbers:* wooden harrows; *breed:* bread; *kye:* cattle; *rigs:* tricks or flashy clothes

The Dunnie was said to be a reiver spirit which wandered the fells of the Cheviots where his loot lay hidden, the most famous being the Hazelrigg Dunnie from Chatton, a shape-changer which took the form of a horse or donkey.

The Tweed Near Berwick

On thy banks, classic Tweed, still my fancy shall wander,
Though far from the Land of the Thistle and thee,
And follow thy course to its latest meander,
The place of my birth where thou meetest the sea.

Though the memory of those early friendships did cherish,
Will fade and is fading, thou still art the same,
For though dear to remembrance young feelings must perish
And the friends of our youth will exist but in name.

But there is a language in thee, sweeping river,
A voice in the woodlands that shadow thy braes,
A home and a heart by thy side that shall ever
Be one with existence, be dear to my lays.

Midst the daydream of boyhood, ere glowing ambition
Had sung the fond thrillings of beauty and love,
Thy banks were my study – my only tuition
The sounds of thy waters, the coo of thy dove.

Stream of maturity, can I forget thee
When my birthplace's threshold thy waters will lave?
Forget thee! When Nature's omnipotent set thee
To wash the green sod by my forefather's grave?

Yet if these were forgot thou art witness with heaven
Of my vow on the breath of thy murmurs conveyed,
When, pure as the fountain, confiding was given
To me the fond heart of my Favourite Maid.

In this, deep and keenly, my soul's dearest feeling
Now tells me that thou art remembered indeed,
For to think of the Maid of my Heart is revealing
A tale that revisits the banks of the Tweed.

(Tweedmouth, 1834)

JOHN MACKAY WILSON
Berwick Grammar School Magazine, c.1965

John Mackay Wilson (1804–1835) was born in Tweedmouth. His first literary work seems to have been the poem 'A Glance at Hinduism' (1824). Wilson spent some time in Edinburgh, where his plays included *The Gowrie Conspiracy* (1829) and *Margaret of Anjou*. He returned to Berwick and became editor of the *Berwick Advertiser* in 1832. By then, however, he had become addicted to the bottle. He is buried in the crowded graveyard at Tweedmouth church. The six volumes of his *Tales of the Border* (1834–40) had originally appeared in weekly parts and after Wilson's death they were continued for his widow, with Alexander Leighton as editor. A new edition by Leighton extended to 20 volumes (1857–59) and his 1869 revision added four more volumes. [AM]

from **Tweed**

Under the A1's arterial hurry
Old Tweed spreads out, broad and slow and easy,

Its surface feathered by the breeze. All blowsy,
It slops, laps, toothless, at the undercut mud-bank,

A glacial boulder, a traffic cone, a stone-age fish-trap,
Slowly sinking into ooze and slime, or slowly uncovered.

High overhead, their wings up-lit at sunset,
Armies of herring gulls row their white ghosts downriver.

Over the flat haugh, over the salt-marsh, they muster
Out of two countries – over the wheat fields, the ramparts,

The sewage plant, the housing estates, the rotting dockyards,
And drift on Yarrow Slakes like snow – one flock.

At Whitesands and Abstell, Calot and Blakewell,
At Carr Rock, at Crow's Batt, at Gardo an' Hallowstell,
Haul in your gear, lads, it's time we were leavin'
From Canny and Pedwell to Farseas and Sandstell.

Ahead, the Royal Border Bridge. It is a gate
Sorting this side from that side. It combs the broad water.

Beached on the mud-bank, the haughty swans clap their wings:
Here's Berwick, perched on its high horse, looking down on England.

The tide is sucking out. Its swirls and eddies claw away

The knuckled roots of pines and fossil forests, cones and seeds,
The silts, soils, stones of prehistoric oceans dragged from far upstream,

The spawn, the snails, the shrimps, the eels, the smolting salmon – millions
    strong,
Their populations scattering

To far-flung places of migration and desire, tumbled and whirled
And rolled together in the dark, the cold

Salt, shifting place where river ends and sea begins

To wind all journeys back to where they came from.

It's this that I was looking for,
Says Tweed:

Oblivion.

On Spittal beach, among the sticks and broken shells, strips torn
From desiccated black
Plastic bin-bags metamorphose into crackling scraps
Of bladderwrack,

And tubes of polypropylene become the whumlick kex,
And strands of willow bough,
The hitches, bends and splices of a thousand long-discarded
Nylon tows;

As if, in this great glittering meeting, weaving, marrying, relaxing,
Tweed lets go
Its cumulative weight of contradictions; memories, imaginings – all borders
Flow

Into one another, and the line – the human, managed, measurable shore –
Is lost
To whirling currents; and, beyond, the spiral stream
Of stars and dust.

On the farthest spit of coarse brown grit,
Sandstell,
Wind shivers a few blades of lyme-grass, and the sun picks out
A bleached sheep's skull,

And wound around it, rags and tatters that were once
A salmon net;
So tangled up, their fortunes river-ravelled and impossible
To separate.

KATRINA PORTEOUS
Tweed Rivers, 2005 | *Two Countries*, 2014

The Harbourmaster's Daughter
(for Sylvia Secker)

Retired, she has returned to the town
Where she was born, taken a flat
Whose bay embraces estuary, lighthouse,
Pier, the white line where river and sea
Contend, and on the other shore, a
Harbour which she has, with love,
Reclaimed.

Monthly she sends in the shipping news,
Amazes *Advertiser* readers with what comes,
What goes, the where and what of cargoes,
Ships and ports, stirs unsuspected longings,
Creates a kind of music we can share.

The *Ambience* from Howdendyke, to Bremen
With malt. *Erica H.* from the Tees, loading
Barley for the Azores. *Hoo Dolphin* from Leith
Sailing to Terneuzen with stone.

'Trading is brisk,' she notes. 'Four vessels
Outward bound.' And describes the *Osiris*,
'Spick and span in dazzling blue and white,
Sporting a snappy replica of Donald Duck,
Just below her bridge.' She adds: 'There's no
Better place to be on a fine June night
Than Berwick Port.'

Nautica from Belfast with oats for Bruges.
Kerin from Methil, loading barley for Bergen.
The *Shetland Trader*, inward with fertiliser,
Outward for Terneuzen with stone.

She summons up the past with photographs
Of bygone cargo ships, remembers girlhood
Trips on coasters up to Leith and down to
Whitley Bay... Daily looking out to sea,
She focuses on shifting depths, faint horizons,
Follows dwindling vessels till they vanish
In the mist.

The *Barentree* from Grangemouth,
To Laerdal with cement.
Vera from Amsterdam,
Loading barley for Belfast.
The *Torquence*, empty, from Huff,
Sailing for Terneuzen, with stone.

VINCENZA HOLLAND

Midsummer Night, Berwick

The half-hearted darkness at eleven,
a sliver of night that is and is not a night.

I run my mind over the land, the surprises
of its plunging, coves with no footprints.

So many thresholds. Sea and stone
left words and prayers behind long ago.

Castles appear closer than they really are,
signs are hazy – *To the North* –

yet we follow, transhumant creatures
always climbing to remoter pastures.

Sometimes I wish I rose at dawn
to bake bread or deliver letters in the mist

but summer is just an interlude here
like loganberries or happiness.

ANNE RYLAND
The Unmothering Class, 2011

Duddo Stones
(for my wife)

Summer grips us in its damp
grey palm. But there, across a quarter-mile
of perfect wheat, are blinks of sunlight choosing,
one by one, grooved faces of five megaliths
to celebrate, beyond the wind-stroked crop
that balks us, and by balking speaks
for stones whose prime contemporary role
is surely the dumb oracle.

We'll hike back here at harvest time
to put more closely what it is
we can't quite ask,
and meanwhile leave, beside untrodden wheat,
a miserly libation
of lukewarm coffee from a Thermos flask.

PETER BENNET
All the Real, 1994

Roughting Linn, Northumberland
(for Sid Chaplin)

Tucked out of sight of the Cheviot massif,
the site itself was convenient
for defence: to south and west
a deep-wooded gorge echoing with the Celts'
bellowing cataract – even withered
to a trickle, the noise seems to hiss through the copse,
overflowing birdsong and the easing
of wind through trees across the scarp.
To north and east four giant ramparts and ditches
grooved in an arc still reek of man
through the dry March bracken and rampant
shrubbery. Blackbirds and throstles cluck off
in pairs, an affronted cock pheasant
squawks upwards in a russet feathering of alarm,

glinting red and green.
Picnic litter flakes the grass.
On the edge of the road a dead mole bares
its pale-furred belly to the sky's predators.
At the edge of the camp
there's a massive grey sandstone boulder
as if frozen at a point
where it has not quite freed itself
from peaty earth and last year's ling.
It is studded with sculptured signs
all but erased by the precipitation
of perhaps three thousand years: time and man
co-operators of this alien delicacy,
these hermetic markings that fuel
our hermeneutic urge.
Most are concentric rings centred by cup-holes,
chipped out by stone or bronze, roughly tooled,
often with a downward extended radius
like soaring ideograms of a comet.
Some, plainly, are ripples of rain falling
in a pool of stone.
Other carvings: overturned U-shapes
stacked on top of each other,
primitive stalk and flower forms, as full of grace
as a passionate hope, yet arcane
as the roots of worship.
Some could be signs of one-eyed death
or the lapidary emblems of life-force,
reverberating planets and analogues of divinity;
fertile tree-rings, patternings of birth
or sacrifice, or prosaic maps of *oppida*. They mingle
familiarly with natural hieroglyphs,
and give to elemental groovings and groins of rock
where rain stagnates
and to the cavities and quarry-traces
of later farmers, a sense of latent design.
After so many centuries their purpose
seems immanent in the stone, but secretly larval.
They might be symbols of transmigrating souls,
as Berwick naturalists thought a hundred years ago,
or metaphors of the flux of blood and time,
to placate the supernatural.
They might.

They offer a meaning that is imagistic
yet obscurely discursive: imponderable
echoes rippling in the mind. The fading
beauty of their bas-relief excites
seductive dreams of ancestral mysticism – why not
say only that such signs are there still
to strike a spark
in imaginations that hold
a streak of flinty reasoning?

RODNEY PYBUS
Bridging Loans, 1976

Acknowledged Land
(Northumberland, 10,000-700 BC)

One beginning is *cold*. It freezes our lips
like ice, hungry for the white of our bones.

Light and dark make shadows in the stretch of waking,
wild beasts of dreams that catch you in their teeth,

sweating under rancid skins, huddling for the warmth
of blood. This place here and now is only us,

more or less cold, stone chiselled from the silence
of winter. Even our fires are hungry, spitting

out orange snakes of heat; one half of us always
shivering. Flames tempt like lovers' eyes,

moons in black mirrors; leave you cold and sad
when you must rise with the sun and walk away

alone, another rampart raised around the settlement
of your heart. Every third child dies. We burn

the bones and make another mark in stone,
a cup of blood, a ring of milk. We are silted

with loss, morning frost on blades of grass, fine white
on, brave green; so many blades, knives

we whittle from the sharp sound of flint, dreaming
of words out of our lips' kenning, glinting

like the kiss of metal, a memory we've not forged
yet, can't forget. The moon keeps on, keeps on

turning into herself and back again. And so
do we, the year, freezing and melting.

No one remembers all the beginnings any more.
All we know is it keeps on happening.

*

We don't say second. What we wait for is *next*,
this, what, and after; try to remember

what came before, the shape it made in the sky,
the white abacus of stars, colour of days,

the texture of soil, grit of seed. The moon is our best
next, drawing us on, white as milk and good magic.

In her mirror we see the invisible becoming visible;
make her shapes with our mouths, our eyes,

our faces, build our safe places in the same way,
ring after ring of safe. We bracelet

our hearts; all her people, who want to live,
sow wheat and barley, in terraces of sense,

fields of healthy children whose faces
make the same shapes as ours, our eyes,

our mouths, the moon, their mother.
The women's bodies open into miracles, white

globes, and our children float down their rivers,
crying droplets of *O*s. We drink the blessing,

our hearts roaring. There are only two things we need
to know and they are one: what we need and

what is possible. We know these things are many.
Together they make grain and water in a clay bowl,

warmed in the glow of a fire, the good and round
in your belly, the come and go of your breathing.

The imaginary is only a thought that exists
to make something happen: come and come and go.

*

Here is a place where we are born, where our children
are born, where we and our children will die.

This place is where we live, the light
and shadows in between. We are people

breathing the green and purple of a vast land,
colonies of bees, beautiful, dangerous, orange

and black, feeding on honey. We choose high places
to build our homes. We hold up our heads, watch

horizons for changes in the weather, warning signs of danger.
Our foundations are strong shapes the earth makes, circles

we draw around ourselves, ring upon ring and stone
upon stone, beat back wild beasts, wilder weather.

From this hill top we can surrender, never stop
fighting. And what we see are more hills, mountains

capped in snow, greening in sunlight; rivers we call
Till or Tyne, winding like silver snakes, shedding

their skins in the dry: what time does over and over,
the great dissolver. The hill, the law of the land

is the lie of it we need to believe in since
this is the place where we are born. We call it

home; every day feel it touch the soft places
at the centre of our eyes, grateful

for its gift of good grain, fresh water, remember
its dangers; bury our dead beneath its thick brown

blanket, wind cutting the wet cheeks of those
left behind who must fight and surrender, stay safe.

*

Land of natural borders, rearing contours,
we watch them shift with the seasons, borrow

the shapes they make, find answers
to their questions. We acknowledge this land,

our debt to it, a pact of clasped hands,
the maps we carry on our open palms.

The spaces between cold and hungry and lost
we fill with the red of our blood,

our children and blessings. And so we make maps
of all our safe places, to remind us where they are,

how to find our way home in the dark. We carve
them out of the stone of our hearts, catch

the blood in crimson spirals, charting the gradient
of our country, the land where we live; know

how much geography we carry inside us, a home roaring
with rings of fire, oranges and blacks.

And all the places we know are safe, Old Bewick
and Dod Law, Yeavering Bell

and Lordenshaw, we see their names in lights,
beacons blazing gold under the silver-studded shield

of dark. In the cold, hungry and lost, they seem
to say we are not alone. We light fires

for each other in the dark. We are all
different and we are all the same; our skins,

our own natural borders, simply contours
exposed that need protection, feeding, warming.

*

Forest is menace, is mystery, a match fit
only for fools or the fearless. We don't know

which till after: either a deer to be skinned
and roasted, mead to be drunk, or just

an empty space round the fire at nights wearing
a fool's face. Water is also dangerous, gorgeous

with fish and flowing. Rivers are maps we can trace
the route of, follow up or down: to the place

where the water falls, a cauldron of earth and air
and this water, this Roughting Linn, a bull, bellowing.

And we bellow like bulls, spray fresh on our cheeks;
slake our thirsts and lift our heads. This place

is a special safe, holy days free of horizons,
a mirror of wisping prisms where we can see

our dreams dance and melt, what we need and what is
possible, what can be real. Whatever happens,

we go home with cleaner faces and lighter hearts,
strong as bulls, the red ball of the sun at our backs.

Beyond the borders of home in a grove of trees,
a rock lies sleeping. We sing it awake with rings

and cups, a wild garden of eyes. And sleeping,
dreaming, waking, stone outlives us all,

doesn't melt in fire or crumble in the fist
of weather. Its one surrender is to tricks of light.

So we play tricks too, make our mark on rock
with picks of stone, share the blisters.

*

Naming a thing is giving birth to it, a blessing
or a curse, an imaginary cloak of real power:

the magic works. The moon, its waxing and waning,
the women's blood, taught us that. We imagine

we want to hear the sounds of our own names, a word
like *the*, definite as granite, that always stays

the same. After a spell of thinking, it happens
and so we give birth to the name of the sun,

its power and glory. Though its heat may wax and wane,
the shape of its face stays the same. We want

to know the summer shapes our children's faces make
are the same as ours. We learnt that from the moon.

And still the women hold up half the sky
alone. Always changing, always bleeding, without

even the grace to die. So we name the sun
who knows what death really is, has power over life

and death, earth-scorching, thirst-making. Warriors
we are, hunters, who know the power and glory

of death. Our sun battles with the moon for the sky
and its strength splits day and night in two, a cracked egg,

yellow yolk, liquid white. One thought leads
to another and we dig our ditches deeper, raise

our ramparts higher, mine the earth and make metals,
copper, bronze and iron, our fires roaring.

Forging coins like little suns, we trade our lives
for seeds of ideas, with minds of their own.

*

Whatever we do, something new keeps on
happening, a new name. We etch alphabets

in wood or stone so we remember how we invented
the beginning of things, know the difference

between left and right, light and shade,
this man's wife, this man's son, and his neighbour's,

his enemy's: the lines we draw to divide
our territory. This is our land, the place where

we are born. We acknowledge it only with the brand
of our different names. There are many

uses of fire; blessing or curse, we imagine we know
the difference, kindling brittle sticks into orange

and black. Our skins grow coarse from the heat.
But we feel like gods and say it is good.

Only the earth keeps the silence of stone,
chanting its song of the seasons. We stop

our ears with wax, blind to our reflections
in other eyes. Too busy chasing the tail of time,

we never surrender, never stop fighting. Too busy
with the business of staying alive to know

what living is. We imagine this is vital and say it,
write it: it is *good*. Our hearts in their stockades

of one and one and one grow colder. Ice
splinters our blood, moon's not bold enough to melt.

We weave our stories into woollen cloth,
call our freedom *fate*. And the unravelling.

LINDA FRANCE
Acknowledged Land, 1994 | *The Gentleness of the Very Tall*, 1994

'Acknowledged Land', a collaboration with the artist Birtley Aris, was first published in book form by Northumberland County Council in 1994. The poem spans 9000 years of Northumberland's prehistory, charting changes from the early Stone Age right through to the early Iron Age. The seven sections of thirteen couplets represent the diurnal (the days of the week) and the lunar (the moon months of the year). The named places in Northumberland are sites of prehistoric settlements where cup and ring marks (petroglyphs) can be found on exposed rocks. These include Roughting Linn (see Rodney Pybus's poem, page 149), as well as Duddo (Peter Bennet, page 149).

acknowledged land
coalburn, eglingham, northumberland

weep november cold tears,
make this ford impassable.

hide us in the mizzle caul of ancient fears,
protect us from this reiver dark.

fox cry, plangent grace,
the wearing lines

of history on her face:
the ghost of static mines,

the broken ribs of rusted ships,
of shoulders laden with flaccid chips.

inscribe a legend on your map,
no longer whippet & cloth cap

but totem statuary here & there,
a culture raped, the cupboard bare.

this north, this cold, acknowledged land
where rule is cheap & underhand

where heritage is all the rage
& all our rage now heritage.

PAUL SUMMERS
Union, 2011

Stately Home

> Behold Land-Interest's compound Man & Horse.
> EBENEZER ELLIOTT

Those bad old days of 'rapine and of reif!'
Northumberland's peles still seeping with old wars –
this year's lawful lord and last year's thief,
those warring centaurs, scratch their unscabbed sores.

But here, horned koodoo and okapi skulls,
the family's assegais, a Masai shield,
the head of one of Chillingham's white bulls,
this month's *Tatler, Horse & Hound, The Field*.

Churned earth translucent Meissen, dusted Spode
displayed on Sundays for the pence it makes,
paintings of beasts they'd shot at or they'd rode,
cantered grabbed acres on, won local stakes,
once all one man's debatable demesne,
a day's hard ride from Cheviot to sea –

His scion, stretching back to Charlemagne,
stiff-backed, lets us put down 40p.

TONY HARRISON
Selected Poems, 1984 | *Collected Poems*, 2007

from Marmion
CANTO SECOND

VIII
And now the vessel skirts the strand
Of mountainous Northumberland;
Towns, towers, and halls successive rise,
And catch the nuns' delighted eyes.
Monk-Wearmouth soon behind them lay,
And Tynemouth's priory and bay;

They marked, amid her trees, the hall
Of lofty Seaton-Delaval;
They saw the Blythe and Wansbeck floods
Rush to the sea through sounding woods;
They pass'd the tower of Widderington,
Mother of many a valiant son;
At Coquet-isle their beads they tell
To the good Saint who owned the cell;
Then did the Alne attention claim,
And Warkworth, proud of Percy's name;
And next, they cross'd themselves, to hear
The whitening breakers sound so near,
Where, boiling through the rocks, they roar
On Dunstanborough's cavern'd shore;
Thy tower, proud Bamborough, mark'd they there,
King Ida's castle, huge and square,
From its tall rock look grimly down,
And on the swelling ocean frown;
Then from the coast they bore away,
And reached the Holy Island's bay.

IX

The tide did now its flood-mark gain,
And girdled in the Saint's domain:
For, with the flow and ebb, its style
Varies from continent to isle;
Dry shod, o'er sands, twice every day,
The pilgrims to the shrine find way;
Twice every day, the waves efface
Of staves and sandall'd feet the trace.
As to the port the galley flew,
Higher and higher rose to view
The Castle with its battled walls,
The ancient Monastery's halls,
A solemn, huge, and dark-red pile,
Plac'd on the margin of the isle.

X

In Saxon strength that abbey frown'd,
With massive arches broad and round,
   That rose alternate, row and row,
     On ponderous columns, short and low,
        Built ere the art was known,

By pointed aisle, and shafted stalk,
The arcades of an alleyed walk
   To emulate in stone.
On the deep walls, the heathen Dane
Had pour'd his impious rage in vain;
And needful was such strength to these,
Expos'd to the tempestuous seas,
Scourg'd by the winds' eternal sway,
Open to rovers fierce as they,
Which could twelve hundred years withstand
Winds, waves, and northern pirates' hand.
Not but that portions of the pile,
Rebuilded in a later style,
Show'd where the spoiler's hand had been;
Not but the wasting sea-breeze keen
Had worn the pillar's carving quaint,
And moulder'd in his niche the saint,
And rounded, with consuming power,
The pointed angles of each tower;
Yet still entire the Abbey stood,
Like veteran, worn, but unsubdued.

XIV

Nor did Saint Cuthbert's daughters fail
To vie with these in holy tale;
His body's resting-place, of old,
How oft their patron chang'd, they told;
How, when the rude Dane burn'd their pile,
The monks fled forth from Holy Isle;
O'er northern mountain, marsh, and moor,
From sea to sea, from shore to shore,
Seven years Saint Cuthbert's corpse they bore.
   They rested them in fair Melrose;
      But though, alive, he lov'd it well,
   Not there his relics might repose;
      For, wondrous tale to tell!
   In his stone-coffin forth he rides,
   A ponderous barque for river tides,
   Yet light as gossamer it glides,
      Downward to Tilmouth cell.
Nor long was his abiding there,
For southward did the saint repair;
Chester-le-Street, and Rippon, saw

His holy corpse, ere Wardilaw
   Hail'd him with joy and fear;
And, after many wanderings past,
He chose his lordly seat at last,
Where his cathedral, huge and vast,
   Looks down upon the Wear:
There, deep in Durham's Gothic shade,
His relics are in secret laid;
   But none may know the place,
Save of his holiest servants three,
Deep sworn to solemn secrecy,
   Who share that wondrous grace.

SIR WALTER SCOTT
Marmion, 1808

Sir Walter Scott (1771-1832) wandered much about his beloved Border country in his youth. In Northumberland he climbed the Cheviot, and in 1791 spent the autumn at the old white-washed farmhouse at Langleeford. In the summer of 1797 the young Walter, his brother and a friend made their headquarters in Gilsland, where the brothers became rivals for the attentions of Charlotte Mary Carpenter. After a whirlwind courtship, Scott is alleged to have proposed at the Popping Stone at Gilsland, giving her purple pansies gathered on the Roman Wall. The marriage took place in Carlisle. The countryside here forms much of the background to Scott's novel *Guy Mannering* (1815).

   The future Laird of Abbotsford (formerly Clarty Hole) gained fame as a poet, particularly with *Marmion* (1808), before he began his career as a novelist. Flodden Field, near Ford Castle in Northumberland, where the Scots army was overthrown and King James IV killed in 1513, gave rise to verse on both sides of the border. Scott describes the scene in the sixth canto of *Marmion*. He gives credit to Robert Surtees, the celebrated Durham antiquary, for inspiring him to set about writing the epic at all. [AM]

   See also second note on Scott and *Rokeby* on page 473.

Lindisfarne

Jet-black the crags of False Emmanuel Head
Against the winter sunset: standing stark
Within the shorn sun's frosty glare, night-dark,
A solitary monk with arms outspread
In worship or in frustrate tense desire
Of racked and tortured flesh: still young and spare,
With drooping head he seems to hang in air
Crucified on a wheel of blood-red fire.

The red sun dips, and slowly to his side
His slack arms fall, and in the clear green light
Of the frosty afterglow where coldly burns
A lonely star, a very pillar of night
He stands above the steely shivering tide,
Then slowly to the darkening east he turns.

WILFRID GIBSON
Chambers, 1920 | *Collected Poems 1905-1925*, 1926
➤ AUTHOR NOTE PAGES 232-33

Holy Island Arch

Against the buffeting wind and the sea's growl
The crafted stone
Soars overhead in the high blue forever,
Thin as a wishbone.

Nothing so fragile should stand so strong.
Leaping, unbound,
As if quarried blocks were weightless; as if wind
Could not suddenly dash them down,

The sandstone balanced by the mason's hand
Impossibly, holds.
All grace defies weight, logic, weather –
Bends, a bow –

Hope, launching itself
Into cold space.
The breaking sun transfigures it. An equal,
Opposite embrace

Is all that keeps the stones from crashing,
And the heart,
That has one longing only – to be met and held
In such an arch.

KATRINA PORTEOUS
Two Countries, 2014

Causeway

Beneath the rain-shadow and washed farmhouses,
in the service of the old shore,

we waited for the rising of the road,
the south lane laden in sand,

the north in residue and wrack;
the tide drawing off the asphalt

leaving our tyres little to disperse;
still, the water under wheel was forceful –

cleft between the chassis and the sea –
that clean division that the heart rages for.

But half way out the destination ceases to be the prize,
and what matters is the sudden breadth of vision:

to the north, a hovering headland,
to the south, a shoal of light –

the sea off-guarded, but hunting:
our licence brief, unlikely to be renewed.

Between mainland and island, in neither sway,
a nodding of the needle as the compass takes its weigh.

MATTHEW HOLLIS
The Guardian, 2015

St Cuthbert on Inner Farne

How the small boat rode the swell
   tossed like flotsam
      steadied by prayer

a cloud of curious fulmars
   circling calling

He left the shared bread
   the community
      of compline

for the kittiwake colony
   the turmoil of terns

choosing solitude among sea birds
   the salt lash of the storm
      inhospitable hermitage

sea cresting and crashing
   sending spray swirling

no silence in the buffeting wind
   but the silence within
      stillness gathered

divine contemplation
   among puffins and eiders

How his spirit grew strong
   icy shallows his abbey
      the night sky his dome

CYNTHIA FULLER
Shadow Script, 2013 | *Estuary*, 2015

Making the Book
(FROM *Good News from a Small Island*)

1 *Eadfrith in the Scriptorium*

old and coming to the end, in the seventh year,
of his Great Labour for God and St Cuthbert;
fingers the skins he has smoothed and gathered,
the pages ruled with stylus and that good knife;

the feathers pulled from a goose wing,
cured in boiling sand, slit to the strongest point;
dipped in ink of lamp black and soot;

and now Good Eadfrith mouths all
he has written in sturdy half-uncials as a soldier
of Christ, each word another wound
on Satan's skin, every letter a preaching
with the hand, a glimpse of the Godhead

and now Good Eadfrith sees his illuminations
before him: the first words, evangelists, crossed pages
of pelta and fret and unsmiling he leaves one wing
without feathers, that interlace unreddened,
those few letters empty; in order to remain imperfect,
in order once more to please his God.

2 *The Binding of Aethalwald*

He squares up the pages, the thirty-three gatherings,
trapped between oak boards; he rubs beeswax on the threads
to ease each sewing, glues the spine, hammers it curved;
then lays out the almost book on crimson goatskin,
well pared and pasted, folds the leather inwards and inwards,
smooths it with his hand, rests his fingers on the words;
his opus manuum, his binding.

3 *Billfrith the Jeweller*

who has stood outstretched with the silence
of waves for some time; now bends,
lifts from the pile two garnets,
red and hard, holds them over the Book's
freshly grown skin, whispers
a question and waits for instructions
and waits as the moon crosses
the glassless window, as the bells
sound beyond the narrows,
as the wind scatters straws
from the thatch and again waits
for the tide that rises then falls

as this late frost gathers
to hold and kiss,
to whiten and kiss
his dirty hands.

4 *Aldred the Glossator*

wrote between the lines his thick mouthed translation
in insular minuscule, cursive and quick
as if it were business or the Law; thinking himself unworthy
and most miserable, seeking the help
of God and his saint for a steady hand and hard eye
as the snow fell and the snow fell
in Chester-le-Street that winter and the light moved on elsewhere.

ANDREW WATERHOUSE
2nd, 2002

The monastery of Lindisfarne was founded by St Aidan around 635 AD. St Cuthbert was made Prior around 665, spending his last years on Inner Farne. The Lindisfarne Gospels were made during the early 8th century. Eadfrith was the scribe and illustrator, Aethalwald bound the book and Billfrith the Anchorite decorated its cover with gold and jewels. Aldred, a priest of Chester-le-Street, wrote an Old English translation between the lines of the original Latin text 250 years later. Due to Viking raids, the monks left the island around 875, taking with them Cuthbert's body and the Lindisfarne Gospels. The remains seen today are those of a later priory built on the site in Norman times and wrecked during the Reformation.

A Short History of Bamburgh

There are many histories: first,
The iron-red castle
Lording over the red-gold sand at sunset.

Next, the sea. How it roars
And quarrels with the islands: Longstone,
Its cold pulse of light.

Then bent-grass and sand. Wind.
Squat willows, bones;
Skylarks' knotwork, twining the whins to Spindlestone;

The Gamestone; the King's Baulk; the Worm Well –
Scraps and make-believe
Forged in the village smithy. What is forgotten

Between the Whistle Wood and the Blue Hemmel
Matters most of all. Tomorrow
There are fields to sow. Deep in the Grove

Rooks, like old priests, squabble.

KATRINA PORTEOUS
Bamburgh Parish Council plan, 2005 | *Two Countries*, 2014

Bamburgh Wind

Nebody knaas the will o' the wind
And its wilful vagary;
It caresses wi' luv, or screams wi' hate;
Unpredictable as can be.
Which airt it'll choose ye nivvor can tell.
It might cum howlin' wi' glee,
Upruttin' trees – an' then ripplin' the corn
Like a sea in sorenity.
So divvn't hatch schemes like yon King Penda did;
In wind's pooer he put his trust,
But it torned on him wi' its thick blindin' smoke
An' the flames of devourin' lust.

FRED REED
Northumbrian Miscellany, 1978 | *The Northumborman*, 1999

knaas: knows; *airt:* sense, mood, direction

In 672, Penda, King of Mercia, attempted to burn an early Bamburgh castle by setting fire to piles of wood and brush laid against its walls, but the wind blew, then blew contrary, flames and thick smoke caught his camp, and he was obliged to raise his siege.

Grace Darling

Take, O star of all our seas, from not an alien hand,
   Homage paid of song bowed down before thy glory's face,
Thou the living light of all our lovely stormy strand,
   Thou the brave north-country's very glory of glories, Grace.

Loud and dark about the lighthouse rings and glares the night;
   Glares with foam-lit gloom and darkling fire of storm and spray,
Rings with roar of winds in chase and rage of waves in flight,
   Howls and hisses as with mouths of snakes and wolves at bay.
Scarce the cliffs of the islets, scarce the walls of Joyous Gard,
   Flash to sight between the deadlier lightnings of the sea:
Storm is lord and master of a midnight evil-starred,
   Nor may sight or fear discern what evil stars may be.
Dark as death and white as snow the sea-swell scowls and shines,
   Heaves and yearns and pants for prey, from ravening lip to lip,
Strong in rage of rapturous anguish, lines on hurtling lines,
   Ranks on charging ranks, that break and rend the battling ship.
All the night is mad and murderous: who shall front the night?
   Not the prow that labours, helpless as a storm-blown leaf,
Where the rocks and waters, darkling depth and beetling height,
   Rage with wave on shattering wave and thundering reef on reef.
Death is fallen upon the prisoners there of darkness, bound
   Like as thralls with links of iron fast in bonds of doom;
How shall any way to break the bands of death be found,
   Any hand avail to pluck them from that raging tomb?
All the night is great with child of death: no stars above
   Show them hope in heaven, no lights from shores ward help on earth.
Is there help or hope to seaward, is there help in love,
   Hope in pity, where the ravening hounds of storm make mirth?
Where the light but shows the naked eyeless face of Death
   Nearer, laughing dumb and grim across the loud live storm?
Not in human heart or hand or speech of human breath,
   Surely, nor in saviours found of mortal face or form.
Yet below the light, between the reefs, a skiff shot out
   Seems a sea-bird fain to breast and brave the strait fierce pass
Whence the channelled roar of waters driven in raging rout,
   Pent and pressed and maddened, speaks their monstrous might and mass.
Thunder heaves and howls about them, lightning leaps and flashes,
   Hard at hand, not high in heaven, but close between the walls
Heaped and hollowed of the storms of old, whence reels and crashes

All the rage of all the unbaffled wave that breaks and falls.
   Who shall thwart the madness and the gladness of it, laden
     Full with heavy fate, and joyous as the birds that whirl?
Nought in heaven or earth, if not one mortal-moulded maiden,
     Nought if not the soul that glorifies a northland girl.
Not the rocks that break may baffle, not the reefs that thwart
     Stay the ravenous rapture of the waves that crowd and leap;
Scarce their flashing laughter shows the hunger of their heart,
     Scarce their lion-throated roar the wrath at heart they keep.
Child and man and woman in the grasp of death clenched fast
     Tremble, clothed with darkness round about, and scarce draw breath,
Scarce lift eyes up toward the light that saves not, scarce may cast
     Thought or prayer up, caught and trammelled in the snare of death.
Not as sea-mews cling and laugh or sun their plumes and sleep
     Cling and cower the wild night's waifs of shipwreck, blind with fear,
Where the fierce reef scarce yields foothold that a bird might keep,
     And the clamorous darkness deadens eye and deafens ear.
Yet beyond their helpless hearing, out of hopeless sight,
     Saviours, armed and girt upon with strength of heart, fare forth,
Sire and daughter, hand on oar and face against the night,
     Maid and man whose names are beacons ever to the North.
Nearer now; but all the madness of the storming surf
     Hounds and roars them back; but roars and hounds them back in vain:
As a pleasure-skiff may graze the lake-embanking turf,
     So the boat that bears them grates the rock where-toward they strain.
Dawn as fierce and haggard as the face of night scarce guides
     Toward the cries that rent and clove the darkness, crying for aid,
Hours on hours, across the engorged reluctance of the tides,
     Sire and daughter, high-souled man and mightier-hearted maid.
Not the bravest land that ever breasted war's grim sea,
     Hurled her foes back harried on the lowlands whence they came,
Held her own and smote her smiters down, while such durst be,
     Shining northward, shining southward, as the aurorean flame,
Not our mother, not Northumberland, brought ever forth,
     Though no southern shore may match the sons that kiss her mouth,
Children worthier all the birthright given of the ardent north
     Where the fire of hearts outburns the suns that fire the south.
Even such fire was this that lit them, not from lowering skies
     Where the darkling dawn flagged, stricken in the sun's own shrine,
Down the gulf of storm subsiding, till their earnest eyes
     Find the relics of the ravening night that spared but nine.
Life by life the man redeems them, head by storm-worn head,
     While the girl's hand stays the boat whereof the waves are fain:

Ah, but woe for one, the mother clasping fast her dead!
    Happier, had the surges slain her with her children slain.
Back they bear, and bring between them safe the woful nine,
    Where above the ravenous Hawkers fixed at watch for prey
Storm and calm behold the Longstone's towering signal shine
    Now as when that labouring night brought forth a shuddering day.
Now as then, though like the hounds of storm against her snarling
    All the clamorous years between us storm down many a fame,
As our sires beheld before us we behold Grace Darling
    Crowned and throned our queen, and as they hailed we hail her name.
Nay, not ours alone, her kinsfolk born, though chiefliest ours,
    East and west and south acclaim her queen of England's maids,
Star more sweet than all their stars and flower than all their flowers,
    Higher in heaven and earth than star that sets or flower that fades.
How should land or sea that nurtured her forget, or love
    Hold not fast her fame for us while aught is borne in mind?
Land and sea beneath us, sun and moon and stars above,
    Bear the bright soul witness, seen of all but souls born blind.
Stars and moon and sun may wax and wane, subside and rise,
    Age on age as flake on flake of showering snows be shed:
Not till earth be sunless, not till death strike blind the skies,
    May the deathless love that waits on deathless deeds be dead.

Years on years have withered since beside the hearth once thine
    I, too young to have seen thee, touched thy father's hallowed hand:
Thee and him shall all men see for ever, stars that shine
    While the sea that spared thee girds and glorifies the land.

ALGERNON CHARLES SWINBURNE
Grace Darling, 1893 | *Astrophel and Other Poems*, 1904
➤ AUTHOR NOTE PAGES 50-52

Grace Darling (1815–1842) was the daughter of the lighthouse keeper on Longstone Island, one of the Farne Islands, who became a national heroine for her role in rescuing nine survivors from the wreck of a paddlesteamer, the SS *Forfarshire*, in the early hours of 7 September 1838, when she and her father rowed out from their lighthouse to the wreck on the rocks in seas too rough for the lifeboat to set out from Seahouses. She was the subject of numerous poems, songs, books, paintings and plays, and died at 26 from tuberculosis. Buried with her parents at St Aidan's, Bamburgh, she is commemorated in an elaborate cenotaph in the churchyard and at the Grace Darling Museum.

Grace Darling

After you had steered your coble out of the storm
And left the smaller islands to break the surface,
Like draughts shaking that colossal backcloth there came
Fifty pounds from the Queen, proposals of marriage.

The daughter of a lighthousekeeper and the saints
Who once lived there on birds' eggs, rainwater, barley
And built to keep all pilgrims at a safe distance
Circular houses with views only of the sky,

Who set timber burning on the top of a tower
Before each was launched at last in his stone coffin –
You would turn your back on mainland and suitor
To marry, then bereave the waves from Lindisfarne,

A moth against the lamp that shines still and reveals
Many small boats at sea, lifeboats, named after girls.

MICHAEL LONGLEY
The Echo Gate, 1979 | *Collected Poems*, 2006

Charlie Douglas
(Beadnell)

'We're gan' tyek hor off, th' morn,'
Said Charlie, squatting in his black-tarred hut;
And the other old fishermen muttered, spat, swore.
So after a thin night, cracked by storm,
I arrived by the harbour kilns at dawn,
Where the sour *Jane Douglas* smoked and heaved,
Rocking her burden of dans and creeves.
And Charlie, a tab in his toothless jaw,
Stared blindly out to Featherblaa',
Tiller in hand. And away she roared,
Her proud bows rising, blue and white,
The same cold colours as the changing light
Bowling over the wind-torn sea.

Now, all the creatures that creep below,
Lobster and nancy, crab and frone,
From many million years ago
Have secret places, and Charlie knows
The banks and hollows of every part.
He's learnt their lineaments by heart
And mapped the landscape beneath the sea.
O, I was the blind man then, not he.
Now Charlie's quiet. His words were few:
'Aah'll tell ye somethin'. Now this is true –
We're finished, hinny. The fishin's deed.
Them greet, muckle traa'lers – it's nowt but greed.
Whae, there's nae bloody chance for the fish t' breed...
An' the lobsters! Y' bugger! In wor day
W' hoyed aa' th' berried hens away!'
'And they don't do that now?' 'Darsay noo!'
As he spoke, I watched the steeple grow
Smaller, still smaller, marking where
His folk, for the last three-hundred years,
Were christened and married and laid to rest.
So I urged him to tell me of all the past,
That other, hidden, deep-sea floor;
And whatever I'd cherished in life before –
Home, friends – just then, I loved him more,
This crined old man of eighty-two;
I wanted to trawl him through and through
For all the mysteries he knew
About the sea, about the years.
I wanted to haul his memories free
Like a string of creeves from the troubled sea,
Shining with swad and water-beads.
But turning his fierce, blind gaze on me,
His eyes said, 'Hinny, ye'll nivvor see –
Ye divvin't tell them aa' ye kna
Or aal your stories in a day.'

KATRINA PORTEOUS
The Lost Music, 1996

dans: marker buoys; *nancy:* squat lobster; *frone:* starfish; *berried hens:* female lobsters carrying eggs; *swad:* the green, fringed seaweed that clings to ropes.

The Marks t' Gan By

I asked Charlie what a fisherman must know.
'Aal bloody things!' he answered me. 'How so?'
'A fisherman hetti hev brains, y' kna, one time;'
His fingers twisted round the slippery twine
In the stove's faint firelight. It was getting dark.
'Them days,' he said, 'w' hetti gan b' marks.

'Staggart, the Fairen Hoose; Hebron, Beadlin Trees...'
Thus he began the ancient litany
Of names, half-vanished, beautiful to hear:
'Ga'n roond the Point, keep Bamburgh Castle clear
The Black Rock, mind. Off Newton, steer until
Ye've Staggart level the Nick a the Broad Mill.'

Novice, I listened. In the gloom I saw
The rolled-up sail by the long-unopened door,
A traveller, stiff with rust, a woodwormed mast –
All the accumulation of the distant past.
'Now, keep the Chorch on Alexandra Hoose,
An' yon's the road...' 'Oh, Charlie, what's the use?'

I said. 'These memories! I know they're true,
And certainly they're beautiful. But how can you
Compete with all the science of these modern days?
The echosounder's finished your outdated ways.
Efficiency. That's what they want; not lore.
Why should the past concern us any more?'

I could not see his face. The stove had died.
'There's naen crabs noo,' said Charlie sadly, and he sighed,
And seeming not to hear me, sealed the knot.
'When ye see lippers comin', when t' stop
An' when t' gan – that's what ye need t' kna.
The sea's the boss. Me fatther told me so.

'Them marks,' he said; 'he handed aal them doon
Like right an' wrang. Them buggers for' the toons,' –
He sliced the twine he sewed with, savagely –
'Th' divvin't kna what's right. Th' gan t' sea –
Their only mind's for profit. They'll no give
Naen thowt t' hoo their sons'll hetti live.'

I saw, then. 'So,' I said, 'as we embark,
The past is map and measure, certain mark
To steer by in the cold, uncertain sea?
We leave it, like the land. But all we know –
What to hang on to and when to let go –
Leads from it...' 'Aye,' said Charlie. 'Sic an' so.'

KATRINA PORTEOUS
The Lost Music, 1996

traveller: iron ring attaching sail to mast; *lippers:* breaking waves.

Stinky

When you draw up here,
Down the hill to the rocket house,
The whitewashed Square

Brined in the past, that redolence
Of tarred rope, oak bark,
Rum casks,

And you lie awake
In the early dawn to catch the sun
Crawl up between

Billy, the coastguard watch-house,
And the castle;
While a robin

Scries from the pan-tiles
Of the hemmel,
And not one coble

Carves its wake
Through the flawless blue silk
Of the Haven,

You might be forgiven
For forgetting
This: the place

Was pigs, middens, yeddle,
Rotten kelp,
Fish livers reeking in the yetlin;

That the roof above your head
Is a tree, its roots
In herring guts.

KATRINA PORTEOUS
Two Countries, 2014

'Stinky' was the local name for Low Newton-by-the-Sea. The Square is now in the care of the National Trust. 'Billy' is the fishermen's name for the coastguard watch-house at Low Newton, *c.* 1829. *yeddle:* liquid run-off from manure; *yetlin:* a three-toed iron pot.

Dunstanborough

Over the unseen September tide the mist
Sweeps ever inland, winding in a shroud
Stark walls and toppling towers that in the cloud
Of streaming vapour soar and twirl and twist,
Unbuilded and rebuilded in grey smoke
Until the drifting shadowy bastions seem
The old phantasmal castle wherein man's dream
Seeks shelter from time's still-pursuing stroke.

And I recall how once above a sea
That under cold winds shivered steely clear,
Fresh from the chisel, clean-cut and white and hard,
These towers, rock-founded for eternity,
Glittered when Lancelot and Guinevere
One April morning came to Joyous Gard.

WILFRID GIBSON
Chambers, 1920 | *Collected Poems 1905-1925*, 1926

from **Dunstanburgh**

Loud kittiwakes on an echoey crag:

There is a castle by the sea
That no road leads to any more –

On the height of a cliff, the farthest edge
Of land, a wind-rucked field; a wall

And gatehouse, ruled across the sky;
A city, seen from miles away;

A promise, pledged in tall stone towers
That, more than battle, passing years,

Winter on winter of wind and rain,
Have battered down to a great ruin:

There's a secret as old
As the stones to unlock:
There's a riddle, a mystery
Trapped in the rock,
   In the rock,
   In the rock,
   In the rock,
   In the rock,
   In the rock.

Fade into kittiwakes, merging with them completely.

And nobody visiting listens or stays
Long enough to tell that the noise

Of the sea on the cliff-face does not cease,
Or to say when the swallows and gulls that roost

In its loud, rocky hollows are suddenly gone
To the tug of winter; and nobody sees

How, in its hours of solitude,
The ruin is endlessly reclaimed.

[…]

Inside tower:

All day, all night, the wind explores
The gaps, the cracks. The stones resist.

As if it was searching for something lost,
The wind interrogates the walls.

Through arrow-slit, down parapet,
Round inaccessible, remote

Corners – a peaceful window-seat,
Marooned like something beyond the tide –

The wind inquires. Round battlements,
Up spiral stairs, through chambers, halls,

Brimful of voices, the way a shell
Fills with remembered sounds of the sea,

It pries. It probes.
The castle echoes:

It has become the wind's instrument.

Outside. Kittiwakes:

It's an island of rock.
It's a dragon, asleep,
With a dinosaur back
And the tail of a beast.
   It's a beast,
   It's a beast,
   It's a beast,
   It's a beast,
   It's a beast.

Fade out kittiwakes.

Hanging Stones:
Who?
     A dozen
Basalt towers,
Faceless, frozen;

Iron-armoured,
Rust-red,
Hacked, cracked,
Cold blood

Automata, black and blind,
Prehistory, glowering out,
They hold the tower aloft,
Offering it to the sky,
Lifting it up, cold hands
Raised in sacrifice
To sun and star and wind.

Wind that brings iron and timber,
Takes sons, brings strangers,
Wind that fans the fire's hunger –
   Whisper. Whisper. Who lives here?

What did he have on his mind,
The architect who planned
The hilt of a sword, stuck
In the spine of the rock –
What was he thinking of?

We know, hiss the stones.

[...]

Far-off sea and one melancholy oystercatcher:

On King Henry's shore, a heap
Of filthy rags and bone – a sheep,

A shipwreck, trailing spars and rigging,
Beards of fleece and skin. The straggling

Seaweed streamers of its guts –
Rubber bands, ravelled mats –

Hang from its rafters, ribs and spine;
And round its forelegs tangle twine,

Fishing nets and bladderwrack.

It has begun the long road back

To element and mineral.

Its socket glares. A blue-black fly
Sizzles in its empty eye,

And in the clean, salt, cold sea wind
Among the stones, its jawbone grins.

Queen Margaret has come from France.
The wind blows, and the grass
Trembles before it. Ice
Cracks on the pools like glass.

Over Queen Margaret's Tower
Five white swans,
Straight and clean as arrows,
Head for the south. My friend,

Who can we trust? Whose word
Is neither ice nor grass
Nor the shifting wind?
Over the field in-bye,

Shadow under its wings,
Hunger in its belly,
A chestnut kestrel bends,
Its eye stitched to its prey.

                                                            Quiet sea:

The immense quiet of evening: things
Returning home.
Stone that was bone in the morning and gold at three
Is only stone.

Now the flat, slate sky is feathered
Like a pigeon's breast,
Lilac, fiery pink and smoky grey
And, in the west,

Over Alnwick Moor and Hedgeley, flags
Of crimson flame
Blaze up from Cheviot, turning
Rock-pools to bloodstains.

KATRINA PORTEOUS
Dunstanburgh: A Secret as Old as the Stones, 2004 | *Two Countries*, 2014

'Dunstanburgh' is a radio poem, first broadcast by BBC Radio 4 in 2004 and performed with the children of Seahouses First School. The whole work is half an hour long on air and takes up nearly 30 pages in Katrina Porteous's *Two Countries* (and can be heard on the e-book with audio edition). This extract can only serve as a taster.

Katrina Porteous writes: 'One of the great mysteries about Dunstanburgh Castle is why it exists at all. It was used by the local community as a refuge during raids by the Scots in the 15th century; but it would appear that its purpose was more than purely defensive. It was built by Thomas, Earl of Lancaster, whose opposition to King Edward II is well known. While I was researching this poem, a team of archaeologists from English Heritage were unearthing evidence for a series of freshwater lakes, or meres, surrounding the castle. They proved beyond doubt that it was once a man-made island. Thomas of Lancaster went to considerable expense to design his castle as a massive visual reference to the Isle of Avalon, mythical home of King Arthur. This was a provocative symbol, designed to suggest that he, Thomas, had greater legitimacy to the English throne than the King himself. In a part of the country where law and order were impossible to maintain, Thomas promised alternative "good lordship". But his promise came to nothing. Northumberland remained lawless, and Dunstanburgh, ruined a century and a half later during the Wars of the Roses, stands as a visual reminder of Arthurian ideals which were never realised.'

Deposition

Take me to Dunstanburgh – in your pack
(no entry fee) – up through the sun-warmed towers
to that wild meadow, for a few last hours
together where the charming insects talk
and walk in the grass, and you can almost hear
the gossip between nests along the cliff.

And when you tire of nature, or to relieve
some natural need, run down the slope to where
Master Elias (a relation?) built
the castle's clean latrines, washed by the sea.

There you can pour me in a heap, to scour
the box where centuries of waste were spilt.
There I shall wait for waves to carry me
away from land, to my drowned ancestors.

ALISTAIR ELLIOT
Telling the Stones, 2017

Alnmouth

Something unassuageable about an estuary.
Black ooze, oily,

Clinging. Dragging east,
Miles of cloud rubble.

Acres of sea-purslane.
Redshank, dunlin,

Camouflaged. Dissemblance.
Chains of footprints

Snaking through mud. Loops
Of old rope. A curlew

Letting go its rinsed notes.
Abandonment.

And, slowly filling with water,
A boat

Rotten beyond rescue, its anchor-chain
Stiff; paint, lichen,

Flaking from its timbers, revealing
Strong, clear lines. What matters

Is sunk, uncovered
And sunk. On the far bank, a train,

A straight line on the heugh,
Hauling its troubles south.

And between them, the river
Slipping from green fields, Scots pines, gables –

Pink, blue, terracotta –
From the gull-squabble,

Towards something sparer:

Wormcasts.
Ripples.

On the far side of the water,

Walls, roofless.
Gleaming bent-grass.

Its surface wind-hatched, stippled with light,
The river

Is letting go
At the end of its life, an old man

Catching sight of what matters –
That muffled roar,

The stern white line of the breakers.

KATRINA PORTEOUS
Two Countries, 2014

At the Friary in Alnmouth
(for Marian Goodwin)

We are looking at Coquet Island in the long blue evening light.
How awkward we are at Compline.
We have no habits.
The smell of the sea is in our hair yet, after supper.
Our hearts are stranded here, transparent, lit
Like jellyfish in the afternoon.
How awkward it is to be at Compline in the long blue evening light
With my old shoulder-bag lying there yet, at my feet.

GILLIAN ALLNUTT
Sojourner, 2004 | *How the Bicycle Shone*, 2007

Druridge Bay

I can't remember being at Druridge Bay –
It was going that was important.
We might not get there, anyhow:
It might rain, or Father change his mind.

But going! The car's leather smell,
The bright blue drive, mile after mile
Down shimmering tarmac lanes.
    At last, the sea –
Can you see it yet? – the magic line
Rising over coarse dune grass.
I could stand on the seat to gaze though the open roof
Or ride on the running-board
For the last few thrilling miles.

The silent engine's petrol smell in sunshine.
Father's first picnic cigarette.
Heaven about to happen.

R.V. BAILEY
Marking Time, 2004

kye: cattle ➤

Felton Lonnen

The kye's cam yame but I see not me hinny
The kye's cam yame but I see not me bairn
I'd rather loss aal the kye than loss me hinny
I'd rather loss aal the kye than loss me bairn

Fair faced is me hinny, his blue eyes are bonny
His hair in curled ringlets hangs sweet to the side
So mount the auld pony seek after me hinny
Bring back to his mammy her only delight

He's always oot roaming the lang summer day thro'
He's always oot roaming away from the farm
Thro' hedges and ditches and valleys and fellsides
I hope that me hinny will cam to nae harm

Well I've searched in the meadow and in the far acre
Thro' stackyard and byre but nowt could I find
So off ye gan Daddy seek after yer laddie
Bring back tae this Mammy some peace tae her mind.

TRADITIONAL

The Complaint of the Morpethshire Farmer

On the up-platform at Morpeth station
in the market-day throng
I overheard a Morpethshire farmer
muttering this song:

Must ye bide, my good stone house,
to keep a townsman dry?
To hear the flurry of the grouse
but not the lowing of the kye?

To see the bracken choke the clod
the coulter will na turn?
The bit level neebody
will drain soak up the burn?

Where are ye, my seven score sheep?
Feeding on other braes!
My brand has faded from your fleece,
another has its place.

The fold beneath the rowan
where ye were dipt before,
its cowpit walls are overgrown,
ye would na heed them more.

And thou! Thou's idled all the spring,
I doubt thou's spoiled, my Meg!
But a sheepdog's faith is aye something.
We'll hire together in Winnipeg.

Canada's a cold land.
Thou and I must share
a straw bed and a hind's wages
and the bitter air.

Canada's a bare land
for the north wind and the snow.
Northumberland's a bare land
for men have made it so.

Sheep and cattle are poor men's food,
grouse is sport for the rich;
heather grows where the sweet grass might grow
for the cost of cleaning the ditch.

A liner lying in the Clyde
will take me to Quebec.
My sons'll see the land I am leaving
as barren as her deck.

(1930)

BASIL BUNTING
Active Anthology, ed. Ezra Pound, 1933 | *Complete Poems*, 2000
➤ AUTHOR NOTE PAGES 60-61

coulter: ploughshare; *cowpit:* overturned; *hind:* farmhand.

Butterwell

Nightdriving. Going to pick dad up from work.
Singing *Dance to Your Daddy* as the road unwinds,
a cine-film pitted with potholes. Cat's-eyes.
An allotment flae-craa sucking its fangs
by the stob where they hanged the last Ranter.
Where Jesus met the woman with five husbands.
Where the tigers turn to butter. Where they bury
men alive, black torchlight on the livid faces,
Netherton to Widdrington,
Widdrington to Seaton Burn.
Sedimental generations eking & hawking,
cavilling in Jolson monochrome. Butterwell.
A double scoop of Peroni's ice cream, the finest in Ashington
and the world. And the recipe gone: snow melt
from the hills of Butterwell. 'Somebody wants
to make the guy an offer really: patent it, they'll make a mint.'
A housing estate rechristened by council officials
in the wake of a scathing ITV documentary.
Our childhood word for cabbage whites: *butterlowie*.
Butterwell. Asking mam to tell us again
how the road was sinking because it was built
over the mine where granddad was buried alive
so often they nicknamed him *Jonah*. Driving on
past the watchtower in St Mary's churchyard, built
in 1830 to deter body snatchers from Makemland;
where I saw Aidan & Cuthbert knock the dirt off their boots;
where I saw slag heaps rise like smouldering hills of buttermilk;
where I saw Barabbas scabs
and selected representatives of the Tory party
in smurf-blue boiler suits & white hard hats
with red tape surveyors creep at night
to snatch our milk and poison every well. Butterwell.
The warning sign on the gate to the site.
The whistle at lowse, the wire fence, the floodlit watchtower.
The full moon poaching itself in the clouds.
Mam changing sides, winding the seat with a sheet,
while we press our noses to the glass & squeak
a cross in the mist to ward off the vampire
who is sliding up to the car on silent Nosferatu-rails;
who is climbing into the car, his donkey jacket heavy

with the odour of the mine (old earth freshly turned:
a smell that sticks to you, dogged as a lesson,
dogged as a lesson you wish you'd never learned);
who plants a kiss on mam's cheek & leaves a bruise.
And my brother & I nodding our pumpkin heads
and grinning our pumpkin grins.
And him reaching behind his seat
and grabbing our knees, his hand swinging like a shovel.

PAUL BATCHELOR
The Sinking Road, 2008

The Pit Heap

    Horray! They've teun the blot away!
The pooers that be are funny'ns.
    Us thowt its stench wuz heor t' stay
Phew! Rotten eggs and onions!
    But noo the canny folks that dwell
In collory raa abodes
    At last can let thor lung-box swell,
For noo blokes mekin' roads
    Need dort t' feed thor speedway lust,
An' wor reed ash 'n' clinkors
    That med' the hairt-ache wesh-day dust
Frum such sulphuric stinkors
    Hes gyen in screamin' trucks aall day,
That thunderin' doon wor lane
    Hev med yung parents waatch 'n' pray
An' mebbies wax profane.

    Yon heap filled hyems wi' dust 'n' stink
An' tarnished paints 'n' brasses –
    A plague, a fiendish corse, Aa think,
On aall wor hooseprood lasses.
    At neit the man-made moontain glowed
An' reeked 'n' spat 'n' twinkled,
    An' when the westorn air-stream flowed
Offended noses crinkled.

Aw! whaat a day of temper strain
When claes weshed wi' high hairt
    Should aall be tyekin' in agyen –
The wind had changed its airt!
    An' while the wives wad sniff 'n' froon,
An' t' thor claeslines horry,
    A swarm of specks wad settle doon
On clean weshed tarritory.

    Abeun the heap the pit pond lay –
A foul subsidence pool
    Wheor, with wor jamjars, bairns wad play
When on the wag frum scheul,
    Plodgin' roond wi' soaken beuts,
The education-hators,
    For tadpoles, frogs 'n' little newts
Us thowt war alligators.
    Aa mind when jist an impish pup,
A smaall playmate 'n' me
    Once pulled an oval bath-tin up
The steep-sloped pitheap scree.
    We both got in 'n' slid away,
An' cheered 'n' yelled 'n' chortled,
    An' nivvor war two bairns mair gay
As doon the slope wuh hortled.
    But, aw dear me, when halfway doon,
The bath-tin cowped its creels.
    Two imps spilled oot upon thor croon
Aall scratches, scrapes 'n' squeals!

    The big wheels 'n' the pitheap geor,
The waggons 'n' the sidin's,
    Us viewed each day withoot a feor
The morn wad bring dark tidin's,
    And aall wor labours heor wad cease,
King Coal wad abdicate,
    His subjects findin' sad release,
A lang dole queue thor fate.
    Aa knaa the blot hes gyen at last,
Green fields cum inta view,
    Strange silence broods wheor once the blast
Of despot buzzors blew.
    But if them wheels could torn agyen

Wor joy ne tungue could tell.
    We'd put up wi' the blot 'n' stain
An' dust 'n' reek 'n' smell.

FRED REED
Cumen and Gannin, 1977 | *The Northumborman*, 1999
➤ AUTHOR NOTE PAGE 63

teun: taken; *us thowt:* we thought; *canny:* nice, kind, good, OK (so not like Scots *canny*); *collory raa:* row of mining cottages; *noo:* now; *hyem:* home; *claes:* clothes; *tyek:* take; *airt:* sense, mood, direction; *on the wag frum scheul:* playing truant; *beuts:* boots; *us thowt:* we thought; *cowped its creels:* did a somersault; *knaa:* know; *gyen:* gone.

Seacoaling
(Lynemouth)

A January man scrapes the sea for coal,
hauls it from its froth still
shining –
soft necklaces of jet, strands
of a gypsy woman's hair
scribbled across the shallows.

Shirtless, smoking, he lugs
bucket after bucket
the long stagger to the dunes
and his bored mare, strapped to her cart,
grinding sea grass down between
bone-yellow gums.

An easterly rips in across his shoulder blades,
so flesh, wishy-washy round a florid heart
and indigo anchor, cringes –
like teeth marks, the coal-bits mottle
his forearms and chest to a samurai armour
or Steptoe overcoat.

More and more now he thinks he hears them
from the undersea shaft, long unworked,
their tappings and callings: no fathers

or grandfathers of his.
Poor leavings, these,
that keep a needy fire alive.

PIPPA LITTLE
Overwintering, 2012

See also George Charlton's 'Sea Coal' on page 460 (which relates to Seaham).

The Earthen Lot
(for Alistair Elliot)

> From Ispahan to Northumberland, there is no building that does not
> show the influence of that oppressed and neglected herd of men.
> WILLIAM MORRIS, *The Art of the People*

Sand, caravans, and teetering sea-edge graves.

The seaward side's for those of lowly status.
Not only gales gnaw at their names, the waves
jostle the skulls and bones from their quietus.

The Church is a solid bulwark for their betters
against the scouring sea-salt that erodes
these chiselled sandstone formal Roman letters
to flowing calligraphic Persian odes,
singing of sherbet, sex in Samarkand,
with Hafiz at the hammams and harems,
O anywhere but bleak Northumberland
with responsibilities for others' dreams!

Not for the Northern bard the tamarinds
where wine is always cool, and *kusi* hot –

his line from Omar scrivened by this wind 's:

Some could articulate, while others not.

(Newbiggin-by-the-Sea, 1977)

TONY HARRISON
from the School of Eloquence and other poems, 1978 | *Collected Poems*, 2007

The Blackleg Miner

It's in the evening after dark,
When the blackleg miner creeps to work,
With his moleskin pants and dirty shirt,
There goes the blackleg miner!

Well he takes his tools and doon he goes
To hew the coal that lies below,
There's not a woman in this town-row
Will look at the blackleg miner.

Oh, Delaval is a terrible place.
They rub wet clay in the blackleg's face,
And around the heaps they run a foot race,
To catch the blackleg miner!

So, divint gang near the Seghill mine.
Across the way they stretch a line,
To catch the throat and break the spine
Of the dirty blackleg miner.

They grab his duds and his pick as well,
And they hoy them down the pit of hell.
Doon ye go, and fare ye well,
You dirty blackleg miner!

So join the union while you may.
Don't wait till your dying day,
For that may not be far away,
You dirty blackleg miner!

(1844)

ANONYMOUS

Miners from the villages of Seghill and Seaton Delaval in Northumberland faced mass evictions during the national lock-out of 1844, which lasted for about 20 weeks and largely collapsed through blackleg labour being brought in.

'Two hundred men and eighteen killed...'

Two hundred men and eighteen killed
    For want of a second door!
Ay, for with two doors, each ton coal
    Had cost one penny more.

And what is it else makes England great,
    At home, by land, by sea,
But her cheap coal, and eye's tail turned
    Toward strict economy?

But if a slate falls off the roof
    And kills a passer-by,
Or if a doctor's dose too strong
    Makes some half-dead man die,

We have coroners and deodands
    And inquests, to no end,
And every honest Englishman's
    The hapless sufferer's friend,

And householder's or doctor's foe,
    For he has nought to lose,
And fain will, if he can, keep out
    Of that poor dead man's shoes.

But if of twice a hundred men,
    And eighteen more, the breath
Is stopped at once in a coal pit,
    It's quite a natural death;

For, God be praised! the chance is small
    That either you or I
Should come, for want of a second door,
    In a coal pit to die.

Besides, 'twould cost a thousand times
    As much, or something more,
To make to every pit of coal
    A second, or safety door,

As all the shrouds and coffins cost
    For those who perish now
For want of a second door, and that's
    No trifle, you'll allow;

And trade must live, though now and then
    A man or two may die;
So merry sing 'God bless the Queen',
    And long live you and I;

And, Jenny, let each widow have
    A cup of congo strong,
And every orphan half a cup,
    And so I end my song,

With prayer to God to keep coal cheap,
    Both cheap and plenty too,
And if the pit's a whole mile deep,
    What is it to me or you?

For though we're mortal too, no doubt,
    And Death for us his sithe
Has ready still, the chance is small
    We ever die of stithe.

And if we do, our gracious Queen
    Will, sure, a telegram send,
To say how sore she grieves for us
    And our untimely end;

And out of her own privy purse
    A sovereign down will pay,
To have us decently interred
    And put out of the way;

And burial service shall for us
    In the churchyard be read,
And more bells rung and more hymns sung
    Than if we had died in bed:

For such an accident as this
    May never occur again,
And till it does, one door's enough
    For pumps, air, coal, and men;

And should it occur – which God forbid! –
    And stifle every soul,
Remember well, good Christians all,
    Not one whit worse the coal.

JAMES HENRY
Poematia, 1866 | *Selected Poems*, 2002

congo: coffee; *sithe*: scythe; *stithe:* stythe, blackdamp or choke damp, a mixture of unbreathable gases left after oxygen is removed from the air.

'At ten o'clock on the morning of Thursday, January 16, 1862, the great iron beam of the steam-engine which worked the pumps of the Hester coal pit near Hartley in Northumberland, snapped across, and a portion of the beam, 40 tons in weight, fell into the shaft, tearing away the boarded lining so that the earthy sides collapsed and fell in, filling up the shaft in such a manner as not only to cut off all communication between the interior of the pit and the outer world, but entirely to obstruct all passage of pure air into, and of foul air out of, the pit. All the persons who were at work below at the time, two hundred and eighteen in number, were of course suffocated, nor was it until the seventh day after the accident that access could be had to the interior of the pit, or anything, beyond the mere fact of their entombment, ascertained concerning the helpless and unfortunate victims of that 'auri sacra fames' which so generally, so heartlessly, so pertinaciously refuses the poor workers in the coal mines of England, even the sad resource of a second staple or air shaft.'
Illustrated London News, January 25 and February 1, 1862.

James Henry (1798–1876) was a classical scholar, physician and poet from Dublin who spent many years travelling around Europe, on foot, to carry out research on Virgil, crossing the Alps seventeen times. His five poetry collections were printed at his own expense and little known in his lifetime. His work was rediscovered by Christopher Ricks in Cambridge University Library, which led to his poems being included in several of the standard anthologies of Victorian verse, and to the publication by the Lilliput Press of his *Selected Poems*, edited by Ricks, in 2002.

The Hartley Calamity

The Hartley men are noble, and
    Ye'll hear a tale of woe;
I'll tell the doom of the Hartley men –
    The year of Sixty-two.

'Twas on the Thursday morning, on
    The first month of the year,
When there befell the thing that well
    May rend the heart to hear.

Ere chanticleer with music rare
    Awakes the old homestead,
The Hartley men are up and off
    To earn their daily bread.

On, on they toil; with heat they broil,
    And streams of sweat still glue
The stour unto their skins, till they
    Are black as the coal they hew.

Now to and fro the putters go,
    The waggons to and fro,
And clang on clang of wheel and hoof
    Ring in the mine below.

The din and strife of human life
    Awake in 'wall' and 'board',
When, lo! a shock is felt which makes
    Each human heart-beat heard.

Each bosom thuds, as each his duds
    He snatches and away,
And to the distant shaft he flees
    With all the speed he may.

Each, all, they flee – by two – by three
    They seek the shaft, to seek
An answer in each other's face,
    To what they may not speak.

'Are we entombed?' they seem to ask,
    'For the shaft is closed, and no
Escape have we to God's bright day
    From out the night below.'

So stand in pain the Hartley men,
    And swiftly o'er them comes
The memory of home, nay, all
    That links us to our homes.

Despair at length renews their strength,
   And they the shaft must clear;
And soon the sound of mall and pick
   Half drowns the voice of fear.

And hark! to the blow of the mall below
   Do sounds above reply?
Hurra, hurra, for the Hartley men,
   For now their rescue's nigh.

Their rescue nigh? The sound of joy
   And hope have ceased, and ere
A breath is drawn a rumble's heard
   Re-drives them to despair.

Together now behold them bow;
   Their burdened souls unload
In cries that never rise in vain
   Unto the living God.

Whilst yet they kneel, again they fell
   Their strength renewed – again
The swing and the ring of the mall attest
   The might of the Hartley men.

And hark! to the blow of the mall below
   Do sounds above reply?
Hurra, hurra, for the Hartley men,
   For now their rescue's nigh.

But lo! yon light, erewhile so bright
   No longer lights the scene;
A cloud of mist yon light hath kissed,
   And shorn it of its sheen.

A cloud of mist yon light has kissed,
   An see! along must crawl,
Till one by one the lights are smote,
   And darkness covers all.

'Oh, father, till the shaft is cleared,
   Close, close besides me keep;
My eye-lids are together glued,
   And I – and I – must sleep.'

'Sleep, darling, sleep, and I will keep
   Close by – heigh-ho!' To keep
Himself awake the father strives –
   But he – he too – must sleep.

'O, brother, till the shaft is cleared,
   Close, close besides me keep;
My eye-lids are together glued,
   And I – and I – must sleep.'

'Sleep, brother, sleep, and I will keep
   Close by – heigh-ho!' – To keep
Himself awake the brother strives –
   But he – he too – must sleep.

'O mother, dear! wert, wert thou near
   Whilst sleep!' – The orphan slept;
And all night long by the black pit-heap
   The mother a dumb watch kept.

And fathers and mothers, and sisters, and brothers –
   The lover and the new-made bride –
A vigil kept for those who slept,
   From eve to morning tide.

But they slept – still asleep – in silence dread,
   Two hundred old and young,
To awake when heaven and earth have sped,
   And the last dread trumpet rung!

(1862)

JOSEPH SKIPSEY
Poems, Songs, and Ballads, 1862 | *Selected Poems*, 2014

The Collier Lad

My lad he is a Collier Lad,
   And ere the lark awakes,
He's up and away to spend the day
   Where daylight never breaks;

But when at last the day has passed,
    Clean washed and cleanly clad,
He courts his Nell who loveth well
    Her handsome Collier Lad.

CHORUS
There's not his match in smoky Shields;
    Newcastle never had
A lad more tight, more trim, nor bright
    Than is my Collier Lad.

Tho' doomed to labour under ground,
    A merry lad is he;
And when a holiday comes round,
    He'll spend that day in glee;
He'll tell his tale o'er a pint of ale,
    And crack his joke, and bad
Must be the heart who loveth not
    To hear the Collier Lad.

At bowling matches on the green
    He ever takes the lead,
For none can swing his arm and fling
    With such a pith and speed:
His bowl is seen to skim the green,
    And bound as if right glad
To hear the cry of victory
    Salute the Collier Lad.

When 'gainst the wall they play the ball,
    He's never known to lag,
But up and down he gars it bound,
    Till all his rivals fag;
When deftly – lo! he strikes a blow
    Which gars them all look sad,
And wonder how it came to pass
    They played the Collier Lad.

The quoits are out, the hobs are fixed,
    The first round quoit he flings
Enrings the hob; and lo! the next
    The hob again enrings;
And thus he'll play the summer day,

      The theme of those who gad;
And youngsters shrink to bet their brass
      Against the Collier Lad.

When in the dance he doth advance,
      The rest all sigh to see
How he can spring and kick his heels,
      When they a-wearied be;
Your one-two-three, with either knee
      He'll beat, and then, glee-mad,
A heel-o'er-head leap crowns the dance
      Danced by the Collier Lad.

Besides a will and pith and skill,
      My laddie owns a heart
That never once would suffer him
      To act a cruel part;
That to the poor would ope the door
      To share the last he had;
And many a secret blessing's poured
      Upon my Collier Lad.

He seldom goes to church, I own,
      And when he does, why then,
He with a leer will sit and hear,
      And doubt the holy men;
This very much annoys my heart;
      But soon as we are wed,
To please the priest, I'll do my best
      To tame my Collier Lad.

JOSEPH SKIPSEY
The Collier Lad and other songs and ballads, 1864 | *Selected Poems*, 2014

'Get Up!'

'Get up!' the caller calls, 'Get up!'
      And in the dead of night,
To win the bairns their bite and sup,
      I rise a weary wight.

My flannel dudden donned, thrice o'er
  My birds are kissed, and then
I with a whistle shut the door,
  I may not ope again.

JOSEPH SKIPSEY
A Book of Lyrics, 1892 | *Selected Poems*, 2014

The collier poet **Joseph Skipsey** (1832–1903) was born in the Percy parish of Tynemouth, where his father was shot dead in a clash between pitmen and special constables. Skipsey himself worked in the pits from the age of seven; he had no schooling, but taught himself to read and write. In 1852, he walked most of the way to London, found work on the railways, married his landlady and returned north to work in Scotland, and later at Choppington and the Pembroke collieries near Sunderland.

In 1859 he published a volume of *Poems* in Morpeth, though this seems not to be extant. It attracted the attention of the editor of James Clephan, editor of the *Gateshead Observer*, who obtained a job for him as under-store-keeper at Hawks Crawshay and Son in Gateshead. In 1863, after a fatal accident to one of his children in the works, he moved to Newcastle, where Robert Spence Watson had secured him a position as assistant librarian to the Literary and Philosophical Society. The work did not suit him, however, and the pay was none too good. He returned to the mines until 1882. Skipsey became part of Robert Spence Watson's wide circle of acquaintance; his table talk is said to have been trenchant and to the point.

In 1883 he delivered his lecture 'The Poet as Seer and Singer' to the Literary and Philosophical Society in Newcastle and subsequently published a number of books, including *Carols from the Coalfields* (1886), drawing praise from Rossetti and Oscar Wilde, who likened the poems to those of William Blake. Rossetti met Skipsey, apparently brought to London by Thomas Dixon and records: 'I found him a stalwart son of toil, and every inch a gentleman. In cast of face, he recalls Tennyson somewhat, though more bronzed and browned. He is as sweet and gentle as a woman in manner, and recited some beautiful things of his own with a special freshness to which one is quite unaccustomed.'

In 1889 Skipsey was appointed custodian of Shakespeare's birthplace at Stratford-upon-Avon on the recommendation of Burne-Jones, Tennyson, Rossetti, Bram Stoker and other eminent men. He resigned two years later, and the episode prompted Henry James to write his story 'The Birthplace'. Skipsey returned north and died at Harraton in 1903.

Basil Bunting contributed an interesting preface to the Ceolfrith Press edition of Skipsey's *Selected Poems* (1976), and in comparing Skipsey with Burns makes the telling point that Burns saw Ayr and Dumfries vividly, but from outside. Skipsey was so much inside the pit village, he hardly notices Cowpen or Percy Main at all. Dignified and austere as a man, Skipsey could be windy and rhetorical as a writer. 'The Hartley Calamity', a tribute to the miners who died in the 1862 disaster, is both heartfelt and clumsy. He is at his best when describing his own experience as a pitman. Rossetti called him: 'Joseph Skipsey, the Northern Collier Poet, a man of real genius' and considered 'Get Up!' equal to anything in the language for quietly direct pathos.

A second edition of the authoritative *Selected Poems*, edited by R.K.R. Thornton, Chris Harrison and William Daniel McCumiskey, was published by Rectory Press in 2014. [AM]

NORTH TYNE, REDESDALE, COQUETDALE

from The Lay of the Reedwater Minstrel
illustrated with notes historical and explanatory, by a Son of Reed

from PART I

And I will bring a *Minstrel sweet*,
   A son of *famed Woollaw*,
And with his strains he shall you greet,
   And loud his pipes shall blaw.

He'll sing Reedwater's muirlands wild,
   Where whirring heath-cocks flee,
Where limpid wells and heather bells
   Delight the Sportsman's E'e.

He'll tell of hapless *Parcy Reed*,[1]
   And how each traitor Ha',
The squire betray'd, all reft of aid,
   By Crosier's brand to fa'.

The feudal frays of former days,
   The Minstrelsy shall tell,
How on the *Hare-haugh's bloody plain*[2]
   The Pride of *Coquet* fell

When doughty *Parce* and *Ellick Ha'*,
   The heroes of the *Reed*,
In battle stout the foe did rout
   Wi' mony a *broken head!*

Dire was the clattering cudgel's thud,
   When frae the Reedsdale clan,
The foe pursued thro' Coquet's flood,
   In wild disorder ran.

---

   1. Parcy Reed. The particulars of the traditional story of Parcy Reed of Troughend, and the Halls of Girsonsfield, the Author had from a descendant of the family of Reed. From

his account it appears that Percival Reed, Esquire, a Keeper of Reedsdale, was betrayed by the Halls (hence denominated the false-hearted Ha's) to a band of moss-troopers of the name of Crosier, who slew him at Batinghope, near the source of the Reed. The Halls were, after the murder of Parcy Reed, held in such universal abhorrence and contempt, by the inhabitants of Reedsdale, for their cowardly and treacherous behaviour, that they were obliged to leave the country.

2. Hare-haugh's bloody plain. In former days the inhabitants of Reedsdale and Coquet-side entertained an antipathy to each other, which, when the parties happened to meet at a race or cock-fight, was generally productive of dissension. Their only offensive weapons, however, being fists and cudgels, these quarrels, tho' very fruitful in broken pates and bruises, seldom proved of more serious consequence to any of the combatants. The battle here alluded to, was fought at a *Cocking* on the *Hare-haugh*, close by the stream of *Coquet*; where the *Sons of Reed*, led on by two champions of herculean strength and stature, named *Percival* and *Alexander Hall*, attacked the *Coquetors*, and after a desperate and bloody conflict, obtained a decisive victory, numbers of the routed and flying enemy being in their panic driven into the river, to avoid the vengeance and fury of the conquerors.

from PART II

And thou, romantic sweet Tod Law,[3]
   Shalt grace the Minstrel's humble lay,
'Thou bear'st the bell amang them a',’
   When clad in verdant spring's array;

Thy heathy hill, thy waving wood,
   Thy clustering nuts and jetty sloes,
The limpid Reed's meand'ring flood,
   That round thy flow'ry meadow flows;

The early primrose too is thine,
   And violet sweet of glossy dye,
Crane-berries on thy border shine,
   And glad the school boy's searching eye:

The skilful angler hies to thee,
   His pleasing pastime to pursue,
Wi' cautious art he *thraws the flee*,
   And ling'ring bids the streams adieu!

Of Deadwood stor'd wi' *Black* and *Gray*
   The Minstrel he shall sing,
Of *brave Sir John* o' the Cleugh-brae,
   And Woollaw's *little king*;

Of Cottonshope and Gowden Potts,
   Of Ramshope and Whitelee,
The Birkhill, Bagraw, and the Hotts,
   Silloans and Pity-me;

Nor shall he pass by Ratten-raw,
   The Smart-side and Ash-trees,
The Stobbs and Horsley, *Thrisley Ha'*,
   Mill-haugh and *Jamie's Bees*.[4]

And Overacres, Shittleheugh,
   Hope-foot and Monkridge Ha',
The Birness,[5] Blakehope, and Catcleugh,
   Shall shine amang them a'.

And thou, Elishaw,[6] too, shalt claim
A share of tributary fame;
Though wretched now thy Mansion seems,
Thy splendor fled like fading dreams,
The sumptuous feast, the sparkling wine,
The Lordly visitor was thine;
But now no more within thy walls
Resounds the roar of Bacchanals;
Thy noble guest is wrapt in clay,
And the sweet Songster's far away;
Whose merry glees and tuneful song,
Oft charm'd the social, jovial, throng;
Whose artless strains, so witching wild,
The dreary winter night beguil'd.

---

3. On the Tod Law were three stone columns, placed in a triangular order, twelve feet distant from each other, and each column nearly twelve feet in diameter. These, it is presumed, were sepulchral, or monuments of some memorable event. It was the custom of the Danes, at the solemn in vestiture of their kings, or men of chief authority, to erect monuments of this nature; and to that people it is most reasonable we should attribute such erections. HUTCHINSON.

4. Jamie's Bees. Alluding to a well known inhabitant of the Mill-haugh, an honest weaver, *James Mair*, celebrated for his successful management of these curious insects, and for the delicious honey with which he supplied the neighbouring country. The author still remembers with pleasure the happy moments he has spent in Jamie's garden amongst his busy bees and fragrant flowers, when tired with fishing in the *Durtree-burne*, and weary with the weight of his well filled creel, he has quaffed with delight the hospitable weaver's 'milk and honey'.

5. Birness, a corruption of Buryness. Mr Wallis says, there was at this place a 'British temple, the stones numerous, of various sizes, in a circular order'.

6. Elishaw. A place of note in the vale of Reed, famous for being the scene of many a merry meeting, and night of revelry.

Here was the rendezvous of the 'vagrant train' of *faa's, tinklers, &c.* The celebrated *Wull Allen* frequently sojourned here, in the progress of his fishing and otter-hunting expeditions; and here often resounded the *drones* of his no less celebrated son, *Jamie Allan*, the Northumberland piper. At Elishaw were held the rustic races for the *hat* or *saddle*, and, to sum up all, at Elishaw will long be recorded the fame of its hospitable and noble resident, the late *Lord Cranstoun*, of convivial memory. But alas! these days are gone, and the grandeur of Elishaw is no more. 'Sic transit gloria mundi.'

ROBERT ROXBY
The Lay of the Reedwater Minstrel, 1809

Robert Roxby (1767–1846) grew up on farms near Hartburn and in Redesdale, turning to clerking in Newcastle when his fortunes foundered: 'In early youth Mr Roxby began to cultivate the poetic faculty. For some time the outward manifestation of his abilities in this direction was limited to the production of rhythmical letters, addressed to friends in Redesdale and Coquetside. […] An enthusiastic disciple of Izaak Walton, Mr Roxby added zest to his favourite pursuit by contributing to its poetical literature. In 1821, in conjunction with his friend Thomas Doubleday, he published what proved to be the commencement of a series of lyrical productions, known to sportsmen with rod and fly as 'Fisher's Garlands'. These Garlands, illustrated with appropriate cuts by Bewick, were published annually, till 1843.' (Richard Welford, *Men of mark 'twixt Tyne and Tweed*, 1895)

Winter on the Carter Fell

Oh! it's dour and snell on the Carter Fell
On a cauldrife winter's morning
When the sna' lies deep where the Marches meet
And the Northern wind is storming
When the powdery drift drives fierce and swift
Filling hagg and syke and hollow
And Crozier's pack at the plantin' back
Are pairting wie' their tallow.

When ower the fell danders Crozier's sel'
And he looks baith dour and sulky
The sna's lain lang 'and O! my sang'
The hay in the shed's no' bulky.
Dark sorrow's trace has marked his face
Each day he's getting thinner,
He lang has ser'ed as a moorland herd
But he soon will be a skinner.

When up the hill marches roadman Bill
And faces these regions colder.
With an action swift he tackles each drift
And heaves it o'er his shoulder.
By his side there works these willing Turks
Brave Bod and Alexander
And that steam machine the famous Green
With a hiss like an angry gander.

With anxious eyes they view the skies
For a sign of the Western breezes
And then with a scowl and angry growl
Each gapes his gab and sneezes.
They swing their arms till each cauld hand warms
And stamp their feet wie ire
Crying Oh! dear me for a cup o' tea
And a seat by the kitchen fire.

E'en Auld Nick himsel' on the Carter Fell
Wadna' stay in sic' stormy weather
We hae guid proof unless his hoof
Was held by a hempen tether.
And it's weel we ken that the smoky den
O' this famous brimstone charmer
Whate'er it be we can plainly see
Will indeed be a wee thought warmer.

Oh! it's dour and snell on the Carter Fell
On a cauldrife winter's morning
In that lone retreat where the Marches meet
And the Northern wind is storming
It's infernal cauld when ye're getting auld
And yer bluid is turning thinner
So ye're no' tae blame if ye stay at hame
As I'm a leevin' sinner.

(1917)

BILLY BELL
Billy Bell: Redesdale Roadman, Border Bard, 2013

Billy Bell (1862–1941) lived his whole life in a small cottage at Low Byrness, north Redesdale, apart from a short time spent working as a groom at Dunnshouses, Troughend, near Otterburn. Around 1882 he became a roadman for the district council which had taken over the former toll road to Scotland in 1880, a job he held for the next 48 years, responsible for keeping ditches and verges clear, and for pot-hole filling and snow clearing, on the eight-mile stretch south of the border at Carter Bar. He always wore clogs and finally retired at the age of 71. Known to locals as 'the Bard of Redesdale', he was known for giving impromptu recitals and was a regular contributor of poems to the *Hexham Courant*, but were it not for the actions of a neighbour, who rescued his surviving manuscripts after his widow died in 1951, his work would not have survived. Three of his poems are about the Bellingham Show [220]. In 1988 the 'Billy Bell project' was set up to try to collect more information about Billy and his poems at the Border Library, which was later moved to Hexham's Old Gaol, where a volunteer, Susan Ellingham, revived the research in 2011, finally leading to the publication of Billy Bell's poems in book form by Bellingham's Heritage Centre in 2013.

Wild Hills O' Wannys

O my heart's in the west, on yon wild mossy fells,
Amang muircocks, an' plovers an' red heatherbells;
Where the lambs lie in clusters on yon bonny brae,
On the wild hills o' Wannys sae far, far away.
There's Aid Crag, an' Luma, an' Hepple Heugh, too,
Hartside and Darna, I've oft been on you,
Ottercaps, Hareshaw, an' Peaden sae hie,
An' the wild hills o' Wannys for ever for me.

There the muircock he becks in his wild mossy hame,
O'er the tops o' the heather ye ken his red kame;
The plover is tilting on yon mossy flowes,
The black-cock is crooing on Fernyrigg knowes.
The cranberries creep where they scarce can be seen,
The blaeberries peep from the heather between,
An' the sweet-scented wild thyme on yon bonny brae,
On the wild hills o' Wannys sae far, far away.

O Wannys, wild Wannys! thou rears thy proud head,
And boldly thou stand'st 'tween the Wansbeck and Reed,
Thou rears thy proud crest o'er hill, dale, and knowe,
Whereof yore Rob o'Risinghame bent his strong bow.
The dark ravens bield on thy grey cliffs sae hie,
The fox rears her young anes, auld Wannys, in thee;
The wild flashing falcon he darts on his prey,
On the wild hills o' Wannys sae far, far away.

O Wannys, wild Wannys! the scene it is grand,
On a clear summer's morn on thy summit to stand,
The hills o'er the Carter and Cheviot to view,
An' listen to the lapwing an' lonely Curlew.
The shepherd he climbs thee his fair flocks to see,
An' woo that fair mountain nymph – sweet Liberty;
On the braes by the burnie the lambs loup and play
Round the wild hills o' Wannys sae far, far away!

Round the wild hills o' Wannys 'twas glorious to tread,
When we went otter hunting to the Tyne or the Reed,
When Rockwood an' Ringwood an' Bugle's clear cry,
An' Ranger was warning the otter to die.
Then we track't the sly fox to his den in the snow,
An' howkt him or trapt him for a grand tally ho,
An' wak'd the wild echoes by Sweethope and Rae,
Round the wild hills o' Wannys sae far, far away!

Round the wild hills o' Wannys in the morn's early gleam,
O 'twas grand to gan fishin' away by the Leam,
Wi' the flee o' the woodcock, the green drake, or teal,
Wi' gould-speckl't trouts we filled monie a fine creel.
There's the Reed an' the Wansbeck, where the dews sweetly fa',
The Lyles Burn and Reasey we oft fished them a',
Aye, there's monie a burnie and sweet heather brae
Round the wild hills o' Wannys sae far, far away.

Here's to the hills o' the brave an' the free,
And the red waving heather sae bonnie to see;
An' the bright gushing streams wimplin' doun to the dell,
By wild thyme an' gowan an' sweet heather bell;
Here's to the wild Wannys' ilk hill, dale, and stream,
Still, still I am there in my thoughts an' my dream;
Here's health, peace, an' plenty, for ever and aye,
Round the wild hills o' Wannys sae far, far away!

(c. 1860)

JAMES ARMSTRONG
Wanny Blossoms, 1879

Rockwood, Ringwood and *Ranger*, famed otter hounds belonging to Mr Harrison, Woodburn. *Bugle*, a celebrated otterhound, the property of William Turnbull of Bellingham.

James Armstrong lived during the mid-19th century in the Wilds o' Wanney at Aid Crag near Wanny Crag. A new printing of his *Wanny Blossoms* (1879) included not just the ballads for which he was well-known in Northumberland but also 'a brief treatise on fishing with the fly, worm, minnow and roe', as he noted: 'The welcome reception given to my first venture of "Wanny Blossoms" encourages me to give a second edition, to which I have added (in verse and prose), several new subjects, including Songs, Fishing, Fox and Otter Hunting, and other Border Sports and Pastimes, in which many of my readers doubtless take an interest.' He also notes that his best-known poem, 'Wild Hills O' Wannys' was not written there but at Dewlaw Mill near Matfen. Another of his poems, 'The Kielder Hunt' [227], has long been a favourite for many Northumbrian singers, including Willy Scott.

The Raw

A razor wind slashed as she douked below dykes,
following dips and shake holes, taking detours along dales.
Her skirts tacked the storm that stropped her face
with the sharp icy edge of a blade.

High Carrick, Elsdon, late May 1791
When her daughter Jane fell sick Jean Clark asked Isabel
if they could board in a barn
and begged milk for her up and down the road for days.

Three months later she called in to light her cutty.
Isabel's eighty-year-old mother, Maggie, was just leaving
with a bundle of merchandise to sell from The Raw.
When Isabel asked after her own two lasses
Jean lit her pipe and said 'away past wi the asses,'
and 'Does your mither deal in more than baccy?
And does she live in yon muckle hoos hersel?'

William Winter met the Clarks at Edington Mires
and travelled to Stannerton Heugh, where they camped.
He was just back from a seven-year stretch in the Hulks.

Jean told him they were penniless
but when she'd bought baccy at The Raw
she saw fifty guinea worth of goods on the table.
And she knew the way 'brawly. The lasses can tek ye there.

Gan by Black Heddon, Little Harle, and Kirkwhelpington,
north owa the moors, across the Elsdon turnpike to

Whiskershiel. Then meet me and Nell's bairn
at Huntlaw the morra.'

Nell and Jane left with Winter
who stole a sheep and killed it, then got a coulter
in a haugh near Little Harle.

Whiskershiel Fell
A merlin harried a singing lark over a chased sky.
It flipped and dived without missing a note.

Young Abraham, tending his master's flock,
climbed a steep slope to a sheep fold
where Nell and Winter were girthing an ass
and Jane wrapped a large gully in straw rope.
Fresh picked bones lay scattered.

When he saw Abraham, Winter sang
a few lines about a shepherd boy
and asked 'whet o-cleck is it?'

Jane led away, north over the moor towards East Nook,
to a narrow clough where they fastened the ass to a dike
and waited for the lights in the hoos to gan oot.

The Raw
Shadows flit across the vaulted ceiling
to a high winding jig that pipes through every crack and gap.
The isolated bastle was exposed to the sweep of a reiving wind,
drilling the shell of her home with the bit of its beak.

Winter used the coulter to jemmy a gap between door and jamb
and pulled back a wooden bar to get in.
The sisters, lying on each side of her, kept Maggie Crozier still
while he broke the locks off two chests and a cupboard
and took much lawn, four or five silk handkerchiefs, some cambric
and fifteen yards of blue shalloon.
And from a small chest seven gowns, nine bed gowns,
fifty yards of red, blue, black and spotted ribbon.

He took an old striped petticoat from the bed head
and from the cupboard four or five pounds of white thread,
nine pair of women's white cotton stockings,
two pounds of currants and raisins and half pound of starch.

From a dresser he took one dozen handkerchiefs and shawls
and ate a piece of cut cheese and bread from the cupboard.

The sisters held the old woman down while he took the gear outside
to wrap in two aprons, sewn together for the purpose.
When he came back to fetch them Jane said 'she's got coin,'
and showed him a hidden pocket near Maggie's head.
But Winter said 'it's time to gan and if yi divvin shift I'll skelp yiz.'

He went to the bedside but old Maggie was still.
He took hold of her shoulders and began shaking her.
He raked the fire to make a flame. Lit a candle
and found a cut on her face,
and a handkerchief tight around her neck with two knots.
He raised her and laid her down again.
He threw cold water on her.

'You've done bad lasses, she'll not speak again.'
They put the gear in sacks on the ass's back
and set out for Kirkwhelpington
but got lost in the dark and sheltered behind a hay pike
where they ate bread and cheese,
and gave the ass some green peas
found amongst the swag.

TOM PICKARD

hoyoot: Collected Poems and Songs, 2014
➤ AUTHOR NOTE PAGE 413

William Winter and sisters Jane and Eleanor Clark were found guilty of the murder of Margaret Crozier and executed at Gallowgate in Newcastle on 10 August 1791. Winter's body was taken afterwards to Steng Cross on the drover's road above Elsdon, not far from the Raw, and hung up in a gibbet cage as a warning to all felons, while the bodies of the two women were donated for medical dissection. Birds, maggots and insects fed upon Winter's body in the gibbet cage, with wild animals taking what fell down to the ground. Eventually only his bones remained, and these were said to have been scattered and his skull sent to a Mr Darnell in Newcastle. One of Northumberland's more unusual landmarks, the original Winter's Gibbet was replaced around 1867 with a replica which used to hold a dummy, then just a wooden head. While Winter's ghost left his body on the scaffold in Newcastle, it is said to haunt the area around his gibbet 40 miles away, most often next to a nearby cattle grid. Another local story has it that the nearby village of Elsdon is the resting place of the dead from the battle of Otterburn (1388). [NA]

Epitaph for Ned Allan

Here lies old Ned in his cold bed,
For hunting otters famed,
A faithful friend lies by his side,
And 'Tug 'em' he was named.
Sport and rejoice ye finny tribes
That glide in Coquet river,
Your deadly foe no more you'll see
For he is gone forever.

The amphibious otter now secure,
On Coquet's peaceful shore,
May roam at large for Ned and Tug
Will never harm him more.
Up Swindon burn he may return,
When salmon time comes on;
For poor old Ned in his cold bed
Sleeps sound at Holystone.

(early 19th century)

ROBERT HUNTER
P. Anderson Graham, *Highways and Byways of Northumbria*, 1920

This epitaph was written for Ned Allan, a weaver and celebrated local fisherman, of Holystone, Northumberland, by village schoolmaster Robert Hunter.

Northumborland (1)

For scenory sum seek a foreign land,
The highor 'n' the caador, the mair grand!
But soft-corved hills 'n' trees 'n' leas for me –
The signs of luv's artistic husbandry;
Corn, coos, cool streams, a lamb that's gyen astray
An' ye can heor its baa a mile away.
Corlews 'n' herons ower sumpy sedges,
An' fussy little spuggies in the hedges.

Nature a mottled luvliness attains
Wheor trees in majesty arch ower the lanes,
And as ye gan alang the regal arch
Raised spirits move in a triumphal march
Inta the green expanses fresh 'n' fair
That heal the mind noo shaken free of care.
Theor's fells wheor infant streams cum oot t' play
An' romp 'n' giggle on theor tumblin' way
In escapades of liquid ecstacy
That mek wor Coquet full of coquetry.

FRED REED
Cumen and Gannin, 1977 | *The Northumborman*, 1999
➤ AUTHOR NOTE PAGE 63

caador: colder; *coos:* cows; *gyen:* gone; *spuggies:* sparrows.

'Stones trip Coquet burn…'

Stones trip Coquet burn;
grass trails, tickles
till her glass thrills.

The breeze she wears
lifts and falls back.
Where beast cool

in midgy shimmer
she dares me chase
under a bridge,

giggles, ceramic
huddle of notes,
darts from gorse

and I follow, fooled.
She must rest, surely;
some steep pool

to plodge or dip
and silent taste
with all my skin.

(1970)

BASIL BUNTING
Agenda, 1970 | *Complete Poems*, 2000
➤ AUTHOR NOTE PAGES 60-61

from Hen Harrier Poems

§

There are, were, four couples south of Cheviot:
one prospecting Gled Scaur flatt by fair Dod Law
not to nest there by Doddington, but in a flaw
of the shining glidder-slacks westward, alight
with the glow off those stones as those dotterels.
White Moss's birds have gone off to Sundaysight
of mixed fortunes, another pair in the forest
favoured a bit of blow-out – but found no rest,
shot-off, like those others far out on the fells…

(1980s)

§

Formerly on traditionally-managed haughland
just as the harriers have, much declined
but didn't we see them at Elsdon, Eglingham?
we were above; the Tarset below and bright-lined
when her 'old-timer's' eye turned to me bright
with what was not what I call the light
from the birds of prey, glimpsed in flight
from her Reenes Farm, hill over Bellingham

no, the harrier had caught her eye, but the white
in the greensward on the fell by Sundaysight
the little white orchis *Pseudorchis alba*
now inseparable from her own remaining aura

for Brenda Richardson, deceased (2005)

Katharine Macgregor – of The Sneep, Tarset

She said, graceful lady of wisdom, 'they will be back'
this is their land, especially so before the forestry;
Gleedlees their pastures, hunted Bimmer (when I was a boy)
Ridley Shiel an egg laid as bright as moontrack
good sense since of the likes of Wilson, McCracken...

there we were, me more trouble to the sheep,
each prospecting a place to live near Sneep.
Blackburn Common, the Tarret, and the Dargues Hope*
and led by big huntring Kestrel from Woodhead

fell in with a harrier that spring which,*
cockbird, forced our kestrel into the ditch
toward Heathery Hill, and later, perhaps
killed her by Pit Houses, pierced corpse
not scavenged, but post mortemed; instead of course...

(1990)

* Hen Harrier tried to nest some seasons I watched them there, by Tarset and Tarret.

§

The cadence of a Strathspey, played slow
yet with its opening bars' urgency
she took off and started quartering into the blow
and buffeting the 'winds o' Kielder's' sashay

They say the Tynedale fells for miles
seem 'nowt but nothingness'
whilst all the whiles
round and round flee these indigenes
regular over the same bit o' ground
even after they *must* have found
summat ti eat for the nest!

For such a bird all the dales are one
every common and fellside could be available
but too many of their 'smitt-spots' are gone…

For Bill Lancaster of Blaydon and Haydon Bridge
his Northern Review *promoting Northern sense and letters*

COLIN SIMMS
Hen Harrier Poems, 2015

Between Lord's Shaw and Pit Houses
(Sheet 80 NY821926)

At the back end of beyond
the only signpost musters
a rimless wheel of arrows
pointing everywhere.
You let the engine idle
– the wind exhaling
through an open slit of window,
a ditch of rushes
bowing to the inevitable –
and could almost reach and pluck
from that faintly ringing metal
it beckons not; it beckons
each place-name like a petal
till the obvious is clear
where was it you were going?
It must be somewhere here.

PETER ARMSTRONG
The Capital of Nowhere, 2003

Sundaysight

By Seven Pikes to Blackmoor Skirt
And so to Sundaysight
Is a rough road for travelling
For him who walks by night.

In rain or snow for seven years
Each night he took the track
That he might see a window-light,
And ere the dawn walked back.

By moon or stars to Sundaysight
He came to ease his mind
In gazing on a glowing pane
And the shadow on the blind.

He never spoke to her by day,
Who could not be his wife,
And naught she ever knew of him
Who loved her more than life.

'Twixt Sundaysight and Seven Pikes
A man may come to hurt;
And with a broken neck he lay
One dawn on Blackmoor Skirt.

By Seven Pikes to Blackmoor Skirt
And so to Sundaysight
Is a rough road for travelling,
But ghosts can travel light.

WILFRID GIBSON
Whin, 1918 | *Collected Poems 1905-1925*, 1926

Hareshaw

The heather's black on Hareshaw
When Redesdale's lying white:
When grass is green in Redesdale
Dark Hareshaw blossoms bright.

They harvest hay in Redesdale
For beasts within the byre:
The heather upon Hareshaw
Is harvested with fire.

WILFRID GIBSON
Chambers, 1920 | *Collected Poems 1905-1925*, 1926

Hareshaw Linn

At length the din
Of battle dulls in dying ears…
And now his spirit hears
Once more the well-remembered roar
Of Hareshaw Linn –
Of Hareshaw Linn at flood,
In snowfed torrent dashing down
From the high fells: and now the blood
From his young body seems to pour
And mingle with the gleaming brown
Untrammelled waters that ere long shall be,
Merged in the sweeping current of the Tyne,
Borne on towards the bitter brine
Of the oblivious sea.

WILFRID GIBSON
The Outpost, 1918 | *Collected Poems 1905-1925*, 1926

Hareshaw Linn

is inching nearer
its beginning.

However hard its teeth are gritted,
stone is bitten. Water fumes,
squeezed by its entourage of oak, of beech –
earth lifter, rummaging in spate.

Among this crockery of cliffs,
outriding trees
have dangled wishbones of their dead
like timber lightning.
Resentful of your footsteps, they
discharge, through loopholes in the rock,
their weaponry
in bursts of rooks.

There's no way home
except the route you got here by.

Go back.

High moorland has been scoured for snow,
the melt
leans forward in an upright thunder.

Sandstone pressure
bends rainbows to the neck of water.

PETER BENNET
All the Real, 1994

An Old Shepherd's Adventure at Bellingham

Aw am an aad herd and Aw live far oot bye
Aw seldom see owt but the sheep and the kye
So Aw says te wor Betsy Aw think Aw will go
To hev a bit leuk at the Bellingham Show.

Ah weel, says the aad wife, if the money's to spare
No doot it's a lang time since ye hev been there.
Wor pack lambs hev seld weel, they've a lang time been low
So Aw think ye might gan te the Bellingham Show.

So Aw gets mesel' drest in me braw Sunday claes
And me brass nebbed shoon polished black as twa shaes,
A big stand up collar, and me tie in a bo'
Aw looked quite a masher at Bellingham Show.

Well Aw got te the show ground, and managed first rate
And paid me bit shilling to git in at the gate.
Aw met wie some aad friends who cried oot hal-lo
Hes thou really gitten te Bellingham Show.

Aw was feeling gay dry so in we all went
Just tae hev a wee drop an a crack in the tent,
Aw said mine was a half but the rest all cried no
There's to be no half glasses at Bellingham Show.

Well we all had a glass or it might hev been two
Or to tell ye the real truth, we maybe hed three,
The wee drop that we got set oor heart in a glow
As we talked ower aad times at Bellingham Show.

Aw then hed a look at the tups and the hoggs
The horses, the cows, the fat pigs and the dogs,
And all ower the showfield Aw went to and fro
Determined to miss nowt at Bellingham Show.

Aw got me eye on a chap that was selling half croons
There wad nee body buy them but Aw thout they were cloons
The fook all did laugh as they stood in a row
When Aw bought three for two shillings at Bellingham Show.

When Aw opened the purse to take oot the tin
Aw saw at a glance Aw was weel taken in
A brass broach and two pennies, how ma temper did grow
When Aw saw aw'd been cheated at Bellingham Show,

Aw was hevin' a look at the butter and eggs
And sat doon on some boxes to ease me aad legs,
Up comes a fine lady fat, forty and slow
Contented and jolly at Bellingham Show.

Excuse me she says but I do hate mistakes
Now which are the duck eggs and which are the drake's,
I just have been wondering, I thought ye might know
There's intelligent people at Bellingham Show.

Aw can tell ye that Mistress, it's quite plain to be seen
The duck eggs are white and the drake ones is green,
Oh! how simple, she cried, and how wise one may grow
By making enquiries at Bellingham Show.

Aa stept up to a chap what was shaved te the lips
Says Aw, canny man, three pennorth o' chips.
He cursed and he sent me to the regions below
He was a motor car driver at Bellingham Show.

Excuse me, cries Aw, but Aw doot Aw am green
Aa thought ye were minding a fried chip machine,
Whey man that's a motor belongs Lord So and So
And we're hevin a day at the Bellingham Show.

So Aw dodged away round by the edge o' the crood
And smoked me aad pipe in a nice happy mood,
When up comes a young queen and cries oot Uncle Joe
I am glad to have met you at Bellingham Show.

She flung her arms roond me neck and gav me a kiss
And Oh! te an aad man nee doot it was bliss
But Aw wasn't her uncle and aw told her straight so
That Aw hadn't a niece at the Bellingham Show.

She gave a bit scream and Aw thout she wad faint
But Aw sometimes jaloose that the women folks paint.
Oh excuse me says she, and your pardon bestow
Mistakes sometimes happen at Bellingham Show.

It's all right now hinny it's all right Aw did cry
While Aw stooped down a minute me shoelaces to tie.
When Aw looked up again and me eyes roond did throw
Me relation had vanished at Bellingham Show.

Me heart begen jumpin and Aw felt fairly spent
So Aw thowt Aw wad hev a bit glass in the tent,
So inside Aw got, felt ma pockets and lo
That fly jade had robbed me at Bellingham Show.

Not a copper Ad left not a cent did remain
And gean were ma aad specks ma watch and ma chain
The watch Aw had bowt masel lang years ago
When Aw first courted Betsy at Bellingham Show

Well Aw went te the Bobby an telt him me tale
But he said Aw was nowt but a silly aad feul,
Twas time Aw knew better as aad men should know
Not to meddle the lasses at Bellingham Show.

Aw got see excited and lood Aw did yell
That the policeman took me right off te the cell,
Through the door he did send me with the tip o' his toe
Saying 'Keep theesel' quiet ower Bellingham Show'.

Aw got oot the next morning and made me way hame
But te wor aad wife not a thing did Aw name
She'll knaw suen enough they'll be plenty to blow
Aboot me misfortunes at Bellingham Show,

Now Aw've a blue paper and it says that next week
Aw hev to appear 'fore his worship the beak
Seven days teasing oakum Oh! My poor heart is low
Aw'll gan ne mair back te the Bellingham Show.

(1905)

BILLY BELL
Billy Bell: Redesdale Roadman, Border Bard, 2013
➤ AUTHOR NOTE PAGES 206-07

Show Saturday

Grey day for the Show, but cars jam the narrow lanes.
Inside, on the field, judging has started: dogs
(Set their legs back, hold out their tails) and ponies (manes
Repeatedly smoothed, to calm heads); over there, sheep
(Cheviot and Blackface); by the hedge, squealing logs
(Chain Saw Competition). Each has its own keen crowd.
In the main arena, more judges meet by the jeep:
The jumping's on next. Announcements, splutteringly loud.

Clash with the quack of man with pound notes round his hat
And a lit-up board. There's more than just animals:
Bead-stalls, balloon-men, a Bank; a beer-marquee that
Half-screens a canvas Gents; a tent selling tweed,
And another, jackets. Folks sit about on bales
Like great straw dice. For each scene is linked by spaces
Not given to anything much, where kids scrap, freed,
While their owners stare different ways with incurious faces.

The wrestling starts, late; a wide ring of people; then cars;
Then trees; then pale sky. Two young men in acrobats' tights
And embroidered trunks hug each other; rock over the grass,
Stiff-legged, in a two-man scrum. One falls: they shake hands.
Two more start, one grey-haired: he wins, though. They're not so much fights
As long immobile strainings that end in unbalance
With one on his back, unharmed, while the other stands
Smoothing his hair. But there are other talents –

The long high tent of growing and making, wired-off
Wood tables past which crowds shuffle, eyeing the scrubbed spaced
Extrusions of earth: blanch leeks like church candles, six pods of
Broad beans (one split open), dark shining-leafed cabbages – rows
Of single supreme versions, followed (on laced
Paper mats) by dairy and kitchen; four brown eggs, four white eggs,
Four plain scones, four dropped scones, pure excellences that enclose
A recession of skills. And, after them, lambing sticks, rugs,

Needlework, knitted caps, baskets, all worthy, all well done,
But less than the honeycombs. Outside, the jumping's over.
The young ones thunder their ponies in competition
Twice round the ring; the trick races, Musical Stalls,

Sliding off, riding bareback, the ponies dragged to and fro for
Bewildering requirements, not minding. But now, in the background,
Like shifting scenery, horse-boxes move; each crawls
Towards the stock entrance, tilting and swaying, bound

For far-off farms. The pound-note man decamps.
The car park has thinned. They're loading jumps on a truck.
Back now to private addresses, gates and lamps
In high stone one-street villages, empty at dusk,
And side roads of small towns (sports finals stuck
In front doors, allotments reaching down to the railway);
Back now to autumn, leaving the ended husk
Of summer that brought them here for Show Saturday –

The men with hunters, dog-breeding wool-defined women,
Children all saddle-swank, mugfaced middleaged wives
Glaring at jellies, husbands on leave from the garden
Watchful as weasels, car-tuning curt-haired sons –
Back now, all of them, to their local lives:
To names on vans, and business calendars
Hung up in kitchens; back to loud occasions
In the Corn Exchange, to market days in bars,

To winter coming, as the dismantled Show
Itself dies back into the area of work.
Let it stay hidden there like strength, below
Sale-bills and swindling; something people do,
Not noticing how time's rolling smithy-smoke
Shadows much greater gestures; something they share
That breaks ancestrally each year into
Regenerate union. Let it always be there.

(3 December 1973)

PHILIP LARKIN
High Windows, 1974 | *The Complete Poems of Philip Larkin*, 2012

Philip Larkin (1922–1985) made frequent visits to the North East. He was known to have been in Newcastle before 1953, was in Durham in the summer of 1958, and in Newcastle again in 1963, this time professionally to study the layout of the university library. Larkin dedicated *The Less Deceived* (1955) to Monica Jones, with whom he spent many holidays in the flat she owned at 1A Ratcliffe Road in Haydon Bridge. Monica's mother came from St

John's Chapel in Weardale, and as Monica approached Haydon Bridge by rail from Newcastle (she didn't drive) she always felt she was coming home. She had bought the cottage in 1961, and when Larkin visited in April of the following year, he wrote: "I thought your little house seemed…distinguished and exciting and beautiful…it looks splendid and it can never be ordinary with the Tyne going by outside… You have a great English river drifting under your window…' When Monica bought the house, this view could be seen from the living-room. The cottage has since been altered.

According to Andrew Motion's biography, Larkin and Monica 'lazed, drank, read, pottered around the village and amused themselves with private games'. Larkin used to buy the *Telegraph* and the *Observer* from the newsagents. The place always cheered them both up. 'As always, the place worked its spell,' wrote Larkin. From here they journeyed to the Lake District and elsewhere (Larkin passed his driving test at the first attempt in 1963). They visited Hadrian's Wall, Langley Castle, Allendale and Allenheads. They certainly crossed into Scotland at Carter Bar and Larkin has some jocular lines in a letter substituting Morpeth for Macbeth. He also mentions Holy Island in passing, as well as Corstopitum (Corbridge). The pair occasionally dined out with friends at the Lord Crewe Arms in Blanchland, where Auden had stayed with Gabriel Carritt in 1930. Despite Larkin's admiration for Auden, however, he seems to have been unaware that this whole area was the older poet's 'great good place' and figured prominently in his verse throughout his life.

Larkin and Monica used to attend the spectacular New Year's Eve 'tar barrel' celebrations in Allendale; they were certainly there in 1966 and again in 1970 and 1976. Larkin was, rather uncharacteristically, thrilled by it all. His notable poem 'Show Saturday' is a description of the 1973 Bellingham show in the North Tyne valley. He refers to Haydon Bridge and its California Gardens allotments in the sixth stanza.

On *Desert Island Discs* (17 July 1976) one of Larkin's choices was what he calls a Newcastle street-song of the 1790s, 'Dollia' ('Dol-li-a') sung by Louis Killen [see page 297]. Though folksong was not one of Larkin's keenest interests, he did own Killen's LP (with Johnny Handle and Colin Ross) *Along the Coaly Tyne* (Topic, 1962). Moreover, one of Larkin's notable later poems 'The Explosion' (1970) is based, according to him, on 'a song about a mine disaster, a ballad, a sort of folksong. I thought it very moving… It made me want to write the same thing, a mine disaster with a vision of immortality at the end.' This strongly suggests Tommy Armstrong's famous 'Trimdon Grange Explosion' of 1882, Killen's version of which appears on the LP. One also notes the use, in both works, of the word 'explosion' rather than the more usual 'disaster'.

In 1982, Monica retired to live in Haydon Bridge. Larkin called her 'Bun', a Beatrix Potter allusion, and both called 1A Ratcliffe Road her 'Rabbit Hole'. Larkin was fond of animals, particularly rabbits; they were also Monica's favourite animal. She often asked to see the pet rabbits of the Willis family next door. On one occasion, Larkin asked to photograph them with Monica in the back yard. When Merlin, the cat at the General Havelock pub, was locked in Monica's cottage, Larkin drove her to Haydon Bridge to let it out.

Monica finally left the cottage in 1984, when ill-health prevented her living alone. She continued to enquire about it, however, asking Mrs Willis by phone: 'How is my little house?' 'How is my river, is it high?' A prospective buyer recalls that Monica talked about Haydon Bridge as if it were paradise; she was still desperately reluctant to sell the property and even nurtured thoughts of an eventual return. Andrew Motion visited to retrieve letters left lying about. The cottage had been left empty for over five years and broken into three times. When she died on 15 February 2001, Monica, who had become a major beneficiary of Larkin's will some months before his death, left a quarter of a million pounds each to Hexham Abbey and Durham Cathedral. [AM]

Bellingham

> Farewell Secret Bellingham,
> The capital of Nowhere –
> Nowhere, since it never seems
> Quite possible to go there.
> SEAN O'BRIEN

> Let it stay hidden there like strength...
> PHILIP LARKIN

Even Nowhere has its capital,
mispronounced by foreigners
who visit by an accident,
sunlight having camouflaged
the drifting kelp of coal-smoke.

Its histories will be going on,
the grey stone ticking over in the sun,
the four-wheel drives and pick-ups
collecting heat behind the windscreen.
Its grace-notes and its labours blur.

Beyond, there is the forest;
its deep green quilt drawn over
the sleeping figure of the border.
Hidden down its firebreaks
the feral species muster.

But what were you expecting?
Grass is bending double
over the spoil-heaps of the giants,
and imperial roads gone native
lose themselves down farm-tracks.

Here a modest statuary
accommodates the weather,
and the names on stones and shop-fronts
negotiate from era
to different-spoken era.

The bus pulls out; the street-lights
flicker up and spell
You Are Where You Can Get.

The valley settles round that alphabet
hidden there like sense, initiate;

and the wind planes down the reservoir,
the broken wave-heads iridesce;
miles off on the trunk-road
headlights frame a signpost;
they pan across your ceiling and they pass.

PETER ARMSTRONG
The Capital of Nowhere, 2003

The Kielder Hunt

Hark! hark! I hear Lang Will's clear voice sound through the Kielder glen,
Where the raven flaps her glossy wing and the fell fox has his den;
There the shepherds they are gathering up wi' monie a guid yauld grew,
An' wiry terrier game an' keen an' fox-hund fleet and true.

   CHORUS
Hark away! hark away!
O'er the Bonnie Hills o' Kielder, hark away!

There's Moudy frae Emmethaugh an' Royal frae Bakethinn,
There's hunds frae Reed an' Kielderhead, an Ruby by the Linn;
An' hunds of fame frae Irthingside, they'll try baith moss an' crag,
Hark! hark! that's Moudy's loud clear note, he has bold Reynard's drag.

Away an' away o'er hill and dale, an' up by yonder stell,
The music o' this gallant pack resounds o'er muir an' dell;
See yon herd callant waves his plaid, list yon loud tally-ho,
The fox is up an' breaks away o'er the edge o' Hawkhope Flowe.

Hark forrit! hark! ye gallant hunds, hark onwart, hark away,
He kens the hauds on Tosson hills, he kens the holes at Rae;
There's no a den roun' the Kailstane but he kens weel I trow,
An' a' the holes on Lariston he kens them thro' and thro'.

There's Wannys Crags, an' Sewingshields, and Christenbury too,
Or if he win to Hareshaw Linn ye may bid him adieu;
At the Key-Heugh an the Cloven-Crags, the Cove, an Darnaha,
Chatlehope-Spout an' the Wily-holes, auld foxy kens them a'.

Away an away o'er bank and brae they drive the wily game,
Where Moudy, Ruby, Royal still uphaud their glorious fame;
An' see the lish yald shepherd lads how Monkside heights they climb,
They're the pride of a' the borders wide for wind and wiry limb.

Thro' yon wild glen they view him noo right for the Yearning Linn,
By cairn an' crag, o'er moss an' hagg, sae glorious is the din;
Weel dune, hurrah! they've run him doun, yon's Moudy twirls him now,
The hunt is dune, his brush is wun, I hear the death hal-loo.

Here's to Will o' Emmethaugh, he is a sportsman true,
An here's to Robie o' Bakethinn, an' Rob o' Kielder too;
At the Hope, Bewshaugh, an' Kersie Cleuch, Skaup, Riggend, an' the Law,
In Tyne, an' Reed, and Irthinghead, they're gallant sportsmen a'.

JAMES ARMSTRONG
Wanny Blossoms, 1879
➣ AUTHOR NOTE PAGE 209

How Mackie Did the Drowning, Plashetts

To begin, he moved into her kitchen,
slouched on a chair while she fried up *hinnies*.
He brought in pine cones, dubbin, swamped
her smell of cotton-scorch and Bibles.
Every night, to dry their tongues, he hung his boots
from bedrails near the stove. He slaked himself
on her, before he told her how he'd dammed
her river, how a flood would come. He stayed
a while, until the first wave reached the hearth,
until it climbed the panelling. He left
for higher ground, the day the waters floated
Jesus off the wall, back turned forever.

That's when he edged up Belling Hill, to watch
her rooftop disappear, her chimney brim with water.
The lake he made weighed four years.
Some days he thought he'd drink the lot
to fill the space inside him. Instead, he cast stones.

CHRISTY DUCKER
Skipper, 2015

The North Tyne valley west of Falstone was flooded in 1982 to create Kielder Water, the biggest man-made reservoir in Europe, with the loss of many farms and wildlife habitats along with the drowned village of Plashetts.

'Out Northumberland, Out!'

(a favourite phrase of his in moments of depression over the future of the Northumbrian and Northumbria)

The North Tyne was next:
Bewshaugh and Bakethin unfleshed and 'earnstand out
Gowanburn and Lewisburn
cleared out places butted down, and out
flitted unflinching but Northumberland, out
Plashetts and Wellhaugh, Hawkhurst, Mounces
Otterstone Lee and the Law, and the Iron Age huts at Belling,
Emmetthaugh and Shilburnhaugh, Whickhope cottages
watter to be   over rowan and eller selling
the only humanity
fingers up to the Authority!   but 'out, Northumberland, out'
linked   outline urge edge to be submerged
long-ley and planting, garden and   'out, Northumberland, out'
stunned   stone ancient homestead
camp and field-museum, ageless track and lazy-bed
droveway and lintel, dyke and tumbled biggin   out, out
otterholt, badgersett, martenden and weasel-cranny away
foxearth, rabbitwarren haresform   blackcockplay 'out, out'
        (not 'go-back, go-back')

their balances mangled discontent   'out, out'
lost   under   cold weight gley supersaturated clay

the cormorant still wings (higher) yowes and kine leaking
beat and bleat (gone) echo and carry of voices
                              'out, Northumberland, out'
haze   so that there were neighbours, these places
bound by   'evict, evict'   the same owl calls, speaking
redshank and oystercatcher, sandpiper and kestrel staint   out

to B.B. Nov. 1982 and posted in the Moorcock Inn

COLIN SIMMS
Bewcastle and Other Poems for Basil Bunting, 1996

The Water of Tyne

I cannot get to my love if I should dee,
    The water of Tyne runs between him and me;
And here I must stand, with the tear in my e'e,
    Both sighing and sickly, my sweetheart to see.

O where is the boatman? my bonny hinny!
    O where is the boatman? bring him to me –
To ferry me over the Tyne to my honey,
    And I will remember the boatman and thee.

O bring me a boatman – I'll give any money
    (And you for your trouble rewarded shall be).
To ferry me over the Tyne to my honey,
    Or scull him across that rough river to me.

TRADITIONAL
Rhymes of Northern Bards, 1812

This song is said to relate to the old ferry crossing at Haughton Castle in the North Tyne.

TYNEDALE, SOUTH TYNE, NORTH PENNINES

In Hexham Abbey

Like spirits resurrected from the tomb
We stept from the dark slype's low-vaulted gloom
Into the transepts' soaring radiancy
Where from the lancets of the clerestory
Noon-sunshine streaming charged the pale sandstone
Of wall and pillar with a golden tone
Rich as the colour of the rock, fresh-hewn
From sheer Northumbrian hillsides to the tune
Of clinking hammer and chisel, in the days
When the aspiring spirit in life's praise
Soared in exultant fabrics of delight –
Earth quarried stuff exalted to the height
Of man's imagination, heaven-entranced.

And, as with eager footsteps we advanced
Through the South Transept with enraptured eyes,
From off our hearts fell the perplexities
Of these calamitous times; and we forgot
Awhile the warring of nations and the lot
Of the battalioned youngsters doomed to march
Into annihilation – pier and arch
Springing in sunshine seeming still inspired
With the adoring ecstasy that fired
Those early craftsmen: and we recalled how man,
Builder and breaker since the world began,
Betrayed by frailties of the mortal flesh,
Is yet a phoenix soul that springs afresh
Resilient to the imperishable gleam
Out of the self-wrought havoc of his dream,
From devastation fashioning anew
His vision; and that to his best self true
Man, the destroyer, is Man, the builder, too.

WILFRID GIBSON
The Alert, 1941

The Abbey Tower

On the parapet of the crenellated tower
He leans, fire-watching in the Summer night:
And, as with clear reverberating chimes
The clock below prepares to strike the hour
Of midnight, he recalls the far-off times
When his forefathers from this very height
Kept watch for other enemies, the bands
Of Scottish reivers, bearing fiery brands,
Descending to maraud the market-town;
Hoping to ford the river Tyne and raid
Its merchant-riches and to batter down
The Abbey gates and pillage the Abbot's store,
Putting all to sack and slaughter. And he once more
Recalls how in an even earlier age
When the town was threatened by the heathen rage
Of Northern hordes all night Saint Wilfrid prayed
Among his monks, invoking the swift aid
Of God to thwart the invaders; when suddenly
The valley of the Tyne was filled with blind
White mist in which the baffled Norsemen strayed
Nightlong in scattered bands that failed to find
A ford; and how next day the river came down
In spate and barred all access to the town.
And now he muses, wondering if, maybe,
Over the town he loved in days gone by
Saint Wilfrid's spirit hovers protectingly
To shield it from the foreign foes who fly
Threatening it with destruction from the sky.

WILFRID GIBSON
The Searchlights, 1943

Wilfrid Gibson (1878-1962) was born on Battle Hill, in Hexham, though only the room above an archway on the street remains. He wrote the lines for the fountain erected in the market place in 1901. Despite the fact that he went to London in 1912, and later lived there and in Gloucestershire, many of Gibson's poems both then and later are set in rural Northumberland and deal with poverty and passion amid wild landscapes. Others are devoted to fishermen, industrial workers and miners, often alluding to local ballads and the rich folk-song heritage of the North East. Though occasionally powerful, they are often conventionally melodramatic and do not convince nowadays, despite all the Northumbrian names they use. Gibson must be the only poet to set a dialogue on Bloodybush Edge.

His war poems are more immediate and every schoolchild used to know his 'Flannan Isle' about the three lighthouse-keepers, mysteriously missing. Gibson was published in Edward Marsh's *Georgian Poetry* and was a friend of Rupert Brooke, who made him one of his heirs. His work influenced Auden's *Paid on Both Sides* and he could certainly produce thrilling effects on occasion, as in the opening stanza of 'Lindisfarne' [162]. [AM]

Devilswater

Up the hill and over the hill,
Down the valley by Dipton Mill,
Down the valley to Devilswater
Rode the parson's seventh daughter.

Her heart was light, her eyes were wild –
Seventh child of a seventh child –
Down the valley to Devilswater
Rode the parson's black-eyed daughter.

Down she rode by the bridle-track,
Down she rode, and never came back –
Never back to the Devilswater
Came the parson's black-eyed daughter.

Up the hill and over the hill,
Down the valley by Dipton Mill,
High and low the parson sought her,
Sought his seventh black-eyed daughter.

He tripped as he trod the bridle-track,
A bramble tore his coat of black,
And he stood on the brink of Devilswater
And cursed, and called her the devil's daughter.

.   .   .   .   .

Up the hill and over the hill
Rode a black-eyed gipsy Jill,
Down the valley to Devilswater
Rode the devil's black-eyed daughter.

Rode in a yellow caravan,
By the side of a merry black-eyed man;
Down to the bank of Devilswater –
Rode the devil's merry daughter.

Her heart was light, her eyes were wild,
As kneeling down with her little child,
She christened her bairn in the Devilswater –
The black-eyed brat of the devil's daughter.

Low she laughed – as she hugged it tight,
And it clapped its hands at the golden light
That glanced and danced on the Devilswater –
To think she was once a parson's daughter.

WILFRID GIBSON
Whin, 1918

Mother and Maid

And where be you stravaging to at such an hour of night?
To look on Allen Water in the full moonlight.
Go your wilful ways then; but you will learn too soon
That no good comes to any lass from looking on the moon.

And where be you stravaging to at this unearthly hour?
To hearken to the hoolet that hoots by Staward Tower.
Round the Peel at midnight the brags and horneys prowl,
And no good comes to any lass from listening to the owl.

So don't say I've not warned you whatever may betide.
And what should I be fearing with Robert at my side?
What should you be fearing? Since the world began
No good has come to any lass from walking with a man.

WILFRID GIBSON
I Heard a Sailor and Other Poems, 1925 | *Collected Poems 1905-1925*, 1926

Terry Conway (1943–2013) was a singer and songwriter from Tynedale who worked as a council roadman for much of his life. Performing on guitar, often with Liz Law on dulcimer, he played a huge repertoire of traditional songs as well as others he wrote himself, some of these about Northumberland and in Northumbrian dialect, such as 'The Bus to Morpeth' and 'Hawkhope Hill'. He recorded 'Fareweel Regality' for Kathryn Tickell's album, *The Northumberland Collection* (1998); it was included on the 20 CD *Northumbria Anthology* boxed set from MWM Records (2002) and is available on *Songs from the North of England* by Terry Conway and Liz Law with Julie-Ann Morrison (Stonehouse Music, 2014).

Fareweel Regality

And now it's time te say fareweel,
Though Aa hope that we may meet again,
And aall things may be reet again,
We've lived and spent the day.

   CHORUS:
And we'll cry, farewell Regality,
And cry, farewell the liberty,
Te honest friend civility,
Te winter's frost and fire,
And there's nowt that Aa could bid yer,
But that peace and love gan with yer,
Never mind wherever caal the fates,
Away from Hexhamshire.

And what is time, that flies se free,
But just a bird that flies on merry wings,
And lights us down in happy spring,
When winter's neet is past.

Aye, but the curlew sings her sang,
And winds her sorrows doon the Rowley Burn,
As drear as winds the hunter's horn,
The caall is aall fareweel.

And as aa set the mossy stanes,
And de me bits o' jobs and gaff the dykes,
Aa hear the whisper doon the sykes,
Fareweel, the sang fareweel.

De aa remember, de aa dream,
And did we rightly meet on Bewleyside,
For aal this and much more beside,
Has got me sair beguiled.

But on some gowlden autumn morn,
Or when July is hazin' Dipton slopes,
By Whitley Mill or West Burnhope,
We'll live and spend the day.

TERRY CONWAY

Fallowfield Fell

Soldier, what do you see,
Lying so cold and still?
Fallowfield Fell at dawn
And the heather upon the hill.

Soldier, what do you see,
Lying so still and cold?
Fallowfield Fell at noon
And the whin like burning gold.

Soldier, what do you see,
Lying so cold and still?
Fallowfield Fell at night
And the stars above the hill.

WILFRID GIBSON
Chambers, 1920 | *Collected Poems 1905-1925*, 1926

At Bywell

This earth is dense with days, lived through
and left behind in long-repeated seasons.
We read of villagers who 'in these parts'
received the travellers who walked
the Roman Bridge across the Tyne
a thousand years ago, bringing
Border gossip, news no doubt of
the murdering Scots not sixty miles away.

Hushed on this later summer afternoon
by their remote yet homely presences,
we walk the spongy grass with some idea,
I think, of treading lightly on a soil
so pungently composed; passing each other
heads down pondering our closeness
above the churchyard ground to those
who've gone within with all their gear –

the woven tunics, mantles, breeches,
heel-less shoes, the treasured oxen, children's
breakfast bowls, the sunlit harvestings
of barley, groats, round smoky kitchens
jumpy with tallow flames, their bright
or clouded eyes...foolish to think we hear them
in the shadow of the limes – and yet
they do speak, for a moment, when we stand

by the north wall, close enough to touch
the dusty stone, mellow as trapped sunlight
– surely it's their prayers we hear, as in
the squat Saxon tower we see their knuckling down
to the severer ecstasies of God. In the nave
I touch with a kind of shyness the Frosterley
marble column – black sheen with grey
stone flowers alive, alight within it.

LAURIS EDMOND
Summer Near the Arctic Circle, 1988 | *New and Selected Poems*, 1992

Allendale Dog

A lean tyke, supple
As the long winds that ripple
Counties cool as ivory,
He wills the moving reverie
Of northerly-fathered flocks.
Prick-eared, he lurks
To leeward, patiently bold;
Lift arm or lift an eyebrow,
He'll weave his sky-brow
Spell round the offender
Who has taken leave to wander,
Re-knotting as if by chance
The cordon of Providence.

His fibre of wit is spun
From the careful brain of man,
Yet gleams in its own right;
He skims gay light
From mountains gaunt with cold;

Certain as love, brings home
The blundering ewe, the lamb
By snows in March confounded;
You storm-bound Jill or Jack,
Me too he has befriended.

Fells under heaven are his;
The poet he is
Of dawns that wring new gold
Like dew from danger's fleece,
And the sheep-bell's travelling peace.

Oh comrade emperors lack!

LILIAN BOWES LYON
A Rough Walk Home, 1946 | *Collected Poems*, 1948

Allendale

The smelting-mill stack is crumbling, no smoke is alive there,
Down in the valley the furnace no lead ore of worth burns;
Now tombs of decaying industries, not to survive here
        Many more earth-turns.

The chimney still stands on top of the hill like a finger
Skywardly pointing as it were asking 'What lies there?'
And thither we stray to dream of those things as we linger,
        Nature denies here.

Dark looming around the fell-folds stretch desolate, crag-scarred,
Seeming to murmur 'Why beat you the bars of your prison?'
What matter? To us the world-face is glowing and flag-starred,
        Lit by a vision.

So under it stand we, all swept by the rain and the wind there,
Muttering 'What look you for, creatures that die in a season?'
We care not, but turn to our dreams and the comfort we find there,
        Asking no reason.

(December 1924)

W.H. AUDEN
Juvenilia: Poems 1922-1926, 1994/2003

A Rough Walk Home

A rough walk home! I shan't forget
The fells that day and the sting of the sleet;
A black north-easter seemed to have torn
From sheltering womb the elf unborn.
From shivering child his shattered toy;
Terrible Satan sang with joy.
I thought, as up the hill I plodded,
Hoping the cow and calf were bedded,
Thought it strange our whetstone life
Should labour to sharpen winter's knife,
Be ground to give perpetual edge
To Fate that blows, that freezes ridge
And furrow, sears a man like sedge.

Who was I, though, hale and strong,
Crunching the adder-coloured dung,
The bracken's rag-and-bone, to bother?
Braced against the brutish weather
On I ploughed; a mile at most
And damn the blizzard, I could rest.
Just for once would Jean be waiting,
Soft in the lamplight, softly knitting?
Only a hungering mile to go;
But closer and denser gloomed the snow
To snuff the earth out; heaven had thickened.
Ten more minutes and I reckoned
Half the worst would lie behind me.
How it blew! As if to blind me,
Tear me asunder, left and right
Spew me eternally into the night.
Not my self but kinsmen stronger
Dared the universe's anger;
Furious body, wedge of fire,
I drove towards a heart's desire
Beyond my own; though grimly fared
That host in me who fought, despaired,
Faster reeled, and crazily cursed
What still pursues yet gets there first:
Doom that plants in moss, in mould,

In milk-warm side or the marigold
The abiding death-seed of the cold.

God leans, at times, forethoughtfully, on hands
That build; or maybe wonders work by chance.
Right in my tortured path it stands,
The great stone husk that was a tithe-barn once.

I'm gathered in by stones that housed a grain
Hard-got; and centuries after,
These cobweb aisles remain, have grown immense.
A pinion hoary, each protective rafter
Ponders the ripening orient of our pain.
Corn-swelled, you comprehend (as in my bones
I feared to adore) the future's ancient laughter,
Nor tire of dawn's irrevocable darkening.
What's two is one here, in slow-motion trance.
So buried let me lie profoundly quickening.
Far I have come, to you I loved long since,
Forgotten, yet the core of my remembering.
Asleep, and not aware yet they are slumbering,
Men walk alone. Is this, then, the awakening?

How kindly the farm windows winked
And gave me a bearing. God be thanked,
My luck had turned. A fiend can falter.
Downhill clumping, helter-skelter
Home out of the storm I sped.
Life is a hearth and new-made bread,
Oh life is warmth! And there was Jean;
As if no chasm yawned between
Our separate safeties. Rockhouse Barn
Was farther away than Lindisfarne.
We kiss the hem of an alien peace!
Though soft, in her forget-me-not dress,
She set the board, and delicate fell
Some tears – like me, unskilled to tell
A tale in full – the kitchen seemed
Less golden than a dream I had dreamed.

A year or twenty years may pass,
Carting muck, or scything grass,
But now I've done with discontent.
I can't say where or when I learnt

To bear in mind what no man knows
Yet always knew. It comes and goes,
For ever wears a different guise,
The ghost, the given-again surprise.
It's Jean, my constancy, who cries.

LILIAN BOWES LYON
A Rough Walk Home, 1946 | *Collected Poems*, 1948

A cousin of the Queen Mother, **Lilian Bowes Lyon** (1895–1949) was born and grew up at Ridley Hall, near Bardon Mill, where Augustus Hare stayed and described the haunting beauty of the grounds. Her observations of the country life she loved form the subject of her early poems, but after her move to the East End of London in 1942, her poetry is concentrated on the war. Her only novel *The Buried Stream* (1929) treats of the power of the unconscious. Her verse appeared in many periodicals and her *Collected Poems* came out in 1948, when C. Day Lewis wrote of the influences on her work of Emily Dickinson, Hopkins and Christina Rossetti in an introduction. She suffered greatly from arthritis, and her last book of poems, *A Rough Walk Home*, is as much about this as the war.

Her *Uncollected Poems*, not published until 1981, were written after she had lost both legs and the use of her hands. These poems include powerfully direct accounts of the pain she suffered. Her papers are in the William Plomer collection at the University of Durham. [AM]

The Old Lead-mine

This is the place where Man has laid his hand
To tear from these dark hills his gold
He found it not, they say, but left his brand
Of greed upon the spot for all men to behold.

I peered a moment down the open shaft
Gloomy and black; I dropped a stone;
A distant splash, a whispering, a laugh
The icy hands of fear weighed heavy on the bone

I turned and travelled quickly down the track
Which grass will cover by and by
Down the lonely valley; once I looked back
And saw a waste of stones against an angry sky.

(February 1924)

W.H. AUDEN
Juvenilia: Poems 1922-1926, 1994/2003

Rookhope (Weardale, Summer 1922)

The men are dead that used to walk these dales;
The mines they worked in once are long forsaken;
We shall not hear their laughter or their tales
Now, as in bygone days, all these are taken.
Dead men, they say, sleep very soundly, nought
Remaineth as a mark to signify
The men they were, the things they did, nor aught
That this unheeding world may know them by.
Yet – I have stood by their deserted shafts
While the rain lashed my face and clutched my knees,
And seemed to hear therein their careless laughs,
To glimpse the spirit which engendered these;
    Feel in the might of that exulting wind
    The splendid generous Soul, the simple Mind.

(April 1924)

W.H. AUDEN
Juvenilia: Poems 1922-1926, 1994/2003

The Pumping Engine, Cashwell

It is fifty years now
Since the old days when
It first pumped water here;
Steam drove it then.

Till the workings were stopped,
For the vein pinched out;
When it lay underground
Twelve years about.

Then they raised it again,
Had it cleaned a bit,
So it pumps still, though now
The beck drives it.

As it groans at each stroke
Like a heart in trouble,

It seems to me something
In toil most noble.

(1924)

W.H. AUDEN
Juvenilia: Poems 1922-1926, 1994/2003

Lead's the Best

The fells sweep upward to drag down the sun
Those great rocks shadowing a weary land
And quiet stone hamlets huddled at their feet;
No footstep loiters in the darkening road
But light streams out from inn doors left ajar,
And with it voices quavering and slow.
'I worked at Threlkeld granite quarry once,
Then coal at Wigan for a year, then back
To lead, for lead's the best' –
                            – 'No, sir, not now,
They only keep a heading open still
At Cashwell' –
             – 'Yes, the ladder broke and took him
Just like a pudding he was when they found him' –
'Rich? Why, at Greenearth Side the west vein showed
Ten feet of ore from cheek to cheek, so clean
There weren't no dressing it' –
                                steps closed the door
And stopped their mouths, the last of generations
Who 'did their business in the veins of th'earth,'
To place a roof on noble Gothic minsters
For the glory of God, bring wealth to buy
Some damask scarf or silken stomacher
To make a woman's body beautiful,
Some slender lady like a silver birch,
A frozen dream of a white waterfall,
Slim-waisted, and hawk-featured, for whose love
Knights sought adventure in far desert lands
And died where there was none to bury them;
Nor thought of those who built their barren farms

Up wind-swept northern dales, where oftentimes
The Scot swooped suddenly on winter nights
And drove their cattle back across the snow
By torchlight and the glare of blazing homes,
Where torn men lay, that clutched their wounds,
And bonnie forms face downward in the grass
As in old ballads very pitiful.

   Here speak the last of them, soon heard no more
Than sound of clarinets in country churches;
Turf covers up the huge stone heaps, green ferns
The dark holes opening into hollow hills
Where water drips like voices from the dead.
A pile of stone beside the stream is all
Left of the 'Shop' where miners slept at nights;
(Within, tired crowded sleepers, far from home;
Without, the torrent, darkness, and the rain);
Nor will they start again in early dawns
With bags like pillows slung across their shoulders
And watched by children enviously, who wish
Themselves grown-up to climb like that, for whom
Soon after it was all the other way;
Each wished himself a child again to have
More hours to sleep in.
                All their memory fades
Like that two-headed giant slain by Jack
Who lay for years in the combe-bottom, where
Men flocked at first, then fewer came, then ceased,
And only children visited the spot to play
At hide-and-seek in the dark, cavernous skulls
Or gather berries from the thorns which hid
The arched ribs crumbling in the grass.
                              They go
And Hodge himself becomes a sottish bawd
Who takes his city vices secondhand
And grins, if he hears Paris mentioned. Naught
Remains but wind-sough over barren pastures
The bleak philosophy of Northern ridges
Harsh afterglow of an old country's greatness
Themes for a poet's pretty sunset thoughts.

(March or April? 1926)

W.H. AUDEN
Juvenilia: Poems 1922-1926, 1994/2003

The Watershed

Who stands, the crux left of the watershed,
On the wet road between the chafing grass
Below him sees dismantled washing-floors,
Snatches of tramline running to a wood,
An industry already comatose,
Yet sparsely living. A ramshackle engine
At Cashwell raises water; for ten years
It lay in flooded workings until this,
Its latter office, grudgingly performed.
And, further, here and there, though many dead
Lie under the poor soil, some acts are chosen,
Taken from recent winters; two there were
Cleaned out a damaged shaft by hand, clutching
The winch a gale would tear them from; one died
During a storm, the fells impassable,
Not at his village, but in wooden shape
Through long abandoned levels nosed his way
And in his final valley went to ground.

Go home, now, stranger, proud of your young stock,
Stranger, turn back again, frustrate and vexed:
This land, cut off, will not communicate,
Be no accessory content to one
Aimless for faces rather there than here.
Beams from your car may cross a bedroom wall,
They wake no sleeper; you may hear the wind
Arriving driven from the ignorant sea
To hurt itself on pane, on bark of elm
Where sap unbaffled rises, being spring;
But seldom this. Near you, taller than the grass,
Ears poise before decision, scenting danger.

(August 1927)

W.H. AUDEN
Poems, 1928 | *Poems*, 1930 | *Collected Poems*, 1976

Wystan Hugh Auden (1907-1973) was born in York and grew up in Birmingham but spent term times away from home at boarding schools from the age of eight. He had little mechanical aptitude but acquired in childhood a lifelong fascination with underground spaces and mining machinery.

Despite living in Birmingham and attending school in East Anglia, Auden's mind was irresistibly drawn towards the North. In December 1947, in an article for *House and Garden* entitled 'I Like it Cold', he wrote:

> Though I was brought up on both, Norse mythology has always appealed to me infinitely more than Greek; Hans Andersen's *The Snow Queen* and George Macdonald's *The Princess and the Goblin* were my favourite fairy stories and years before I ever went there, the North of England was the Never-Never Land of my dreams. Nor did those feelings disappear when I finally did; to this day, Crewe Junction marks the wildly exciting frontier where the alien South ends and the North, my world, begins.

His family bought a holiday cottage near Keswick in the early 1920s, and Auden stayed there frequently until his departure for America in 1939. It was Alston Moor across the Eden valley in the North Pennines, however, and the adjoining regions of Durham and Northumberland, which Auden came to love more than any other locality. He kept an Ordnance Survey map of the area on the wall everywhere he lived throughout his life, and told Geoffrey Grigson in a letter of 17 January 1950: 'My great good place is the part of the Pennines bounded on the S by Swaledale, on the N by the Roman wall and on the W by the Eden Valley.'

What gripped Auden's imagination was the once-thriving lead-mining industry, whose poignant remains lie scattered around these wild whaleback moors. A poem of the early 1920s entitled 'The North' celebrates the high fell country. 'Alston Moor' and 'Allendale' [238] also date from 1924, as does the poem entitled 'Rookhope (Weardale, Summer 1922)' [242]. What Auden indicated as the seminal moment in his creative life seems to have occurred when he dropped a stone down an abandoned mine shaft in Rookhope, probably in 1919, when he first visited Weardale [as in 'The Old Lead-mine', 241, and the extract from 'New Year Letter', 45-46]. It is a recurring image in his verse. The poem regarded as the first of the mature Auden, 'The Watershed' (1927) [245], was originally entitled 'Rookhope'. Auden describes the hard life of the lead miner (and alludes to the Border ballads) in his 'Lead's the Best' of 1926. His 'charade' *Paid on Both Sides* (1928) openly uses Pennine village names – Rookhope, Brandon Walls and Garrigill, for example. The two houses named in the play, Lintzgarth and Nattrass, still stand. London reviewers took these strange names to be saga-based inventions.

At Easter 1930, Auden and his friend Gabriel Carritt stayed at the Lord Crewe Arms in Blanchland after a walk along the Roman Wall. Carritt recalls Auden loudly calling for champagne in the public bar, before striding over to the 'honky-tonk' piano and launching into Brahms. Next day, the pair bathed in the freezing Derwent before setting off to inspect abandoned mine workings. Auden's poetry and plays at this period are studded with references to northern locations. *The Dog Beneath the Skin* (1935), for example, mentions Bellingham and Scot's Gap, together with a sonorous roll-call of Pennine fells. The village of Pressan Ambo in the drama is probably based on Blanchland.

In his unfinished and unpublished alliterative epic 'In the Year of my Youth…' (1932) Auden describes Blanchland and the Lord Crewe Arms in some detail. He also dreams of visiting a cathedral on a rock. The cathedral is floodlit and Auden is overwhelmed:

> Casting the shadows upwards was a cairn so noble
> That I though born in earshot of the Minster
> Learnt all my standards to be second-rate.

Clearly Durham Cathedral is meant here, the Minster being of course York Minster.

Auden continued to make use of North Pennine imagery at intervals for the rest of his life, and made it clear that the area constituted one of the bedrocks of his poetry. 'Amor Loci' (1965) is a particularly poignant evocation of his 'great good place'.

In 1937 he visited Newcastle with Benjamin Britten for the broadcast of their radio documentary Hadrian's Wall [64]; and the last public readings given by Auden (wearing carpet slippers, as was his wont in later years) were in Newcastle and Ilkley, close to the landscapes he cherished. After reading at the University Theatre, Haymarket (now Northern Stage), on Sunday, 17 December 1972, he stayed at the Turk's Head in Grey Street. Perhaps the ringing lines from 'New Year Letter' [45] can stand as testimony to what the northern hills meant to one of the great poets of our century: 'An English area comes to mind, / I see the nature of my kind / As a locality I love, / Those limestone moors that stretch from BROUGH / To HEXHAM and the ROMAN WALL. / There is my symbol of us all. […] Always my boy of wish returns / To those peat-stained deserted burns / That feed the WEAR and TYNE and TEES.' [AM/NA]

Killhope Wheel, 1860, County Durham

1860. Killhope Wheel, cast
forty feet in iron across, is swung
by water off the North Pennines
washing lead ore crushed here.

And mined, here. Also fluor-spar.
In 1860 soldiers might kill
miners if they struck.

A board says that we're free to come in.
Why should it seem absurd to get
pain from such permission? Why have

I to see red-coat soldiers prick
between washed stones, and bayonets
tugged from the flesh?

Among the North Pennines what might
have seeped the flesh of miners, who chucked
their tools aside?

I can't work out what I have
come here for; there's no mineable land
or work of that kind here now.

Why does a board, tacked to wood,
concerning my being free to visit
nourish my useless pain?

Like water. I am its water, dispersed
in the ground I came from; and have footage
on these hills, stripped of lead,

which the sheep crop, insensibly white.
The mist soaks their cries into them.

JON SILKIN
Killhope Wheel, 1971 | *Complete Poems*, 2015

Strike

The earth comes moist-looking, and blackens;
a trickle of earth where the feet pressed,
twice a day, wearing off the grass.
Where the miners
were seen: a letter blown damply
into the corner of a hut: 'Oh dear love, come to me'
and nothing else.

Where are they?
The sheep bleat back to the mist balding
with terror; where
are they? The miners
are under the ground.

A pale blue patch of thick worsted
a scrag of cotton;
the wheel is still that washed the pounded ore.
They were cut down.

Almost turned by water, a stammer of the huge wheel
groping at the bearings.
Their bayonets; the red coat
gluey with red.

The water shrinks
to its source. The wheel,
in balance.

JON SILKIN
Killhope Wheel, 1971 | *Complete Poems*, 2015

Spade

George Culley, Isaac Greener?

A want of sound hangs
in a drop of moisture from the wheel that
turned and washed the ore.

A rustling of clothes on the wind. The water does not move.

I have come here to be afraid.
I came for love to bundle
what was mine. I am scared
to sneak into the hut to find your coat.

When you put down your pick,
when others wouldn't sprag
the mine's passages; when you said no:

soldiers, who do not strike,
thrust
their bayonets into you.

They were told to.

The young mayor, shitting, closeted
with chain on his neck. I want to

push my hands into your blood
because I caused you to use yours.

I did not die; love, I did not. All the parts
of England fell melting like lead away,
as you showed me the melting once, when you and the men
with you were jabbed,

and without tenderness, were filled over;
no psalm, leaf-like, shading the eyelid
as the eye beneath is dazed abruptly
in the earth's flare of black light
burning after death.

The spade digging in the sunlight illuminates the face of my God.
Blind him.

JON SILKIN
Killhope Wheel, 1971 | *Complete Poems*, 2015

Killhope

Mist rolling down Killhope
as smoke billowing from dead rubble
or dust from approaching war horses.

And another morning walk,
pulled up Newhouse Bank onto the top road;
a better view of the carnage.

Past Whitestones and
down into the Clough;
the muffled sounds of sword and shield, grenade and gun
and silence when all's done.

Centre road, two ears stick up,
hairy and recognisable,
from the grey, red, brown squash that was a rabbit;
dual cairn,
marking the easiness of killing,
the hardness of death.

Three more dogs at the top of Carroway Bank
set us downwards past the blue zone, the war zone, the murder zone;
and back through the lead-filled void
of West Black Dene, silenced by the bones
of patient pit ponies and buckled miners.

Then, along the Wear's bank, the heron
catches another fish
and flies high home with it,
competing hopelessly with the practising Tornado.

PRU KITCHING
All Aboard the Moving Staircase, 2004

What's It Like Up There?

above Harehope and beyond the lake is the bleak winter horizon
not softened by snow
dirty green patches sectioned by stone walls
improbably perched on the aggressive slopes
the odd off-white dot of a nibbling sheep

and then the farmhouse   sunk into itself
not Cotswold-nestled but dogged   northern
gritting its teeth in the teeth of a Weardale winter

where are the dogs   people   tractor   landrover?
hiding from the grimness of subsistence?

a life different from Ruth and Herbie's
whose cottage down near the wooden bridge
wobbles with each wagon to-ing   fro-ing   going
from quarry to kiln and endlessly back again

different from Lenny Burrup who see-saws out and in
back and forth with sandwiches   pop   a bit or a drill
for the open-cast packers   the movers and shakers
the gelignite drillers   society pillars

what is it like up there   above the explosions
away from the grit the grime the lorries' vibrations
the cordite taste   the rising smoke   the dusty waste
and Ruth and Herbie falling off their chairs

PRU KITCHING
The Kraków Egg, 2009

Road

I take the Weardale road,
Witton-le-Wear,
the sign to Hamsterley.

Through Fir Tree
where my eighteen-year-old mother
sat for a photograph coquettishly,
gingerly posed on a fence,
hockey legs shining in twenties silk stockings.

Then Thornley –
my five-year-old mother
walked there to school, two miles over fields
dragging a sledge for the winter ride home.

Like her, I plunge down Harperley Banks
to the Lodge at the foot,
where she was born in a hexagonal room,
the fifth girl, named by her sisters.

My eleven-year-old mother
took the track to the station
for the train to Wolsingham Grammar
(head girl in '28, her name is on the board).
Now there's no station, no hamlet,
but under the hedge, white violets.

Grandad's wood is on the right,
he planted it before the War.
His trees are a blur through the windscreen
scrolling a story of a hundred years
writing the memory
of lives I didn't live.

DOROTHY LONG
No Random Loving, 2013

No Buses to Damascus

Wonder Pearl distemper pale, queen
of Blanchland who rode mare Bonny
by stooks and stiles in the land
of waving wings and borage blue
and striving storms of stalks and stems.
Pearl, who could not speak, eventually
wrote: Your family feuds are ludicrous.
Only my eyes can laugh at you.
She handed over springwater under a stern look.
We fell asleep at Blackbird Ford
named by princes Bar and Paul of Sparty Lea.
We splashed and swam and made the brown trout mad.
Dawdled in our never-ending pleasure over
earth-enfolded sheephorns
by rivermist webs, half-hidden moss crowns.

Up a height or down the dale in mist or shine
in heather or heifer-trampled marigold
the curlew-broken silence sang its volumes.
Leaning on the lichen on the Leadgate Road,
Pearl said: a-a-a-a-a-, pointing with perfectly poised
index finger towards the rusty coloured dry stone wall
which contrasted so strongly with her milky skin.

The congenital fissure in the roof of her mouth
laid down with priceless gems, beaten lustrous copper
and barely hidden seams of gold.

BARRY MACSWEENEY
Pearl, 1995/1997 | *Wolf Tongue*, 2000

Cushy Number

Much desired landscape loved keenly several lifetimes
Our unregenerated soil-heap hillsides, bleak
and bare of plastic life: one everyday religion.

Your ghost spindrifts in the lead-crusted law,
in mist combed by bracken and fern. The old school
where you were humiliated and betrayed, thrown

back to the riverbank and cribs of marigold, head
shaved, now up for sale: bijou conversion possibilities
for the turbo-mob, weird souls dreaming of car-reg

numbers and mobile phone codes. They are taking
over from the Barbour vegetarians, who couldn't
stand the nailed-down winters. Inside you, spectre,

an inarticulate fury. Me, tongue-boy, lathered with words,
and you, thee, fern-haired and Pearl naked. We swam
against all Tyne tides which rose from the sea. When you sink

towards the head of the hush, where the beck runs
out of the tunnel towards the west, brewing foam
as it goes, we'll meet my adverbs ad infinitum:
tongue-stoned invisible prelate of the shaking holes.

BARRY MACSWEENEY
Pearl in the Silver Morning, 1999 | *Wolf Tongue*, 2000

High Fells April 2011

The mood-music goes a little ahead of the action
to anticipate, for we have hunter's brain, reaction
this morning the golden-plovers each take up the same strain
of warning; territory after territory, gain
urgency from each other, three-dimensional chain –
or, if you like, just emphasising a people's refrain
of solidarity facing an unknown intrusion.

———

for the alarm is general, they don't yet know quite who
approaches and traverses; though at the head of the queue
the first-responder may have a clue, a code to relay
as to whether fox or dog or crow or a bird-of-prey
a heron or mankind, raven or cat or 'weasel', say

but today I see low over the wathe for once, grey
the Goshawk, not the grey Bluehawk harrier anyway...

and the sentinel cock plovers rise almost together
away from their mates in unbailing in moss and heather;
their crying and apparently wild haphazard flying
as the hawk dither at first, then he's forcefully trying
to climb on his tail; soaring here would be just tieing
himself in knots in the confusion and mobbing and crying...
he's away; today none of this community is dying.

COLIN SIMMS
Goshawk Poems, 2017

Where Rise Watters of Tyne, Tees, Wear

The ringtail no longer visible
has merged into the winter brown
wingstroke by wingstroke down
under the sky, into the deceivable

Using the spillway channel left over
from the great ice melt not so long ago
when we consider pedigree of this rover
know more than the genome will show

Off the spiky blanket-bog peatlands spread
for the smallest falcon as for our rare gled
where becks rise from and burns are born
and so the Three Rivers some southrons scorn...

Let hawks hold the upland, 'empty' or 'bare'
and let us guard *their* territory up there
from 'playground' development, FWDs
– there's more than human greed to please...

COLIN SIMMS
Hen Harrier Poems, 2015

NEWCASTLE

News from Newcastle

England's a perfect world, hath Indies too;
Correct your maps, Newcastle is Peru!
Let the haughty Spaniard triumph till 'tis told
Our sooty minerals refine his gold.
This will sublime and hatch the abortive oar
When the sun tires and stars can do no more.
No mines are current, unrefined and gross;
Coals make the sterling, Nature but the dross.
For metals Bacchus-like two births approve.
Heaven heats the Semele and ours the Jove.
Thus Art doth polish Nature; 'tis the trade.
So every madame hath her chambermaid.
Who'd dote on gold? A thing so strange and odd
'Tis most contemptible when made a god!
All sin and mischief hence have rise and swell;
One India more would make another Hell.
Our mines are innocent, nor will the North
Tempt poor mortality with too much worth.
They're not so precious; rich enough to fire
A lover, yet make none idolater.
The moderate value of our guiltless ore
Makes no man atheist, nor no woman whore.
Yet why should hallowed Vestals' sacred shrine
Deserve more honour than a naming mine?
These pregnant wombs of heat would fitter be,
Than a few embers, for a deity.
Had he our pits, the Persian would admire
No sun, but warm his devotion at our fire.
He'd leave the trotting whipster and prefer
Our profound Vulcan 'bove that Waggoner.
For wants he heat, or light, or would have store
Of both? 'Tis here. And what can suns give more?
Nay, what's the sun but, in a different name,
A coal-pit rampant, or a mine on flame?
Then let this truth reciprocally run,
The sun's Heaven's coalery, and coals our sun;
A sun that scorcheth not, locked up in the deep;

The lions chained, the bandog is asleep.
That tyrant fire, which uncontrolled doth rage,
Here's calm and hushed, like Bajazet in the cage.
For in each coal-pit there doth couchant dwell
A muzzled Etna, or an innocent Hell.
Kindle the cloud, you'll lightning then descry;
Then will day break from the gloomy sky;
Then you'll unbutton though December blow,
And sweat in the midst of icicles and snow;
The dog-days then at Christmas. Thus is all
The year made June and equinoctial.
If heat offends, our pits afford us shade,
Thus summer's winter, winter summer's made.
What need we baths, what need we bower or grove?
A coal-pit's both a ventiduct and stove,
Such pits and caves were palaces of old;
Poor inns, God wot, yet in an age of gold;
And what would now be thought a strange design,
To build a house was then to undermine.
People lived under ground, and happy dwellers
Whose jovial habitations were all cellars!
These primitive times were innocent, for then
Man, who turned after fox, made but his den.
But see a fleet of vitals trim and fine,
To court the rich infanta of our mine;
Hundreds of grim Leanders do confront,
For this loved Hero, the loud Hellespont.
'Tis an armada royal doth engage
For some new Helen with this equipage;
Prepared too, should we their addresses bar,
To force this mistress with a ten years' war,
But that our mine's a common good, a joy
Made not to ruin but enrich our Troy.
But oh! These bring it with them and conspire
To pawn that idol for our smoke and fire.
Silver's but ballast; this they bring on shore
That they may treasure up our better ore.
For this they venture rocks and storms, defy
All the extremity of sea and sky.
For the glad purchase of this precious mold,
Cowards dare pirates, misers part with gold.
Hence is it when the doubtful ship sets forth
The naving needle still directs it north,

And, Nature's secret wonders to attest,
Our Indies' worth, discards both east and west
For Tyne. Not only fire commends this spring,
A coal-pit is a mine for everything.
We sink a jack-of-all-trades, shop and sound,
An inverse bourse, an exchange under ground.
This Proteus earth converts to what you ha't;
Now you may wear it to silk, now come it to plate,
And, what's a metamorphosis more dear,
Dissolve it and 'twill turn to London beer.
For whatsoe'er that gaudy city boasts,
Each month doth drive to attractive coasts.
We shall exhaust their chamber and devour
Their treasure of Guild Hall and mint of the Tower.
Our staiths their mortgaged streets will soon deride,
Blazon their Cornhill-stella, share Cheapside.
Thus shall our coal-pits' charity and pity
At distance undermine and fire the City.
Should we exact, they'd pawn their wives and treat
To swop those coolers for our sovereign heat.
'Bove kisses and embraces fire controls;
No Venus heightens like a peck of coals.
Medea was a drug of some old sire
And Æson's bath a lusty sea-coal fire.
Chimneys are old men's mistresses, their inns,
A modern dalliance with their meazled shins.
To all defects a coal-heap gives a cure,
Gives youth to age and raiment to the poor.
Pride first wore clothes; Nature disdains attire;
She made us naked 'cause she gave us fire.
Full wharfs and wardrobes, and the tailor's charm
Belongs to the collier; he must keep us warm.
The quilted alderman in all his array
Finds but cold comfort in a frosty day;
Girt, wrapped, and muffled, yet with all this stir
Scarce warm when smothered in his drowsy fur;
Not proof against keen Winter's batteries
Should he himself wear all his liveries,
But chillblain under silver spurs bewails
And in embroidered buckskins blows his nails.
Rich meadows and full crops are elsewhere found.
We can reap harvest from our barren ground.
The bald parched hills that circumscribe our Tyne

Are no less pregnant in their hungry mine.
Their unfledged tops so well content our palates,
We envy none their nosegays and their sallets.
A gay rank soil like a young gallant grows
And spends itself that it may wear fine clothes,
Whilst all its worth is to its back confined.
Our wear's plain outside, but is richly lined;
Winter's above, 'tis summer underneath,
A trusty morglay in a rusty sheath.
As precious sables sometimes interlace
A wretched serge or grogram cassock case.
Rocks own no spring, are pregnant with no showers,
Crystals and gems are there instead of flowers;
Instead of roses, beds of rubies sweet
And emeralds recompence the violet.
Dame Nature, not like other madames, wears
Where she is bare, pearls in her breasts and ears.
What though our fields present a naked sight?
A paradise should be an adamite.
The northern lad his bonny lass throws down
And gives her a black bag for a green gown.

JOHN CLEVELAND
News from Newcastle, or Newcastle Coal-Pits, 1651

Semele: mortal mother of *Bacchus* (Dionysus) by *Jove* (Jupiter/Zeus); *bandog:* huge mastiff guard dog; *Bajazet:* sultan of Turkey imprisoned by Tamerlane in a public cage, described by Richard Knolles in his *Historie of the Turkes* (1603); *ventiduct:* ventilation duct; *Æson:* king of Iolcus in Thessaly whose throat was cut by Medea who then put his corpse in a pot in some versions of the story; *sallet:* helmet with outward curve over back of the neck; *gogrom:* coarse fabric made of silk, often combined with mohair or wool and stiffened with gum; *adamite:* adherent of an early Christian sect from North Africa who wore no clothing during their religious services.

John Cleveland (1613–1658), 'the last of the Metaphysicals', was the most popular poet of his age (far more so than Milton, for example) and no fewer than 25 editions appeared between 1647 and 1700. His reputation declined, however, after Dryden's criticism that the poet was apt to deliver 'common thoughts in abstruse words'. His often dazzling conceits and comparisons were termed 'Clevelandism'.

Cleveland was an ardent Royalist during the Civil War and served as judge advocate at Newark, where King Charles I surrendered to the Scots in 1646. Charles was taken to Newcastle, and a plaque in Market Street indicates the house where the king was held for some eight months of tense bargaining, until the Scots, much to Cleveland's disgust, handed him over to Parliament. One of his most savage satires, 'The Rebel Scot', was written on that occasion.

Cleveland seems to have been a destitute wanderer between 1646 and 1655, dependent on Royalist sympathisers for support. His actual whereabouts, however, are a mystery. It is not impossible that he was in the North East for some of this period, and the poem 'News from Newcastle' (first printed in 1651) is ascribed to him. It certainly has more of Clevelandism than other poems so ascribed, and whoever wrote it was a poet of more than usual accomplishment. He clearly also knew the Tyne (and possibly Cleveland's work) very well. The beginning is arresting – and Newcastle is pronounced Geordie fashion: 'England's a perfect world, has Indies too; / Correct your maps, Newcastle is Peru!' Then follows a wonderfully convoluted set of conceits in praise of coal. The poet mentions 'the bald parched hills that circumscribe our Tyne' and with surprising fervour, now writing as if he were a Tynesider, mentions Blaydon and Stella, as he sees London's wealth draining northwards: 'We shall exhaust their chamber and devour / Their treasures of Guildhall, the Mint, the Tower./ Our staiths their mortgaged streets will soon divide, / Blathon own Cornhill, Stella share Cheapside.' [AM]

Newcastle Is Peru

>Correct your maps: Newcastle is Peru!
>JOHN CLEVELAND

>Venient annis saecula seris,
>Quibus Oceanus vincula rerum
>Laxet & ingens pateat tellus,
>Tethysque novos detegat orbes,
>Nec sit terris ultima Thule.
>SENECA, *Medea*, 375-9

For defending in our Civil Wars
the King's against the better cause,
Newcastle got its motto: FORTIT-
ER TRIUMPHANS DEFENDIT.
After Nigeria and Prague I come
back near to where I started from,
all my defences broken down
on nine or ten *Newcastle Brown*.

A sudden, stiff September breeze
blows off the sea along the quays
and chills us; autumn and I need
your shoulder with a desperate need.
A clumsy effort at control,
I faff with paper chips and coal,
and rake out with elaborate fuss
one whole summer's detritus.

A good draught and the fire roars
like muted Disney dinosaurs,
and last week's Sunday paper glows
yellowish, its urgent prose,
like flies across a carcass, spreads
and fattens on the voiceless dead.
A picture shows lobbed mortar bombs
smashing down Onitsha homes.

The fire sucks in the first cold air
under the coverage of massacre.
The fire chatters, almost flies,
a full-fledged bird of paradise.
I lay down, dizzy, drunk, alone,
life circling life like the Eddystone
dark sea, but lighting nothing; sense
nor centre, nor circumference.

A lifelong, sick sixpennyworth
of appalling motion round the Earth;
scared, moonrocketing till Pop-
eye and blurred planets stop;
Switchback; *Helter Skelter*; *Reel*;
the Blackpool Pleasure Beach Big Wheel,
its million coloured lightbulbs one
red halo like an empty sun.

The *Caterpillar*, Hunslet Feast;
one hand on my first woman's breast;
darkness; acceleration so
we're desperate with vertigo;
then chained in solitary *Chair-
o-planes* through whistling air
as all the known Leeds landmarks blur
to something dark and circular.

Venus, Vulcan, Cupid stare
out vacantly on City Square,
and *Deus invat impigros*
above the bank where God helps those
who help themselves, declares
Leeds purposeful in its affairs.
Mercator; *miles*, school chapel glass
transparencies to blood and brass.

And *Self Help* Samuel Smiles was said
to have waltzed round our first bed
in our partitioned ballroom flat
with hardly room to swing a cat.
Worthies! Loiners! O King Dick
Oastler and his rhetoric,
and William Hey, the first to show
syphilis *in utero*.

O highlife crocodiles that went
round one palm tree in the bare cement!
The dizziness! That spiral stair
up St Vitus's Cathedral; there
the golden cockerel and great Prague
before us like a catalogue;
slides. Bloodless mementos, all
Time-Life International.

And now with vistas like Earl Grey's
I look out over life and praise
from my unsteady, sea-view plinth
each dark turn of the labyrinth
that might like a river suddenly
wind its widening banks into the sea
and Newcastle is Newcastle is New-
castle *is* Peru!

Swirled detritus and driftwood pass
in state the 1880 *Sas-
inena Cold Storage Co.*,
and Neptune gazes at the Tyne's flow
seawards, where the sea-winds 'boast
and bluster' at the North East coast,
the sluggish Tyne meandering through
the staithes and shipyards of Peru.

Shadow girders faced with sun
shimmer like heaped bullion.
Commerce and contraceptive glide
and circle on the turning tide;
Plain, *Gossamer* and *Fetherlite*
and US *Trojan*, knotted tight,
ferry their unborn semen, free
for ever from discovery.

Discovery! Slaves, now trains,
like *spirochetes* through dark brains,
tunnel the Andes, spiralling for zinc
and silver, gold and lead; drink
still makes me giddy; my mind whirls
through all my wanderings and girls
to one last city, whose black crest
shows all the universe at rest.

At rest! That last red flash
as life's last ember turns to ash
and riddled dusts drop through the grate
around the heart. O celebrate,
as panic screws up each charged nerve
to cornering the next sharp swerve,
Earth, people, planets as they move
with all the gravity of love.

First this Victorian terrace, where
small scars of the last World War –
those wrought-iron railings made
into shrapnel and grenade,
acanthus leaf and fleur-de-lys,
victorious artillery –
are enough reminder that we brave
harsh opposition when we love.

This cluttered room, its chandelier
still spinning from the evening's beer,
this poor, embattled fortress, this strong-
hold of love, that can't last long
against the world's bold cannonade
of loveless warfare and cold trade,
this bed, this fire, and lastly us,
naked, bold, adventurous.

Discovery! wart, mole, spot,
like outcrops on a snowfield, dot
these slopes of flesh my fingers ski
with circular dexterity.
This moment when my hand strays
your body like an endless maze,
returning and returning, you,
O you; you also are Peru.

And just as distant. Flashing stars
drop to the ashpit through the bars.
I'm back in Africa, at ease
under the splashed shade of four trees,
watching a muscled woman heave
huge headloads of dead wood; one bare leaf
for covering wilts in the heat,
curls, then flutters to her flat, cracked feet.

And round each complex of thatched huts
is a man-high cactus hedge that shuts
out intruders and the mortars thud
like a migraine in the compound mud.
Night comes, and as drunk as hell
I watch the heavens and fireflies, and can't tell,
here at my Shangri-la, Pankshin,
where insects end and stars begin.

My fingerprints still lined with coal
send cold shudders through my soul.
Each whorl, my love-, my long life-line,
mine, inalienably mine,
lead off my body as they press
onwards into nothingness.
I see my grimy fingers smudge
everything they feel or touch.

The fire I laid and lit to draw
you downstairs to the second floor,
flickers and struts upon my bed.
And I'm left gazing at a full-page spread
of aggressively fine bosoms, nude
and tanned almost to *négritude*,
in the Colour Supplement's *Test
Yourself for Cancer of the Breast.*

TONY HARRISON
Newcastle Is Peru, 1969 | *Collected Poems*, 2007

Newcastle is Benidorm

girls on Friday exit routes
in flimsy skirts & skimpy t shirts
all brandish castanets
& form a human party chain
to dance thru Eldon Square

with the skill & dexterity
of bullfighters depicted
on trinkets & souvenir ashtrays
the 'lads' in the bravado after hours
hover in doorways makin moves

& safe sex hasn't been invented
& all the bars tonight were hivin
& the sky's the colour of sun tan lotion
& I'd give a million to be so neutral
& everywhere has become a haze
of free offers & tabloid slogans
& disco rhythms insidious & thumping
& the crowd from the Pizza House jumping
into litter bins & pissin on windows
selling fridge freezers & community singing
& groping hands & fumbling tongues at bus stops
& football arguments & the ringing
of alarm bells set off for 'high jinks'
& the stale boke on the floor of the Bacchus tavern
& all down the cubicles in nightclubs – stinks
& there will never be an armed uprising
against the Capitalist Conspiracy here
or anywhere else for that matter –
what a crying shame!...

'Here we go, Here we go, Here we go'...

BRENDAN CLEARY
Newcastle Is Benidorm, 1988 | *goin' down slow*, 2010

Bacchantes

Into the dark forests of the city
they dance, loosely-clad limbs
skimming air, light-headed
before the serious business begins.

They signal to each other
across lamplit paths
alive with flesh and striped skins,
eager for the heart of the ritual.

They stumble from vomitories
into the irregular amphitheatre
of violent delights: tribal fights,
catcalls, broken glass and takeaways,

bus-stop sex and smeared
tears of disappointed dramas;
girls who re-create the world,
stamp their heels and scream,

break from the centre,
flailing arms, celebrating
carnage but fall down
lost alleyways, beehives for a pillow.

Clamped to phones, they travel
backwards into the past. Blood
on their hands, they wake
to the pale-fingered dawn.

ELLEN PHETHEAN
Breath, 2009, 2014

Newcastle Is Lesbos

Sweating in the Turkish baths
or breast stroking in Elswick pool.
Driving buses, besuited, unrooted,
or regularly walking The Barking Dog.

Browsing in the bookshop.
Camping with Vamps in twilight,
rocking with Doris afterwards.
Teaming into the Tyneside.

Plotting on allotments on Sundays.
Playing footsie in the park,
on television, on telephones.
Flirting in Fenwicks.

Newcastle is Lesbos.
They have infiltrated. Look behind you,
under your desk, in the garden,
in your pink rose bushes.

Sappho, come here on holiday instead.
We are in commune with our own Powerhouse.
Come, give praises to our Northern ladies.

The Heat is On.
There's Spit on our Tongues.
We're best in the West,
Walker or Byker
or cruising the wide waters
of the Tyne.

Remember that nice doctor,
social worker, dentist (dammit)
and the woman who winked at you
by the pyjamas in Marks and Spencers?

Newcastle is Lesbos.
They seem quite ordinary,
they are quite ordinary.
We are.

JULIA DARLING
Sauce, 1994 | *Incredible, Miraculous*, 2015

The Entry of Don Quixote into Newcastle upon Tyne

He comes by Lambretta over the Tyne Bridge
with a lamppost for a lance, having just crashed
a transit van into the Angel of the North
declaring 'Protect the South from drear Boreas.'
The compressed and screeching van still follows
with Oliver Hardy at the wheel, his Panchez,
still dressed in his coonskins à la *The Fighting Kentuckians*,
with a soundtrack of Handel via Zappa blaring
from a large rectangular megaphone.
Quixote, played as always by Peter O'Toole
as in The Man of La Mancha, ignores
the drivers who hiss, 'Don't sing!'
Having just slung seventeen bowling balls
at the Metro Centre-as-Leviathan and
attempted to liberate the pensioners from
the singalong at Harry Ramsden's,
he steps on the northern shore of the Tyne.

And has the crap beaten out of him at once by lasses
outside *The Pitcher and Piano* on a Friday night
for singing madrigals in Foreign.
He is thrown out of the Civic Centre
for interrupting every marriage ceremony with,
'Think of the unborn: give Limbo a chance.'
He is moved on from the War Memorial for yelling at
the frieze of marching dead, those who answered 'The Call',
'Look! Look the other way!' while Ollie
drops a vast banana skin before them.
He is given a cup of tea in St Thomas the Martyr's
for explaining they shouldn't 'Hate Evil'
as their slogan advises. He charges the Magpies during
a crucial fixture, convinced that eleven
cannot be a lucky number. Quixote is played,
as always, by Miguel de Unamuno.
The Toon Army chant 'Get back, get back,
get back to Le Pays Basque!'

He is chased by a herd of Range Rovers from Acorn Road
for attempting to give the rather plush contents of *Oxfam*
to the man selling *Big Issues* opposite,

then releasing tilapia and witch sole down
the drain outside Taylor's fish shop.
He is thrown out of an architectural salvage company
for brandishing a lump of wormy wood
and shouting, 'This is the stool
of Ignatius de Loyola: I can smell upon it
the buttocks of my physician father!'
He delivers a skipful of cigarette butts to the tenants
of the yuppified Wills Building; tries
launching Hardy down the slipway at Swan Hunters;
mans the reconstructed section of Hadrian's Wall
exhorting the Scandi-looking passers-by
to 'help defend us from these monstrous Picts'.
He breaks into the Formica factory with a petition
signed by obviously-fictitious anteaters
demanding they stop extracting formic acid from
queen ants just for kitchen worktops.

Quixote is played as always by Pierre Menard:
the queen ants squeak, 'Now write something by Borges!'
His Dulcinea is a lollypop lady in North Shields
sighted trailing the disk of her lollypop along the pavement
until it sparks, and puffing on a Regal. Just for her
he joins in the medieval joust at Tynemouth Priory
a little too vigorously, armed only
with a magican-opener and a melamine ladle.
While Hardy winces and eats a kipper stotty,
he has the crap beaten out of him yet again.

W.N. HERBERT
The Big Bumper Book of Troy, 2002

Song of the Longboat Boys

Well we've been sailing all day through the ice and snow,
we've got this little wooden compass tells us where to go;
now some folks say we like to ravish and rage
but a viking's got a right to earn a living wage
in
      Northumberland thumber thumberberland
      Northumberland thumber thumberberland.

Well our boss is Erik Bloodaxe he's a bit of a dork:
he wants to settle down in this place called York,
but we're all far too young we wanna filch and fight
and gan oot wi the lasses on a Saturday night
in the
      Bigg Bigg Bigg Bigg Mar-ket Biggbigg Mar-ket
      Bigg Bigg Bigg Bigg Mar-ket Biggbigg Mar-ket.

Well we hear there's aal these lads who like to dress in gray
and sing their Christmas carols in the kirk aal day:
they get a lot of leather and they call it a book,
then they cover it in gold – we'd like to take a look
in
      Lindisfarne disfarne Lindisdisfarne
      Lindisfarne disfarne Lindisdisfarne.

Well Olaf's got an axe and Gunnar's got a spear
and you oughta see our boat cause we made it last year;
we're gonna crack your skull and burn your neighbourhood
but then we'll build this cool store and sell you bits of wood
in
      Northumberland thumber thumberberland
      Northumberland thumber thumberberland
      Northumberland thumber thumberberland
      Northumberland thumber thumberberland…

(Continue until interrupted by a chorus of Geordies):

'Woh! We're gannin to IKEA! Doodleoodleoodoo…
Woh! We're gan to buy some flat-packs! Doodleoodleoodoo…'

W.N. HERBERT
The Big Bumper Book of Troy, 2002

Newcastle Beer

When Fame brought the news of Great Britain's success,
    And told at Olympus each Gallic defeat;
Glad Mars sent by Mercury orders express,
    To summon the deities all to a treat:
        Blithe Comus was placed
        To guide the gay feast,
And freely declared there was choice of good cheer;
        Yet vowed to his thinking,
        For exquisite drinking,
Their Nectar was nothing to Newcastle Beer.

The great God of war, to encourage the sun
    And humour the taste of his whimsical guest,
Sent a message that moment to Moor's for a tun
    Of Stingo, the stoutest, the brightest and best:
        No Gods – they all swore,
        Regaled so before,
With liquor so lively – so potent and clear:
        And each deified fellow,
        Got jovially mellow,
In honour, brave boys, of our Newcastle Beer.

Apollo perceiving his talents refine,
    Repents he drank Helicon Water so long:
He bowed, being asked by the musical Nine,
    And gave the gay board an extempore song;
        But 'ere he began,
        He tossed off his cann:
There's nought like good liquor the fancy to clear:
        Then sang with great merit,
        The flavour and spirit,
His godship had found in the Newcastle Beer.

'Twas Stingo like this made Alcides so bold;
    It braced up his nerves, and enlivened his powers;
And his mystical club, that did wonders of old,
    Was nothing, my lads, but such liquor as ours.
        The horrible crew
        That Hercules slew,

Were Poverty – Calumny – Trouble – and Fear:
       Such a club would you borrow,
       To drive away sorrow,
Apply for a jorum of Newcastle Beer.

Ye youngsters, so diffident, languid and pale!
  Whom Love, like the cholic, so rudely infests;
Take a cordial of this, 'twill probatum prevail,
  And drive the cur Cupid away from your breasts:
       Dull whining despise,
       Grow rosy and wise,
Nor longer the jest of good fellows appear;
       Bid adieu to your folly,
       Get drunk and be jolly,
And smoke o'er a tankard of Newcastle Beer.

Ye fanciful folk, for whom Physic prescribes,
  Whom bolus and potion have harrassed to death!
Ye wretches, whom Law and her ill-looking tribes,
  Have hunted about till you're quite out of breath!
       Here's shelter and ease,
       No craving for fees,
No danger, – no doctor, – no bailiff is near!
       Your spirits this raises,
       It cures your diseases,
There's freedom and health in our Newcastle Beer.

JOHN CUNNINGHAM
Poems, chiefly pastoral, 1766

Stingo: strong, sharp beer; *Alcides:* Hercules.

In the churchyard of St John's in Newcastle stands the table-tomb of Dublin-born actor and poet **John Cunningham** (1729–1773), author of the play, *Love in a Mist* (1747). He is described as a pastoral poet in this least pastoral of settings. Though of Irish-Scots extraction, he regarded Newcastle as his home. After many wanderings as an indifferent actor, he turned to poetry, also writing newspaper articles for the *Newcastle Chronicle* to make a scant living; after giving his last performance in Darlington, he returned to Newcastle, was taken ill and died aged 44 in 1773. Though much of his poetry has a gentle charm, he can show enthusiasm (and an Irish accent) in his best-known poem, 'Newcastle Beer'. [AM/NA]

'Our Friends in the North'
(for Jon & Elaine Glover)

They were like – (fists raised)
'Like what? Go on, then, like what?'

Like something this child could dance to
with such a rhythm,
the words don't matter yet,
                                      it's the speech-flow
full-guttering from the back of the throat like

Like what?

Irish, Norse, Scots and burred
Northumbrian, stirred into a dancing reel
rising and falling and rising –
                                  so harshly tender, luvver –
before the passion's flattened right out of it down south

'Howaay, man, hoy the bal ower heor!'
or *'The spuggies are fledged'*

And in the early years it was said
'If you are going to talk like that
you can go to the school up the road'

(A flat tone is generally best
for menace and threat, with no warm scurries
and hullabaloo of anything like feeling.)

Even then, not always
so *canny toon, Geordie*
for all the whisper-quiet yellow trolleys
addressed to Two Ball Lonnen,
and before them
the climbing trellised roses of scenty Moorside,
the Great North Road trams, rattling and roofless to sky

'Gissaride-onyer-bike-kidda?'
'Eee-lissen-him – gerr'im! Gerr'it-off-'im-Billy!'

I saw a window with a hole
splattered like black mud –

'Ah-seen'im-hoy-it-Mam!'

and my stomach melting
down my strengthless tiny legs

'Eee-ya-dortypig-smash'is-fyess!'
'Howaay-let's-do'im!'

What tales can you tell, canny bairn?
                                        The first ones, always
in the right language.

And more than a thousand books later I was watching
moving pictures of a grey river still holy to me,
and those lovely garths and wynds climbing ancient from the Side
      of the town
with, above, the Tyne Bridge's sea-green coathanger
and my grandfather's stone towers bulking at each end

That's two per County, like

and the screen's arguing families fell out of focus –
all I could hear through the broken black hole was

Like what? Go on, then, like what?

Like words do when they dance,
like the rhythms that undo
the bindings of the heart,
                                  so close to the border
it's easy to forget they were once my own.

RODNEY PYBUS
Darkness Inside Out, 2012

'Our Friends in the North': the BBC television serial written by Peter Flannery, shown in 1996.

A Return to Newcastle

I'm up from the South and back to it:
Brown Ale in the cryptic pubs full
Of the lilt of Geordie accents.
A frog-prince back, too thirsty for release
From terraced streets' truncated ends,
Those old bricked-off perspectives.

Under roof tops hatched like herringbone
Jobless men read paperbacks till dawn
At a loss. Time-served engineers
Done with the sea, return to river towns –
Prodigal salmon spawning in the Tyne,
That unrepeatable, one-off gesture.

As a youth on a summer Saturday night
I waited in a shop door for a girl,
Head into the sports page. In those days
A soft curve could draw the eye downwards
Where Grey Street, tawny in late sun,
Defined its limits – my own inelegance.

GEORGE CHARLTON
Ten North-East Poets, 1980 | *Nightshift Workers*, 1989

Hyem

When a place puts its hands round your heart
you feel the gentle grip, experience
an inner lift of spirit, a smile
that claims your face, even when alone.
A sinking sun falling on fields
across the valley, the sense of space
and peace as lives in scattered houses
turn on lights along the river – *hyem*.

Home, where trains ran alongside shipyard cranes
until the morning one of them knocked
our carriage off the line as its jib swung through
the driver's cab. Yet, after the screams,
through shattered glass, voices reassured.
Firemen, who sounded like my dad, lifted us
onto ladders and Scotswood Road soothed
by being dusty and noisy, as it usually was.

When the shipyards closed, cranes were last to go –
sold to India along with the dry dock.
I wondered how they dealt with the shock of heat:
our sky was never the same again.
Yet now, in this southernmost county,
cranes draw me to the water as I drive
down Tebourba Way, hoist my heart high enough
to swing me over the estuary, as if I'm travelling home.

ROBYN BOLAM
Hyem, 2017

Moving On

In the Haymarket a bus station has been transformed
from cattle crush to airport lounge. I no longer miss
Marlborough Crescent, open to weather. From there, I'd rush
for the trolley bus to school while the abattoir let
blood flow unchecked along the gutter, stinking through fumes
as drivers climbed in their cabs and, one by one, engines
vibrated, buses pulled into stands. I'd leap across,
never connecting that red stream with the death it meant
or managing to link this to cattle sometimes glimpsed.
Our city made blood, tanks and ships. It still stood on coal.

Near to where we waited in the cold, suits with laptops
raise glasses in the lobby of a high-rise hotel.
Phones vibrate silently; clean shoes press the shining floor.
Automatic doors open, close by a subdued road.
Multi-glazed rooms gaze across the river. It must be
better; no more leading to slaughter. Downstream they dredged

the Tyne at Wallsend for the deepest vessel ever
to sail there – fifty feet of it underwater – so
they could load the last remains of shipbuilding up for
Dahbol. Blood down the gutter: water under the bridge.

ROBYN BOLAM
Hyem, 2017

Satsumas

She is gliding out of Marks and Spencers,
carrying a clematis, a pound of satsumas.
It's just after five. Her legs are heavy.

There is the bus station, green wrought iron,
a woman in blue, selling *The Big Issue*,
a long coated man with a face like a lion.

She sees the stone angel that flies from a column.
And a child is laughing, a bell is ringing;
the bones of the city breath in a rhythm.

The starlings gather. She peels a satsuma
seeing a bank that was once a tea room,
before that a hairdresser, before that a lane.

She is bulging with maps, with lost streets,
threaded through her like silver. Stone faces
look from the cornices. Perhaps she is turning

into stone? *It's all right*, she says out loud
to the closing shops. *I'm still here. Actually*
dropping her bag of satsumas

watching them fall onto the tarmac, rolling
bright and orange, against the grey.
Living fruit and stone. The kernel of things.

JULIA DARLING
Sudden Collapses in Public Places, 2003 | *Incredible, Miraculous*, 2015

A Short Manifesto for My City

This city shall treasure its pedestrians
and its small places, its irregular shops.

It shall hang onto its pink lanes, its towers,
Dog Leap Stairs and Pudding Chares.

And the city shall never try to be Barcelona,
or dress itself in luxury underwear.

Let it be salty, and rusty with iron,
keep secrets beneath its potent river

and be proud to be radical, afraid
of refurbishment. It doesn't need fireworks,

or Starbucks; for it knows its interior.
Let it always be ready to take off its hat.

My city is hard stone, canny and clever.
Don't give it a mirror. Let it be itself.

JULIA DARLING
Apology for Absence, 2004 | *Incredible, Miraculous*, 2015

Old Jezzy

I went to old Jesmond Graveyard
to find my plot, to mark a place.
Doug from Bereavement showed me a spot
green and reflective, under a willow.
He apologised for the trimming of the weeds,
he liked it messy, overgrown,
but the government had made stipulations
for health and safety, things must be neat,
in case of gravestones squashing children,
so raggy old Jezzy was having a clean up.

But you know, said Doug, death isn't tidy.
It's a plague of knotweed, a bed of nettles,
a path through thistles, that's how it should be.

JULIA DARLING
Apology for Absence, 2004 | *Incredible, Miraculous*, 2015

The Wild Life on Newcastle Town Moor

It is true that there are kestrels;
I have seen them hover like capitals
over their columns of air set up on the Moor,
                then bat off fast as pigeons.
It is true that there are skylarks,
I have heard them above green earth-heaps
shifted in making the motorway through the Moor;
                and every eave spawns starlings:
but the dominant species is student,
though not a resident, but passage migrant.

It is true there's a herd of cattle
and an assortment of dogs with attendant people,
and all their spoor and spraint spread on the Moor
                for naturalists to observe;
and, once in a wind, an undulating kite
tugs at its cord and soars to a great height
like a papery, air-swimming tapeworm over the Moor
                above the budding grove:
but the typical species present
is still the gregarious student.

It is true that the Hydra cheers
through its ten-thousand throats, so roars
of joy spread out across the darkening Moor
                from St James' football ground
where sudden exploding flowers
or seedheads scatter their spores
of light against the dusk above the Moor
                with festive thunder-sound:

but the student remains a constant
perennial in this environment.

It is true that they are a threatened
species; their narrowing strand
of tidal ground between clear pools and the sea
                must soon be overwhelmed,
but the student seems unalarmed.
The fleet androgynous young run hand in hand,
or play, at midnight, in the New Year snow,
                and survive by being transformed
to citizens: to doctors, chartered accountants,
authors, explorers, teachers, and even parents.

ANNA ADAMS
Nobodies, 1990 | *Open Doors: Selected Poems*, 2014

Temperance Festival: Town Moor, Newcastle

Licking ices on the Town Moor in the middle of Race Week,
A bob or two in our pocket and no end of cheek,
This is the time of our lives, so come on chaps,
Come and see the girls with the kiss-me caps.

Come on, Neddie, who's your pick-up,
The one with the squint or the one with the hiccup?
The Ghost Train's starting, if you're out for a lark
There's nothing like a bit of slap and tickle in the dark.

Come on, girls, on the figure-of-eight,
I've got the tickets and the chap won't wait,
Hold on, hinney, hold on tight,
What's the use of loving if you don't love right?

Come and smell the tigers, come and smell the zoo,
You hold me, and I'll hold you.
We've lost Tom Rutherford, and Chinese Ben
Is looking for his mother in the lost kids' pen.

The three-headed woman, the five-legged goat,
The Zulu with the daggers sticking in his throat,
The mysteries of Paris, the performing fleas,
And old fat Kate on the big trapeze,
The lady wrestlers with their writhing muscles,
The Siamese Twins with the whalebone bustles –
We ain't seen nothing, and we'll soon be dead,
Come and heave a brick and chuck a lady out of bed.

Hoopla, jugglers, the Wall of Death,
The fortune-teller with the beery breath,
The man with the tail, and a face like a toad,
– Or come and see the lights on the Great North Road?
Come on, kiddie, the grass won't grow,
The cat won't tell and your mother won't know.

– I knew a chap who came in on a boat,
He had a monkey who got him by the throat –
Chuck it hinney.
                I knew a kid,
Burned herself to death on Byker Tip she did.

   The lads of the village were up at dawn
   With nothing to sell and nothing to pawn,
   Nothing to break and nothing to mend,
   Squatting on their hunkers at the four-ways end.

Then there was the one on Jarrow Slake.
Stole five bob and didn't get a break.

   Jennie's had a kid, and she can't come;
   Liz works late, and Nell drinks rum;
   Kath got pinched in the British Home Stores
   With five pair of knickers and some woollen drawers.

Come and see the clowns – they ain't half low –
And the Hottentots from Cardiff in a Show-Boat show,

– I knew a chap sold tips for the Plate,
Made five quid just standing at the gate –

Come on, Sal, come on, Gert,
You ain't seen fun if you ain't seen dirt.

See you in the morning, see you in the church,
See you down in Byker and leave you in the lurch.
Ha'way, lads!

MICHAEL ROBERTS
Orion Marches, 1939

Poet, critic and editor, **Michael Roberts** (1902–1948) taught at the Royal Grammar School in Newcastle for 16 years after 1925, apart from an interval in the early 30s in London. Oddly enough, one of the fellow boarders in his Jesmond guest-house in 1925 was Biggles author Captain W.E. Johns. Later, Roberts lived at Red Lodge in Longbenton, now gone, where he papered a wall up to the ceiling with rejection slips. Subsequently, his anthologies *New Signatures* (1932) and *New Country* (1933), containing work by William Empson, Auden, Spender, Day-Lewis and others, had made him, in T.S. Eliot's phrase, 'expositor and interpreter of the poetry of his generation'. Roberts edited the influential *Faber Book of Modern Verse* (1936).

In 1935 Roberts married Janet Adam Smith (1905–1999), also a gifted writer and anthologist (as well as a renowned champion of Scottish literature). She was the editor of *The Faber Book of Children's Verse* and had been assistant editor of *The Listener* in 1933, when she incurred the wrath of the formidable Lord Reith, the BBC Director General, by having Auden's poem 'The Witnesses' printed in the magazine's poetry supplement. Lord Reith found it incomprehensible.

The couple lived at 13 Fern Avenue, Jesmond, from June 1935 to April 1939, then at no. 73 for the birth of their second child, Henrietta (and still later in Penrith, 1939-41, when the RGS was evacuated). Janet Adam Smith wrote of those Newcastle years as 'a tale of poems, children, books, anthologies, reviews, climbing, ski-ing, school camps and holidays in Lakes, Highlands and Alps'.

Auden had written to Roberts in 1932 for advice on his teaching career and, later, about his play *The Ascent of F6*. On 27 September, 1937 he came to dinner at 13 Fern Avenue, Jesmond, when the couple's first baby Andrew was three weeks old. Always fascinated by medical matters, he talked much with the midwife in attendance, Nurse Laverick, and elicited a fund of stories drawn from her Newcastle experience.

Michael Roberts' own poetry is often about the mountains where he and his wife were very much at home, but 'HMS *Hero*' (see page 341) and 'Temperance Festival: Town Moor, Newcastle' have local interest – and 'Hymn to the Sun' begins:

> 'Voy wawm' said the dustman
> one bright August morning –
> but that was in Longbenton,
> under the trees.

[AM]

from Twelve Songs

O lurcher-loving collier, black as night,
Follow your love across the smokeless hill;
Your lamp is out, the cages are all still;
Course for heart and do not miss,
For Sunday soon is past and, Kate, fly not so fast,
For Monday comes when none may kiss:
Be marble to his soot, and to his black be white.

(June 1935)

W.H. AUDEN
Coal Face, 1935 | *Collected Poems*, 1976

Traditions
(The Hoppings, Newcastle upon Tyne)

Last night was the last: today
the lorries and dormobiles
are ready to go, the dodgems are stowed away,
dive bombers and ferris wheels
are packed as neat as biscuits. Jack the Ripper
is roping canvas, Dracula's Daughter brings
the baby's wind up, and the stripper
(naughty but nice) is clearing the breakfast things.

Where children play in the sun,
under the lights the servants of the Lord
advanced their placards against the Evil One:
they wake to Sunday, the promise of their reward
bright for another spell. But rich and poor
are points of reference here, not body and soul:
loud engines jam the larksong over the moor,
and the big trailers roll.

RICHARD KELL
The Broken Circle, 1981 | *Collected Poems 1962-1993*, 2001

The Hoppings

Time to run the futures' gauntlet, between
the fortune-tellers' Alice-banded caravans,
that open croc jaw pegged with wooden teeth
which promise to unsheathe your only truth,
the way their signs assure you of descent
from one prognosticator's faultless descant.

Each one must brew the facts from scattered fates
like rain impelled into neat glassy beads
between the petals of her brain. Walk on
through scent collisions – candy and adrenaline –
the airbrushed purple mouths on waltzers,
the horses grinning at the wurlitzer,
nearly extinct, this conjured hysterical shake
of all our children's sugared vertebrae.

But you're still reading from her freckled back,
that woman, strapless on a mattress, slack
outside a pair of mobile homes once seen
cornered with horses on a municipal green.
Heading for the helter skelter, you want to know
the one sharp life which she would not have told.

W.N. HERBERT
Bad Shaman Blues, 2006

Divisions

I

All aggro in tight clothes and skinhead crops
they think that like themselves I'm on the dole.
Once in the baths that mask of 'manhood' drops.
Their decorated skins lay bare a soul.

Teenage dole-wallah piss-up, then tattoos.
Brown Ale and boys' bravado numbs their fright –
MOTHER in ivy, blood reds and true blues
against that North East skin so sunless white.

When next he sees United lose a match,
his bovvers on, his scarf tied round his wrist,
his rash NEWCASTLE RULES will start to scratch,
he'll aerosol the walls, then go get pissed...

So I hope the TRUE LOVE on your arm stays true,
the MOTHER on your chest stays loved, not hated.

But most I hope for jobs for all of you –

next year your tattooed team gets relegated!

II

Wartime bunkers, runways overgrown,
streets named for the town's two England caps;
cricket played with shovelblade and stone,
the daylight's rotten props near to collapse.

HEALTH (H changed to W) FOR ALL
with its *Never Have Another Haemorrhoid*
is all that decorates the tap-room wall
of this pub for pensioners and unemployed.

The Brewery that owns this place supports
only the unambiguously 'male'
Northern working-class spectator sports
that suit the image of its butch *Brown Ale*,
that puts hair on your chest, and makes you fight,
and when you're legless makes a man of you!

The *Brown Ale* drinkers watch me as I write:

one front door orange in a row all blue!

TONY HARRISON
Continuous, 1981 | *Collected Poems*, 2007

Brazen Faces
(tune: 'The Blaydon Races')

We dandered roond bi Gallowget
When us went ti the toon
Nineteen hundred 'n' sivinty eight
On a Seterda efterneun.
Skinheads, yakkors, lud-brained louts,
The tousled haired disgraces,
Aall gannin' in ti St James' Park
Ti show wor brazen faces.

Oh, me lads, ye shud hev hord us yellin',
Offensive blue 'n' blasphemous
An' crude abeun the tellin'.
A bunch of hooligans ti blare
Aall wi' brazen faces
Ti mek folks wundor whaat the future
O' the human race is.

FRED REED
Northumbrian Voice, 1978 | *The Northumborman*, 1999

dander: saunter; *yakkor:* bloke, pitman, also hooligan; *gannin':* going; *abeun:* above, beyond.

Grainger Market

I

The colour scheme of remembering:
those white geese who lost their heads,
their necks paralysed by sudden loss of thought,
their bodies cold as snowmen.

Meat hooks, claws, rabbits hung by paws,
second-hand bookstalls, hams and eggs,
red-feathered hens, leather smells,
and cold damp hands, wiped pink.

Empty pigs beside trotters and snouts
that once were theirs. Butchers' fingers
in silver mincers, stained cleavers
on worn wooden blocks. Candles,

Dolly Mixtures, spiked brushes
propped outside hardware shops.
Women in headscarves laden with greens,
a juggle of juicy Jaffas.

Orange nylon nighties fluttering
from awnings, golden slippers
with cream fleece linings
and dark thick-soled socks.

II

We patrol the walls of Elswick
like guards of the ancient city
waiting to greet her bus.

Greedy for what she might have
we attack the fat Saturday bags
as soon as she alights.

III

She has been round all the stalls
in the thick expanding clatter
under that glittering glass,
tiptoeing sawdust, sidestepping clots,

weaving from the record shop
to Oliver's and Dodd's, past greeting cards,
the Penny Bazaar, Northern Opticals,
the flower stands and the Weigh House.

Through endless rows of fruit and veg
to rest her heavy bags and legs
by the plastic grass beside the caf'
before one last stop at Farnons

where she buys all our vests,
where you can get anything in white:
Communion dresses, pillows, sheets and nets,
all you need to keep body and soul intact.

Except those magic colouring books
she sometimes brings us back:
their grocery of greens,
barrows of reds;

just add water,
see the colours spread.

KATHLEEN KENNY
Firesprung, 2008

Gift of the Gab
(Grainger Market)

Closing time. The market traders wrap
their gifted tongues in greaseproof paper.
They transplant the vivid steaks

to cold drawers and the walk-in fridge,
from where now my granddad steps
with a chilled-blue face, calling last reductions.

His language is foreign to me.
I can't translate the weights and measures
on this avenue of butchers' shops.

It should be in my blood,
his knack for selling, his spiel and patter,
but I'm more at ease with the cleanliness

of what the market has become.
An emporium of the artisan: bistros,
vintage clothes and specialist obsessions,

cup cakes and paella dishes – silent
and arranged where the dead still slash
the sacks of sawdust open. They hang

rabbits like wrung-out rags,
singing with their strong tongues of kilogram
and stone, of shilling, pence and pound.

JOHN CHALLIS
Steps in Time, 2017

Street Song

Pink Lane, Strawberry Lane, Pudding Chare:
someone is waiting, I don't know where;
hiding among the nursery names,
he wants to play peculiar games.

In Leazes Terrace or Leazes Park
someone is loitering in the dark,
feeling the giggles rise in his throat
and fingering something under his coat.

He could be sidling along Forth Lane
to stop some girl from catching her train,
or stalking the grounds of the RVI
to see if a student nurse goes by.

In Belle Grove Terrace or Fountain Row
or Hunter's Road he's raring to go –
unless he's the quiet shape you'll meet
on the cobbles in Back Stowell Street.

Monk Street, Friars Street, Gallowgate
are better avoided when it's late.
Even in Sandhill and the Side
there are shadows where a man could hide.

So don't go lightly along Darn Crook
because the Ripper's been brought to book.
Wear flat shoes, and be ready to run:
remember, sisters, there's more than one.

FLEUR ADCOCK
Selected Poems, 1983 | *Poems 1960-2000*, 2000

A riddle on the steeple of St Nicholas's Cathedral, Newcastle

My Altitude high, my Body foure square,
My Foot in the Grave, my Head in the Ayre,
My Eyes in my sides, five Tongues in my Wombe,
Thirteen Heads upon my Body, four Images alone;
I can direct you where the Winde doth stay,
And I Tune Gods Precepts thrice a Day.
I am seen where I am not, I am heard where eye is not,
Tell me now what I am, and see that you misse not.

ANONYMOUS

This riddle on the steeple of St Nicholas's Church (now St Nicholas's Cathedral) was formerly attributed to **Ben Jonson**, who had visited Newcastle in 1618-19. It was published as Jonson's work in *Gentleman's Magazine* (1866) and appears in volume 11 of Jonson's *Complete Works* (1952) but with editors Herford and Simpson indicating that later scholarship had cast doubt on this.

Though bulky and getting on in years, Jonson walked all the way from London to Scotland to visit William Drummond of Hawthornden, near Edinburgh. He passed through Newcastle on his way north in August 1618, having bought a new pair of shoes in Darlington to replace those he had worn out: he was still wearing them when he came back through Newcastle in January 1619. John Taylor, the 'Water Poet', is thought to have burlesqued Jonson's enterprise in *Penniless Pilgrimage*, but Jonson, who met Taylor in Leith, good-naturedly gave him money to continue his journey. [AM/NA]

Thin Riddle

After the scrabble to the top,
   the scrape of hooves
      escaping over the cobbles

   soaks into stone
   and a cloak evaporates
from under a gaslamp.

Engines roll overhead.
   A Roman, or maybe Norman
      sentry watches on the wall

  while, in no time at all
 a boy in a flatcap
strikes a match against its ruins.

Spray-paint on masonry.
 Stroll back to the bottom
  where hen-dos huddle

  in the same strange archways
 as sea-weary sailors
and the neon kebab-light

illuminates a glossy top hat.
 A city riddled with cracks,
  spaces to slip between,

  where history lurks
 with the homeless under railway arches,
the way the pubs sit

in shadows of bridges. Metal rails
 press down from above, squeezing
  past against the present.

  A quick skip through time,
 a dog-leap. Look up and imagine
some adventurous terrier

daring the gap between windows.
 Except this is a spot
  where the crack has outlasted

  the rock, a thin riddle running
 through the foundation of the town
from quay to castle keep.

PETER HEBDEN
Steps in Time, 2017

According to legend, Bessie Surtees eloped on horseback up Dog Leap Stairs with John Scott, 1st Earl of Eldon (later Lord Chancellor of England), on 18 November 1772. The unusual name means 'a narrow slip of ground between houses'.

On Falling Up Dog Leap Stairs

Already your tongue's
checked your front teeth twice. One shin
is stinging, your forehead's intact

but those minutes you'd saved, precious
coins in your pocket, lie spent
on the steps. You notice your legs

have you upright again, and your feet,
ignoring the interruption,
have carried you on – suede-booted,

weightless – but now they've given in.
You're on your own, half-way up,
illuminated by a yellow lamp.

You hold on to what's left of your breath
they slowly exhale, listening for footsteps
not coming, still

not coming out of the dark, the silence above
and behind your thudding pulse. In the beats between
you offer a deal to the ancient

hiding close by, watching. Then you stop
having thoughts – you make a move, go
with what the shadow-cat in you knows, in her bones.

JOAN JOHNSTON
An Overtaking, 2016

Salvaging

This has grown a friendless town,
its open heart begins to close;
heavy plant is moved in
and more than slums go up in dust.

Doric columns, pediments as pale as Bamburgh sand,
clean acanthus, lose their order,
receding into concrete scenarios.
What we have long trusted
has been powdered and dispersed;
money has blackened every vision
of spire, bridge or castle –
the repeated grab of centuries.
Now imitation marble flakes
from shopfronts like dandruff:
one symptom of our rateable blight.

An old woman, in headscarf
and many-wintered coat, urges
her pram of sliced bread and tins uphill
through July heat; her face unsunned,
shadowed by gaslight on walls
where the paper would hang in desperate foliage,
she tries to dare
to cross the street, in this town
she once knew
as her own kitchen.

Places have been torn up by the roots,
and only the roots resist, secretly
among such abrupt excavations –
this cordial salvage of chamomile and goosefoot,
grass tufting itself from broken Flemish brick,
bearding rooftops and stairways
of our abandoned quarters:
white and yellow stars seeding
their green sky.

Grains of pollen are borne like menace
on windy fumes – let
things bud importunately
in planners' dreams.

RODNEY PYBUS
At the Stone Junction, 1978 | *Cicadas in Their Summers*, 1988

The Side

I tread the precipice of this descending city –
all twisting expectations, suspended
cunning vantages.
The very steepness of land falling
beneath arching currents of stone
down to water, conjures up
high stepped abutments of space;
its split levels force shifting
planes on my gaze, angled round
structures of brick, air and stone.
With the crucial obliqueness of city places,
this old quarter makes the mind
bend backwards: smell of fresh bread,
rank sewage in the gutters,
fever-carts groaning in the fog.

Shadows take substance from mass,
driving the street sinuously upward
where it should be anchored;
perpendiculars lose their hung strength,
foreground and distance fail to grip
and mesh: unendingly
the picture re-sets, for human scale,
its own vanishing-points.

RODNEY PYBUS
At the Stone Junction, 1978 | *Cicadas in Their Summers*, 1988

Down to the Waterline
(lyrics)

Sweet surrender on the quayside
You remember we used to run and hide
In the shadow of the cargoes I take you one time
And we're counting all the numbers down to the waterline

Near misses on the dogleap stairways
French kisses in the darkened doorways

A foghorn blowing out wild and cold
A policeman shines a light upon my shoulder

Up comes a coaster fast and silent in the night
Over my shoulder all you can see are the pilot lights
No money in our jackets and our jeans are torn
Your hands are cold but your lips are warm

She can see him on the jetty where they used to go
She can feel him in the places where the sailors go
When she's walking by the river and the railway line
She can still hear him whisper
Let's go down to the waterline

MARK KNOPFLER
Dire Straits, 1978

Mistress of the Crown

He would dock on the Tyne, lure me in, reel me
up Side to The Crown; time and again I'd resist
then give in to the promise of silk and port wine.

I'd leave my pinny on Paddy's Market, the fish-
gutters on their stalls, the bone-lasses on Butcher
Bank with a stench of Lort Burn at their doors.

I'd leave them on Breakneck Stairs to meet him
at Castle Keep; I'd turn my back at Black Gate
for the glister of Silver Street.

Each time he sailed I'd go down
to the river and feel it slap me like a mother
with tales of his Spanish bride.

I'd dream of mantillas, tortoiseshell peinetas,
petticoats that foam on the tide, flamenco roses
like blood-red dresses floating on the waterline.

I'd dream her on Dog Leap Stairs and leave her
at Castle Keep; I'd watch her from Lantern Tower
swirl down Pilgrim Street.

He would dock on the Tyne, lure me in, reel me
up Side to The Crown; time and again I'd resist
then give in to the promise of silk and port wine.

BERNADETTE McALOON
Steps in Time, 2017

One of Newcastle's oldest pubs, the Crown Posada was originally The Crown. The Spanish word 'Posada', meaning inn or resting place, was added in the 19th century when it was owned by a sea captain.

The Keel Row

As I went up Sandgate, up Sandgate, up Sandgate,
As I went up Sandgate I heard a lassie sing –

Weel may the keel row, the keel row, the keel row,
Weel may the keel row that my laddie's in!

He wears a blue bonnet, blue bonnet, blue bonnet,
He wears a blue bonnet, a dimple in his chin:

And weel may the keel row, the keel row, the keel row,
And weel may the keel row that my laddie's in!

c. 1770

TRADITIONAL
Northumberland Garland, ed. Joseph Ritson, 1793

Keels were large shallow-draught boats manned by keelmen which transported coal from the banks of the Tyne and Wear to collier ships waiting downriver.

Dol-li-a

Fresh aw cum frae Sandgate Street,
Dol-li, dol-li,
Maw best friends here to meet,
Dol-li-a,
Do-li the dil-len doll,
Dol-li, dol-li,
Dol-li the dillen doll,
Dol-li-a.

The Black Cuffs is gawn away,
Dol-li, dol-li,
And that will by a crying day.
Dol-li-a.

Dolly Coxon's pawned her shirt,
Dol-li, dol-li,
To ride upon the baggage cart.
Dol-li-a.

The Green Cuffs is cummin' in,
Dol-li, dol-li,
An' that'll make the lasses grin.
Dol-li-a.

(1790s)

TRADITIONAL
Rhymes of Northern Bards, 1812

Cuffs: different regiments' uniforms.

Fog on the Tyne
(lyrics)

Sittin' in a sleazy snack-bar
Suckin', sickly sausage rolls
Slippin' down slowly, slippin' down sideways
Think I'll sign off the dole

'Cause the fog on the Tyne is all mine, all mine
The fog on the Tyne is all mine
The fog on the Tyne is all mine, all mine
The fog on the Tyne is all mine

Could a copper catch a crooked coffin maker
Could a copper comprehend
That a crooked coffin maker is just an undertaker
Who undertakes to be a friend?

And the fog on the Tyne is all mine, all mine
The fog on the Tyne is all mine
The fog on the Tyne is all mine, all mine
The fog on the Tyne is all mine

Tell it to tomorrow, today will take its time
To tell you what tonight will bring
Presently we'll have a pint or two together
Everybody do their thing

We can swing together, we can have a wee wee
We can have a wet on the wall
If someone slips a whisper that it's simple sister
Slapped them down and slavered on their smalls

'Cause the fog on the Tyne is all mine, all mine
The fog on the Tyne is all mine
The fog on the Tyne is all mine, all mine
The fog on the Tyne is all mine

Fog on the Tyne is all mine, all mine
The fog on the Tyne is all mine
The fog on the Tyne is all mine, all mine
The fog on the Tyne is all mine

The fog on the Tyne is all mine, all mine
The fog on the Tyne is all mine
The fog on the Tyne is all mine, all mine
The fog on the Tyne is all mine

ALAN HULL
Lindsfarne, 1971

Big River
(lyrics)

Walking on cobble stone,
little bits of skin and bone
jumping on the tram car for a ride
I can remember then,
I was just a boy of ten
hanging out along the old quayside
not all the capstans and the cargo boats
and stevedores are gone
to where all the old ships go
but memories just like the seas live on

That was when coal was king,
the river a living thing
and I was just a boy, but it was mine,
the coaly Tyne.

This was a big river,
I want you all to know that I was proud
this was a big river, but that was long ago,
that's not now, that's not now.

My father was a working man,
he earned our living with his hands.
He had to cross the river every day
he picked up a union card out of the Neptune yard.
Mouths to feed and the bills to pay
then came a time for him to sail
across the sea and far away.
Finally when the war was won
you brought him home and home he stayed.

And when his days were done,
under a golden sun
you carried him to where he longed to be,
back to the sea.

This was a big river,
I want you all to know that I was proud
this was a big river, but that was long ago,
that's not now

The Neptune was the last to go,
I heard it on my radio.
and then they played the latest number one
but what do they do all day?
And what are they supposed to say?
What does a father tell his son?
If you you believed that there's a bond
between our future and our past
then try to hold on to what we had,
we build them strong, we built to last

'cause this is a mighty town,
it's built upon solid ground
and everything they tried so hard to kill,
we will rebuild

This was a big river
I want you all to know that I was proud
this was a big river, but that was long ago,
that's not now
this is a big river,
And in my heart I know it will rise again
the river will rise again.

JIMMY NAIL
Big River, 1995

Tyneside, 1936
(a photograph by Humphrey Spender)

Darkness falling on the dead
quiet of the Quayside cobbles
where groups of laid-off men
in overcoats and flat black caps
are killing time, sad silhouettes,
lost shades waiting for the pubs to open.

The goods train tracks all lead
into the empty river, lit by a dying
winter sky's chaotic clouds, on which

the Victorian High Level and the static
black rainbow of the Great Tyne Bridge
define a total absence of animation.

Those men with useless hands in empty pockets
walk silently into the growing mists.
The Swing Bridge will not swing for them;
the distant lorries unloading beer barrels,
the moored freighter with smokeless stack
echo their aimlessness, a hopeless peace.

Among those groups of bitter ghosts, without
a job, without a name, waiting for another war,
is that my dead father I see walking there?

JAMES KIRKUP
Throwback, 1992

Bridging Loans

> Camden calls Newcastle, Ocellus, the eye of the north, the harth that warmeth the south parts of this kingdome with fire... This towne hath been famous in foure ages of the world.
>
> WILLIAM GRAY, *Chorographia* (1649)

Backlit by the caustic flare of neon
they mix together at dusk, like a film dissolve
not carried through, and filtered
through a half-life span of memories.
At midnight bridges, water, lights gleam
and blare speciously, like a politician's cant
of a northern Venice.
Even in sunlight they mingle,
the bridges, now airlocked in their intense patterning.
High-slung or low-swinging,
or Victorian Stephenson-solid – these three bridges
yoke me to childhood and native parts,
when Durham was a foreign land
across a thin fingering sea: their foundations
rooted deeper than family.

Each bridge a chare into the past:
stone, iron, water, form
my city's outlasting triptych.
Horizontals and verticals sprung
into the twin arcs of the Tyne Bridge –
a steely sea-green rainbow promising gold
at neither end.
Somewhere above the river
the fulcrum of two counties preserves
balance and imbalance:
of Duke and Prince Bishop, rich and poor,
North and South. And the affluence
rides its own discharge
on the regiment of grudging tides –
the rusty old saga of the North.

Each well-keeled bridge implies
land fissured by water and the conjunction
of lands that never quite meet, a cracked
region stapling the map of its self-doubts,
and the severance of my needs from what is.
Traffic back-tracking across and above
the course of ships – cross-currents fix
the angles and axes of my life: a way out
and a road in, flight and return. An illusion
of control over the hours that seep
under arches. Reflection speeds them.
They support an eternity of migrations,
endure the corrosion of possibilities.
Routes across the graves of travellers
who never went, paths across water,
mediating between us and our indifferent selves,
hyphenating what we love to hate.
Below them, liquid echoes float like exhaust fumes
from invisible black sails.

Now sepia and foggy blankness laps
over the memory of salmon teeming like silver
bars into the nets,
or bridges built and tumbled,
the spans and abutments of centuries:
a medieval Pontevecchio stiffened by the stumps
of the *Pons Aelii*, mid-river bartering and flourish

of tradesmen in wooden shops;
the traffic of horses and pilgrims drawn northwards
by Our Lady of Jesmond drowned, sinking
into the scalding roar of iron and steam,
the life and death spasms of the Victorian
Juggernaut. After wood and stone, crafted by men
but fallen to fire and *sudden inundations,*
have come steel links that weld now
concrete to concrete. Craftless, total
images of despair. No forging.
It's commerce builds bridges, makes certain
contacts, money, contracts, all
the profitable placements of industrial generals –
bridges which soon no man will dare to cross
to reach his empty cell: *fortiter defendit triumphans*
the capital that's spent.

They did, remember, manufacture
the longest swing-bridge in the world
to let Italians sail the world's biggest gun –
one hundred and four killer tons –
to Spezia, from Armstrong's upriver rural
Elswick. And that bridge Victoria opened
with a gracious, imperial gesture, clanged
shut on the keelmen's life.
As one bridge shuts another closes – that's always
been the Geordie's joke of self-betrayal.

Three tales of Tyne bridges deserve
resurrection and testimonial:

Seven hundred years ago those who offered to help repair the old bridge destroyed by fire were promised prayers and indulgences by the Bishop of Waterford, Ireland. Whose the favours?

Five hundred years ago a bearded recluse on the bridge sang in his hermitage for the soul of the late Roger Thornton, not to mention the twenty-nine other priests– figure how many desperate requiescats *for six marks a year?*

In the Tower on the old Tyne Bridge poor Harry Wallis, master shipwright, was remanded in his cups for telling the honourable Alderman Barnes to 'Piss Off!' Hung over in his cell above the river, he found a quantity of malt, and in disgust shovelled it out of the window –

>   *'Oh base mault'* he groaned
>   *'Thou didst the fault,*
>   *And into the Tyne thou shalt...'*
> *'What ails you, Harry Wallis?'* laughed the keelman down below.

Dog-Leap Stairs and Break-Neck Stairs tumble
down the streets to water, sprinkled with the blackened
brick and stone, crooked names crouching
round breathless corners. Names afraid
to hear the delving rampage of bulldozers
set loose on the homely fabric of citizens.
Some already buried for ever – All-Hallow-Pant
in the Foot of The Side; vanished like steam,
the cries from Pudding Chare –
'A nice black pudden, man!'
'A nice hot pudden, hinnie!'
'A nice fat pudden, smoken het, ma jewel!' –
and Painter Heugh below Nether Dean Bridge,
when boats sailed high into the old city,
up the gullied veins of the Tyne, to moor
in its heart. And the buildings of ageing, golden stone
fresh-skinned of their sooty patina,
whose fastidious yet sturdy delights
are now obscured, overlooked by the thousand
blank eyes of monolithic grey:
the towering slaughter of innocent vistas.
Yet spires will needle the smoky blue.

There's a sourness in that water now,
a river whose palm has been greased
by the coinage of the century, the slick
of departing life.
In a dark light, where dank timber staithes
and quays cast shadows beyond their reach,
the water even moves like oil-waste, drudging
and sucking at its own depths, and scummed
with the flotsam of aborted hopes.
The sprightly freshness of sea and river
congealed in sludge
now bears the stench of industrial catacombs.
From those depths over the years have come
Roman altars, coins, and prayers to Neptune
and Oceanus, marked with trident, anchor, dolphin

and gratitude; golden rings recovered
from the bellies of trapped salmon by some tale-spinner
who conned Herodotus and his friends...

Those medieval arches sustained bookshops, mercers,
cheesemongers and cobblers, above trading ships
stuffed with cargoes of pepper and ginger,
lead, wool and hides, toing and froing
from this shivering ultimate colonial Samarkand.
And coal, always coal. Mined from the seized heart.
Pennies, carbon-cold, lie on the tongues of the dead
and the living. Death has dusted the yellow
of their phlegm. Its gold built bridges, ships
and shops, respectable mansions, filled the Quayside
with trade figures in top hats, and paid painters
for their celebrations: there are not many portraits
of pitmen or keelmen gracing
our marbled civic galleries.
The gilt has been unfairly doled.
But even wood and stone were weak in the face
of brute water: and after the deluge, iron and steel.
In every High Level pile is sealed
the thunder-bolting heartbeat
of Nasmyth's Titanic Steamhammer,
whose tonned smashes at sixty a minute
made the pile-heads flame like iron matches,
bellowing louder than Railway King Hudson's war
against Isambard Kingdom Brunel.
It's a pallid echo now as the InterCity sidles
into the Central Station.

Swing open contrarily
into reflections: on Turner's exploding
moonlight. No keels, no
cinematic Barge Day processions now
up and down river, trumpeting its life-blood.
Precious few ships at all – we have come to that.
Few seamen to drink the 'Baltic' dry, or mourn
the empty grave of the 'Anchor'
weighed for ever, where we bought mussels
and bootlaces with our beer,
and plied the mad fiddler.
No 'Tommy on the Bridge' in Stan Laurel gear,

scrounging coins in mid-river, feeding
stingy ha'pennies to the fish,
dodging the police with a shifty, nifty sidestep
over the mid-Tyne boundary
and back again.
It's Sunday sees the pulse and bustle now
of trade and barter at Paddy's quayside market –
Indian carpet-sellers with Geordie accents
and Brown Ale wit; microscopic goldfish
circling in plastic bags, and the gibberish
of exotic moth-eaten finches, caged by the dozen;
surplus of Army Surplus, warm bags
of chips like white snails slumped
in their own grease; all the formica, tinny kitsch
that's bright – barrows beckoning a thousand bargains
fallen from the back of a hundred lorries;
the odd solar topi from colonial days,
dirty Edwardian postcards or World War One
binoculars with the green trench-mould of Flanders,
antique Queen Elizabeth Coronation mugs.
All meet for an easy sneer, but the life's there
on Sunday mornings, to the tune of pock-marked
clicking solos from Tauber seventy-eights.
Sunday shoals swarm the riverside, ready
for the catch-penny, purse-mouths open.

I look again at that million-pound Tyne Bridge,
strutting Sydney harbour prototype,
opened by the golden key of George the Fifth:
that steel-arch bowstring's taut
enough still with optimism to lend
a spurious tension to the numbness.
Yet it doubles typically its sodium lights
with old street-lamps in pairs, like illuminated
belt and faulty braces.
And who does ride now
up one of my grandfather's blunt grey lift-towers
for a view of multistorey car parks,
multistorey offices, multistorey sewage,
and multistorey millionaires too far away to see?

Beneath all that soaring overcast of steel
I often stand on the desolate quayside and glower

at the broken promises of bridges.
I scuff the sleazy cobbles, summoning bile.
People, cars, lorries, swish by me
like parts of speech to a deaf man or the rumble
of syntax to a man struck dumb:
were – used to be – could have been –
will be – might have been –
We read of suicides who leap vainly
from these bridges into the imagined grave of the Tyne;
and need their stomachs flushed
for another day.
The power of those bridges over water,
over me, is mighty. But might-be,
might-be, is what I catch
from the drab wake of their refractions.
Only the Swing Bridge turning still opens up
the possibility of possibilities.
Too often I go on looking at that wanting space
that no bridge spans: the leaking interregnum
of the present.

RODNEY PYBUS
The River Project, 1974 | *Bridging Loans*, 1976

Passed By

Scented ghosts: spice from a dry Orient,
the greasy tang of whalers;
men sweat under the fruits
of distant trading.

Sailors moor their curses
in this ultimate Samarkand;
smiling merchants pass coin,
fondle their percentages.

Downstream, echoes from the shouting boy
on grubby-sailed keel:
surprise of his white smile.
Coal-dust billows on the labouring quay,
moonlight brazing the sky.

Salmon barter for space with their own silver
teeming, slip clear waters
through wood and stone.
Men pass over bridges with their women
clutching their dreams.

January, and the river sets
into curdled rock;
screws the month tight
till the hunger-pangs bite.

RODNEY PYBUS
At the Stone Junction, 1978 | *Cicadas in Their Summers*, 1988

Down the Town

Glass and concrete towers move
into their own shadows, dwarfing
battlements and an obelisk spire
of thwarted delicacy: the eye shifts
to replenish the filigree of stone
with its due transparency.

A tiled roof-top sprouts broken aerial
and a smudge of plants
against the declining light;
the old warehouses, empty of hide and bark,
crack-windowed above the cobbles.
Strings drop from the curved bridge
to hidden waters;
stranded railings portcullis the sun, swept
by a tidal clatter of starlings.

On grimy neo-classical
night has seemingly always fallen,
as it comes now, slowly,
on All Saints and its yard of troubled dead.
The weathercock shifts and sighs
at the flung clouds,
of rain and unseen changings.

Below, spaces of spanned clearance
where names tell lies: a dumb Cowgate,
a silent Stockbridge.
The lying derelict of it all.

Somewhere there has to be a true dwelling,
to hold that infant's telling cry,
a dog's chained barking.

RODNEY PYBUS
At the Stone Junction, 1978 | *Cicadas in Their Summers*, 1988

Where Home Started

I used to cross the Tyne to school. Days raced
on a rattling, crowded bus, hands gripping
fingered chrome, knees braced against straining seats.
Once, reading *The Return of the Native*
in too-dull light – the Tyne below Scotswood,
dark and silent under the bus's roar –
wheels left the road and we slipped down a bank
to halt feet away from lapping water.
Cocooned in gabardine, I was handed
out through the upturned emergency door,
clutching my satchel.

Then, while the shipyard lads lit cigarettes,
we huddled, stamping, at the river's edge,
watched the steady lights of a pilot boat
speed uptide, bringing in cargo too big
to go it alone, and a police launch
on its routine patrol. Still shivering
in near-dark, I could smell the river tang,
sense submerged lives and deaths, feel a current
pull, inside me, as it does whenever
I think of home. Whatever depths there were,
we never reached them.

ROBYN BOLAM
Hyem, 2017

The Devil's Destroying Angel Exploded

    no sound
but horns of Southern ships
    and flapping wings

no colour
    but dancing black

producers of heat
    confused in the cold

moon full above the dole

    sleep children of chilled night
whose fathers were black men

    sleep bairns, shiver now
ya fathers' gold is stolen

strong fathers of a harsh past
    despondent now
slag faces rot against the dole

your hands held hammers
    & demanded much
the moment passed
    bairns curled cad in the womb

    you worried troops and churches
suffocated in the Durham bishop's stables
    when Londonderry's jails were full

    the coal you hewed
should have burnt them alive
instead you begged another shilling

    you should have thrown it
in their faces like a bomb
    fed your children joyful stories

    of the blood of those
who cheat us

where we live
shattered smiles
   break on haggard faces

   manufacturers of filth
marry our wealth
   in a confetti of votes

no breath of slum air

councillor, elected by my father,
   he said you wore a worker's cap
called everybody *marra*
   the word I heard was slave

bloodfluke in the brain of an ant
   that gold chain scraped
from the lungs of pitmen

your gown is a union leader
   gutted and reversed

   look dozy fathers look
your masters have changed
   drawn by the rivermist
you drift in a dream

ah father, your flesh is overrun with lice
and all your life you nurtured many parasites

TOM PICKARD
The Order of Chance, 1971 | *hoyoot: Collected Poems and Songs*, 2014

When first published this poem included a reference under the title to the painter John Martin (1789–1854), whose apocalyptic landscapes were inspired by the rugged Northumberland landscape and the forges and ironworks of the Tyne valley he would have known in his youth.

I Looked Down On a Child Today

I looked down on a child today, not because he or she was smaller than me
or because I was being in my middle-aged way bairnbarren and condescending
but because he or she was dying or dead between the kerbstone and the wheel

I stepped down from the steps of a 39 bus today with sudden blood on my shoes
The lesions and lessons and the languorous long-winged stiff-winged fulmars
chalked against the sky and white against the unpainted lips of her

I looked down at a child today, Gallowgate, the bus was turning left
the child stepped out, leaving its mam's hand behind partly swept by the wind
and partly by blind wonderful enthusiasm for life we guard against increasingly

She stepped into the path of something she or he would never know forever
in an elegant but unassuming place where as a living they hanged prisoners
       for bread-theft
it was the eve of St Valentine's Day on the wild side of Geordieland

The white dresses were being collected from dry cleaners Darn Crook to
       Sidgate
the strategy of the masses was being unaddressed once more except through
       the tills
where paper receipts come clicking out increasingly slowly to everyone's
       annoyance

What a beautiful, brilliant day, tart with expectation of love and romance in
       Chinatown
or down the Bigg Market as lager casks were moved into station and the
       dance floors cleaned
I looked down at a child today, never having had one of my own, and having
       no kid

I can call mine in a very old-fashioned romantic Barry MacSweeney Elvis
       Orbison Highway 61 way
O Robert it was almost where you left on the bus O Aaron O Dusty O
       Blackened Eyelids
I looked down upon a child today under the buswheels and knew whatever
       your name you would see

heaven and it would shine and be filled with pianos and trumpets and not be
       suppressed

and freedom would be written in moth-dust on every angel's wings
and there will be the music of Shostakovitch and Poulenc when you wanted
> to hear it

and the monumental poetry of MacDiarmid and Mahon and all spirits would
> gather there
and tell you when you awake again what lemonbalm was and you and say
I looked down on a child and bonnybairn in blood today the day before St
> Valentine's Day

(Newcastle, 13 February 1998)

BARRY MACSWEENEY
Wolf Tongue, 2000

Barry MacSweeney (1948–2000) was born in Newcastle and attended Broadwood primary school and Rutherford Grammar School. He left school at 16 to join the Newcastle *Evening Chronicle* as a cub reporter (where he met Basil Bunting, one of the paper's sub-editors), and subsequently worked on several provincial newspapers, including the *South Kentish Times*, Darlington's *Evening Dispatch* and the *South Shields Gazette*. He contracted the journalist's industrial disease, alcoholism, which eventually cost him his life.

MacSweeney started writing early, and was part of – and influenced by – Newcastle's lively literary and cultural scene during the 1960s: involved with Morden Tower, hosting a chaotic poetry festival at Sparty Lea in Allendale in the summer of 1967, and running his own imprint, Blacksuede Boot Press (he was a sharp dresser). His own view of poetry was formed round a myth of failure and belated recognition, somewhat on the lines of Rimbaud. He also detested the destruction of communities and the consequent impact on individual lives. He contrasted social and personal crisis with exalted recollections of a natural world of plants, creatures and the elements.

MacSweeney published more than two dozen titles between 1968 and 1999. These included *Black Torch* (1977), which deals with North-East working-class culture and political dissent in mining communities from the Industrial Revolution to the 1970s, while *Ranter* (1985) reflects on the Levellers and other dissenting figures. His later sequence *Pearl* (1995), often tender or celebratory, evoked the figure of a mute childhood sweetheart from Allendale, and was reprinted with *The Book of Demons* (1997), his last substantial collection, where he projects himself as a hapless yet percipient victim of the demon drink, in writing which is both comic and terrifying. He had almost completed the preparation of a retrospective selection of his work at the time of his death, *Wolf Tongue: Selected Poems 1965-2000*, later published posthumously by Bloodaxe in 2003. See pages 253-54 for two *Pearl* poems. [AM/NA]

Baltic Mill

Though you maintain the elements
have conspired against us we still
inch the cobbled street past Castle
Keep down to the Quayside's rain-
slick paving slabs all for the whim
of standing across from Baltic Mill
in a turbid mist lifted from the Tyne.

We planned to catch a talk at the Laing
or the Biscuit but, pushed for time,
plumped for a backstreet pizzeria, throw-
back to another world, a haberdasher's
maybe or greasy spoon for blackface
minstrels from Gateshead mines and
iron works. The North Sea wind-chill

bids us leave behind this city of faces
cast in stories passed down, vestige
of years when hundreds of miles stood
between us. The exact course that brought
us here is unimportant. It is that we met
like this river, drawn from two sources,
offered up our flaws, our sedimental selves.

KAYO CHINGONYI
Bedford Square 5, 2011 | *Kumukanda*, 2017

Treading Water

I was birthed in the Tyne on a fluorescent buoy
kept afloat by its placenta. Both of us ballooned.

My eye a coin of seagulls, mothering.

We all come out of these wombs
swimming: for six months we can breathe like that.

On his lunch my father threw crumbs from the Biscuit Factory.
A prayer I'd stay afloat. To begin with there were warm cookies.

Those first Sundays people with cameras came. Snapped me
screaming on my back. Like an apple bobbing before the pie.

I lay as a longboat twisting to reach our old Valhalla –
my plastic mother drowned below. The first word was anemone.

I farmed myself: a kick for every Christmas day
I wouldn't sit under a moulting tree. Some tried to baptise me

from the river banks, and The Baltic where locals looked out
from sky-top floors. Binoculars to count the salt I cupped.

Umbilically I was a long line of fishermen and lasses.
A northern starfish. A pink, fleshed bomb waiting for my tail to grow.

I smiled gums for ships I'd one day sink.
I hovered in the river mouth, touching neither one side nor the other.

JEN CAMPBELL
The Hungry Ghost Festival, 2012

The West End

This is the place where men
throw gobs of phlegm
at ladies' feet, though
they've never seen inside a mine
or any place of work enough
to warrant an industrial disease.

Netto lays on spectacle:
a moonfaced couple scrabble
with Security, locked in classic
wrestling pose between the aisles
of mushy peas and knockdown Belgian biscuits;
shoppers stare, but wander at their ease.

Thin women pushing buggies
roll their eyes at families
up ahead who speak too loud
a language they can't comprehend;
May sells mooli, bottle gourds,
English apples in dwindling varieties.

Here nothing looks familiar
under the single bulb. And we're
not sure if this is something new
or what we're facing is the end
and where, if we could rewrite
history, we might begin.

ELLEN PHETHEAN
Breath, 2009, 2014

Rebuilding the West

Today, there's a rainbow over Scotswood
protecting the cranes from the northern rain
so they can flatten the terraces again,
remix the tricks of my birthplace.
For the third time in my life Violet Walk
will be bulldozed. Cruddas Park drug dealers
and pimps, sellers of Tags from Thailand
will get new garden fences and fresh
urban views. In Benwell (home of the fifty
pee street), they'll build shopping centres
in the style of prisons, next door
to the enterprise park.

The *Chronicle* will burst with jobs,
as the men who have drunk their ship-
building skills in the Gold Cup will
wake up and smell the mortar and smell
the bricks they will carry for their Gosforth
bosses. The same men will plant
                                        barbs,
razor wire on the roof of the office

block that will cut the knees of their own
sons when they're twockin to get a fix,
the cost of which is a fax machine. But
today, there's a rainbow over Scotswood,
children are out, vandalising the new road.

STEVIE RONNIE
The Thing To Do When You Are Not In Love, 2008

from The Collier's Wedding

   Now all the country lads around,
That get their living under ground,
For to prepare themselves are told,
When *Tommy*'s wedding-day will hold:
The maids have warning, friends beside
Must all be there to mense the bride
At *Benwell*, at her mother's house,
For *Tommy* gave the bride her choice,
The wedding-dinner must be there,
Provided with the greatest care.
Now joy in every face is seen,
The lads are pleased, the lasses keen:
Old men, and wives, do all declare,
They'll come to taste the bridegroom's fare.
[...]

   Tom comes in trumph o'er the plain,
With collier lads, a jolly train;
They smoke along the dusty way,
Whips crack for joy; the horses play,
The bridegroom rides in state before,
'Midst clouds of dust the bagpipes roar,
The echo's born on wings of air,
Make all the *Benwell* folks prepare:
Like streamers in the painted sky,
At every breast the favours fly.
[...]

   They all rise up, and think it time

To haste for church, the clock struck nine.
Two lusty lads, well dressed and strong,
Stept out to lead the bride along:
And two young maids of equal size,
As soon the bridegroom's hands surprise.
The pipers wind and take their post,
And go before to clear the coast:
Then all the vast promiscuous crowd,
With thundering tongues, and feet as loud,
Toss up their hats, clap hands, and hollow,
And mad with joy, like *Bedlam* follow;
Some shout the bride, and some the groom,
Till just as mad, to church they come;
Knock, swear, and rattle at the gate,
And vow to break the beadle's pate,
And call his wife a bitch and whore,
They will be in, or break the door;
There rave and tear, and make a noise,
Like rude distracted fools or boys.
[…]

   At last the beef appears in sight,
The groom moves slow the pond'rous weight;
Then haste is made, the table clad,
No patience till the grace is said.
Swift to the smoking beef they fly,
Some cut their passage through a pie;
Out streams the gravy on the cloth;
Some burn their tongue with scalding broth:
But rolling spices made them fain;
They shake their heads, and sup again.
Cut up that goose, cries one below,
And send us down a leg, or so:
A honest neighbour tries the point,
Works hard but cannot hit a joint;
The bride sat nigh, she rose in prim,
And cut, and tore her limb from limb.
   Now geese, cocks, hens their fury feel,
Extended jaws devour the veal;
Each rives and eats what he can get,
And all is fish that comes to net.
No qualmish appetites here sit,
None curious for a dainty bit.

The bridegroom waits with active force,
And brings them drink 'twixt every course,
With napkin round his body girt,
To keep his clothes from grease or dirt,
With busy face he runs about
To fill the pots which are drunk out.
[...]

Now all are full, the meat away,
The table drawn, the pipers play.
The bridegroom first assumes the floor,
And dances all the maidens o'er;
The rubs his face, and makes a bow,
So marches off, what can he do?
He must not tire himself outright,
The bride expects a dance at night.
In every room, both high and low,
The fiddlers play, the bagpipes blow;
Some shout the bride, and some the groom,
They roar the very music dumb.
Hand over head, and one through other,
They dance with sister and with brother:
Their common tune is *Get her bo*,
The weary lass cries, music so:
Till tired in circling round they wheel,
And beat the ground with toe and heel.
[...]

And thus the day in pleasure flies,
Till shining *Phoebus* quits the skies.
The gladsome night doth now approach;
The barrels found, no more to broach;
There's but a pipe for every one,
The dear tobacco's almost gone;
The candles in their sockets wink,
Now sweal, now drop, then die and stink,
Intoxicating fumes arise,
They reel and rub their drowsy eyes;
Dead drunk, some tumble on the floor,
And swim in what they drank before.
Hickup, cries one, reach me your hand,
The house turns round, I cannot stand.
So now the drunken senseless crew
Break pipes, spill drink, piss, shit and spew.

The sleepy hens now mount their balk,
Ducks quack, flap wings, and homeward walk;
The lab'ring peasant, weary grown,
Embraces night, and trudges home;
The posset made, the bride is led
In great procession to her bed;
The females with an edict come
That all the men depart the room,
On pain of scandal and disgrace,
If any one stay in the place.
The proclamation is obeyed,
The men walk out till she be laid,
But with this cautious reprimand
The posset should have leave to stand,
Be unmolested, feel no lip
Nor any one attempt to sip;
They all declare they'll be accursed
If bride and bridegroom drink not first.

   When young and old, and all are out,
They shut the doors and spy about;
A general search is quickly made
Lest any lie in ambuscade;
So when they think all places sure,
And holes and corners all secure,
That none could see, nor none could hear,
Nor none rush in to make them fear;
The one, far wiser than the rest,
Who knew their way of wedding best,
Steps up to *Jenny* bathed with tears,
And thus with counsel fills her ears:
Come, wipe your face, for shame, don't cry;
We all were made with men to lie;
And *Tommy*, if I guess but right,
Will make you have a merry night.
Be courteous, kind, lie in his arms,
And let him rifle all your charms;
If he should rise, do you lie still,
He'll fall again, give him his will:
Lie close, and keep your husband warm,
And as I live, you'll get no harm;
Be mannerly in every posture;
Take this advice from *Nanny Forster*.

Thus spoke, she ran, and catched the bowl
Where currant cakes in ale did roll;
Then with a smile said, *Jenny*, lass,
Come, here's thy health without a glass.
Her arm supports it to her head,
She drinks, and gobbles up the bread;
So everyone their courses took,
Some watch, for fear the men should look:
Their hasty promise soon was broke
For they must either drink or choke.

Now some prepare t' undress the bride,
While other tame the posset's pride;
Some loose her head, and some her stays,
And so undress her sundry ways;
Then quickly lay the bride in bed,
And bind the ribbon round her head:
Her neck and breasts are both displayed,
And every charm in order laid.

Now all being ready for *Tom*'s coming,
The doors are opened by the women;
Impatient Tommy rushes in,
And thinks that they have longsome been:
The maids unwilling to withdraw;
They must go out, for that's the law.

Now *Tommy* next must be undressed;
But which of them can do it best?
It is no matter, all assist,
Some at his feet, some at his breast:
Soon they undress the jolly blade,
And into bed he's fairly laid.

Between the sheets now view this pair,
And think what merry work was there;
The stocking thrown, the company gone,
And *Tom* and *Jenny* both alone:
No light was there but *Jenny*'s charms,
And *Tom* all those in his own arms.

Now he is master of his wishes,
And treats her with a thousand kisses:

Young *Tommy* cocked, and *Jenny* spread,
So here I leave them both in bed.

(1729)

EDWARD CHICKEN
The Collier's Wedding, 1779 edition

Edward Chicken (1698-1746) lived opposite the Three Tuns (demolished 1907) on the corner of Low Friar Street and Newgate Street in Newcastle. Like his parson brother, he was educated at St John's charity school, and later became a teacher himself. Regarded as man of wisdom in the town, he arbitrated minor disputes and became known as 'The Mayor of White Cross' after the ancient monument close by. He was also clerk of St John's Church for 25 years, and was buried there. Written in 1729, his long poem *The Collier's Wedding* was said to have circulated widely in manuscript before a transcription of the text, with dialect phrasing regularised, was finally published many years after Chicken's death, probably in 1764. This remarkably frank poem (unthinkable in the next century) offers fascinating glimpses of marriage observances in the coalfield. The drunken wedding reception is described with startling realism, while even the church ceremony is somewhat rowdy: 'For some perhaps that were three score / Were never in a church before.' [AM/NA]

About Benwell

Perhaps there will always be yellow buses
passing and Presto's
and people with faces like broken promises

and shops full of stotties and butties and buckets and bubble bath
and bones for broth
where the poor may inherit the earth

and women who will
wade into the wind and waste with hope eternal
and kids like saplings planted by the Council

and William Armstrong's endless line
of bairns, whose names, in sandstone,
rehabilitate their streets of rag and bone

where bits of paper, bottle tops and Pepsi cans blow up and down
despondently, like souls on their own.
Perhaps there will always be unremembered men

and maps of Old Dunston and Metroland and the rough blown rain
and the riding down of the sun
towards Blaydon.

GILLIAN ALLNUTT
Blackthorn, 1994 | *How the Bicycle Shone*, 2007

After the Blaydon Races

Look how the big yellow bus of the sun bowls breakneck into
      Benwell also.

Shall it not, for a while, be still, with its wheel flown off?

Shall the old yellow bus, October, stop and beautifully steep us
in its pennyworth of ale, its picnic

cloth of gold unfolded on the rough grass?

Look how it briskly bowls by the rough sky-grass where houses were
and the forgotten, poor, affectionate people are,

berates us not as does the law in its bald helicopter

but, like that ribald bus on its breakneck way to Blaydon,
braves us, hedging bets

before our houses, waving, wild at heart and unrepentant
as the river, with its staithes and bridges.

GILLIAN ALLNUTT
Blackthorn, 1994 | *How the Bicycle Shone*, 2007

The Blaydon Races

Aa went to Blaydon Races, 'twas on the ninth of Joon,
Eiteen hundred an' sixty-two, on a summer's efternoon;
Aa tyuk the bus frae Balmbra's, an' she wis heavy laden,
Away we went 'lang Collin'wood Street, that's on the road to Blaydon.

CHORUS (REPEAT BETWEEN EACH VERSE):
Ah me lads, ye shudda seen us gannin',
We pass'd the foaks alang the road just as they wor stannin';
Thor wis lots o' lads an' lassies there, aal wi' smiling faces,
Gannin' alang the Scotswood Road, to see the Blaydon Races.

We flew past Airmstrang's factory, and up to the Robin Adair,
Just gannin' doon te the railway bridge, the bus wheel flew off there.
The lassies lost their crinolines off, an' the veils that hide their faces,
An' aw got two black eyes an' a broken nose gannin' te Blaydon Races.

When we gat the wheel put on away we went agyen,
But them that had their noses broke they cam back ower hyem;
Sum went to the Dispensary an' uthers to Doctor Gibbs,
An' sum sought out the Infirmary to mend their broken ribs.

Noo when we gat to Paradise thor wes bonny gam begun;
Thor was fower-an-twenty on the bus, man, hoo they danced an' sung;
They called on me to sing a sang, aa sung them 'Paddy Fagan',
Aa danced a jig an' swung my twig that day aa went to Blaydon.

We flew across the Chain Bridge reet into Blaydon toon,
The bellman he was callin' there, they call him Jackie Broon;
Aa saw him talkin' to sum cheps, an' them he was pursuadin'
To gan an' see Geordie Ridley's concert in the Mechanics' Hall at Blaydon.

The rain it poored aall the day an' mayed the groons quite muddy,
Coffy Johnny had a white hat on – they war shootin' 'Whe stole the cuddy'.
There wis spice stalls an' munkey shows an' aud wives selling ciders,
An' a chep wiv a hapenny roond aboot, shootin' 'Noo, me lads, for riders'.

[REPEAT CHORUS]

GEORDIE RIDLEY
Allan's Tyneside Songs, 1891

George 'Geordie' Ridley (1835–1864) was a Tyneside concert hall song writer and performer. He was sent to Oakwellgate Colliery as a trapper-boy at around the age of eight, but soon moved on to the Goose Pit (The Gyuess), where he worked for ten years. Working next as a waggon-rider for Hawks, Crawshay and Co (see 'Maw Bonny Gyetside Lass', page 335), he was crushed by a wagon, leaving him unfit for manual work. For the last five years of his life he trod the boards of first the Grainger Music Hall, as a singer of Irish comic and old Tyneside songs, before switching to the Wheatsheaf Music Hall (previously Balmbra's, later the Oxford). Ridley sang the song which became Tyneside's adopted anthem at a concert in Balmbra's Music Hall on 5 June 1862. According to family claims, Eric Burdon of The Animals is his great-great-nephew.

The Blazing Grater, *or*, The Olympic Torch Passes Through Tyneside

(A variation on 'The Blaydon Races')

I saw the Blazing Grater on the fifteenth day in June
two thousand Geordie years and twelve, on a summer's afternoon
the Metro ran to Whitley Bay, where the mad and caald go bathing
haway we went to St Mary's Light – that's where the torch was blazing.

Oh me lads, what is this light that's passing?
the miner's lamp that foond the seam or the little fame we're rationed?
Aal the lads and lasses there, with fish and fried potaters
Gaan by Spanish City just to see the Blazing Grater.

By the Priory at Tynemouth and the guiding lights at Shields
the Roman baths at Waalsend and the Rising Sun's bright fields
the runners bypassed Meadowell, told the shipyards 'smell you later'
the unpaid stewards lined the route to cheer the Blazing Grater.

Oh me lads, what is this light that's passing?
the spark that fired the Rocket or the North run oot of passion?
Aal the lads and lasses there, with ice cream in a wafer
Gaan by the aald Wills Factory to see the Blazing Grater.

By the hyame of Hughie Gallagher, Wor Jackie and of Shearer,
the temple called St James's Park – each year wor faith grows dearer,
the flame it ran doon Grey Street to the Baltic and the Sage
a Monument to hoo the Toon found culture aal the rage.

But oh me lads what is this light that's passing?
the rushlight lit at Jarrow or a Southron sporting fashion?
Aal the lads and lasses there with suncream on your faces
Would you rather gaan to London Toon or to the Blaydon Races?

While the rest of Britain was still living in a barn
Bede picked up the Gospels' torch and welded Lindisfarne
But the Grater skipped the Scotswood Road, and poverty and trouble –
it's looking like a monkey show performed inside a bubble.

Oh me lads, this light has left us stannin
I fear it is the sort of flame that passeth understannin
Aal the lads an lasses there, aal smiling in a crater,
just wave goodbye to cash for growth and to the Blazing Grater.

W.N. HERBERT
Omnesia (Alternative Text), 2013

from Great North
Mile 1-2

> There must be a job gannin' in Sooth Sheels!
> VOICE OF SPECTATOR

The crowd is still too dense to pick up pace,
    You have to watch your step at every step,
And though your breathing's good you can't quite place
    The feeling in your knee as on you schlep
Towards the City Centre, past the Quayside,
    And up towards the bridge, the gateway South,
A fleshy flood-tide running to the seaside
    To meet the river foaming at the mouth,
Via Jarrow, Hebburn, Harton, up to Westoe,
    And all the pitless, pitiless estates
Where living is a well-thumbed manifesto
    In praise of unredeemed one-party states.
Now Britain has its first North-East PM,
    But power's no longer weighed in tons of coal
Or block votes from the Durham NUM
    And 6.8% are on the dole.

Where public loss flows into private gain
    The River Tyne conjoins the Acheron,
And private profit meets with public pain,
    And Government-North-East is known as GO-NE!
Below, the swollen, muddy river flows;
    Above, the pealing city's Sunday bells;
And linking heaven and earth's a bridge that goes
    Across to Gateshead, where the angel dwells.

This is tomorrow's *Guardian* front page,
    The usual Tyne Bridge long-lens/aerial photo,
One of those half-true clichés which our age
    Believes can show what Britain is in toto –
As though the last two decades of defeat,
    Industrial neglect, decay, decline,
Could be redeemed by 80,000 feet
    In unison across the River Tyne.
Like Glasgow junkies, say, or Eton scholars
    Seen waving wads of starred GCSEs,
Or striped-shirt traders selling us for dollars,
    Ibiza clubbers stoned on whizz and Es;
Like England fans who drink in foreign bars,
    Or vigilantes looking for a nonce,
Redundant miners doing up old cars,
    Or like New Labour branches in Provence,
Such images suggest we understand
    Our neighbours rather better than we do,
Until we see ourselves at second-hand
    And think the sepia images are true:
The Boro red, Toon Army/Maccam stripes,
    Brown ale, brown bread and avocado peas,
And all the browned-off, browning calotypes
    That separate the Tyne, the Wear, the Tees.

Part Mardi Gras, part May Day march, part Mela,
    This bannerless and minerless Big Meeting
Is like a weird, post-modern Miners' Gala
    (Without the beer, the speeches or the eating);
Our sweat's not spent to make the world's improvement,
    Our sponsors' banners aren't quite so exalted,
But right now we're not that much of a movement –
    This is the forward march of labour halted!
This carnival North East's a mummer's play

    Where old Misrule rides round on Shank's mare,
The world's turned upside-down for just one day
    And every tortoise gets to beat the hare;
A race with over 40,000 losers
    Where every loser knows themselves a hero,
The biggest heroes are the wheelchair users,
    And Newcastle is Rio de Janeiro!
There's something in this sweating, chugging throng
    Of runners caught in Northern monochrome,
A place and time that's yours, where you belong,
    That makes you feel as though you're almost home.
Well not quite home – there's still a long way yet,
    (11.1 miles to be exact)
A lot more miles of agony and sweat
    Until your knee is well and truly knacked.

ANDY CROFT
Great North, 2001

Cutty Sark Race, 1986
(for Jeanne Harvey)

Eighty names under eleven flags,
the tall ships are preparing.
Consensus of the skippers will decide
the winner of the trophy –
not for coming first, but for doing most
to promote friendship among the nations.
No walls, no warheads. Germany, Poland, Russia,
Britain, Ireland, Italy share the wharves
downriver from Tyne Bridge.
Its great bow spans the water like a sign.

Yesterday we joined the people strolling
among the snackbar smells and the funfair's clamour,
to gaze at booms and rigging, the strakes' long curves
lifting to perfect union at the bows.
Sailors aboard and citizens on the quay
decoded syllables, smiles, gesticulations
to touch each other's lives. When night fell,

the air was salt with jazz and roistering shanties,
then subtler compounds festively exploded
and glittering sprays of colour drenched the sky.

Now we are two among the early thousands
gathered on Tynemouth grass.
With monumental pride, above the guns
that thundered at Trafalgar,
Collingwood stares across the estuary
where no one stopped the Danes.
But friends and families peer upriver,
watching for shapes that will recall
the trade routes, cargoes of tea or wool,
stress and courage the same in all races.

We wait for hours, then masts as fine as needles
appear at the last bend.
Applause crackles like flame along the crowd
as yawl, brig, schooner and barquentine
grow to their full splendour and glide past,
all afternoon lighting the people's eyes,
winning their love and their understanding.
We raise binoculars, pick out names and flags.
Ships from eleven countries
remind us what we deeply care about.

Someone says 'Look, she was nesting here.'
We weren't prepared for this, a small brown bird
– some grass dweller, lark or pipit maybe –
fluttering back and forth over the crowd,
holding a scrap in her beak, plaintively crying.
Yes, we care – her kindred, makers of homes,
packed like aliens on her territory.
But what can be done? We watch her, equally helpless,
in pity sharing her torment, filled with anger
at randomness and irony even here.

There's fallout in our minds; but eighty ships
now line abreast beyond the harbour
have something more to say, and we're attending.
Brief celebrants, we watch our purest hope
declared in full sail on the open sea.
Kruzenshtern, Dar Młodziezy, Falken, Outlaw,

Kaliakra, Eendracht, Asgard, Malcolm Miller,
far from the presidents and the armies,
are slowly melting into light and rain
under a spectral arc.

RICHARD KELL
Rock and Water, 1993 | *Collected Poems 1962-1993*, 2001

Zamyatin in Heaton

conceived of Jesmond as the icy keel
of class conformity, and laid it down;
here English bergs cut scones with stainless steel,
sank tea Titanics, watched each other drown –
a quaker Archangel of publessness
where vicars trapped their dicks in sharp routines.
He saw that fear of flesh, of hope, of mess,
made people turn themselves into machines,
and realised the Revolution's grip
on its own *muzhiks'* soft interior gears
was also prudish, crude, mechanical;
just as the top Range Rovers brusquely slip
down Acorn Road today, it crushed its fears,
since what it couldn't measure it could kill.

W.N. HERBERT
Bad Shaman Blues, 2006

The Russian novelist Yevgeny Zamyatin (1884–1937) lived at 19 Sanderson Road, Jesmond, during part of 1916, while overseeing the construction of a number of icebreakers at Armstrong Whitworth in Low Walker and Swan Hunter in Wallsend for the Imperial Russian Government. His novella *Islanders* (1918) has savage fun at the expense of the inhabitants of Jesmond. Much of its companion novella, *A Fisher of Men* (1921), supposedly set in London, relates to Newcastle settings, including Leazes Park, while his masterpiece, *We* (1921), includes many hidden references to the city and to working practices in the Tyne shipyards. In 1931 Zamyatin produced a screenplay set in a colliery on the Tyne, which was an adaptation of the pitman writer Harold Heslop's novel *Goaf* (1934), which had been published first in a Russian translation in 1926, a copy of which Heslop had presented to Zamyatin during a visit to the USSR in 1930. Shortly after this screenplay was rejected by the censors, Zamyatin was allowed by Stalin to leave the Soviet Union. [AM/NA]

Fantasia on a Theme of James Wright

There are miners still
In the underground rivers
Of West Moor and Palmersville.

There are guttering cap-lamps bound up in the roots
Where the coal is beginning again.
They are sinking slowly further

In between the shiftless seams,
To black pools in the bed of the world.
In their long home the miners are labouring still –

Gargling dust, going down in good order,
Their black-braided banners aloft,
Into flooding and firedamp, there to inherit

Once more the tiny corridors of the immense estate
They line with prints of Hedley's *Coming Home*.
We hardly hear of them.

There are the faint reports of spent economies,
Explosions in the ocean floor,
The thud of iron doors sealed once for all

On prayers and lamentation,
On pragmatism and the long noyade
Of a class which dreamed itself

Immortalised by want if nothing else.
The singing of the dead inside the earth
Is like the friction of great stones, or like the rush

Of water into newly opened darkness. My brothers,
The living will never persuade them
That matters are otherwise, history done.

SEAN O'BRIEN
The Drowned Book, 2007 | *Collected Poems*, 2012

GATESHEAD

from **The Pitman's Pay**

I sing not here of warriors bold,
   Of battles lost or victories won,
Of cities sacked or nations sold,
   Or cruel deeds by tyrants done.

I sing the Pitman's plagues and cares,
   Their labour hard and lowly lot,
Their homely joys and humble fares,
   Their pay-night o'er a foaming pot.

Their week's work done, the coally craft,
   These horny-handed sons of toil,
Require 'a right gude willie-waught',
   The creaking wheels of life to oil.

See hewers, putters, drivers too,
   With pleasure hail this happy day –
All clean washed up, their way pursue
   To drink and crack, and get their pay.

The BUCK, the BLACK HORSE, and the KEYS,
   Have witnessed many a comic scene,
Where's yel to cheer, and mirth to please,
   And drollery that would cure the spleen.

With parchéd tongues, and geyzen'd throats
   They reach the place where barleycorn
Soon down the dusty cavern floats,
   From pewter-pot or homely horn.

The dust washed down, then comes the care
   To find that all is rightly billed;
And each to get his hard-earned share,
   From some one in division skilled.

The money-matters thus decided,
    They push the pot more briskly round:
With hearts elate and hobbies strided,
    Their cares are all in nappy drowned.

'Here, lass,' says JACK, 'help this agyen,
    It's better yel than's i' the toun;
But then the road's se het it's tyen,
    It fizzed, aw think, as it went doun.'

Thus many a foaming pot's required
    To quench the dry and dusky spark;
When ev'ry tongue, as if inspired
    Wags on about their wives and wark –

The famous feats done in their youth,
    At bowling, ball, and clubby-shaw –
Camp-meetings, Ranters, Gospel-truth,
    Religion, politics, and law.

With such variety of matter,
    Opinions, too, as various quite,
We need not wonder at the clatter,
    When ev'ry tongue wags – wrong or right.

The gifted few in lungs and lare
    At length, insensibly, divide'em;
And from a three-legged stool, or chair,
    Each draws his favoured few beside him. [...]

See on their right a gambling few,
    Whose every word and look display
A desperate, dark, designing crew,
    Intent upon each other's pay.

They're racers, cockers, carders, keen
    As ever o'er a tankard met,
Or ever bowl'd a match between
    The POPPLIN WELL and MAWVIN'S YETT.

On cock-fight, dog-fight, cuddy-race,
    Or pitch-and-toss, trippet-and-coit,
Or on a soap-tail'd grunter's chase,
    They'll risk the last remaining doit.

They're now at cards and GIBBY GRIPE
   Is peeping into HARRY'S hand;
And ev'ry puff blown from his pipe
   His party easily understand.

Some for the odd-trick pushing hard –
   Some that they lose it pale with fear –
Some betting on the turn-up-card –
   Some drawing cuts for pints of beer.

Whilst others brawl about JACK'S brock,
   That all the Chowden dogs can bang;
Or praise LANG WILSON'S 'piley cock',
   Or DIXON'S feats upon the swang.

Here TOM, the pink of bowlers, gained
   Himself a never-dying name,
By deeds wherein an ardour reign'd
   Which neither age nor toil could tame.

For labour done, and o'er his doze,
   Tom took his place upon the hill;
And at the very evening's close,
   You faintly saw him bowling still.

All this display of pith and zeal
   Was so completely habit-grown,
That many an hour from sleep he'd steal,
   To bowl upon the hill alone. […]

THOMAS WILSON
The Pitman's Pay; or, A Night's Discharge to Care, 1826-30

'*a right gude willie-waught*': a draught of good fellowship, quoting Burns's 'Auld Lang Syne'; *the* BUCK, *the* BLACK HORSE *and the* KEYS: pubs in Low Fell; the Buck became the Beaconsfield, and the Keys (the Belle Vue) gave its name to Cross Keys Lane; *yel:* ale; *geyzen'd:* thirsty for strong drink; *nappy:* ale; *tyen:* taken; *clubby-shaw:* game played with a globular piece of wood and a stick; MAWVIN'S YETT: bowling green on Gateshead Fell; *cuddy:* donkey; *brock:* badger; *bang:* rush, surpass; *piley:* mottled, speckled; *swang:* swamp.

Thomas Wilson (1773–1858) was born in Low Fell, Gateshead. He received very little education and went to work from the age of eight. He studied in his leisure time, left the pit at 19, and made two abortive efforts to establish himself as a schoolmaster; then from 1799 to 1803, he worked for John Head, a Newcastle merchant and underwriter before entering the counting house of Losh, Lubbin, which later became Losh, Wilson and Bell. Within two years Wilson became a partner and remained so for the rest of his life. In 1835, Wilson was elected one of the first two councillors of Gateshead. His bust was sculpted by the younger Dunbar and is now in the Shipley Gallery.

Throughout his life, Wilson devoted all the time he could to intellectual pursuits, and collected an excellent library. He contributed to the local *Diaries* for sixty years and acquainted himself with every aspect of mining life. *The Pitman's Pay*, Wilson's chief literary work, appeared originally in *Mitchell's Newcastle Magazine* in 1826-28 and 1830. Other poems were contributed to the *Tyne Mercury* and some of these were reissued with notes by John Sykes, compiler of local records. *The Pitman's Pay* is a metrical description, much of it in mining language, of the incidents and conversations of colliers on their fortnightly pay nights. Others of Wilson's verses, the poem entitled 'On seeing a mouse run across the road in January' for example, show him to have made a close study of Burns. Some consider that in the 'Tippling Dominie' Wilson is perhaps seen at his best.

Wilson died at Fell House, Gateshead, and was buried in the family vault at St John's, Gateshead Fell. His funeral was attended by the Mayor and town council. [AM]

Maw Bonny Gyetside Lass

Aw warned ye hevent seen me lass, – her nyem aw winnet menshun,
    For feer ye gan an' tell her hoo aw like her, so aw de!
But it's just for lads an' lasses te whispor thor affecshun,
    The bonniest lass o' Gyetside's bonny fyece's bothered me!

The forst time aw saw her, whey aw's sure aw diddint knaw her,
    Tho' aw thowt aw'd seen her fyece afore, but cuddint think o' where;
Her blue eye met mine i' passin' up High Street, i' the mornin',
    An' her luik wes se intrancin, that me heart wes mine ne mair!

Aw diddint see her for aweek, till one neet at the Bridge End,
    When aw strampt upon her goon, an' the gethors com away;
She said that aw wes clumsy, an' aw said that aw wes sorry,
    An' aw humbly begged her pardon, – aw wes lickt for what te say.

But av wawked on biv her side just as if aw had a reet te did,
    The convorsayshun forst wes shy, at last it turned forst-class;
We byeth spoke aboot the weather, – an' she menshundd that her fethur
    Wes a puddlor doon at Hawks's – Oh, maw bonny Gyetside Lass!

She menshuned confidenshly that her unkil wes a grossor,
    An' his muther's fether's cussin wes a fiddler doon the shore;
An' she spoke se nice an' frindly, an' smiled se sweet an' plissint,
    That aw thowt aw'd nivor seen a lass se charmin' like before.

She said her muthor kept a shop, an' selled het pies an' candy,
   An' her bruther wes a cobbler at the high pairt o' the toon;
An' she wes a dressmaker, – we got se kind tegithor,
   That aw blis't aw'd been se awkword as aw strampt upon her goon.

Aw myed her laff an' slap me lug, wi' tawkin' lots o' nonsense,
   But, bliss ye, when yor curtin thor's nowt se gud 'ill pass;
Aw askt her wad she be me lass, an' aw'd tyek her oot on Sunday,
   To maw delite, she said aw might, maw bonny Gyetside Lass!

JOE WILSON
Tyneside Songs and Drolleries, 1890

strampt upon her goon: stamped on her gown; *gethors:* gathers; *puddlor:* worker in charge of puddling in an ironworks; *Hawks's:* Hawks, Crawshay and Co. operated Gateshead ironworks, and were contractors for the ironwork on the High Level Bridge.

Joe Wilson (1841–1875) was one of region's most celebrated songwriters and poets, best-known for 'Keep Your Feet Still Geordie Hinny'. He was a music hall performer and kept a pub, the Adelaide in New Bridge Street, Newcastle, from 1871, before becoming a temperance reformer. He died of tuberculosis.

Originally meant for the printing trade, Wilson had his first book published at 17. Influenced, however, by Geordie Ridley and Ned Corvan, he turned to the popular song. Among his other well-loved pieces are 'Aw wish your Mother wad cum' , 'Dinnet clash the Door' and 'The Row upon the Stairs' – as well as the exquisite 'Bonny Gyetside Lass'. His later temperance songs received no such welcome from his tolerantly thirsty audience.

Wilson said of himself: 'It's been me aim to hev a place i' the hearts o' Tyneside, wi' writing bits o' hyemly sangs aw think they'll sing'. These words are inscribed on his tombstone. [AM]

Gateshead

sea monsters chalked on the asphalt road
stride the alley
as though it were a long cave

we sit half way up on the pyramid to our back door
sun swallowed in the coke oven flame

mammal bodies swim beneath the flapping clouds
which women hang in zigzag lines across the lane

there are beast with wings in the cellar
beaked and mucky faces contemplate each other

the children have built a toad-run
we sit and watch the sun down

there is nothing else
to do

TOM PICKARD
Hero Dust, 1979 | *hoyoot: Collected Poems and Songs*, 2014

Gateshead Grammar

There must be hundreds like us now,
Born since the war, brought up
In terraced streets near factory yards
And on expansive council estates.

We were the ones who stayed on at school
In academic quarantine. Others
Took apprenticeships in the skilled trades
And left us indoors to finish homework.

And we didn't notice it at first –
All the literature that wasn't written
For us: passing an exam
Was an exercise in its own right.

To live like Spartans, think like monks
Had something heroic about it...
Now we dress carefully, and at
Introductions in expensive restaurants

Suppress the local accent in our voice,
Not to give ourselves away.
And little by little we go home less
To parents who seem to have fostered us:

We are like those bankrupt millionaires
With our own social success stories
And personal failures. Remaindered
Fashions at give-away prices.

GEORGE CHARLTON
Ten North-East Poets, 1980 | *Nightshift Workers*, 1989

Angel of the North, Gateshead
(FROM *The Dunno Elegies*)

What use are angels when the wind blows back
our sighs with the sand? What use this song, nosing
through undergrowth like a dog roots out smells,
tired of its own hot-blooded clichés, bored
with knowing how lost and forgetful we are
here in this reciphered, recycled world.
If we knew how terrible it would feel
to be reminded that beauty exists
just a fleet moment from the walkers' path,
in mould on a leaf or mud in a footprint,
what would we do, would breath catch or guilt grip?

No, if I were to shout, now, on this hill
above the Team Valley Business Park,
how many angels would hear it? How many
would care that my grief had blown their cover?
The change in my pocket occupies me
for a cold minute or two. The sobbing dark
chokes on my whistling, a tune that visits
and then forgets to leave. Forgive me.
I only mean to console myself.
This is a song for my mother, the past,
an echo I hear of a better world,
a trail worn out of knotted grass, folly
that pushes you on into the woods,
a place torn down that started again,
dark native mud still on its boots,
unilluminated wings stretched out.

Magpies croon and croak and try to catch it,
trees sway bare and brown, wind-blown
hedges mime the river rushing seawards
while it takes in this hopeful new song.

The angel rusts a welcome to its brothers,
its wings embrace prayers, its sore heart escapes
the buried pithead in a gasp of song,
over the seasoned museum of the land
where the worm is king, turning like a screw
in a rawlplug, a bradawl into wet bark.
The keening rises on the valleys thermals,
rolling and tumbling into low hinterland.

But there are shadows left even by angels,
where the coal sleeps soundly, silent miles down.
The wild coast between here, there, now and then
is not so solid as it used to be.
This song was only meant to warm the air.
If it could do more it would be unbearable.
There are things only angels can forgive.

MARK ROBINSON
How I Learned to Sing, 2013

The Angel

was moulded when I was seven, further down the country.
It was the same day we copied the world in Lego.
She was made in parts, then glued together
hauled back up again on the back of a truck, sleeping.
We mocked her on the way home from Thurston Outdoor Education Centre
flapping our arms like wings as the minibus rocked.
She is rusted like ridges along the tops of tin cans.
Ten thousand naked tin cans.
Birds try to bring her hair so they can make homes in the ears she does not have.
Her arms reach out to touch the sky. I think she does not touch it.

JEN CAMPBELL
The Hungry Ghost Festival, 2012

Angel Metal

We stand underneath and pray to her.
We do not know why we pray. Sometimes
the sheep come to look before the fires start.
It is hard, the grass. It's the frost here.
We are all of us the worm on a higher ground.
You hold my hand like it's the theatre.
The applause is too low down
winding under us like electric rabbits. You
pick my arms up and spread them out
so we are matching. Our woollen scarves
touch our noses – catch our breath
like cloth balloons. We dig our feet into the soil
and stamp down into the very deep.
Somewhere below, the river sleeps with a lady
screeching. She has arms that could carry boulders
to the edge of cliffs. We wait for her
to throw us down. Our parents, stiff, pretend
they are not watching. They sit on sofas behind
their damning newspapers. We are not children.
We wait alone in the coldest times while people read.
They say we have taken something
they can never put back inside of us. They say
we are building blocks, and purse their ragged lips.
I picture barren fields transformed into supermarkets
with bars across their naked windows.
I am warm inside. We wait.
We fill our pockets up with frozen peaches.

JEN CAMPBELL
The Hungry Ghost Festival, 2012

NORTH TYNESIDE

H.M.S. *Hero*

Pale grey, her guns hooded, decks clear of all impediment,
Easily, between the swart tugs, she glides in the pale October sunshine:
It is Saturday afternoon, and the men are at football,
The wharves and the cobbled streets are silent by the slow river.

Smoothly, rounding the long bend, she glides to her place in history,
Past the grimed windows cracked and broken,
Past Swan Hunter's, Hawthorn Leslie's, Armstrong's,
Down to the North Sea, and trials, and her first commission.

Here is grace; and a job well done; built only for one end.
Women watch from the narrow doorways and give no sign,
Children stop playing by the wall and stare in silence
At gulls wheeling above the Tyne, or the ship passing.

(1936)

MICHAEL ROBERTS
Orion Marches, 1939
➤ AUTHOR NOTE PAGE 282

Tyne Ferry: Night

The turnstile's enigmatic tongue
reluctantly announces the impending passage.
Row-boats nibble at the long,
floating body of the landing-stage.

The passengers embark, anonymous
beneath the swinging arc-lamp's
gesticulating melodrama. Their elastic shadows
rage suddenly and vanish down the heaving ramps.

From the leaning smoke-stack, cables
of heroic steam are hauled. The broken
water glitters when departure's
hidden bells are shaken.

The boat gently valses, and a course is set
across the unseen harbour's springing darkness.
Louder the winds leap through the black proscenium of night,
and slowly now the landing's floodlit emptiness

glides like the setting for a nameless play
with sinister, deceptive urgency away.

JAMES KIRKUP
Northern Review, 1949 | *A Correct Compassion and Other Poems*, 1952

Night Fishing

    Lightbuoys bob red on the sea
Through blue fog: bell-stick tugs in the sand
Till taut line slipped through a hard hand
    Heaves a whiting to the bay.

    Arm arcs, swings a whistling line,
Dwindling the coil till the plunger's splash
Spurts spray like blood in the lighthouse flash
    At the lip of the green Tyne.

    Salt north-easter peels the beach,
Plaits flaxen tracery as it combs
The dunes' thin tresses: curlew cries come
    Craven from the sheer cliff's ledge.

    Moon gilds weeds on the split rock
Where once I sat in the wishing-chair
And yearned, Kathleen, for your golden hair:
    Thoughts drift, and are lost, like wrack.

FRANCIS SCARFE
Underworlds, 1950

Trawlers

Red sail on tan sail and black sail by white,
Swell and swing out of the banking green river,
Heeling the squattest of Tyne trawlers over.
Set south-east-by-east on a moonlit night,
Veer, haul and tack, trim canvas, trim deck,
Till you gather the gold nets and pack the catch tight,
And ride home with the dawn and the wind at your back.

(March 1941)

FRANCIS SCARFE
Forty Poems and Ballads, 1941
➤ AUTHOR NOTE PAGE 367

When the Boat Comes In

Come here me little Jacky
Now ah've smoked me baccy
Let's hev a bit o' cracky
Till the boat comes in.

Dance to thee Daddy, sing to thee Mammy,
Dance to thee Daddy, to thee Mammy sing;
Thou shalt hev a fishy on a little dishy,
Thou shalt hev a fishy when the boat comes in.

Here's thy mother humming,
Like a canny woman;
Yonder comes thy fatha,
Drunk – he cannat stand.

Dance to thee Daddy, sing to thee Mammy,
Dance to thee Daddy, to thee Mammy sing;
Thou shalt hev a fishy on a little dishy,
Thou shalt hev a haddock when the boat comes in.

Our Tommy's always fuddling,
He's so fond of ale,
But he's kind to me,
I hope he'll never fail.

Dance to thee Daddy, sing to thee Mammy,
Dance to thee Daddy, to thee Mammy sing;
Thou shalt hev a fishy on a little dishy,
Thou shalt hev a bloater when the boat comes in

I like a drop mesel',
When I can get it sly,
And thou, my bonny bairn,
Will like't as well as I.

Dance to thee Daddy, sing to thee Mammy,
Dance to thee Daddy, to thee Mammy sing;
Thou shalt hev a fishy on a little dishy,
Thou shalt hev a mackerel when the boat comes in.

May we get a drop,
Oft as we stand in need;
And weel may the keel row
That brings the bairns their breed.

Dance to thee Daddy, sing to thee Mammy,
Dance to thee Daddy, to thee Mammy sing;
Thou shalt hev a fishy on a little dishy,
Thou shalt hev a salmon when the boat comes in.

(1826)

WILLIAM WATSON
Songs of the Bards of the Tyne, ed. Joseph Robson, 1849

Island of Souls
(lyrics)

Billy was born within sight of the shipyard,
First son of a riveter's son,
And Billy was raised as the ship grew a shadow,
Her great hull would blot out the light of the sun.

And six days a week he would watch his poor father,
A working man live like a slave.
He'd drink every night and he'd dream of a future
Of money he never would save.
Billy would cry when he thought of the future.
Soon came a day when the bottle was broken,
They launched a great ship out to sea.
He felt he'd been left on a desolate shore
To a future he desperately wanted to flee.

What else was there for a shipbuilder's son?
A new ship to be built, new work to be done.
One day he dreamed of the ship in the world,
It would carry his father and he
To a place they would never be found,
To a place far away from this town.

Trapped in the cage of the skeleton ship,
All the workmen suspended like flies.
Caught in the flare of acetylene light,
A working man works till the industry dies.

And Billy would cry when he thought of the future.
Then what they call an industrial accident
Crushed those it couldn't forgive.
They brought Billy's father back home in an ambulance:
A brass watch, a cheque, maybe three weeks to live.

What else was there for a riveter's son?
A new ship to be built, new work to be done.
That night, he dreamed of the ship in the world.
It would carry his father and he
To a place they could never be found
To a place far away from this town,
A Newcastle ship with no coals
They would sail to the island of souls.

STING
The Soul Cages, 1991

The Tyneside Widow

There's mony a man loves land and life,
    Loves life and land and fee;
And mony a man loves fair women,
    But never a man loves me, my love,
    But never a man loves me.

O weel and weel for a' lovers,
    I wot weel may they be;
And weel and weel for a' fair maidens,
    But aye mair woe for me, my love,
    But aye mair woe for me.

O weel be wi' you, ye sma' flowers,
    Ye flowers and every tree;
And weel be wi' you, a' birdies,
    But teen and tears wi' me, my love,
    But teen and tears wi' me.

O weel be yours, my three brethren,
    And ever weel be ye;
Wi' deeds for doing and loves for wooing,
    But never a love for me, my love,
    But never a love for me.

And weel be yours, my seven sisters,
    And good love-days to see,
And long life-days and true lovers,
    But never a day for me, my love,
    But never a day for me.

Good times wi' you, ye bauld riders,
    By the hieland and the lee;
And by the leeland and by the hieland
    It's weary times wi' me, my love,
    It's weary times wi' me.

Good days wi' you, ye good sailors,
    Sail in and out the sea;
And by the beaches and by the reaches
    It's heavy days wi' me, my love,
    It's heavy days wi' me.

I had his kiss upon my mouth,
    His bairn upon my knee;
I would my soul and body were twain,
    And the bairn and the kiss wi' me, my love,
    And the bairn and the kiss wi' me.

The bairn down in the mools, my dear,
    O saft and saft lies she;
I would the mools were ower my head,
    And the young bairn fast wi' me, my love,
    And the young bairn fast wi' me.

The father under the faem, my dear,
    O sound and sound sleeps he;
I would the faem were ower my face,
    And the father lay by me, my love,
    And the father lay by me.

I would the faem were ower my face,
    Or the mools on my ee-bree;
And waking-time with a' lovers,
    But sleeping-time wi' me, my love,
    But sleeping-time wi' me.

I would the mools were meat in my mouth,
    The saut faem in my ee;
And the land-worm and the water-worm
    To feed fu' sweet on me, my love,
    To feed fu' sweet on me.

My life is sealed with a seal of love,
    And locked with love for a key;
And I lie wrang and I wake lang,
    But ye tak' nae thought for me, my love,
    But ye tak' nae thought for me.

We were weel fain of love, my dear,
    O fain and fain were we;
It was weel with a' the weary world,
    But O, sae weel wi' me, my love,
    But O, sae weel wi' me.

We were nane ower mony to sleep, my dear,
   I wot we were but three;
And never a bed in the weary world
   For my bairn and my dear and me, my love,
   For my bairn and my dear and me.

ALGERNON CHARLES SWINBURNE
Poems and Ballads, third series, 1889

Bobby Shafto

Bobby Shafto's gyen to sea,
Silver buckles at his knee;
He'll come back an' marry me,
Bonny Bobby Shaftoe.

Bobby Shafto's bright and fair,
Kaimin' doon his yellow hair;
He's my awn for iver mair,
Bonny Bobby Shaftoe.

Bobby Shafto's getten a bairn
For to dandle on his airm;
In his airm an' on his knee;
Bonny Bobby Shaftoe.

Bobby Shafto's gyen to sea,
Silver buckles at his knee;
He'll back home an' marry me,
Bonny Bobby Shaftoe.

TRADITIONAL
Rhymes of Northern Bards, ed. John Bell, 1812

One story has it that Bobby Shafto's sweetheart was one Bridget Belasyse of Brancepeth Castle, Co. Durham, who died two weeks after hearing that he had married Anne Duncombe of Duncombe Park in Yorkshire.

Written at Tynemouth, Northumberland, after a Tempestuous Voyage

As slow I climb the cliff's ascending side,
   Much musing on the track of terror past,
   When o'er the dark wave rode the howling blast,
Pleased I look back, and view the tranquil tide
That laves the pebbled shore: and now the beam
   Of evening smiles on the grey battlement,
   And yon forsaken tower that Time has rent: –
The lifted oar far off, with silver gleam
Is touched, and hushed is all the billowy deep!
   Soothed by the scene, thus on tired Nature's breast
   A stillness slowly steals, and kindred rest;
While sea-sounds lull her, as she sinks to sleep,
Like melodies which mourn upon the lyre,
Waked by the breeze, and, as they mourn, expire!

WILLIAM LISLE BOWLES (1762–1850)
Sonnets, Written Chiefly on Picturesque Spots During a Tour, 1789

William Lisle Bowles (1762–1850) was a clerygyman and minor poet. His literary reputation chiefly rests on a volume of sonnets on places visited on his travels which was praised by Coleridge but viewed less kindly by later critics.

The Coast-Watch

With tingling eyes he stares into the dense
And wool-white fleece of fog that hides the sea,
And harkens to the waves that ceaselessly
Scour the Northumbrian strand,
Until the murmurous monotony
Stealing into his blood lulls every sense
Into a trance-like daze through which he hears
The creak of oars in rowlocks close at hand:
And still in stupor like a man of stone
Who sentinels a dream-enchanted coast
He stands, sense-bound,
As, grinding through the shallow sand,

Boats run aground;
And instantly about him swarms a host
Of helmeted grey figures, armed with spears
And swords and targes.... Then the sound
Of his own rifle shatters in his ears
As in a panic he fires randomly
At those horned Vikings.... And the blind fog clears;
And once again he finds himself alone
Staring across an empty moon-glazed sea.

WILFRID GIBSON
Challenger, 1942

Balloons in Sunrise
(a memory of war)

These quilted pink cocoons, upholstered
silken cumuli on which a star might rest,
bolster the wavelit dawn, the clouds'
menace, dark bristling furs of air-raid light.

Across the raised ends of roads to the beaches
the sea lies stretched and tense. The level
darkness drops in streets and docks,
the chimney-stacks emerge
like broken coral reefs
discovered by an unknown tide.

And here, where a renewed
vista opened lately to a bomb,
between pale-papered gables nestling
sleek, dewy, comfortable, dim,

the bound walrus, pegged and roped, that stirs
uneasily among the tiny huts and men, like Gulliver.

(Tynemouth: Winter 1942)

JAMES KIRKUP
Orbis, 1979 | *To the Ancestral North*, 1983

The Harbour: Tynemouth

The yachts lean on their sea-dark sails
whose masts' swooning tips, like a battalion
of sunlit spears glide down the stone
defences of the mile-long pier.
Like pennants flash the light-paring gulls
whose crying is the creak of pulley, rope and spar.
And, like drowning eyes within the green
forehead of the wave, rolling their shark-bright keels,
the wind-carved whitenesses wheel out across the bar.

The ruined priory stands like a broken harp
above black rocks, and makes the North Sea wind
keen in the sky-strung lancets mute with sand.
A gun emplacement battens on the cliff's dark brows.
Rhetorical, a monument to someone in a sea-fretted park
strides on eroded pedestal against unconquerable foes.
And like a stranded liner, lit with glass from end
to end, a modern hive's horizon-squaring ark
echoes a distant wreck, and floats above the drowning quays.

Within the harbour mouth, whose steepled banks
rise from a scaffolding of ships and crane-hung streets,
the white-belted ferries, pilot-craft, and fleets
of yellow-funnelled trawlers dart like water-flies
round a departing tanker's orange hulk, that drinks
the open sea with haunted, anchor-weeping eyes.
To landlocked mariners among their scale-rimed nets
the moving vessel moans farewell. Early the lighthouse winks
one inland eye, and town hall clocks chime in the sea-wide skies.

JAMES KIRKUP
A Correct Passion and Other Poems, 1952
➤ AUTHOR NOTE PAGE 371

The North Sea at Tynemouth

The sea folds over upon itself
again and again,
sucks and chews the shore
till rocks become sand.

Ships ride along its back.
Sometimes the water invades them
and they drown.

Darkness begins only
a couple of feet below,
extending through acres of cold compression
where the silver shoals graze.

Returning along the pier I watch
the pilot's boat greeting a visitor.
Surely they too have felt,
even on the stillest of days,
a sudden vertigo on the sea's heights?

MICHAEL BLACKBURN
The Prophecy of Christos, 1992

At Tynemouth

Here on the headland the wind whittles away
at blind arcades, broken wall-ends of nave
and crossing, choir and chantry.
                              So bleak
in winter, here they sent backsliding monks
to learn the harsher virtues: sore throats
from the sea-frets, tedious diet of boiled fish,
and the sight of ships driven onto the Middens,
crews pleading in plain view and no means
of effecting rescue. *No ringdove
or nightingale is here; only grey birds*

nest in rocks and prey upon the drowned.
See to it, dear brother, you do not come
to this comfortless place.
                          Today, a soft breeze
ruffles neat grass. South of the chapel
the town's dead have forgotten the kniving air,
the sting of salt; but here too the wind
has worked, riddling sandstone, tracing over
and over birth-dates and death-dates, worming hollows
for fingers, miniature caves like the burrows of martins,
riverbank swallows –
                    indifferent worker,
the wind carves its lovely illiterate script
without purpose or schedule, all the time
in the world at its careless disposal.

HELEN TOOKEY
New Writing North and Carcanet blogs, 2015

View

The moon is a chill of silver
and the sea like tin-foil crushed.
Beyond this wind-rattled window
where the night's thin veiled with cold
the castle edges lonely
to the headland of the Tyne.
And through its grey clenched stone
moan the winds of far horizons.

We too have stared
at that edge of the world
flattened to mystery.
It hints at a wall of water
where someday we may drown, or
tumble laughing, like bath-time babies.

I hear you at my back;
a small arranging of plates.
In the room's quiet warmth
your skirt is softly rustled.
I sense your moon-pale hands
fluttering like moths.
Sometimes I turn when needed;
sometimes, only the sea.

I think of the waves, the waves,
tugging at the coat-tails of the shore.
Come, oh please, come.
And each wave dead
when done with its pleading
and no wave ever
the last wave to plead.

PETER MORTIMER
A Rainbow in its Throat, 1993

Cullercoats

A silence crowds the bay
old men gaze down on;

fifty years from shore
the singing boats
of their youth
returning heavy laden.

MIKE WILKIN
Mugs Rite, 1996

Sonnets from Whitley Bay

> Troubled but not distressed.
> FROM A WINDOW IN DURHAM CATHEDRAL

1

Stretches of this country smell so bad,
I apologise. We laugh at your, 'I'd think
About my love for an Island that stinks.'
Those hours we took to find the North had
Become a straight line: imperceptible curves
Broken by an occasional roundabout,
Until talk ran out and we banned ourselves
From idle thoughts of the distant South.

Wake up love. We've long passed the border.
The South is irredeemable. The slanted light
From the early summer sun is colder,
Now it casts elongated shadows of you and I
Ascending the stairs to our love-nest
Where we smell tired and unwilling to rest.

2

We always star in one another's dreams
In full technicolor and super sixteen.
We fall asleep like spoons and only turn
When one or the other decides to turn.
Morning is a silence that won't fracture.
An elbow-room closeness and the odd gesture
Confirms the other's thoughts in sea-air thick
With desire. We nod our approval at brick
In a city where I first said, I love you,
Climbing the cathedral's 325 steps to view
One shire shouldering the next, like molars,
As God would have it or Buddha, or some polar
Icecap and then the warming of the globe,
Exactly as the heat I feel when inside you.

3

These are the people I told you about,
The ones with mostly goodness in their mouths.
They treat us like old friends come back at last.
The pints you and I lever to nought renew fast,
Faster than we can toast the water of Tyneside.
Late into the evening we find seats side by side.
Our legs touch and when I shift it's to feel your hip
As I see it through this straight glass at my lip.

I've brought you here to be undressed by all
Their kind and hungry eyes, only to take
You to a Hi-Fi lit dark, Motown Soul,
And enough spring water by the bed to slake
The thirst of two flushed, open-mouthed lovers,
Through locked-eyes, locked-arms, hip-locked hours.

4

My love you fill my head to distraction.
I am pacing a room you hardly looked into,
Furthest from the bedroom-cum-granary
Where we lived and loved and woke in an aviary
That quietened as the light intensified
And objects muddled by the dark, clarified.
All that night nothing could come between us,
A sliver of light or dark couldn't separate us.

By morning the bed had split into half –
Us in a dividing current on two rafts;
Us in our deep dreams, private and sweet.
How did we drift apart, even in sleep?
One look from you of panic, loss, love,
And I leapt from my raft to share yours.

5

I hold up your 501s against my waist
To get the measure of you: come back, now,
From that big, big city that pulled you away,
To this one main street, coastal town,
With five-minute jams and one of most things.
I knew between us, me and Whitley Bay,
We couldn't make you stay. We tried everything:
Flora and fauna, the sea's light displays.

Your long, elegant legs opened fluently.
I eased into a wet, warm, silky place
That made us gasp, quicken, then rock gently –
Our eyes searching one another's eyes and face,
When not one of ninety nine cars registered
Passing the house in the rush-hour was heard.

6

This kind of loving wrecks the body,
Makes it impossible to function properly.
You wake up mid-morning feeling like the night before,
But to go back to bed would turn your head forever.

You stay on your feet and sway like a ship
Becalmed, waiting for anything to happen, to slip
Your world back into orbit, but nothing does,
Except the light slips and you register a dull pulse.

The ship is hers and the sea is hers, the light
You see the world by, hers; the loving that night
Was all hers; the feeling that you're wrecked, hers.

The love you think is a blessing is a curse,
A weakness, something not hers, but yours: stop,
Before you have no pulse, before you drop.

7

Your touch, I'd nearly forgotten your touch!
And you've been gone less than a month, much
Less; yet here I am using poetry as hype
To conjure you from a Daguerreotype;
From a past neither of us could have known.
The fine tremor in your hands is mine now,
As is that chain of sweat on your upper lip.
I offer my China silk hanky whose tip
Sticks out of my top left hand jacket pocket
And a half-smile: take it, use it to mop
The sweat beaded on fur so delicate
It might be kissed away, not electrocuted.
All I can do is call you up and hope you'll come,
And pray that in calling you, no harm's done.

8

The miles between you and I open up.
The days stretch out against all my wishes.
I fight betrayal when a hand brushes mine,
Preferring a bruise from an upper cut
Delivered by one of Whitley Bay's British
Movement. A stranger's eyes make four with mine,
I hot up instantly like a four bar blues
Launched by Muddy Waters or B.B. King.

Not so long ago we watched a moon in a shoe
Step from that shoe which changed to something
We couldn't name, as clouds do, then the moon
Perched on a lake big like the sea; that moon
Looked like it owned the lake and all around.
But we watched it fall into that lake and drown.

9

When I turn my back on this North of Norths
And I kiss you goodbye, how come it hurts?

When sea-lit winds loosen a stinging rain
On Whitley Bay, your tears drown out mine.

This curved beach of seaweed and stones
Shows from my wavy footprints I'm all alone.

The waves form an orderly queue to see
Who's the miserable man bringing misery.

When those waves wreck in despair on sandstone,
It's my back breaking with my need for home.

I give up town and sea for glass and concrete,
And a capital adding to itself,

House by red brick house on the *For Sale* shelf,
And new-post-code street by tarmacked street.

FRED D'AGUIAR
British Subjects, 1993

Tyneside in December

(for Bill Bailey)

Here wind and darkness rule;
Have rubbed out the intention
Of landscape, the intrusion of trees.

The race has adjusted, has grown
Four-square, double-glazed houses
For four-square practical people,
And small square gardens for long-
rooted indestructible rose-trees.

Here households practise existence by vivid
Electric embers, hymning home-baked
Hospitality and putting on weight.
Here law-fearing straight streets
Glow orange and violet by night
For ten o'clock's dauntless dog-walkers.
And the lighthouse is saying something
Comprehensible only to men at sea.

By a shivering tallow dip, here
In the old, unimaginable darkness and wind,
Bede soberly sifted miraculous evidence,
Divined the shape of the unmapped
Country's history, keeping the candle
From going out. And out
There, in the darkness, the wind and the rain,
Cuthbert practised the habit of being holy.

U.A. FANTHORPE
Voices Off, 1984 | *New & Collected Poems*, 2010

Whitley Bay

The sun's big moment. Balanced on top of the sea
His shining carpet unrolls. The intent rat,
Scavenging the cliffs, doesn't notice. The sea
Stretches itself; tries a little roar;
Settles down again.

Tides high. Dash in, dash out.
Goosepimpled regulars saltily
Gratefully dash back to breakfast.

Warm enough, in the sun, with your back to the promenade wall.
Crossword, knitting, sunglasses, flask;
Snooze here till lunchtime. Soft sand
Lets everything fall into place.

Gran's with the Chapel trip.
She'll not come next year. It's nippy
Watching the canny bairns,
Watching the sea spread itself
All the way to Tynemouth.

And the bairns can't wait –
Fish and chips and candy floss,
A go on the big wheel,
Hours and hours and hours
On the sands.

The sea's sure of itself,
Knows its own highs and lows,
Comes every day, all year;
Has serious designs on the cliffs.

Under her *kiss me quick* hat, he does.
He makes a deep impression,
On her, on the beach. Sea
Sighs, turns over, sighs again. Sand
Lets it all wash over her.

Tide's right out now. Rocks, ribs,
Ridges: joined up lacy calligraphy
No one can read.

Sun and sea stir themselves.
Where's the wind comes from?
When did the light go
From Bandstand, Esplanade, the Lower Prom?

The lovers have caught the sun. Behind the wind-break
Gran says she's caught cold. The bairns
Have caught it from their Da, for waking him up.

The coach drivers fold their *Mirrors*. On the sands,
Toffee papers, orange peel, crusts,
The forgotten watch.

R.V. BAILEY
Marking Time, 2004

Tunnel of Love
(Lyrics)

getting crazy on the waltzers but it's the life i choose
sing about the sixblade sing about the switchback and a torture tattoo
and i been riding on a ghost train where the cars they scream and slam
and i don't know where i'll be tonight but i'd always tell you where i am

in a screaming ring of faces i seen her standing in the light
she had a ticket for the races just like me she was a victim of the night
i put my hand upon the lever said let it rock and let it roll
i had the one arm bandit fever there was an arrow through my heart and my soul

    and the big wheel keep on turning neon burning up above
    and i'm just high on the world
    come on and take a low ride with me girl
    on the tunnel of love

it's just the danger when you're riding at your own risk
she said you are the perfect stranger she said baby let's keep it like this
it's just a cakewalk twisting baby step right up and say
hey mister give me two give me two cos any two can play

>and the big wheel keep on turning neon burning up above
>and i'm just high on the world
>come on and take a low ride with me girl
>on the tunnel of love

well it's been money for muscle another whirligig
money for muscle another girl i dig
another hustle just to make it big
and rockaway rockaway

and girl it looks so pretty to me just like it always did
like the spanish city to me when we were kids
oh girl it looks so pretty to me just like it always did
like the spanish city to me when we were kids

she took off a silver locket she said remember me by this
she put her hand in my pocket i got a keepsake and a kiss
and in the roar of dust and diesel i stood and watched her walk away
i could have caught up with her easy enough but something must have made me stay

>and the big wheel keep on turning neon burning up above
>and i'm just high on the world
>come on and take a low ride with me girl
>on the tunnel of love

and now i'm searching through these carousels and the carnival arcades
searching everywhere from steeplechase to palisades
in any shooting gallery where promises are made
to rockaway rockaway from cullercoats and whitley bay out to rockaway

and girl it looks so pretty to me like it always did
like the spanish city to me when we were kids
girl it looks so pretty to me like it always did
like the spanish city to me when we were kids

MARK KNOPFLER
Dire Straits, *Making Movies*, 1980

SOUTH SHIELDS

The Town Where I Was Born

At the mouth of a great river rising to the sea
my town was both single and double, here and there,
the North and South, divided by the Tyne.

They were two separate entities, belonging
to different counties, having different speech,
yet united by a name's common denominator.

There was no bridge, no tunnel between the two.
Travelling from South to North Shields and back
we still have to pay our obolus and take the ferry

which to me was a first release, a breath of freedom,
delivering me from home and bringing my disquiet
'ower the watter' to a town familiar but strange.

It was always an enchanted voyage – in storm and calm,
rain and shine – to that other dream place. I was happy
to be leaving, less happy to be returning home.

Those almost daily voyages between my North and South,
loaded with lust and library books and scribbling pads
– presaging later partitions of desire between East and West.

· · · · ·

And now I see it was from that divided town, that Scylla
and Charybdis my lightning-struck divisions came
– the ambiguities of being, thought and action.

It tugged my heart, my loyalties, my dreams, my passions
in opposite directions – made me both love and hate
the sundered town beside the sea, beneath colossal skies,

made me both cherish and abhor my roots, my origins,
my faults, my gifts, and even life itself. I became that ferry
on the great river rising to a sea of doubt and death.

Yet that separation from myself was very nature, an integrity
of twin poles united in a schizoid geography's connected
disconnections – the great river ever dividing, joining –

great river of memory rising to the vast, the open sea.

(c. 1940s)

JAMES KIRKUP
Throwback, 1992

View from the North East

Across the end of every street the piled-up sea,
the sky and the indelible horizon stretch
like some faintly stirring backcloth, in front of which
the pillar-box, the street-lamp and the tree detach
their elemental shapes with spectral poignancy.

Against a background of breakers that detonate
with soft explosions over the damp-stained beaches,
and throw up gulls in clouds of spray; the churches,
roof-tops, waterfronts and salt-cellar lighthouses,
ruins, a deserted bandstand, a broken fort

glide like cut-out toys over panoramic lakes.
A child moves like a ghost across the pink-cemented promenade,
and drags her solitary shadow like a lifeless weed
along the wave-ribbed edges of the sea, where hard
cirrus sand-shapes blanch at every step she takes.

(Beach Road, South Shields, 1945)

JAMES KIRKUP
The Drowned Sailor, 1947

Miners

Whirring down shafts in cages to pith of darkness,
The core of night your gloomy field of labour,
Yours is the heart of the earth, from bedrock granite
Hewing and felling and blasting bare black strata.

Yours the aching back and hacking handaxe,
Trilling of drilling all day in your ears drumming,
As your ripple of muscles strains the vast wall till it cracks,
Cleaving a seam to set new arteries humming.

Down by the lanes and gulleys under the ocean,
Stretching like fingers, you handle sleeping forests,
In the fresh crop discovering distant ages,
Driving a tunnel through nature's oldest secrets.

And every minute of work is a threat of dying,
In drinking tea or wiping sweat from your brow,
Roof giving, prop cracking, or hours in water lying,
Or a ghost of gas that makes the davy glow.

And there are some who having once gone down there,
Found stiffer work than ever man was paid for,
The clash of a tub or a silent struggle for air,
Or a grave behind a gigantic sliding door.

Or there are some who leave the wreck of a limb there,
Or leave forever their heart or the spine of their courage,
Some turn white, who were dark, or ugly who were fair,
Some lose their souls and waste their lives in rage.

Yours is the hard, inscrutable face of the coalseam,
Strong sons of strong fathers, daily darers of doom,
Who give trains speed, who set ships under steam,
And the warmth of whose heart lights a fire in each hearth and home.

(August 1941)

FRANCIS SCARFE
Forty Poems and Ballads, 1941

Tyne Dock

The summer season at Tyne Dock
Hoisted my boyhood in a crane,
Above the shaggy mining town
Above the slaghills and the rocks
Above the middens in backlanes
And wooden hen-huts falling down.

Grass grew vermilion in the streets
Where the blind pit-ponies pranced
While poppies screamed by butchers' stalls
And bulls kicked sparks with dying feet,
And in the naked larks I sensed
A cruel God beneath it all.

Over the pit-head wheel the moon
Was clean as a girl's face in school:
I envied the remote old man
Who lived there quiet and alone,
While in the kitchen the mad spool
Unwound as Annie's treadle ran.

The boyish season is still there
For clapping hands and leaping feet
Across the slagheaps and the dunes;
And still it breaks into my care,
Though I will never find the street,
Nor catch the old, impulsive tune,
Nor ever lose that child's despair.

(1947)

FRANCIS SCARFE
Underworlds, 1950 | *Poetry of the Forties*, 1968

'The nature of the Mss drafts has something to do with the fact that after leaving the Army in 1946, I found it difficult to get back to poetry. I decided on two ways: one was to practise automatic writing, the other was to recall childhood scenes. The first of these led me to write 3 novels in quick succession, and the second brought me back to poetry. [...]
   This poem was sent to *Poetry Chicago*, but I don't know if it was ever printed by them. It has since appeared in *The Listener* and in anthologies, and in my book *Underworlds*.'
   [Author's manuscript note: headed 'final version']

Francis Scarfe (1911–1986) was born at 539 Stanhope Road, in South Shields, where he spent four years at the Royal Merchant Seaman's Orphanage, after his father was lost at sea in 1917. He recalled the military-type discipline (he was number 107), playing the bombardon (though unable to carry it to church), and exchanging notes through a wall with a girl he never met.

Scarfe attended the Boys High School in Shields, and subsequently Armstrong College Newcastle, Cambridge and the Sorbonne. By 1936 he was living in Paris, writing surrealist verse and attending meetings of the French Communist Party – both of which he abandoned in 1938. His books included four poetry collection, *Inscapes* (1940), *Forty Poems and Ballads* (1941), *Underworlds* (1950) and *Grounds for Conceit* (1984); three novels; and the studies *Auden and After* (1942), *Paul Valéry* (1954) and *André Chénier* (1965). His Penguin selection of Baudelaire (1961) was enlarged into *The Complete Verse* (1986, 2011); he also published a translation of *100 Fables* of La Fontaine (1985). Following his war service he held academic posts in Glasgow and London, and was Director of the British Institute in Paris for 20 years.

'In Memoriam' is a touching tribute to Scarfe's mother. His best-known poem, 'Tyne Dock', included in his second collection, *Underworlds* (1950), recalls his 'shaggy mining town' with a sense of loss. In Robin Skelton's Penguin anthology *Poetry of the Forties* (1962), the poem appears with an additional stanza after the third stanza:

> Squat fishing-smacks swung down the Tyne
> And windwards their wide tan sails spread
> With bobbling lights red on the wave,
> While with their lanterns to the mine
> The pitmen clogged, and by my bed
> Night kneeled, and all the day forgave.

This is missing from the 'final manuscript' of the poem in the archive held by his estate.

His son, Bruno Scarfe, has kindly supplied the texts of two poems, 'Tyne Dock Revisited' and 'The Knocker-up', which appear to be previously unpublished. [AM/NA]

Tyne Dock Revisited

The spit-rings under the black arch,
The rags and bones that fought for stubs,
The whippet-man the dole has gripped,[1]
The poetry of singing pubs,
Tuberculosis, syphilis,
The colliers rotting on the slips:

The slagheap glowing overhead,[2]
The North Sea in my nightlit room,
The pit-head wheel's black hangman's rope,[3]
The faded cracked linoleum,
The Burne-Jones angel by my bed,
The Bubbles-boy with pipe and soap:

The foghorn through the briny night,[4]
The widow weeping in her sleep,
The boy whose visions knew no rest[5]
But scoured the drowned Atlantic's deep,[6]
The boy whose code and second-sight
Saw suffering pure and saw it blest:

They've all gone where the years have gone,
The seafarers, the giant horses,[7]
The barefoot girls in coaldust haze,
The sailing-ships on fairy courses:
And now I wake and ponder on[8]
That hell on earth, that cleansing gaze.[9]

FRANCIS SCARFE
(Previously unpublished)

Earlier (undated) manuscript variant lines:
1. the sporting-man the dole has gripped,
2. The smoking tunnel overhead,
3. The pithead wheel's black endless rope,
4. The blue fog churning through the night,
5. The child whose visions knew no rest
6. But probed the drowned Atlantic's deep,
7. The mariners, the giant horses,
8. And I still wake and ponder on
9. That dying world, my loving rage.

In Memoriam

Impossible to go back any more
to the cracked lino the bronze stag
the ragmat flapping under the scullery door

Unless perhaps to remember
wyandottes scratching in the backyard
the tortoise upside-down on the kitchen floor

Though now your imagined lives are over
you're never done with looking forward
through the darkening windows of years

Still wondering if there's any answer
to the first question and the last
your hand was asking as it lived in hers

As you trailed through the Market together
under the gas-jets, squeezing pennies
to bid for bruised enormous oranges

As guiding you into the future
she told such marvels you forget about her
whose hand held yours long after she was gone.

FRANCIS SCARFE
Stand, 1985

The grotto

The sea still plunges where as naked boys
we dared the currents and the stinging tides
that stamped red weals of fury on our thighs,
yet did not know our first love was the sea
that rolled like colts between our shining knees,
while under us the sands in golden curls
coiled round our bodies like the plaits of girls.

We came oblique to passion on that shore
identified with our blind will to danger,
as when we explored the slipping walls of caves
booming with the dark echoes of the waves,
whose silence magnified the heart's deep roar
till senses waked that were asleep before,
and in ourselves we recognised a stranger.

Or when we scaled at Frenchman's Bay the cliff
no man has dared, though boys there in the night
still climb to manhood on its murderous side,
that was our climb from innocence to life:
and yet, if we could be there once again
my love, I'd pause amazed among the gulls,
afraid of both the triumphs and the falls.

In sea and grotto where we found our hearts
our youth remains, and all our days return
in endless dreaming to the mocking sea,
where all that closed the past within us stirred
within the silence like a waiting bird,
and never a dawning day will break as pure
as our grave adoration, immature.

FRANCIS SCARFE
Underworlds, 1950

Marsden Rock

There is a sinuous pathway all along those curving clifftops.
With the fields on one hand, the North Sea on the other,
how often I pedalled idly along its treacherous
humps and hollows! It required a steady touch on
the bouncing handlebars, while under the saddle
the leather toolbag's spanners rattled as I jounced along.

If it had been raining, my tyres imprinted on the clay
those interweaving daisychains whose simple flow diagrams
traced the problems of their undulating graphs.
– There was never any need for the hoarse warnings of
my rather rusty bell, whose squawkings mingled with the cries
of indignant gulls; for I always seemed to be the only one

with the mad impulse to map the great bay's perilous path.
But I always kept a keen eye on the cliff's grassy verge
where the wild flowers – blossoming gorse, dandelions, clovers –
bloomed in a floral fringe above the grander borders down below
of North Sea rollers casting wide lassoos of wind-blown foam
with gentle thunderings upon the rocks and caves and sands.

In this photograph, how brightly those memories shine!
The whole bay seems to be basking in a summer sun
that must be low, because it throws cliff shadows
far out across the beaches and the waves – but it's November
and under unseasonably clear skies we can see as far
as the mouth of the Tyne, the white thimble of our lighthouse.

– And just beyond the creeping shadows there stands the Rock
detached, long battered into shapeless shape by winter storms
that soon will rage again upon its crumbling bastion
where gannets and Arctic gulls would come to nest
and lay their eggs that no intruders' hands could ever reach…
its flat top wild and mossy still and pathless round the edge.

JAMES KIRKUP
Home Thoughts, 2011

James Kirkup (1918–2009), the only son of a carpenter, was born in Robertson Street, South Shields, and grew up on Cockburn Street, and later Ada Street in Westoe. After attending South Shields High School, he took a degree in modern languages at King's College, Newcastle, then part of Durham University. A conscientious objector during the Second World War, he was sent to forestry and agricultural labour camps in Northumberland and North Yorkshire.

After the War he went into teaching, firstly at the Downs School, a Quaker prep school in Colwall, Herefordshire (where Auden had been a schoolmaster in 1932-35), where he completed his first poetry collection *The Drowned Sailor* (1947). He published more than 20 books of poetry, and was also a translator (especially of Japanese poetry), a novelist, dramatist, literary critic, reviewer, children's writer, essayist and obituarist. A selected poems is forthcoming in 2018 from Red Squirrel Press which has published his work in recent years.

He held many academic appointments around the world from 1956, in Sweden, Spain, Malaysia, the US, and most frequently in Japan. From 1977 until his retirement in 1989, he was professor of English literature at the Kyoto University of Foreign Studies. For the latter period of his life he lived in Andorra.

His memoir *The Only Child* (1957) gives an enchanting account of a child's life in 1920s South Shields, and was followed by a sequel, *Sorrows, Passions and Alarms*. He later re-wrote these memoirs, laying much greater stress on his sexual proclivities, a theme he continued with startling frankness in autobiographical works published in the 1990s.

He caused considerable controversy in 1977 when his poem 'The love that dares to speak its name' occasioned the first prosecution for blasphemous libel for fifty years. It concerns the ruminations of a homosexual Roman soldier gazing on the body of the crucified Christ. The editor of Gay News was fined and given a suspended prison sentence.

His books and papers are archived at the James Kirkup Collection in South Shields, established in 2006 by Dorothy Fleet at the Central Library, and shortly to be rehoused The Word, National Centre for the Written Word. [AM/NA]

The Knocker-up

Tyne Dock stirs as the knocker-up
Fettles the brass and joggles on
Stotting through dingy dawn:

Lift your larkbones old man
Scrub on your chin the stiff of night
Chuck with the blankets your daft dreaming of
The whippet fields the pigeon smell of love:

Take on your leather crown and davylamp
And tiptap with your staff and hobnail clogs
Down the backlanes into the mucky dark
A mile under the sea where your stint waits:

Wake up the coal its blinding blacknesses
That glint and glitter like the eyes of bairns
Or the pitponies' deep nightfolded gaze

FRANCIS SCARFE
(Previously unpublished)

The Knocker-up

All the mornings of my early childhood
began at five o'clock, when the knocker-up
tapped on the window with his pole – a sound
that haunted my sleep and wakened me betimes
from nightmares of school sports, the horrors
of weekly visits to the municipal swimming baths –
then the terrors of mathematics, physics, chemistry
that poisoned every day with foul gases of theorems.

But my real education had already begun at home
at six o'clock in the morning (when
my father was 'in work') and I helped my mother
to lay, build and light the kitchen grate
after raking out the remains of last night's cinders –
while my father shaved in the sink's icy water

in the freezing scullery on its dark backyard,
'having a scrape' under the gas mantle's precarious
hive of light shivering at every footfall from upstairs.

After a quick trip to the dark outdoor netty
I sat by the fire, watching it take and slowly
feeling its warmth on my hands and bare knees.
As my mother made the breakfast for my father,
I sat eating a slice of bread and dripping
and drank my mug of scalding tea. – At last,
humping his tool bag, my father in all weathers
set out for the shipyards or the new estates –
steady carpenter who had wanted only
to follow his captain father in a life at sea.

Then I still had a couple of hours to spend at home
before running down the streets to the school bell
with its urgent note of suppressed bullying rage.
I still had two hours with my library books – reading
the whole of Dickens (kids' stuff), Arnold Bennett,
Thomas Hardy, D.H. Lawrence, Wordsworth, Rupert Brooke –
all 'too old for you' – but I never felt it so.

Because I had been awakened early –
even on Sundays I was up at five o'clock
to start the week's new library books –
a solid engagement, habit never grown out of.
– And eighty years later, I know I am still
obeying that tap on the window of life's knocker-up.

JAMES KIRKUP
Home Thoughts, 2011

View from the Town Hall, South Shields

At the end of the narrow, empty room
the entire window, before the drawing of the blinds,
strains like a membrane to contain the sky,
or like a quartered sail upon a mast of air
swells with the coming night, the clouded winds.

Like a vast watercolour framed in bone,
the last blue rectangles of dusk begin
to overlap and darken. The iron Hermes on the dome
dissolves, and unseen statues that with evening rain
will shine beneath the lamps, begin now to exchange

their daylight postures for the attitudes of night.
A balustrade continually crumbles out of sight
into the park's drowning trees, that cover and uncover
shaking stars, an avenue of lamps, a lighted ship's
descending constellation. The clock-tower rises out of falling

waves of traffic, laughter, seas of brick, and streets
of rustling sand. Like a strange face pressed inconveniently close
to mine, the changing features tell, with changeless tick
and tock, that now is forever now. But at no other time
will it be quite the same – the winter loneliness, and four o'clock.

(138, Fowler Street)

JAMES KIRKUP
The Submerged Village and Other Poems, 1951

Spring in the Public Gardens

Around the formal pond,
like huge eggs laid in new grass,
the hulls of model yachts recline,
or like exhausted pets
bare smooth bellies to the sun.
Planes rip the cloud-stuffed blue
and wrap it with loose
fraying bandages. The sly
children crouch under
the threat of summer,
pretending not to see
how the Spring's cold ripples
shiver the top-heavy sky;
how the wind cripples

the shrubbery, stabs
the lake, flusters the sails of toy
arks, while a careless boy
with a barking dog disturbs
the couples who dust each other down,
groaning and rising out of the earth
with resurrected clothes,
the dead town
rising with them, and
with all its living graves,
quietly, in catastrophic re-birth.

(South Marine Park, South Shields: Easter 1950)

JAMES KIRKUP
To the Ancestral North, 1983

The Old Clothes Stall, South Shields Market

The old jackets rub shoulders
on the racks of life and death,
the crumpled trousers all undone
swing in a driving wind,
a boneless abandon,
soft-shoe shuffle in the sands of time.

These skeletons out of their cupboards
are human, still warm with dying.
There are crumbs in their pockets,
dust in their turn-ups,
broken feathers in best hats,
glad rags in the seats of their pants,
in elbows where the striped lining
pokes out like fractured bones.

Laid away, the painter's dungarees
are dingy white, stained with forgotten schemes
for houses decorated out of sight.

The cobbles spread their broken flag.
On wooden stalls, tented with clouds
of canvas, a grimy resurrection lies.

Here are the collier's clogs, the seaman's denims,
the housewife's shifts and Sunday coats.
– These are the limbless ghosts
jumbled here on the old wooden stalls,
heaped in confusion or suspended
like out-of-work puppets in
the north wind of curious hands and faces

stirring them in their graves
like the bones in the churchyard of
St Hilda's, on the resurrection morn.

JAMES KIRKUP
Night Ride and Sunrise, ed. Edward Lowbury, 1978 | *Home Thoughts*, 2011

South Shields Town Hall in Snow

It's ten minutes to five, a snowy day –
brief break in the clouds –
but more snow coming up
from the North Sea.
That model ship – weathervane
perched high on top of the solid clock tower
still seems to be making heavy weather.

But the statue of Queen Victoria,
snow draping the dark folds of iron robes –
is the orb of Empire still in that hand? –
still stands imperturbably on her lone
pedestal, in a fir tree's noble shade.

Is that a glimpse, just behind her, of one
of those naked nymphs who used to surround
the Town Hall plaza, lifting electrical lamps –
but they, too, have long since been cleared away,
as too provocative in their nudity

for working lads whose fathers had taught them
the old Tyneside rhyme?– 'Of all the statues,
great and small, there's none like them outside
the Shields Town Hall' – (Paris Opéra copies;
they had become a hazard for leering drivers).

There is a touch of sun, casting shadows
of passers-by, and of a tall street-lamp.
The stolid main building glows in brief warmth,
but no one has cleared the snow off its flight of steps,
leading to a cherry-red door that offends the stone.

– But soon we shall hear the clock strike five
solemn strokes, the usual pigeons will flutter
briefly and settle again in the tall
openwork tower's curious cage – that bell
haunted the long dreams of my misspent youth

across the road, in Fowler Street, and right
opposite that grave clock face, that seemed to
be pressing its moonful of sinister figures
against my bedroom window with mocking
defiance: 'Time and tide wait for no man…'

But in spite of everything, I am still
keeping those patient guardians waiting –
their every quarter, every hour
is struck for me, however far I roam,
with grave tones that poisoned every day and night

as dream-shadows crept to the beaches down
the weirdly-named Ogle Terrace, that led
to dark parks, and maritime horizons
and the lonely pier of dreams I haunted
night after night, with time's distant warning buoys.

JAMES KIRKUP
Home Thoughts, 2011

The Old Library, Ocean Road, South Shields

I still seem to hear the griping grind and groan
of the monumental double-decker trams to the Pier Head
outside the sober windows of the Newspaper Reading Room
with its smells of fresh newsprint and coal miners' old boots –
four-year-old standing as if for hours with Uncle Martin
among the readers' armies of unemployed trouser legs
– Racing Results, Football Scores, Situations Vacant –
I was lost in forests of sloping racks far overhead
bearing 'The Shields Gazette & Shipping Telegraph'.

'Way above your little head' severe librarians at the issue desk
gravely informed me when I brought my books to be stamped
with expiry dates for Poe and Arnold Bennett as I showed
my first library card, hot in my eager hand – I still
remember the fascinating squeak and metallic thud
of the hand-operated date stamp – modern efficiency –
filling a fresh-labelled book with haphazard days and weeks
of Conrad, Wells, Woolf, Hardy, Shaw, Shakespeare, Shelley…
dark green tomes of music scores – Wagner, Scarlatti, Verdi, Chopin…

The palatial tiled entrance hall contained a sailing ship,
accurate scale model enshrined in fingerprinted glass
forever grounded at the foot of a noble flight of polished stairs
conducting me to the Art Gallery's pastoral landscapes and wild marines
with a gorgeous view of the Scala across the street – Mae West!
Chaplin, Garbo, Fred Astaire, Jack Buchanan, dear Jeanette MacDonald,
enormous Technicolor heads above passing tramcar roofs;
then to the twilit, odorous museum, floor-polished jungle
of stuffed parakeets, cobras, tigers, wolves and walruses,
their glass eyes glaring among fur and feathers, bevies of butterflies
from another world, another life that I dreamed of, and longed
to discover, in lands and oceans far from Ocean Road – the Criterion,
embalmed in beer, the tailor's, pails and spades, and Notarianni's
ice cream parlour rumoured to be a den of adolescent vice…
while outside the soaring ecclesiastical windows the upper decks
of earth-bound tramways sounding foot-pedal warning bells
with chinking trolleys in magical showers of sparks, blue flashes
were my only dreamboats groaning and grinding round the bends

of gleaming, sand-filled tracks and points to the Market, Tyne Dock,
Laygate, the Fountain Inn, the Cut's wild echoings running
to Westoe Village, embowered in ancient trees – on to Harton,
Caldwell and Cleadon Hills, the ghostly White Horse.
– I still go there in dreams – along the mile long South Pier;
lose myself among Trow Rocks' haunted bays, clifftop Marsden's
sea-smelling grottoes, its green bathing-tents, the deckchairs
where the idle rich could mingle with the out-of-work
on sands that were a luxury free to all, the sea a paradise for ever.
Library closing time – distant warnings from the Town Hall chimes.

JAMES KIRKUP
Home Thoughts, 2011

Cross-hatch

It was said a girl I sat beside in biology
charged for sex on Cleadon Hills.

You could see the heads of those from my folks'
top room. We'd peek out from there to see

if boys would walk right past the pond and along
up by the special school. We did not spy it, our noses

burning as we rested them on top of the radiator.
We were birds perching. When it rained I wondered

if she took a tent and if she hitched her skirt up. The thing is
she never came to Guides. Lizzy told me of oral sex on the 525 home

and lit the Bunsen burners up in class. We always wanted
to ask if she went up there for fun. If it was true

the topless windmill was lived in. If she had chiselled
her name on the half-eaten oak bench, and if the grass was long.

She'd walk the corridors, a price tag on her head. Our mouths
were black holes then. Tongues moved quickly throughout our school.

JEN CAMPBELL
The Hungry Ghost Festival, 2012

WEARSIDE

The Lambton Worm
(traditional ballad)

One Sunday mornin' Lambton went
A-fishin' in the Wear;
An' catched a fish upon he's heuk,
He thowt leuk't varry queer,
But whatt'n a kind ov fish it was
Young Lambton cuddent tell
He waddn't fash te carry'd hyem,
So he hoyed it in a well.

Whisht! lads, haad yor gobs,
An Aa'll tell ye aall an aaful story,
Whisht! lads, haad yor gobs,
An Aa'll tell ye 'boot the worm.

Noo Lambton felt inclined te gan
An' fight i' foreign wars.
He joined a troop ov Knights that cared
For nowther woonds nor scars,
An' off he went te Palestine
Where queer things him befel,
An varry seun forgat aboot
The queer worm i' the well.

But the worm got fat an' growed an' growed.
An' growed an aaful size;
He'd greet big teeth, a greet big gob,
An' greet big goggle eyes.
An' when at neets he craaled aboot
Te pick up bits o' news,
If he felt dry upon the road,
He milked a dozen coos.

This feorful worm would often feed
On caalves an' lambs an' sheep,
An' swally little bairns alive

When they laid doon te sleep.
An' when he'd eaten aall he cud
An' he had had he's fill,
He craaled away an' lapped he's tail
Ten times roond Pensher Hill.

The news of this myest aaful worm
An' his queer gannins on
Seun crossed the seas, gat te the ears
Ov brave an' bowld Sor John.
So hyem he cam an' catched the beast
An' cut 'im in twe haalves,
An' that seun stopped he's eatin' bairns
An' sheep an' lambs an' caalves.

So noo ye knaa hoo aall the foaks
On byeth sides ov the Wear
Lost lots o' sheep an' lots o' sleep
An' leeved i' mortal feor.
So let's hev one te brave Sor John
That kept the bairns frae harm,
Saved coos an' caalves by myekin' haalves
O' the famis Lambton Worm.

Noo, lads, Aa'll haad me gob,
That's aall Aa knaa aboot the story
Ov Sor John's clivvor job
Wi' the aaful Lambton Worm.

ANONYMOUS
John Stokoe, *Songs and Ballads of Northern England*, 1892

fash: bother; *hoyed:* threw; *hyem:* home; *haad yor gobs:* shut your mouths; *Pensher Hill:* Penshaw Hill, above the Wear, Co. Durham, near Lambton Castle.

The Walrus and the Carpenter

The sun was shining on the sea,
    Shining with all his might:
He did his very best to make
    The billows smooth and bright –
And this was odd, because it was
    The middle of the night.

The moon was shining sulkily,
    Because she thought the sun
Had got no business to be there
    After the day was done –
'It's very rude of him,' she said,
    'To come and spoil the fun.'

The sea was wet as wet could be,
    The sands were dry as dry.
You could not see a cloud, because
    No cloud was in the sky:
No birds were flying overhead –
    There were no birds to fly.

The Walrus and the Carpenter
    Were walking close at hand;
They wept like anything to see
    Such quantities of sand:
'If this were only cleared away,'
    They said, it *would* be grand!'

'If seven maids with seven mops
    Swept it for half a year,
Do you suppose,' the Walrus said,
    'That they could get it clear?'
'I doubt it,' said the Carpenter,
    And shed a bitter tear.

'O Oysters, come and walk with us!'
    The Walrus did beseech.
'A pleasant walk, a pleasant talk,
    Along the briny beach:
We cannot do with more than four,
    To give a hand to each.'

The eldest Oyster looked at him,
    But never a word he said:
The eldest Oyster winked his eye,
    And shook his heavy head –
Meaning to say he did not choose
    To leave the oyster-bed.

But four young Oysters hurried up,
    All eager for the treat:
Their coats were brushed, their faces washed,
    Their shoes were clean and neat –
And this was odd, because, you know,
    They hadn't any feet.

Four other Oysters followed them,
    And yet another four;
And thick and fast they came at last,
    And more, and more, and more –
All hopping through the frothy waves,
    And scrambling to the shore.

The Walrus and the Carpenter
    Walked on a mile or so,
And then they rested on a rock
    Conveniently low:
And all the little Oysters stood
    And waited in a row.

'The time has come,' the Walrus said,
    'To talk of many things:
Of shoes – and ships – and sealing-wax –
    Of cabbages – and kings –
And why the sea is boiling hot –
    And whether pigs have wings.'

'But wait a bit,' the Oysters cried,
    Before we have our chat;
'For some of us are out of breath,
    And all of us are fat!'
'No hurry!' said the Carpenter.
    They thanked him much for that.

'A loaf of bread,' the Walrus said,
   'Is what we chiefly need:
Pepper and vinegar besides
   Are very good indeed –
Now if you're ready, Oysters dear,
   We can begin to feed.'

'But not on us!' the Oysters cried,
   Turning a little blue.
'After such kindness, that would be
   A dismal thing to do!'
'The night is fine,' the Walrus said.
   Do you admire the view?

'It was so kind of you to come!
   And you are very nice!'
The Carpenter said nothing but
   'Cut us another slice:
I wish you were not quite so deaf –
   I've had to ask you twice!'

'It seems a shame,' the Walrus said,
   To play them such a trick,
'After we've brought them out so far,
   And made them trot so quick!'
The Carpenter said nothing but
   'The butter's spread too thick!'

'I weep for you,' the Walrus said:
   'I deeply sympathise.'
With sobs and tears he sorted out
   Those of the largest size,
Holding his pocket-handkerchief
   Before his streaming eyes.

'O Oysters,' said the Carpenter,
   'You've had a pleasant run!
Shall we be trotting home again?'
   But answer came there none –
And this was scarcely odd, because
   They'd eaten every one.

LEWIS CARROLL
Through the Looking-Glass, 1871

Charles Lutwidge Dodgson (1832–1898), who wrote as **Lewis Carroll**, moved with his family from Cheshire, where Charles had been born in 1832, to the vicarage at Croft-on-Tees, near Darlington, in 1843. It remained the family home until 1868. Charles attended school in nearby Richmond for some two years (1844–46) before moving on to Rugby. At this time he used to write stories and poems, and invent games for the entertainment of the numerous family at Croft, where the large shady garden remains much as the Dodgson children knew it. One of his many amusing early poems begins:

> Fair stands the ancient Rectory,
> The Rectory of Croft,
> The sun shines bright upon it,
> The breezes whisper soft.
>
> From all the house and garden,
> Its inhabitants come forth,
> And muster in the road without,
> And pace in twos and threes about,
> The children of the North.

Carroll also wrote a humorous ghost story called 'The Legend of Scotland', referring to the part of Auckland Castle where Scottish prisoners were once kept. The story, set in 1325, involves Bishop Bek of Durham, so that Carroll could bring in one of his puns as the joke ending. Carroll was a keen photographer and a comical story 'A Photographer's Day Out' was published in the *South Shields Amateur Magazine* in 1860. In the first surviving diary of his early manhood, we find that he met 'three nice little children' belonging to a Mrs Crawshay in Tynemouth on 21 August 1855. He remarks: 'I took a great fancy to Florence, the eldest, a child of very sweet manners...'

Most of his famous poem 'Jabberwocky' which begins:

> 'Twas brillig and the slithey toves
> Did gyre and gimble in the wabe

was written on a visit to his Wilcox cousins in Whitburn, near Sunderland in 1855. Mary Wilcox was the wife of the Collector of Customs in Sunderland; their house, High Croft, was later burned down. The word 'beamish' in the line 'Come to my arms my beamish boy' is assumed to be taken from the Durham village, while the Jabberwocky itself was probably inspired by the Sockburn Worm, a ferocious wyvern which laid waste to the village of Sockburn in Co. Durham, according to local folklore. Each newly consecrated Prince Bishop of Durham, entering the bishopric for the first time over the bridge at Croft, was formerly presented with the falchion (now in Durham Cathedral treasury) that Sir John Conyers used to slay 'the worm, dragon or fiery flying serpent' of Sockburn.

Carroll is said to have composed 'The Walrus and the Carpenter' – who wept like anything to see / Such quantities of sand' – while walking on Whitburn and Seaburn beaches. The distinctive headgear of a ship's carpenter was a common sight in a great shipbuilding centre like Sunderland. The walrus once kept in Sunderland Museum, however, arrived later – a gift from the explorer Joseph Wiggins – and has now disintegrated except for the head. There is, however, a bronze walrus in Mowbray Park in Sunderland.

Carroll was in Whitburn in 1864, 1866 and 1872, when he visited his sister who had married the vicar of Holy Trinity in Southwick. There is a commemorative plaque there. Carroll's connection with Whitburn is commemorated by a statue in the library, removed from Cornthwaite Park to protect it from the children of today. It originally had a child companion, not Alice Liddell as might be thought, but her cousin Frederika, whom Carroll had met at Whitburn Hall, and sketched on Roker beach. [AM/NA]

His Bright Silver

>   The bonny pit laddie
>   The canny pit laddie
>   The bonny pit laddie for me O
>
>   He sits on his cracket
>   And hews in his jacket
>   And brings the bright siller to me O
>   (SONG) TRADITIONAL

1

Pit yackers dance to
Pulley-wheel buzzer

At Kelloe the calf hill
Chipped cross-face of Helen

At Hetton and Elemore
Trimdon and Esh

Little Chance is the gallowa
Putters all bless

2

Beech candles drip wax
Into root-fibre cutting

Full draped bier
Draws empty one up

On twisted steel rope
On gravity bobbins

As children whirl haloes
Discarded hemp-core lit

3

Stephenson's steam theodolite
Spies lay for waggon line

Lambton Hetton and Joicey's logo
Bold on wooden sides

Wheel-squeak and larks
Sing along with fossil birds

Embanked through bowed reapers
Eden's last harvest falls

    4

Brick warren estate
Rabbit Wood overrun

High rise shadow blade
Has steel cord cut

Ghostly crossing keeper
Muffler clay pipe and spit

Old 'face' now 'bank man'
Like Hefænricaes Uard
Dreams and puffs his twist

    5

Hazeldene evensong
Church on green edge

Sunset banner
Starboard tapers lit

Deep bramble harrowing
Chancel-bow dip by Gox

Pit-head Malkuth
In bent barley

    6

Memorial words
Uncial Quarter seam

Bonny May morning
Night shift on the face

Telltale yellow cagebird
First shift in the Gate poor lads

Black explosion banner
Stone names all but one

7

Candles flicker in eviction tents
What Kingdom without common feasting

When they were seated
Silk banners on fellside

Friends after nettle broth
Turned slogans into bread

By the poor for the poor
They taught themselves

8

Street children cry Cockerooso
Generations hop across

Spuggie chorus crack
Cathedral choir sing anthem

'Our feet shall stand
In thy gates O Jerusalem'

Larks rise with brass
Big Meeting last one for Eden

9

The bonny pit laddie
Sits on his cracket

Corf fill the keel
Keel fill the brig

Dark drift or shaft hole
He hews in his jacket

And brings the bright silver
The canny pit laddie

His eye full of silver to me

WILLIAM MARTIN
Cracknrigg, 1983 | *Lammas Alanna*, 2000

Song of the Cotia Lass

    1

The keel took my heart
In full tide it was torn
The keel took my heart
Black blood to his flame

The waggonway fall
Was braked by the river
the horse on its tether
With nose-bag and corn

The keel took my heart
To whistle and wo-lad
Down in his brig of dust
Down to his hot ash breath

    2

On lip of drift crying
I sang the raa up and down
Black the craa hinny
Ivvry day now

I sang over fell where
Grey pocked my
Green stitched hem
Smouldering sway there
Banners to brighten

The keel bought my heart
It was bonded and bound
The keel took my heart
In full tide it was torn

    3

Who rose in the morning
To see the keels row then
Who'll rise in the morning
To see the keels go

It was down by the river
Ventricles pumping there

Shute and flat bottom
Leveller schull

Who rose and who'll rise
With banners and drum thump
The keel took my heart
Silk over it laid

    4

The keel played at morning-tide
Bide and abide with me
Keel-brass for my heart blown
Banner-water bidding

Rite blinds were drawn to
Down staithe banks drawn all the way
Hats doffed and held there
In the ebb-tide hush

Down in yon forest
The keel rang my heart away
Black bells of Paradise
Hutton and Harvey change

    5

Foy-boatman blow the flame
Loosen his rope-fast sail
Scorch the wind southerly
Fill it with fire in flood

Blood rages over bar
Out in the molten toss
Fury and friend are lost days
Where you are

The keel sought my heart
In full tide it was torn
It beats every tree on fire
Wagga-pulse fossil dawn

WILLIAM MARTIN
Hinny Beata, 1987 | *Lammas Alanna*, 2000

Wiramutha Helix
Tell the bairns in their wilderness

> Rosy apple lemon and pear
> A bunch of roses she shall wear
> Gold and silver by her side
> She shall be a bride
>
> Take her by the lily-white hand
> Lead her across the water
> Kiss-her eyes and lips on-the hill so high
> She is yesterday's daughter

THORN HILL

   1

Thorn Hill is grown under
Concrete and tar

How many tongue-ties
Will lick the honey

Thorn Hill has a crack
Full of green fossil stars

How many blinded
Will see them rise

   2

I said to the wind
Blowing crow-smoke about her

How many nest-fires
Will Spring take to come

I said to the solstice-sun
Rolling low into dark

How many yellow beaks
How many tongues

3

Thorn Hill is set groaning
By a silver-touch finger

How many blossoms
Will pollen her quick

Thorn Hill is a black bark
Split open tomorrow-tide

How many sick mornings
Will Eskhatos bring

MAIDEN PAPS

4

Corn over breast blown
Summer into harvest

Jostling ears confused…
Hiss of seed coming…

Path with crows
And golden hatchings

Helix unravels harvest
Crows scare the corn

5

Voices come at last out of the spiral path
Out of twin hills

Cleft alined with
Pensher and Hastings

Due west through Fatfield and the Worm
And Cotia underground

The Tup decked out
Candle bristles singe

6

Sea-root breasts are fossil
Reef dried out to desert

Ice gouging Hope House
Haunted by psyche clay

Well in forbidden wood
Plop pebbles 'a dare yu'

Who dashes in green light
Who holds a bairn's tongue

SILKSWORTH COLLIERY

7

(There will be a special meeting)
We all stand still

(In the Miners' Hall)
I touch your eyes to tears

(At seven o'clock)
I count to fifty while you hide them

I see day turning away from us
The moon is a dark faced Crake Man

8

I am his shakey-down child
Silk banner up to chin

I hold his blue-scarred hand
Deep in cloth cap grass

I am raised to meet dawn
Slow on a green shoulder

I am in the whole field moving
As marra-wind ruffles

9

Drum thumps its common pulse
I felt it all day

Ears and throat connect brass valves
I clip music to my feet

I dance the banner clef
Tassel notes Lodge at the heart of it

I will sing inarticulate words
Next year in Durham again

HASTINGS HILL

10

Path through corn hedgeless
Lone fox under cover

His red tail trailing
To a bronze cist empty

Child bones glassed
Pressed noses steaming

Flesh fades away ageing
To metal classified

11

Virgin from the hill
Crooks her arm under

Virgin on the steps
Guards reconstructed cist

Bone cracks like wood
Painted skin sunk in

She holds the bronze child
Plucked from green corn golding

12

Sunrise March and September
From sea in cleft old breasts alined

Thread drawn out of Thorn Hill
Her bow tied to ravel-hill top

Lovers go on a bit
Pulling it slack again

White triangulation shadow
Leaping over paths

HYLTON CASTLE

13

Harm is out of the way
Lonely tower without light

Silent herald Tupp
(Horned Kronos Moses)

Unable to read the stone
Shielded from eyes

Shielded from her moon
Suddenly on castellation

14

Fly again with puritan crows
Over battlefield housing estate

Spin pitch and toss down Pennywell banks
To 'waes me' castle to singing 'caad lad' ghost

'No acorn has fallen from this tree
To grow the wood to make the cradle

To rock the bairn into a man
Who'll lay me'

15

We touch his apparition
He is a changeling

We lay a table before him
He plots against order

We feed him with greenery
He falls into autumn

We impale him on icicles
He spikes the harvest

FULWELL MILL

16

White foul-well mill…
Empty handed sails…

White bleached limestone
Beacon on bright days

Lost canvas tacking
Her ghostly brig ballast

Dumped flint and sand
I saw three ships trimmed in black

17

White mill her days are ground
To black bread staff

Broken fossil seed
Carbon-copy life

Wind through tarred fingers
Empty cross-arm hands

White mill I saw three ships
Crest-fallen over bar

18

White mill your fixed arms
Are winded and seen through

Unfeathered unturned
Vibrating not pushed aside

Stone is fragmented
(All the King's horses

And all the King's menders)
Cemented into wall

WEARMOUTH

19

Saints come out of age
Under ballast hills dumped

They walk east through shingle
Twined serpents at hand

They walk east out of grassed sand
Go east into shifting sand washed

Saints come out of age
They walk east on our pages

20

He came to be venerable with them
Common words raised by common vision

Morning Star a coble from blackness
Fishers of men told where to cast

Spuggie-sparrow flying to a
Beginning of every wonder

Migrating wings take him
Now should we praise

21

He aches out a history
His cold desert song

Leningrad feeling the nip
This hermitage speaking up

White vapour puffing
Inked words in and out

North arm and south arm
Await the star rising

SALTERFEN

22

Are you coming out of Thorn Hill
Are you coming out of rock

Are you coming out of acorn
Tell the ships

Are you coming hissing white
Are you coming morning tide

Are you coming out of shell twist
Tell the ships

23

I come without helm
To the rising

I come without wind
Salterfen

I come without words
To trap me all over

I come golden bowl
To share now and then

24

Take the bowl west
I will stand on the shore

Take to three women
I come in with ships

Take the thrown line now
I stand in the prow

Take my morning with you
I wait to bake fishes

STONYGATE

25

Crowds cheer Eostre-morning sea on fire
Mackerel burn with gannets

Black-headed gull
Follows flame-breaker

Three cobles beach
Hot shingle hisses back

Children dance
On Vinegar Hill

26

Suffer my children with nets
Ley on Middle Haining

From Guide Post Inn to Cherry Knowle
Nettles Lane ending Rat Hill and Howley

Nack Fields for picnics
Thristley Bank not far now

Felled Black Woods
Stephenson's gravity track

Spawn ponds
Gravel howkers

   27

At Stony Gate
On the road to Durham

Three canny women
Are skipping and singing

'We've got heads in the pot
We've got pease in the pudding

So dance with us now
Joy-days are coming'

PENSHAW MONUMENT

   28

With bells and cymbals
Ring the bounds

Lift with the bearers
Bow to the mourners

Go bare-headed
Sun-ways round

Remember to greet every reaper
On the corn-path to Pensher

   29

Pensher temple guards entrance
Waste land pylons cross over

Reliquary pieces carried to remember
Waste-tip banners and followers a faint echo

Sunset blood reflects
In meander stretch

Blue sky steel
With sharp edge hacks

   30

Ancient bairns cry ancient lament...
Templar knight caaled back from Palestine

Sybil's killing advice and warning...
Death on spiked armour

Older than John-Michael
Our shiny flawed hero

Ancient bairns
Cry ancient lament

BOLDON HILL

   31

On Boldon Hill
There lived a lass

She wore a blood-red
Ribbon she wore it

Around her waist
And around her legs

About her neck
Wrapped over her face

   32

On Boldon Hill
There lived a lass

She penned a weasel
(All around the bishopric)

To nibble at words
While she sang to

Her children to dance
And unwind her

   33

On Boldon Hill
There lived a lass

She was blooded
By knowledge partly

Blinded by rigid words
She was bound facing east

She saw the good morning shepherd
Through her windings turn red

WHITBURN

   34

All around the bishopric
They plough three roods they reap three roods

All around the bishopric
They yield thirty-odd shillings for cornage

All around the bishopric
They send when called their hounds to the hunt

All around the bishopric
They kiss his ringed hand

   35

Where Adam delved
The same Lord holds Esscurr

John of Whitburn
Tends forty acres

Where Eve span a weft
Between cliff and dune

Esscurr holds Hwita's mound

36

All around the bishopric
Uneasy goes my river girl

All around the bishopric
Uneasy goes my girl

From Hwita's mound in Boldon Book
All around the bishopric

They reap three roods they plough three roods
She rises and sails in fret from it

NORTH SEA

37

I can not get to my love
She's out in the cold sea

I can not touch her
She's waiting with outstretched arms

I can not see her face without kisses
I sail in an arc south-east and south-west

I set forth today and yesterday
I can not get to my love

38

All around the white light
I will wear her old green willow

All around the channel shrouds
For twelve months and a day

And if anyone passing should ask me
The reason why I wear it now

It's O that my hinny
Is so far far away

39

As I went out early in the
Morning of summer rising

I once met a fair hinny bird
Just as the sun did shine

What made her go out on
Her journey so brightly

She's lost over rocks all alone
In the grey blinding sea

OLD SEAHAM

40

Hough Foot roots touch worn sea hem
The power gone out no issue stem

Mary Mary tolls the knell
Blackthorn starlings flock farewell

Mason herringbone
Marks the north side

Come to me here
Old fisherbride fisherbride

Bidders halt diesel at
Byron's walk crossing

And Seaton announcing
Another lyke crossing

To Sharpley and Burdon
And grave hillock copses

To quarry the hill
And all to me

42

Tell her to reap it
With a sickle of leather
Dun Cow maid
Oracular time
And bind it up
With a peacock's feather
Oak runes say
She's a true love of mine

WARDEN LAW

43

Thorn Hill is grown under
Concrete and tar

How many tongue-ties
Will lick the honey

Thorn Hill has a crack
Full of green fossil stars

How many blinded
Will see them rise

44

I said to the wind
Blowing crow-smoke about her

How many nest-fires
Will Spring take to come

I said to the solstice-sun
Rolling low into dark

How many yellow beaks
How many tongues

45

Thorn Hill is set groaning
By a silver-touch finger

How many blossoms
Will pollen her quick

Thorn Hill is a black bark
Split open tomorrow-tide

How many sick mornings
Will Eskhatos bring

WILLIAM MARTIN
Hinny Beata, 1987

For many years I walked from my home near Tunstall Hills (Maiden Paps) past Thorn Hill, where there is a Convent of Mercy, to my work at a local hospital. Looking at a map one day I realised that there were a number of major features around the town that were four miles from a centre at Thorn Hill, e.g. Warden Law, which is connected with the Dun Cow Legend and is reputed to be the last resting place of Saint Cuthbert before Durham. From this grew the idea of the Helix, to include further historic and geographical sites.

Worm: The Lambton Worm.

Cotia: Harraton Colliery – after Nova Scotia, because so many Scotsmen worked there.

Reef (Maiden Paps): The remains of a barrier reef which extended down the east Durham coast.

Hope House: House in the valley.

Crake Man: The man appointed by the Union Lodge who used to go round the village (Silksworth) with a 'crake' or rattle calling the men to meetings.

Shakey-Down: A bed made up on the floor.

Marra: Equal, like, comrade, friend, work-mate.

Hastings Hill: There is a re-constructed Bronze Age burial kist from Hastings Hill in Sunderland Museum. At the time of writing this was on the top floor, and on the stairs leading to it is a 15th-century wooden Virgin and Child.

Moses: The horned head of Moses is the crest on the east face of Hylton Castle, home of the famous ghost, the Caad Lad of Hylton.

Twined Serpents: These are carved on the porch doorway of St Peter's church Monkwearmouth, founded AD 674.

Coble or cobble: A fishing boat.

Leningrad: A copy of Bede's History now in the USSR.

Pensher Temple: The classical temple-monument erected on Penshaw Hill in 1844, to commemorate John Lambton the first Earl of Durham.

John-Michael: An earlier John Lambton was the slayer of the Lambton Worm.

Boldon Book: The Domesday Book of the north, initiated by Bishop Hugh du Puiset in 1183.

Byron's Walk: A lane named after the poet Lord Byron who was married in the hall nearby.

Song
A Wearside version

It's O but aa ken well
Ah you hinny bird
The bonny lass of Pennywell
Ah you Ah
She's lang-haired and bonny-fyaced
Ah you hinny bird
With gold and silver on her breast
Ah you Ah

Hetton line comes ower the top
Ah you hinny bird
Waggons bound for Lambton Drop
Ah you Ah
Peter's for owld Bede
Ah you hinny bird
Chapelgarth sunk in a field
Ah you Ah

There's Pans Bank for salters
Ah you hinny bird
And Hope race-track for halters
Ah you Ah
Hendon for taarytowt
Ah you hinny bird
And Silksworth pit for 'aall out'
Ah you Ah

There's Backhouse for artists
Ah you hinny bird
And Old Vic pub for Chartists
Ah you Ah
There's Roker front for bonny lights
Ah you hinny bird
Jack's Maggi shine for dark nights
Ah you Ah

There's Tunstall Hills for Maiden Paps
Ah you hinny bird
With lovers lying in the grass

Ah you Ah
There's Tid Mid and Miseray
Ah you hinny bird
Carlin Palm and Paste-Egg-Day
Ah you Ah

There's Doxfords and Pickersgills
Ah you hinny bird
Riveter's and plater's skills
Ah you Ah
There's collier brigs and keel row
Ah you hinny bird
All gone out in the big tide flow

Ah you Ah

WILLIAM MARTIN
Lammas Alanna, 2000

William Martin (1925-2010) was born in New Silksworth, a mining village near Sunderland. During the Second World War, he was a radio technician in the RAF, based near Karachi, where he was inspired by the Eastern religious and philosophical traditions. After being de-mobbed he became a gas fitter and later served in the Audiology Department of Sunderland Royal Infirmary, retiring as Head of Department. For some years he wrote without any recognition, but in 1971 he had a book of poetry published to commemorate the Wearmouth 1300 Festival (*Tidings of our Bairnsea*). This was later followed by four full-length collections, *Cracknrigg* (1983), *Hinny Beata* (1987), *Marra Familia* (1993) and *Lammas Alanna* (2000).

In a note in *Lammas Alanna*, he wrote: 'My mother was a Methodist, and on Sundays I rarely missed going to chapel three times. This included Sunday School. I was brought up on hymns and preaching, and lodge banners and the solidarity they proclaimed. But there was also the separate secret culture of the street. Games like Cockerooso, Jack Shine the Maggi, Mountykitty and Hoist the Banner were a great joy for the children of that time. There was little or no traffic. The gas lamps produced pools of light in the darkness. This was our contact with an oral tradition that enriched our lives.'

Penshaw Pastoral
(tanka)

Pithead acropolis
    washed in
        saltwater smoke

horizon slagheap
     golden grime
  of a lost boy's

    sad mirage –
  dream mine
varnished by Claude

JAMES KIRKUP
To the Ancestral North, 1983
➤ AUTHOR NOTE PAGE 371

Jack Crawford
(lyrics)

  CHORUS:
Nailed his colours to the mast
Nailed his colours to the mast
And there became the hero
Who nailed his colours to the mast.

Jack Crawford was a Sunderland man
He worked on board a keel
Up and down Wear Valley
He knew the river weel
But then he joined the Navy
Amongst the cannon's blast
And there became the hero
Who nailed his colours to the mast.

Jack sailed aboard the 'Venerable'
The flagship of the fleet
They sailed into the Channel
The Hollanders to meet
The battle was at Camperdown
And shot flew thick and fast
And that's where Jack Crawford
Nailed his colours to the mast.

Six times the flag was shot away
As the chain shot flew like hail
Till the mast top fell to the deck
And the fleet begun to fail
Jack Crawford picked up the flag
And nimble to the last
Climbed atop the main and
Nailed his colours to the mast.

Oh, what a cheer was heard that day!
And the English Tars fought back
The Dutch were torn asunder
And the cry went up for Jack
Admiral Duncan stepped up to him
Saying 'We've won the day at last
For Jack Crawford the hero
Nailed his colours to the mast.'

Now Jack was called to London
Sent for by the King
He says, 'Jack, you're a hero'
As the crowd began to sing
'Here's a pension, thirty pound a year
For you fought them to the last
Raise a cheer for brave Jack Crawford
Who nailed his colours to the mast.'

So if you go to Sunderland
Leave the streets and leave the crowd
See the statue of him
Standin' there se proud
When you're down in Mowbray Park
Pause as you go past
And remember brave Jack Crawford
Who nailed his colours to the mast.

JOHNNY HANDLE
Down In Me Own Backyard, 2003

Johnny Handle wrote his song 'Jack Crawford' in 1977 in celebration of the Sunderland hero who rallied the Royal Navy in a battle against the Dutch Fleet at Camperdown in 1797. Some accounts claim that the Union Flag was renamed 'Union Jack' in honour of this bona fide Sunderland daredevil. It's also feasible that the phrase 'to nail your colours to the mast' might well have been popularised via this historical event…

Where in This Wind

Where in this wind, among the crying gulls,
the screeching seas, the shuffling trucks
and the freshly hewn coal, would a stranger stay?
Where in this abhorrent land of power and pick,
man, muscle, machine, sweat and toil,
could a man find peace and contentment?

Don't follow me down to this river town
where dawn breaks over coal staithes,
the bitter morning eats into the iron
shadows, which will dominate the skyline
for many months, before slipping serenely
shipshape, to the waiting, idle waters.

This seashore town of ragged streets,
webbed back alleys falling on to busy,
booming, shopping centres. The old,
too old. The new, too new.
What fascination does this stumbling
place still hold for me?

RON KNOWLES
Wearmouth 1300 Festival, 1974

Ship 1431
(26th March 1986)

Born
at the ship's launch
on her waxy stocks
slipping down her belly
on hand-greased oak blocks.

Spring on the river
and a blizzard blowing.
Welding all day
on a waltzing cherrypicker.

Sandblasted eyeballs
skinned by flash.

The director drunk,
whipping up waters,
chopping jobs.

Her bulbous bow
bends tank-rats double
knocking-off dogs
in the double bottoms.

Shipwrights over
and under; checking,
tucking her in
to shore her up
to slide her down.

Shot-blast gritting
the greased wax-ways.

Born, my son,
along her butts and seams.

Drag chains
in a quick cloud of rust.

TOM PICKARD
Tiepin Eros, 1994 | *hoyoot: Collected Poems and Songs*, 2014

What Maks Makems

An icy wind bites
   through stocks
whippcd-up
   from the Wear
   where shags in a frozen dive
break black watta.

   A crick-neck welder,
bent
   beneath the boat

with his head in a mask
>   burns her together.

He crawls,
>   in a double bottom gutter,
beneath the engine room
>   tank-top
to the sump
>   where the clatter
>   and rattle of caulkers
shatter the ear.

Drum running shudder
of a bulkhead drop.

The only way oot
in a panic
is backwards
over
>   an extractor pipe and cables
through a hatch
>   shrunk
in a swollen flap.

A Makem can
>   weld himself into
>   a steel box
and seal the lid on
>   afterwards.

TOM PICKARD
Tiepin Eros, 1994 | *hoyoot: Collected Poems and Songs*, 2014

Tom Pickard (*b*. 1946) co-founded Morden Tower as an international forum for poetry readings in a turret room on Newcastle's medieval city walls with Connie Pickard in 1964. Many famous poets of the time came to Newcastle, not just to read at the Tower but to meet and talk to Basil Bunting, who had been living in obscurity in Northumberland since being expelled from Persia in 1952. Bunting's friendship with Pickard and his renewed contact with poets and poetry readers were instrumental in the writing of *Briggflatts* (see page 61).

Pickard's first collection *High on the Walls* (1967) was followed by other books including *The Order of Chance* (1971), *Hero Dust* (1979), *Tiepin Eros* (1994), *The Ballad of Jamie Allan* (2007), *hoyoot* (2014) and *Winter Migrants* (2016). In 1989 he published *We Make Ships*, an account of his experiences as writer in residence – and those of the workforce – at Austin & Pickersgill shipyard in Sunderland, in the same year that the yard was closed.

A19 Hymn

>Down in yon forest
>There stands a hall
>The bells of Paradise
>I heard them ring

   1

Gannet splash

A drowning

Ship marks
Squabbling gulls

Furrow-eyed ploughman
Tumbleweed words…

Leaping ditches
Who goes there after them?

Past sentinel winding heads
Along mourning beaches
Over black shingle…

Distant hills hail steeple rooster
Wind in his tail

No resting place for lost words
Driven across fields

To cliffs and bird-emptied shells
Their secret out

   2

Deep dene wood
Beech tops reaching ploughed edge level

Dry limestone gorge
Word-water sink-hole…

Cliff-seep into stream again
Overgrown kiln

Perchers in crumbling church
Paradise bells hanging...

Kingdom keys and
Lovers ash and elm

Enchanter's nightshade
Wood avens and water avens

Pall purple cover
There stands a bed

Purple orchid spotted orchid
Blackthorn burdock toadflax yew

   3

Blood is west
Of his green day

Gibbet and tar
His trundling cart

White rooks coming
Across field stubble

Crimson-berry sunset
A flaming tree

White birds flock to it
Silently roosting

Corpus inscription
Iron frames his heart

   4

Seven keepers
Follow his morning star

Hollow oak bole
Remains of friendship

Carved wings and keys
Peter acorn's bitter cup

5

Three times denied
To morning cock

Three times
To thistle

Three times
To cuckoo spit

Once for seashore
Sun up out of it

Twice for fish
Baked at the rising

Three times for egg
Stained polished and rolling.

6

Worn hill grass
Friday's worn hill grass
I'll sing you four
For worn hill grass

Four for kestrel
Flesh-eyed the first word

Four for pandect-calf
Flying from pasture

Four for winged cat
Fierce fledgling bringer

Four for bright angel-man
Gathering in

7

Old Kingdom lonnen
Silk banner procession

Lift the gate
Brass blare from dene mouth

Join us says Tom the drummer
Follow say seven green officials

   8

Crab-pot gift
Road near muffled surf

Shoals of mackerel
Moonshadow wrapping sea smells

Saithe-coley also
Companions seek sizzling star

   9

May now beside us
April over the cliff already

Mary's belfry
Bluebells ring grave-stone

Lost wooden rood-screen
Slots and blackthorn north and south...

Moth and rust sermon
Arch baring dog-tooth
Pack howling behind us

Sand-rim paten
Broken sun reflections
Stained shattered window

May alongside us
April-coble morning
Herringbone heading east to chancel sea

WILLIAM MARTIN
Cracknrigg, 1983

A184 Hymn
for Peter Armstrong, William Martin and the Lads. FTM.

Gods of the Felling bypass
Gods of Whitemare Pool

Converse at the castra
reveal Wrekendyke.

Let all the lights
at Heworth and Wardley
turn amber to green.

For the sake
of the *desolate North*
for the sake
of distrustful experts

let Testo's big-wheel sink.
Chase flea circus freaks
down Cut Throat Dene.

No flint knap
no sword clash
no human cannonball.

Whoever watches over
lads in their twenties
whoever's faith goes beyond
donner meat and chips

cap the meter at twenty
and let us care nothing
for the battle of Boldon Hill.

JAKE CAMPBELL
2017

Peter Armstrong's 'A695 Hymn' is on page 453.

DURHAM

Durham
(early 12th or late 11th century)

Is ðeos burch breome   geond Breotenrice,
The city is celebrated   throughout the kingdom of the Britons
steppa gestaðolad,   stanas ymbutan
placed on a steep eminence,   surrounded with cliffs
wundrum gewæxen.   Weor ymbeornad,
wonderfully large.   The Wear surrounds it,
ea yðum stronge,   and ðer inne wunað
a river strong in its current   and therein reside
feola fisca kyn   on floda gemonge.
various kinds of fish   in the midst of the floods.
And ðær gewexen is   wudafæstern micel;
And there grows   a great fortress of woods;
wuniad in ðem wycum   wilda deor monige,
in the recesses of which dwell   many wild animals,
in deope dalum   deora ungerim.
in the deep dales there is   a countless number of beasts.
Is in ðere byri eac   bearnum gecyðed
There is also in the town   illustrious among men
ðe arfesta   eadig Cudberch
the honourable   blessed Cuthbert
and ðes clene   cyninges heafud,
and the head   of the pure king,
Osuualdes, Engle leo,   and Aidan biscop,
Oswald, lion of the English   and bishop Aidan,
Eadberch and Eadfrið,   æðele geferes.
Eadberch and Eadfrith,   illustrious associates.
Is ðer inne midd heom   Æðelwold biscop
Therein, along with them, is   Aethelwald, the bishop
and breoma bocera Beda,   and Boisil abbot,
and the illustrious author Bede   and Boisil, the abbot
ðe clene Cudberte   on gecheðe
who taught   the pure Cuthbert
lerde lustum,   and he his lara wel genom.
willingly in his youth   and well did he receive his instruction.

Eardiæð æt ðem eadige   in in ðem minstre
There abide with that blessed one   within that minster
unarimeda   reliquia,
countless   relics
ðær monia wundrum gewurðað,   ðes ðe writ seggeð,
where many honour them wonderfully   as writers report,
midd ðene drihnes   wer domes bideð.
whilst they await   the just sentence of the Lord.

ANONYMOUS
translated from the Anglo-Saxon by Joseph Stevenson

Arvo Pärt in Concert, Durham Cathedral, November 1998

Sea-otters will be calving soon about the Farnes.

Perhaps you'll go there, in your coat, tonight.
Perhaps you'll go to Coldingham

or Lindisfarne, or, landlocked, wait, as if
you too were

sandstone: wounded, worn by wind, rain, light.

O Lord, enlighten my heart which evil desires have darkened

where the imperturbable pillars stand.

For you have fidgeted through sermons.

Hard to sit still with all your insufficiency about you, isn't it?

But you will listen through your permeable skin as if
this music were

slow wounding, swearing in, osmosis.

Ebba, abbess of Coldingham, will find her nuns forsaken, fidgeting,

but you, as Cuthbert, suffering for all, will make straight
for the sea, to stand all night
waist-deep in it,

in praise and prayer,

in fret, is it, or under the stars' bare
scattering of thorns –

O Lord, give me tears and remembrance of death, and contrition –

until dawn. When you will kneel down on the sand.
Sea-otters will come to warm you then.

But you must be as sandstone.

Make of this music an Inner Farne where you may stand alone.

For it *is* Farne, from Celtic *ferann*, meaning land,

where monks will dig a well for you of wild fresh water,
where you'll find not wheat but barley growing on bare ground,
where you will build a wall so high around
your oratory, you'll know the sky, it only
a while

as instrumental, wearing-in of wind and water. Listen

then, you'll find your own skin, salt, intact
as Cuthbert after centuries of wandering, still
permeable –

O Lord, forsake me not –

and one, as Arvo Pärt in his coat, will stand before
the orchestra, the choir, as if he too had only now
walked out of water

new, renewable, knowing the comfort of sea-otters.

GILLIAN ALLNUTT
Lintel, 2000 | *How the Bicycle Shone*, 2007

The lines in italics are taken from the text of Arvo Pärt's *Litany*, a setting of the 24 prayers attributed to St John Chrysostom for each hour of the day and night. St John Chrysostom, a hermit, became Patriarch of Constantinople in 398.

While Cuthbert, born in 634, was a monk at Melrose Abbey, he visited the religious house at Coldingham, and it was there, according to legend, that he stood all night in the sea and in the morning was warmed by seals. From 664 he was Prior of Lindisfarne and, while Prior, spent three years living as a hermit on one of the nearby Farne Islands. In 685, against his will, he was made Bishop of Lindisfarne. He died and was buried there in 687. Because of Viking raids, the monks took Cuthbert's coffin and embarked in 873 on 'the wanderings', continuing until a final resting-place was found for the saint in 995, on the site of the present Durham Cathedral, which still contains his shrine. [GA]

Durham Beatitude
The Easington Colliery disaster in 1951
remembered at the Durham Miners' Gala, July 1980

Gorse blazing on clifftop
I saw three ships
Thorns and May blossom
Explosion at pit

Saul's Dead March
Common grave and grief
Beatitude their banner
Weeping and drum beat

A gentleness flowered
In each drum silence
A Kingdom confronted
Each green thorn

They that mourn
Came here in July
Field blessed with banners
Thronged comforting hush

I saw three ships
Through the gorse sail in
They came to Death's harvest
They came to pulley-wheels

WILLIAM MARTIN
Cracknrigg, 1983 | *Lammas Alanna*, 2000

Durham

> St Cuthbert's shrine,
> founded 999
>> MNEMONIC

ANARCHY and GROW YOUR OWN
whitewashed on to crumbling stone
fade in the drizzle. There's a man
handcuffed to warders in a black sedan.
A butcher dumps a sodden sack
of sheep pelts off his bloodied back,
then hangs the morning's killings out,
cup-cum-muzzle on each snout.

I've watched where this 'distinguished see'
takes off into infinity,
among transistor antennae,
and student smokers getting high,
and visiting Norwegian choirs
in raptures over Durham's spires,
lifers, rapists, thieves, ant-size
circle and circle at their exercise.

And Quasimodo's bird's-eye view
of big wigs and their retinue,
a five-car Rolls-Royce motorcade
of judgement draped in Town Hall braid,
I've watched the golden maces sweep
from courtrooms to the Castle keep
through winding Durham, the elect
before whom ids must genuflect.

But some stay standing and at one
God's irritating carillon
brings you to me; I feel like the hunch-
back taking you for lunch;
then bed. All afternoon two church-
high prison helicopters search
for escapees down by the Wear
and seem as though they're coming here.

Listen! Their choppers guillotine
all the enemies there've ever been
of Church and State, including me
for taking this small liberty.
Liberal, lover, communist,
Czechoslovakia, Cuba, grist,
grist for the power-driven mill
weltering in overkill.

And England? Quiet Durham? Threat
smokes off our lives like steam off wet
subsidences when summer rain
drenches the workings. You complain
that the machinery of sudden death,
Fascism, the hot bad breath
of Power down small countries' necks
shouldn't interfere with sex.

They *are* sex, love, we must include
all these in love's beatitude.
Bad weather and the public mess
drive us to private tenderness,
though I wonder if together we,
alone two hours, can ever be
love's antibodies in the sick,
sick body politic.

At best we're medieval masons, skilled
but anonymous within our guild,
at worst defendants hooded in a car
charged with something sinister.
On the *status quo*'s huge edifice
we're just excrescences that kiss,
cathedral gargoyles that obtrude
their acts of 'moral turpitude'.

But turpitude still keeps me warm
in foul weather as I head for home
down New Elvet, through the town,
past the butcher closing down,
hearing the belfry jumble time
out over Durham. As I climb
rain blankets the pithills, mist
the chalkings of the anarchist.

I wait for the six-five Plymouth train
glowering at Durham. First rain,
then hail, like teeth spit from a skull,
then fog obliterate it. As we pull
out of the station through the dusk and fog,
there, lighting up, is Durham, dog
chasing its own cropped tail,
University, Cathedral, Gaol.

TONY HARRISON
The Loiners, 1970 | *Collected Poems*, 2007

Durham Seen from the Train

The cathedral glides behind the cutting's
long wave of grass and earth, removed
completely by a window's fractional displacement
and the locomotive's endless moment
that closes like a wall now on the flower-foamed
embankment, now on a bird's unmoving wings.

The traditional escarpment
crumbles out of sight. The prison
and the hollow castle fall upon their knees.
The river turns and disappears into a crust of trees.
The last houses like a rib lie broken
on a temporary field invaded by a token pavement.

The heart imagines what the eye no longer sees.
Though distance seems to kill the things we love
and time preserves the gift beyond the giver,
still in a moment's bead of air the lover
lives within his kiss, hand treasures hand forever; and above
the reappearing river still the city rises where it always rose.

JAMES KIRKUP
The Poetry of Railways, ed. Kenneth Hopkins, 1966 |
To the Ancestral North, 1983

Durham Cathedral

Imagine it a ruin.
A spot-lit arch. Its towers
Toppled. The river
Kerving a jud

In the fading light
At the thin end of the year.
Though its countless sockets
Hold a darkness – ours –

In Elvet, North Bailey,
Cobbled Owengate,
Rising, fugitive
As coal smoke on the breath,

From knotwork on vellum,
Keel, scroll, laced
Branches or, beneath,
From a blacker seam –

Hyeven, Hinny, Hyem –
The old words loom,
High, mysterious,
Lit up from within.

KATRINA PORTEOUS
Front Row, BBC Radio 4 & Durham *Lumiere*, 2009 | *Two Countries*, 2014

Durham Cathedral
(FROM *The Dunno Elegies*)

Traffic besieges the hill, would take it
were it not for some echo of restraint.
There is too much humanity here today,
such a swarm you fear nothing would stop it
should it turn ugly and decide to riot
instead of drifting from shop to shop,
family pillage a subtle pilgrimage.

Beneath these historic cobblestones is not
the beach, but a lecture in rhetoric,
a deconstruction of the newspapers
and their black and white godlessness.

The river's swell embraces the island
and earth-bound angels throng the bridges,
miners and priests mingle, a big meeting
of those whose futures have long vanished,
but who persist, who dream on.

The cathedral knocker will give refuge
but only for forty short days and nights.
It cannot keep the voices of angels out
of your head, choirs rustling down corridors,
harmonies rising like clouds that will flood
the pits in the dark so far underground.
Sediment of slack, the run-off of ages,
wrinkled faces and washhouse hands
behind the scenes still, waiting for learning.
These are lucky angels in such grand halls.
Banners and tapestries clash, purple
and crimson sit awkward together.
Songs drown each other out. Tills are loudest.

Listen to the bells. Listen to the bells
and look down onto the green, a car park
or a postage stamp on a letter to God.
Every carving, every stone laid upon stone,
sings of faith, whilst the shoppers stretch their backs
and complain they must trek down the mountain.
This is success in this world. Silence
a gargoyle's glare from the High Street.
Angels escort them back to the river.
The water is a charm full of lead and coal.
As darkness falls erudite drunks fill the streets.

MARK ROBINSON
How I Learned to Sing, 2013

Durham in February

Snow was still around; in tatters;
a walk to the river to the dark bank;
the water very deep brown, bovine.

The trees drew up from the opposite
curve of woodland like taut sentries
in brown and white uniform;

along the river raced a skiff, a snow white skiff,

the rower dressed in white   dipped
his white oars in the calm chocolate water,
the oars flashed like underwings of birds;

the river held the cameo: the air river-fresh,
snow edges at my feet, the frieze of tree stalks,
the monotint of winter

yet underpainted surely
with the not yet seen spring;
the oarsman sped lightly, a phantom briefly,

a skiff, a snow white skiff, like a sleigh.

S.J. LITHERLAND
Composition in White, 2017

River Wear, Durham

The path is still artificially lit; the darkness
just now outfalling. The river's spate outstays
last night's downpour, churning itself over
like the mind on a worry. Debris wavers on
the weir or is thrashed on an unplanned course.

A cormorant stretches out its wings on the bluff
in the early morning. Making its cross on the crag,
it claims survival space among the colony.
Unlike other water birds, its flight feathers let
the water enter: it must open out to recompose.

At the whim of the weather, the water will drop;
the paths in the distance become merely dark
with the aftermath. The river will outlast this rush
but not mourn it. The cormorant will not grieve
for what it never knew to be its difference.

HEIDI WILLIAMSON
The Reader, 2016

'But with a history of ECT'

But with a history of ECT
And separation Milburn Margaret Mrs
Did not attain the obliterating sea
She got no further than the DHSS
And on a Friday in the public view
Lodged on the weir as logs do.

During the rush-hour she was attended to
And all the terraces of Gallowgate
Watched the recovery of this female who
Went in the river at the age of thirty-eight.
She did not pass unnoticed but instead
Got seen to being dead.

And at the inquest the Acting Coroner
Inquiring as to how and why she died
Exculpated both the hospital and her
Emeritus husband who identified
That frozen woman in the mortuary
He had four children by.

DAVID CONSTANTINE
A Brightness to Cast Shadows, 1980 | *Collected Poems*, 2004

The Pitman's Garden
(for Bill and Diane Williamson)

Man called Teddy had a garden in
The ruins of Mary Magdalen
By Baxter's Scrap. Grew leeks. What leeks need is
Plenty of shite and sunshine. Sunshine's His
Who gave His only begotten Son to give
Or not but shite is up to us who live
On bread and meat and veg and every day
While Baxter fished along the motorway
For write-offs Teddy arrived with bags of it
From home, which knackered him, the pit
Having blacked his lungs. But Baxter towed in wrecks
On their hind-legs with dolls and busted specs
And things down backs of seats still in and pressed
Them into oxo cubes and Teddy addressed
His ranks of strapping lads and begged them grow
Bonnier and bonnier. Before the show
For fear of slashers he made his bed up there
Above the pubs, coughing on the night air,
Like the Good Shepherd Teddy lay
Under the stars, hearing the motorway,
Hearing perhaps the concentrated lives
Of family cars in Baxter's iron hives.
Heard Baxter's dog howl like a coyote
And sang to his leeks 'Nearer my God to Thee'.
He lays his bearded beauties out. Nothing
On him is so firm and white, but he can bring
These for a common broth and eat his portion.

Leaving town, heading for the Ml,
Watch out for the pitman's little garden in
The ruined fold of Mary Magdalen.

DAVID CONSTANTINE
Selected Poems, 1991 | *Collected Poems*, 2004

CO. DURHAM

Rap 'Er Te Bank

[CHORUS]
Rap 'er te bank, me canny lad!
Wind 'er away, keep tornin!
The back-shift men are gannin' hyam,
We'll be back in the mornin'.

My feyther used to call the torn
When the lang shift was ower.
As he went oot bye, ye'd hear him cry;
D'ye knaa it's efter fower?

[CHORUS]

And when that aaful day arrived,
The last shift for me feyther;
A faal of stones and brokken bones,
But still above the clatter, he cried:

[fiNAL CHORUS]
Rap 'er te bank, me canny lad!
Wind 'er reet slow, that's clivor!
This poor aad lad hes tekken bad,
Aa'll be back heor nivvor.

TRADITIONAL

Birtley schoolmaster Walter Toyn collected 'Rap 'Er te Bank' in 1962 from singer Henry Nattress of Low Fell. The miner Jack Elliott of Birtley sang it on the 1965 EP *The Folksound of Britain*. The rapper rope hung from a rapper at the minehead; the miners pulled it as a signal to bring the cage back up to the surface. '"Rap 'er te bank!" is the cry of men at the bottom of the [mine-]shaft, waiting to come up in the cage. The onsetter would rap, and the winding man, hearing the signal would draw the cage to the surface (the 'bank').' (A.L. Lloyd, *Folk Song in England*, 1967)

The South Medomsley Strike

If you're inclined te hear a song, aa'll sing a verse or two,
And when Aa'm done yer gan' te see that every word is true;
The miners of South Medomsley they never will forget
Fisick and his tyranny and how they have been tret;
For in the midst of danger, these hardy sons did toil,
For te earn their daily bread se far beneath the soil.
Te make an honest livelihood each miner did contrive,
But ye shall hear how they were served in eighteen eighty-five.

   CHORUS:
The miners of South Medomsley they're gannin te mek some stew
They're gannin' te boil fat Postick and his dorty candy crew,
The maistors should have nowt but soup as long as they're alive
In memory of their dorty tricks in eighteen eighty-five.

Below the county average then the men was ten percent,
Yet Fisick the unfeelin' cur he couldn't rest content;
A ten percent reduction from the men he did demand,
But such a strong request as this the miners couldn't stand.
The notices was aall served oot and when they had expired,
Aall the gear was brought te bank, and the final shot was fired;
Te hurt his honest working men this low lived man did strive,
He'll often rue for what he did in eighteen eighty-five.

Fisick was determined more tyranny te show,
For te get some candymen he wandered to and fro'.
He made his way te Consett, and he saw Postick, the bum,
He knew he liked such dirty work and he was sure te come.
Fisick told him what te de and where te gan and when,
So at the time appointed, Postick landed with his men,
With pollisses and candymen the place was all alive,
All through the strike that Fisick caused in eigthteen eighty-five.

Commander Postick gave the word, they started with their work,
Though they were done at five o'clock, they dursent stop till dark,
And when they'd done aall they could and finished for the day,
The bobbies guarded Postick and his dorty dogs away.
Fisick was a tyrant and the owners was the same,
For the torn oot of the strike, they were the men to blame,

Neither them nor Postick need expect they'll ever thrive,
For what they did to Dipton men in eighteen eighty-five.

(1885)

TOMMY ARMSTRONG

The Durham Lock-out

In our Durham County I am sorry for to say
That hunger and starvation are increasing every day
For the want of food and coals, we know not what to do
But with your kind assistance, we will see the struggle through.

I need not state the reason why we have been brought so low.
The masters have behaved unkind as everyone will know.
For we won't lie down and let them treat us as they like
To punish us they've stopped the pits and caused the present strike.

The pulley wheels have ceased to move that once went swift around,
The horses and the ponies too have been brought from underground.
Our work is taken from us now, they care not if we die
For they can eat the best of food and drink the best when dry.

While the miner and his marra, too, each morning have to roam
To seek for bread to feed the hungry little ones at home.
The flour barrel is empty now, their true and faithful friend
Which makes the thousands wish today the strike was at an end.

We have done our very best as honest working men.
To let the pits commence again, we've offered to them ten.
The offer they will not accept, they firmly do demand
Thirteen and a half per cent or let the collieries stand.

Let them stand or let them lie to do with them as they choose.
To give them thirteen and a half we ever shall refuse.
They're always willing to receive but not inclined to give
And very soon they won't allow a working man to live.

With tyranny and capital they never rest content
Unless they are endeavouring to take from us percent.
If it was due, what they request, we willingly would grant.
We know it's not, therefore we cannot give them what they want.

The miners of Northumberland, we shall forever praise
For being so kind in helping us, those tyrannising days.
We thank the other counties too, that have been doing the same
For every man who hears this song will know we're not to blame.

(1892)

TOMMY ARMSTRONG

Tommy Armstrong (1848–1919) was born in Wood Street, Shotley Bridge. Though his songs were mostly too local in spirit or language, as A.L. Lloyd puts it, to spread far outside the North East, he is regarded as the bard of the Durham coalfield, and one of the most remarkable of all working-class songwriters. He was a small, bow-legged man, 'cursed with fourteen children and a bottomless thirst' as his eldest son said. Armstrong made up songs, had them cheaply printed, and hawked the sheets round the pubs at weekends at a penny each to raise beer money.

When young, Armstrong was relied upon to compose a song on any event of importance in the life of the mining community, such as a strike or a pit disaster. One such was the moving 'Trimdon Grange Disaster' when 74 miners were killed in an explosion on 16 February 1882. Within a few days, Armstrong was singing his commemorative song in the local Mechanics' Hall. He no doubt felt that the dialect of the pitmen, Pitmatic, was not appropriate here and the text is more Victorian-sententious than is usual with him. Like songs written for similar occasions, it lacks the surge of inspiration or 'holy daftness' as Armstrong himself called it.

Armstrong was aware of his responsibility and once said: 'When ye're the Pitman's poet an' looked up to for it, wey, if a disaster or a strike goos wi'oot a sang fre ye, they say: "What's wi' Tommy Armstrong? Has someone druv a spigot in him and let oot aal the inspiration?" Me aud sangs hev kept me in beer an' the floor o' the public bar has bin me stage for forty year. Aw'd drink, aw'd sing, we'd drink agen, sangs wi'oot end, amen.'

The bardic duel between Armstrong and William McGuire, a newcomer to the district, took place in the Red Roe public house in Tanfield. A few miles away the men of Oakley Colliery were on strike. The owners decided to evict strikers and they scoured the slums for layabouts to move the pitmen's furniture out into the streets. The 'Oakey evictions' was chosen as the theme for the duel. McGuire's song is forgotten but Armstrong's lives on. The last two decades of the 19th century were Armstrong's most prolific years and the strike songs reflect the high feelings of the period when the Miners' Federation was growing rapidly. The words of the songs are not revolutionary and concentrate on bread-and-butter issues. As they were sung to raise money for strikers' families, some tact was required so as not to alienate the sympathy of donors. During the great Durham strike and lock-out of 1892, Armstrong acted as 'court minstrel' to William Patterson, the miners' leader, and one of his most durable songs, 'The Durham Lock-out' dates from this time when the whole Durham coalfield was shut down because miners already living on the breadline wouldn't accept a ten percent cut in their wages.

Armstrong wrote the great 'Wor Nannie's a Mazer', and 'Stanla Market', but perhaps his best-known song is 'Durham Jail'. The song is evidently autobiographical, possibly because of his part in the strike, but allegedly the result of stealing a pair of stockings in West Stanley Co-op. He said he was 'elevated' at the time; and they seemed to him the only bow-legged stockings he had ever seen. In his condition he couldn't resist them. [AM]

The Ponies

During the strike, the ponies were brought up
From their snug stables, some three hundred feet
Below the surface – up the pit's main shaft
Shot one by one into the light of day;
And as each stepped, bewildered, from the cage,
He stood among his fellows, shivering
In the unaccustomed freshness of free air,
His dim eyes dazzled by the April light.
And then one suddenly left the huddled group,
Lifted his muzzle, snuffed the freshness in,
Pawed the soft turf and, whinnying, started trotting
Across the field; and one by one his fellows
With pricking ears each slowly followed him,
Timidly trotting: when the leader's trot
Broke into a canter, then into a gallop;
And now the whole herd galloped at his heels
Around the dewy meadow, hard hoofs, used
To stumbling over treacherous stony tramways
And plunging hock-deep through black steamy puddles
Of the dusky narrow galleries, delighting
In the soft spring of the resilient turf.
Still round and round the field they raced, unchecked
By tugging traces, at their heels no longer
The trundling tubs, and round and round and round,
With a soft thunder of hoofs, the sunshine flashing
On their sleek coats, through the bright April weather
They raced all day; and even when the night
Kindled clear stars above them in a sky
Strangely unsullied by the stack which now
No longer belched out blackness, still they raced,
Unwearied, as through their short sturdy limbs
The rebel blood like wildfire ran, their lungs
Filled with the breath of freedom. On they sped

Through the sweet dewy darkness; and all night
The watchman at the pithead heard the thudding
Of those careering and exultant hoofs
Still circling in a crazy chase; and dawn
Found them still streaming raggedly around,
Tailing into a lagging cantering,
And so to a stumbling trot: when gradually,
Dropping out one by one, they started cropping
The dew-dank tender grass, which no foul reek
From the long idle pit now smirched, and drinking
With quivering nostrils the rich living breath
Of sappy growing things, the cool rank green
Grateful to eyes, familiar from their colthood
Only with darkness and the dusty glimmer
Of lamplit galleries....
                Mayhap one day
Our masters, too, will go on strike, and we
Escape the dark and drudgery of the pit,
And race unreined around the fields of heaven!

WILFRID GIBSON
Fuel, 1934
➤ AUTHOR NOTE PAGES 232-33

from Brandon Pithouse: Recollections of the Durham Coalfield

from 1

grandmother sent me a good door-string
six farthing candles for bait
some of her best currant bread

bait poke over my shoulder
candle-box in my pocket through darkness
along the black wagon-way up

past the pit-pond by the pick shop to the pit-heap
clanking of engines creaking pulleys overhead
hoarse voices of men calling answering

from 3

    William Cowburn
You knew
long before you left school
that's where you were going when you left school that was
what you were

born for really to go down the pit

I should never been a pitman
in them days like
lots of liked the thought of going down
them getting a pony to drive
bit of attraction

but then I'm not frightened to admit
I was terrified when I went down the pit
I think I cried all the first shift

place was infested with rats
used to come out in swarms
come right to your feet
after the ponies' corn

from 4

Broomside Colliery
the cage left the surface with four men

stopped by the banksman's order
at the Low Main seam where
Isaac Rickerby was waiting

rapping the signal as he
passed some gear in he was
stepping into the cage as it
began to move down and
was crushed between the
cage and the shaft timbers
[…]

Thornley Colliery
attempting to cross a staple he
signalled the ascending cage away
started to cross at a diagonal and was
crushed by the descending cage

from 7

Herrington Colliery
cutting out a baulk with a saw on the engine plane
we set some timber
a stay from one side to the other to keep ourselves safe
the slip was not to be seen
before it fell without warning
no dribbling
just a fizzle and the stone came straight off he
died two days after
[…]

Burnhope Colliery he
finished his shift
ravelling out-bye
along a new travelling way
passing the upcast shaft .
there was a door he opened
and stepped into the shaft
and fell
to the bottom
[…]

Struck by tram plate while using it as a lever   Fall of stone   Fall down shaft from upper seam to bottom   Crushed by tubs on horse-way   Fall of stone   Fall of stone fall of stone fall of stone Head caught   against roof while driving Fall of stone of stone Crushed by tubs on engine plane   Struck on head   by horse Crushed between wagons and wall   Fall of stone   Crushed by tubs on engine plane   Crushed by tubs on engine plane   Crushed by the cage starting as   he was getting into it   Explosion of a shot   Run over by four tubs of stone   Head crushed between tub   and timbers   Fall of stone   Fall of coal and stone   Crushed on pulley wheel   Fall of stone   Fell into sump and was drowned while changing cage chains   Run over by trucks   Crushed between two trucks   Severely crushed knocked down by and trampled on by his horse Chain broke and the tub ran back and   killed him   Crushed between wall and door by passing tubs   Fall of

from 8

putting is sore work dragging the coal corves or tubs
using a harness called the 'soames'
a chain passed between the legs hooked to an iron ring attached to a
leather belt blisters as big as shillings and half-crown pieces
blisters of one day broken the next and the
girdle stuck to the wound crawling on hands and knees
dragging the coal through the tunnels from the workings to
the passages where pony putters could be used
dis thoo think we deserve to toil awl day in livin' tombs?
[…]

    George Hancock
I was 15 year old and nine month
when I started to hand-putt
and that is the worst job God ever created
shoving it behind a tub
all day
it was horse's work
it was terrible conditions there was
nobody made
to have to do that
but of course it was there…

and that was it

from 9

50 or 60 yards away I heard a tremendous noise looked round and saw the discharge come out of the pit-mouth like the discharge of a cannon

it continued to blow I think for a quarter of an hour discharging everything that had come into the current   stones came up and trusses of hay

the ground all round the top of the pit was in a trembling state I went as near as I durst go and everything appeared crackling about me

The pit continued to blow every two or three hours for two days some of the explosions equal to the first.
1806
[…]

Heworth morning of the 25th May 1812 about half past eleven darkness like
    early twilight
inverted cone of black dust carried away on a strong west wind
falling a continued shower a mile and a half around
covered the roads so thickly
footsteps of passengers were strongly imprinted in it

clothes, tobacco-boxes, shoes, the only indexes by which they could be recognised

bodies in ghastly confusion: some like mummies, scorched dry baked. One
    wanted its head, another an arm. The power of the fire was visible upon
    them all; but its effects were extremely various: some were almost torn to
    pieces, others as if they had sunk down overpowered with sleep. Some
    much burnt, but not much mangled. Others buried amongst a confused
    wreck of broken brattices, trapdoors, trams, and corves, with their legs
    broken, or their bodies otherwise miserably scorched and lacerated.

>   From the position in which he was found
>   as if he'd been asleep
>   when the explosion happened
>   and never after
>   opened his eyes

William Bell working in the pit morning of the disaster
Hebburn 1849 he was knocked down and rendered deaf and
while he was making his way to the shaft he
fell and knew nothing until he found himself at home
[...]

As I knew many of the pitmen there at Haswell, I walked over to see their
    families.
In the Long Row every house save one had its dead.
In one house five coffins – two on the bed, two on the dresser, and one on
    the floor.

from **10**

>   *Dennis Fisher*
> first job I ever had
> I was placed into the stables to work
> I could have been a horse-keeper if I
> wanted to I liked the ponies

liked working with the ponies
and without those ponies
and we had two hundred of them in Chilton colliery
there wouldn't have been
any coal production whatsoever
without the pit ponies
they were the ones that did all the work
taking the empty tubs in
to the coal-face for the coal-hewers
and bringing the full ones out
and it's not
it's not on the level
when you go down the mine it's not level
you're going up steep hills
and going down steep banks
it wasn't very easy work for the
pit ponies
[…]

Blackhall Colliery 1946 we had to run
quarter of a mile down the pit yard
to the netties

for 500 surface workers in shifts at various times
a plank of wood made for 4 persons to sit

no flush toilets them days
a fire hose

to wash all the excrement down a pipe
onto the Pit Dene

from **18**

three days police road blocks sealed the village off
nothing was allowed in
they stopped the buses at Easington Village
they wouldn't let any ordinary bus come down the main street
or through Horden
they had both ends of Easington Colliery blocked off
they were stopping searching all cars
people were ordered off buses

for three days police marched through the village
Gwent police   police from Northampton
I never thought I'd see scenes like this in Britain I never thought I'd
see what I've seen on the streets of Easington
we're occupied we've been occupied by the police
police some of them
wearing black
uniforms with no markings

from **24**

Everything that was lived
experience has
moved away
into

heritage reclamation landscape

blocked drift-mouths ramps collapsed tunnels disused railway
lines viaducts old coke
ovens spoil heaps slurry lagoons

new grassy fields smooth green slopes not quite
real among rolling upland ridges and valleys

dry stone walls thorn hedge
straight enclosure roads

immediacies of an ordinary afternoon where
something happened

times of the southern dynasties where strikes and closures it
was
always ganna gan

JOHN SEED
Brandon Pithouse: Recollections of the Durham Coalfield, 2016

Forgotten of the Foot
(Langley Park, County Durham, 1983-84)

Equisetum, horsetail, railway weed
Laid down in the unconscious of the hills;
Three hundred million years still buried

In this hair-soft surviving growth that kills
Everything in the glorious garden except itself,
That thrives on starvation, and distils

Black diamonds, the carboniferous shelf –
That was life before our animals,
With trilobite and coelacanth,

A stratum of compressed time that tells
Truth without language and is the body store
Of fire, heat, night without intervals –

That becomes people's living only when strange air
Fills out the folded lungs, the inert corpuscles.
Into the mute dark, light crawls once more.

*

So the hills must be pillaged and cored.
Such history as they hide must be hacked out
Urgent as money, the buried black seams uncovered.

Rows of stunted houses under the smoke,
Soot black houses pressed back hard against pit
By fog, by smoke, by a cobra hood of smouldering coke

Swayed from the nest of ovens huddled opposite.
Families, seven or ten to a household,
Growing up, breathing it, becoming it.

On winter mornings, grey capped men in the cold,
Clatter of boots on tarmac, sharp and empty,
First shift out in thick frost simple as gold

On the sulphurous roofs, on the stilted gantry,
Crossing to engine house and winding gear –
Helmet, pick, lamp, tin bottle of tea.

*

A Nan or Nora slave to each black grate.
Washing on Monday, the water grimed in its well.
Iron and clean on Tuesday, roll out and bake

Each Wednesday (that sweet bituminous smell
No child who grew up here forgets).
Thursdays, the Union and the Methodist Circle;

Fishday on Friday (fryday), a queue of kids,
Thin, squabbling by the chippy. Resurfaced quarrels
After pay day – hard drinking and broken heads.

Wheels within wheels, an England of working Ezekiels.
Between slag-heaps, coke-tarns and black sludgy leavings,
Forges roaring and reddening, hot irons glowing like jewels.

No more, no more. They've swept up the workings
As if they were never meant to be part of memory.
A once way of being. A dead place. Hard livings

That won't return, grim tales forgot as soon as told,
Streaming from the roofs in smoke from a lost century –
A veil of breath in which to survive the cold.

*

When the mine's shut down, habits prolong the story,
Habits and voices, till grandmothers' old ways pass,
And the terraces fold into themselves, so black, ugly

And unloved that all but the saved (success
Has spared them, the angel of death-by-money) move away.
The town's inhabited by alien, washed up innocents.

Children and animals, people too poor to stay
Anywhere else, stray, dazed, into this slum of Eden.
The church is without saints or statuary.

The memorial is a pick, a hammer, a shovel, given
By the men of Harvey Seam and Victoria Seam. May
Their good bones wake in the living seams of Heaven.

He breaketh open a shaft away from where men sojourn.
They are forgotten of the foot that passeth by.*

ANNE STEVENSON
The Fiction-Makers, 1985 | *Poems 1955-2005*, 2005

* Job 28.4: The inscription on the Miners' Memorial in Durham Cathedral.

Salter's Gate

There, in that lost
    corner of the ordnance survey.
Drive through the vanity –
    two pubs and a garage – of Satley,
then right, cross the A68
    past down-at-heel farms and a quarry,

you can't miss it, a 'T' instead of a 'plus'
    where the road meets a wall.
If it's a usual day
    there'll be freezing wind, and you'll
stumble climbing the stile
    (a ladder, really) as you pull

your hat down and zip up your jacket.
    Out on the moor,
thin air may be strong enough to
    knock you over,
but if you head into it
    downhill, you can shelter

in the wide, cindery trench of an old
    leadmine-to-Consett railway.
You may have to share it
    with a crowd of dirty

supercilious-looking ewes, who will baaa
    and cut jerkily away

after posting you blank stares
    from their foreign eyes.
One winter we came across five
    steaming, icicle-hung cows.
But in summer, when the heather's full of nests,
    you'll hear curlews

following you, raking your memory, maybe,
    with their cries;
or, right under your nose,
    a grouse will whirr up surprised,
like a poet startled by a line
    when it comes to her sideways.

No protection is offered by trees –
    Hawthorn the English call May,
a few struggling birches.
    But of wagtails and yellowhammers, plenty,
and peewits who never say *peewit*,
    more a minor, *go'way, go'way*.

Who was he, Salter? Why was this his gate?
    A pedlars' way, they carried
salt to meat. The place gives tang to
    survival, its unstoppable view,
a reservoir, ruins of the lead mines, new
    forestry pushing from the right, the curlew.

ANNE STEVENSON
Four and a Half Dancing Men, 1993 | *Poems 1955-2005*, 2005

To a Remembered Stream, and a Never-Forgotten Friend

Sweet stream, the haunt of solitary hern
    And shy kingfisher, far from busy town
    Or even populous hamlet
Through banks thick fringed with underwood and fern
And hazel thickets, where the ripe nuts turn

Unmarked and slow to Autumn's ruddy brown;
      Where gems thy single rock its feathery crown
(For nought of thine looks ever sad or stern!)
      With berried scarlet of the mountain ash;
      I never hear 'mid waking dreams thy dash
Above the pebbles, but I think on One
Whose course of days hath by thy waters run,
      A course like thine of calm and quietness,
      Nor ever raised a voice except to bless!

DORA GREENWELL
Selected Poems, 1906

hern: heron.

Lilies

> The evening and the morning make our day.
> ELIZABETH BARRETT BROWNING

By woody walks, near pathways dank
With the drip of the thick-wove boughs they grew,
By the side of the garlic, wild and rank,
   The Valley-lilies, pure as dew.
Shrouded and swathed in a tender gleam,
   Gold in the sun, and dim in the shade,
   Lilies globe-like, and orbed, and rayed,
Flashed, afloat on the glittering stream;
   Each on its cool, thick leaf apart,
   Flung eager-wide to day's golden dart,
As a door will ope with a secret thrill,
   To a touch beloved, each warm, trembling heart
For the light of the morning to flood and fill.
   At midday the lilies stood up tall,
   Stood up straight, 'neath the garden wall,
White and regal like queens that bear
   Beneath their crowns disconsolate
A weight of woe and a world of care,
Who are glad when the night bears all away*
Yet are ever queens through their long white day,
   Robed and fair and desolate.
Golden were some, and some had curled

Their leaves back in pride, or in scorn of the world,
And some were tawny, and streaked, and pied,
   And frecked, as if in them something ill
   Had passed, but had left them lilies still.
And after them came a sworded strife
Of lilies that warred with death or with life,
   Flushed or pallid with love or hate
I know not which, for to living flame
   They changed from their rose-bloom delicate,
And strove, so that neither overcame;
   For as I marvelled thereat, day grew
More dim, and the flowers' sweet miracle †
   Went by, and a sudden twilight fell,
And with it brought to my soul the scent
   Of mossy wood-walks drenched in dew,
And of Valley-lilies crushed and bent.

DORA GREENWELL
Poems (Selected), 1889

AUTHOR'S NOTES:
   * The lines 'Be the day never so long / It ringeth at last unto even-song' are written in Queen Elizabeth's *Book of Houres.*
   † 'I die,' said a Dutch botanist who had encountered some deadly exhalations in a Javanese forest, '*but I have seen the miracle of flowers.*'

Dora Greenwell (1821–1882) was born at Greenwell Ford, near Lanchester in Co. Durham, the Greenwell family home since the time of Henry VIII, and setting of the two poems included here. Introducing his 1889 edition of her *Poems*, William Dorling describes Greenwell Ford as 'a large and handsome house, in a delightfully pleasant and secluded situation on the banks of a picturesque little stream, which the poet has invested with all the charm of her intense love of nature and her rich and pleasant fancy. She revelled in the beautiful grounds and the wonderful old garden, with its old-time shrubs and flowers, which provided her with such a wealth of memory and joy.'
   There she was taught by a governess for five years, then taught herself, studying philosophy, political economy and languages. After the loss of Greenwell Ford due to mismanagement of the estate, the family moved to Northumberland in 1848, to her eldest brother William's home at Ovingham Rectory, and where Dora taught local girls and published her first collection of poetry with the esteemed imprint of William Pickering. In 1850, they settled at Golbourne Rectory in Lancashire, the home of her brother Alan, where Dora became friendly with Josephine Butler and supported her work. After the death of her father in 1854, she lived with her mother in Durham at 46 North Bailey. This was the period of Dora's greatest intellectual achievement, and she met many literary celebrities, including Jean Ingelow and Christina Rossetti. After 1874, she settled in London and supported the franchise struggle. She also became addicted to opium.
   Dora Greenwell was a woman of understated elegance and had a melodious voice. Despite

her strong Christianity, her letters are lively and spirited. She was, in fact, a sociable woman, though much restricted by her Victorian sense of duty towards her mother. She was loud in the praise of her friend Christina Rossetti, to whom she has been compared, but her last words on herself reflect a sense of failure to meet her own high standards 'One word would alone tell my story – inadequacy.'

Dora Greenwell's poetry, as exemplified in *Carmina Crucis* (1869), *Songs of Salvation* (1873) and other works, is marked by intense religious feeling. Her prose works include *The Patience of Hope* (1860), *Two Friends, Essays* (1866) and *Colloquia Crucis* (1868). Her essay 'Our Single Women' is a plea for the broader education of intelligent women. [AM/NA]

A Camp in Chopwell Woods
(Durham University OTC, 1916)

How we cursed Consett, caught in the light of her steelworks,
That night the Zeppelins came out of her smoke-stacks,
Like silvery fish of fumes, with pulsing fin-beats,
Seemingly skimming the tops of the trees and our tent-poles,
And smothering us where we lay, furious and afraid,
Confined by order to our senseless shelters of canvas,
Like snow-bright igloos on a seam of gleaming black coal,
A marvellous target of moon-chalked tents set for bombing.

In the centre of Chopwell Woods we wondering lads lay,
Priest-student from Ushaw, Methodist from Woodhouse Grove,
Lying side by side, the dread of dogma departed,
Brothers at last in this Eden of lions and lambs,
Finding a common faith in the blessing of the bomb,
In this khaki corner of the Woods having found the answer.

Let us forget then how we cursed you, Consett, that night
When your furnaces flamed like fountains of blood-streaked gold,
Great gushing beacons on the black ridge above the Derwent,
Guiding the droning dread to our woodland camp.
It was summer then, and the water was warm where we bathed,
The pools dyed dark by the works, grey-black and frothy,
And strewn, in a jumble of islands, with huge square rocks
Where we naked lads lay in the sun or poised to dive
Into the molten slate. Trees towered above us,
Innumerable pillars in an abbey's endless nave,
Where, naked in the great stone font, we saw ourselves
Baptised together in the bloody brotherhood of war,
The sunset purging with its fire the stream's flowing slag.

Back through the dim monastic Woods we walked,
The trees so strange, for the trunks were bare and branchless,
Reaching straight up into space and there putting forth
Leafages of cloud like long level banks of smoke.
No undergrowth ravelled their roots on the clean-swept floor,
And it seemed the whole place had been cleared with mortifying zeal
Of everything save these stony soaring pillars
Stripped to the bone of the bark, as if all we saw,
Our minds so sorely disturbed by what lay ahead,
Was the naked body of the tree upon its own cross.

In solemn silence we walked, suddenly aware
Of a greater silence surrounding us like a fog,
Realising now the absence of sound from the Woods,
Not a song or call from a bird in this birdless place,
Shorn of its bushes and boughs, the cruel dumbness
A mutilation of its grandeur. Then we broke from this mood
And chaffed our companions who had practised their forestry here,
Learning as students the academic management of trees,
Too stern a drill for poets' bird-haunted groves!
Now we, too, were regimented; this was no time
For wild rose, hawthorn or low boughs thick with leaves
Where music was born. What did this silence portend,
We thought, looking down the aisles as an exile might,
Then up at the vibrant vaulting of the towering roof,
While far away could be heard in the gathering dusk
The organ of Derwent playing to the empty choir?

J.C. GRANT
Plough and Coble, 1967

J.C. Grant (1898–1967) was born in Alnwick and grew up there, joining Durham University Officer Training Corps from Armstrong College, Newcastle. He served in the Royal Naval Air Service and later the RAF during the First World War, and worked as a civil servant for much of his life. He published several books of poetry from 1928 to 1970, and a novel, *The Back to Backs* (1930), a depiction of life in a northern pit village.

Two Haiku

View of Ferryhill

Grey slagheaps, black stacks,
dark smoke, pithead winding-gear.
– Meadows green with cows.

Chester-le-Street from the Train

Smoke mists decent brick.
Penshaw: classic pit romance.
– Dainty Dinah Toffee.

JAMES KIRKUP
To the Ancestral North, 1983
➣ AUTHOR NOTE PAGE 371

The Ghost of a Tree
(lyrics)

Riding through Yorkshire we come upon
the ghost of a tree at Buttertubs Pass.
Golden and green, flapping its leaves,
though it is winter and there is no breeze.
Seven little sparrows pale as soldiers
hopping in amongst the curling boughs.

Then comes a shout from one of our party –
old Albert Bausfield's fallen down a hole.
Hope upon hope fastened to a rope –
not able to ascertain how deep it goes.
Albert can you hear me? Make a sound if
you can't make a sound then clap two stones.

Leaving behind our friend in the limepit
we hurry on in quiet dread
into the fog smothering the dales,

the raindrops are falling like the bars of a jail.
Hidden in the arsehole of the world
a row of burned-out huts we made our beds.

Lying awake looking up through the black wooden beams
I can see the Milky Way.
Comes there a scream out of the sky.
A great ball of fire goes hurtling by.
Everyone's awake now. What the hell is
happening today? It's all so queer.

Rising at dawn to find Thomas Knox will
not from his sleep be summoned forth.
Face like a mask fixed in a gasp,
we wrap him in blankets and we cover him with grass.
Onward with our journey through Tow Low and
over Hedley Hill past Hanging Stone.

Called on an inn to fill our bellies with
dark bloody meat and sour black beer.
There we were warned never to stray
far from the road through Kyo Bog.
Several of the children from the village
disappeared last month without a trace.

Three hours later we go in single file
through a maze of moaning soil,
reeking of dung, droning of flies,
the moss on the trees glows as we pass by.
There is something awful alive in this place…
We are most relieved to leave behind.

The moon is a peach in the brown fields of Kibblesworth,
it won't be long till we get home.
Cramp in our guts, bile in our throats,
mischief undulating through our bones…
Suddenly the city lights surround us,
disappearing up into the clouds.
Seven little sparrows pale as soldiers
hopping in amongst the curling boughs.

RICHARD DAWSON
The Glass Trunk, 2013

In the summer of 2012 Richard Dawson took part in a project initiated by Tyne & Wear Archives and Museums called *Half Memory* in which artists were invited to respond to historic material held in the labyrinthine archives of Newcastle's Discovery Museum: 'I spent the following month down there rifling through two-hundred-year-old diaries, unfurling bundles of love letters like flowers, staring into the faces of petty criminals in old photograph albums [...] The stories I stumbled across were often painful, shocking, genuinely fascinating and occasionally joyous. They belong to people living in a different point in time from us. [...] Probably the most startling artefact I came across was a scrapbook begun in 1791 full of newspaper clippings on murders, trials, executions, general misfortune, the arcane, politics and the abolition of slavery, as well as songs, poems and recipes. [...] Amid the usual tales of dejection, horror and woe there are some outstandingly nuts stories to be found the in the great scrapbook. One article recounts, with a beautiful lack of cynicism, the splitting-open of the moon as witnessed by a band of travellers on their way through Yorkshire and the subsequent appearance in the sky of two giant red figures mounted on horseback. Another bemoans the passing of a terrible comet – 'The Prophetic Messenger' – bringing with it an epidemic of cholera. I took these two clippings as my starting blocks for a feverish dash through the villages of Durham and Tyneside.'

All the songs on Dawson's 2013 album *The Glass Trunk* came out of *Half Memory*.

A695 Hymn
(for William Martin)

Meanwhile I'm shifting up to fifth along
this road across the landfill
past all those lyric fictions
villages have taken for a name:
Star Gate, Greenside, Clara Vale
– a glance of street-lights
and a figure in the kitchenette.

The city shrinking in the mirrors,
its strings of neon threading black,
dreams this valley and its southerlies,
this fine rain glazing terrace roofs,
this silhouette the one lit window catches.

PETER ARMSTRONG
The Capital of Nowhere, 2003

William Martin's 'A19 Hymn' and Jake Campbell's 'A184 Hymn' are on pages 414 and 418.

Among the Villages

Stumbling across them among thin pastures
and the gorse-grown relics of rail
you couldn't fail to find
the air heavy with elegy,
the locals wry, but incomprehensible.

Buses going other places
yielded brief epiphanies
through the blurred arc swabbed clear
in fogged upstairs windows,
of streets besieged by weather,
terraces shored against
the ebbing tide of trade,

but you knew all that:
that whole inheritance of shales and spoils
you'd sluice clean into the work of giants.
Maybe even knew this night:
the way the light at the gable corner
lights next to nothing,
that head-scarfed woman hurrying
from history to the neighbours.

PETER ARMSTRONG
The Red-funnelled Boat, 1998

The Singing Pylons

Glumdalclitch, glumdalclitch, glumdalclitch
They mumble on dark summer days. They say *Tch tch*
To the muddle of low-flying larks, bees, gnats and, later on, bat-
Mobiles caught by the light
Of the moon in the pliant wire. *Tch tch*
Grumble these Big Friendly Giants on crutches.
And we who've no share in the profit and loss of it all
Also grumble. For having to live with them makes us ill –

And who's cut an oblong hole in the wood
To make them a road –
And look at the laidly worm of the wire that lollops o'er hill and dale
We say, becoming lyrical
In the midst of our dry ecological battles
Remembering *Palgrave's Golden Treasury* and school.
But here comes a candle to light us to bed.
Here comes a big trade
Wind that would tear not only a land but an ozone layer to tatters –
And what does it matter
Then? For then they sing their one peculiarly lovely tone
Across these half-forgotten
Northern hills. O all night long they sing
Their lonely song, like whales uninterrupted, to Esh Winning
And, if they could, they'd sit down
And weep by the waters of Wear or Babylon
For they are exiles. Lashed in a land of blown plastic bags
They're longing for Brobdingnag.

GILLIAN ALLNUTT
Nantucket and the Angel, 1997 | *How the Bicycle Shone*, 2007

Esh Winning

> which has sprung into existence since the opening of the
> colliery in 1859 may...be called a model colliery village.
>> (*The History, Topography and Directory
>> of the County Palatine of Durham*, 1894)

Next door lives drift through the fence in Sunday
dinner smells, in shrieks of grandchildren
let loose in tidy gardens, metallic
clink of tools under propped-up bonnets,
burst of heavy music from a jaunting car.
I let the house recede, the road fade out.
My garden stretches and the sky moves closer.
The earth is resolute in reclamation,
would take this back to rough ground in a season.
Buttercups spread a net of roots, docks sink deep,

rosebay willow seeds blow across the beds,
a blackbird rifles strawberry plants as if
I was not near, the lettuces I set
show as a wavering line of pin pricks.

When I first saw it someone had parked
a rusty Cadillac in knee-high grass,
a 50s dream in a pitman's garden
left untended – *a large garden is
attached to each house, to be cultivated
as the pleasure of the occupant directs.*
A foot below the surface crumbled
edging was evidence of beds and paths,
an occupant's pleasure blossoming.
It must have been a field of bumps and tussocks
before the colliery, grazing for sheep,
wild rose and hawthorn, stands of willowherb.
Incomer, outsider, gardener, I am
weeding and cutting back to keep it here,
as my pleasure directs, keeping in view
houses *really all that could be desired,
surrounded by a beautiful country*,
and lives I borrow from without permission.

CYNTHIA FULLER
Only a Small Boat, 2001

Lost Landscape

Mist makes the grazing horses almost ghostly
in their drift across the field, tough coats,
rope-rough manes softened by November damp.

Deep below the grass thread narrow passages
where other ponies hauled great tubs of coal
through dust and darkness between walls of rock.

Surfaces reveal nothing – farms, hedges,
sturdy oak trees suggest permanence.
Only the fir plantation gives a hint of change.

The farm that squats on the hill's shoulder
is a landmark in the faded photograph.
Forty years ago it looked down on

three terraces of houses that matched this one,
making four sides of the square around the pit;
the stables, shops, the pithead baths, the tracks,

the rattling trucks, the beehive ovens,
cokeyard chimneys puffing poisonous smoke;
machinery that clanged, whirred, juddered,

winding men and boys deep into the earth
for generations. Now all grassed over.
I scan the uneven ground for signs.

At the fence the horses stand, touch muzzles,
breath steams; a handful of hens scratch
at patchy grass; a man crosses the lorry park.

I overlay the fields, the *Sunbrite* depot
with the photograph, but it will not stay.

CYNTHIA FULLER
Only a Small Boat, 2001

Deerness Valley

The farms were first, before the villages –
East Flass, Hare Holme, Hag House and Rowley,
they saw machines and men brought in
to disturb the landscape, saw terraced rows
spread out into communities.

The pit is local history now
kept under the caps of old bent men
who gather outside the post office.
They marvel at the village youngsters,
with their cars and college courses,
their eyes on the wider skies.

Sunday walkers startle deer and breathe
the windy air of ridge and valley view.
Woods give way to fields, fields to new estates.
High over the farms at night the lights of planes
track pathways out into the world and back.

CYNTHIA FULLER
Background Music, 2009

North

I

Grey slow-jaw comes
home to roost
at Blackhall Rocks
consuming shift by shift the dead
men huddled near the winding-shed.

Fluorescence
weeps the streets
of Pity Me
:next year's children to the soundless
piper throng the recreation ground.

Caesar's joiners
nailed the stairs
at Peterlee
my craftsman father climbed to meet the saw
toothed maker with the slow grey jaw.

See-saw, swing, and
roundabout
at Seaham Harbour
heave and whirl, a swarming tide
piped into the slag mountain side.

Under a callous
crust the pit heap
smoulders
:piper, pipe a song to learn
to walk on singing till we burn.

II *Miners' Gala*

Fancy hats and purple tights
umpteen abreast and buttocky
caper before a banner trimmed
with black for this year's dead

To publish fading banns between
Keir Hardie and a Grecian queen
swaying to the slow drum roll
and labelled Justice on a scroll.

The bands blare past into my head
and in my hand the chilly hand
of whom I was who followed some
bad piper from the promised land
to where that phrase tells lies of it.

Full wagons from the engine yard
pull empty wagons up the slow
two-mile incline from dock to pit.

III

And up and crew the grey
squall morning when I set my face
to kneel important on the verge of laughter
blessing my mother's father back to where
I saw and look in vain to see
the bedsore dead stand singing in their grave.

J.S. CUNNINGHAM
The Powers That Be, 1969

Sea Coal

This is the coal coast. Where Seaham tilts seawards
Splintered suns float on the North Sea's pressure
Compounding best coal squeezed from strata

Between seafloor and rockbed. Below,
Sunken eyes lie back exhausted;
Cold currents unpick the sinews of men

Who rippled in earnest, coaling Imperial flotillas:
Both bone-cage and bulkhead fronds
Have fossilised in sea-salt.

Underwater siftings are washing
From the stokehold of the sea, poor nuts,
For sea coal burns badly, gives off meagre heat.

It has become derelict treasure salvaged
Out of an undertow. Coal has produced
Its own decay: coal-pickers who scrounge

Bent-backed on the water-fringe, balance
Sacks on the cross-bars of clapped-out bikes,
Stretch their spines and look out gazing –

There dead things have come from the sea to tell
Bleached tales to the hard-up and out of work,
Rumouring of desolation riding the slack.

GEORGE CHARLTON
Ten North-East Poets, 1980 | *Nightshift Workers*, 1989

See also Pippa Little's 'Seacoaling' on page 190 (which relates to Lynemouth).

The Box-Eggs

As Aa've sed, Aa wed en'
Mary en' me moved ti Murton;
Aa ettled ti wark i'th'offices –
Aa wizna owerstrang, en' warked at bank.

But the pit-foak they sez ti me
What we need's a Post Office, Tim.
Ti hendle wor parcels
en' everyone's penny post.

Seea they bigged us a house
Wi' a shop en' a woffice
A counter fer stamps
En' a other fer kets.

Aa collectid the mail
Off the train en' sorted it,
Some Aa cudint read reet
Seea Aa gollered the nyem oot i'the street, while it got claimed.

En' we selled paper en' envelopes
Bait en' groceries
A feck o' kets, bullits
Claggum en' such.
En', forbye, EGGS...

Naw Aa wanti tell yer a tale o' thon eggs
Thet woz set oot i' trays i' straa as 'box eggs'.

Naw a pitman we kent woz reet crazy on hens
He raised them hissell' frev egg upti hen.

In his incubator he kept the eggs waam
While they hatched en' the brids wor thrang i' the waam.

This time he was short o' some eggs ti put in
Seea he tiuk chance o' wor box-eggs en' put them in.

They woz fertile as owt, en' turned oot a treat
Thor woz nae birds finer i' the street.

Unusual, mind, en' pawkey them wor
Wi gowden bands, crests, ruffs en' spurs.

When they scratch'd i' the road wiv ither plain hens
Fowk cam jist' ti see them wild forin hens.

But yan day 'General Buller' cam by in his cart –
For he selled ice-cream wi' a pony en' cart.
Naw sum gadjee woz cleanin' his gun wi' nae care

En' by accident let flee a shot i'the air.

It freet the pony, thet ran sharpish away
En' charged thru the hens that wor thor in its way.

Them hens rose up, yan en' all, i' the air
En' flitter'd aroon' in an awful scare.

The forin hens tee, flew up wi' a cry
En' fer the forst time i' thor lives got a taste o' the sky.

They nivor wor seen agien, Aa heerd say.
They mebbe tiuk off fer thor hiem far away.

(A meety fremd land Aa'm thinkin' that'd be
Aal clood en' majic en' mystery...)

Onyways, we moved inti a bigger house,
Mary en' me, en' forgot the access
En' hed ti buy a parcel o' extra land
For that the Ranters wudnat let me cross theirs

BILL GRIFFITHS
The Coal World: Murton Tales Reworked as Dialect Verse, 1995

The Coal World was published by Amra Imprint, Seaham, 'for 111th Durham Miners' Gala, with a preface by Bill Griffiths (1948-2007), who wrote: 'These songs are based on episodes from P.N. Platt's book, *The Canny Man*, written in the 1970s about a Murton family, and especially Tim Platts who was born in the middle of the 19th century.'

The Strike

Naw the owners decided ti change the shifts at the pit
Ti lay doon new wark-patterns, en' it caused a stoppage.

For the maistors wad hae thor pits wark faster en' harder
En' the men was hae sed, Ax us, ax us what's safe en' proper,

Seea the men withdrew frae wark, the maistors stoppt wages en' coal,
En' for the pitmen hed little brass i'hand, thor fam'lies wor siunahunger'd.

Us that wor shop-keepers thowt hard what credit we cud give
En' fowk i' the skiuls set up soup-kitchens ti feed the bairns

The men wor bitter an' fierce ti see thor fam'lies tret seea;
The maistors browt in poliss frev Ireland ti deal wi' them.

The men marched wi' a banner: it woz three vests on a line
Which telled o' the shifts disputed; aal woz riddy fer confrontation.

The wives forbye set oot ti show thor anger:
Wi' thor sho'els they gat buckets o'coal frae the Pea Heap

That woz the small coal nae gud for price.
But the women thowt it splendid ti hoy at the poliss

The under-manager, Mr Bell, read them the law.
But be ran for his life as the women cam up nigh

Then the poliss with truncheons made a firm blue line
En' aal the showers o' coal cud not budge them.

En' as the women flacker'd, the poliss charged,
Brayin' them aal wi' thor sticks, bangin' en' yellin'.

The crowd tiuk off ti Johnnie Bell's hoose, jis' nigh,
En' used the coal left on his greenhoos, iv'ry pane was brokken.

But the bairns en' ithers warked aal day at the spoil-tips
Ti scrabble tegither some bit coal fer heatin' en' cookin'.

Thir wor heaps o' stien en' shale, gert as moontins,
Weird rocks o' reds en' broons, wi' rose-bay grawin' on't.

Sometimes it burned in-bye, en' brust inti low on top,
A mannish volcano o' stithes en' gases.

Thor they wad sieve the weany bits they grov up,
Or mak drift-warkin's o' thor ain fer ti howk oot better coal.

En' seea the strike gann'd on en' on;
Ended Aa knaw, but Aa cannot mak it clear, naw, frae the nex' un.

For ye mind, Aa grew owd, still tuneful, but slaw,
Tiward the day, Mary en' me, we stoppt tegither.

BILL GRIFFITHS
The Coal World: Murton Tales Reworked as Dialect Verse, 1995

Two Up Two Down

In a terrace house in Murton,
a bust of Beethoven is arranged
in a living room window.
Behind drawn curtains,
Annie is letting down a mini-skirt,
Jack is looking through the *Echo*:
holes are cut in Christine Keeler's story.

Upstairs, Pat kicks out at Moira
as Annie uncovers a fresh row of daisies.
Moira rolls over murmuring
of her new skirt from Binns. It is nineteen-sixty-three.
In Murton it is earlier. Annie checks the hem
of her bairn's modesty. I will be born
over her dead body.

ANNA WOODFORD
Birdhouse, 2010

Dalton Park/Murton
(FROM *The Dunno Elegies*)

To join the Dalton angels you must drive past
terraced rows as straight as dentures,
detached from town like a retina, head
for the purple lights of the outlets, the fun.
The backs of shops open like old tallies
used to spill their wires when broken,
lorries emptying themselves into the maws.
The streets are being unmade like sick beds,
cobbles long gone but still no tarmac.
Bassi's Golden Chippy sits the top of a line
of harsh steps and jagged cuttings to the sea.
The wind feels like history. The wind hurts.
It doesn't know, and neither do the angels,
where the backs end and scrubland starts.
Something could get undone here, on these
scrappy municipal football pitches.
Someone could get their name engraved
on the war memorial even now.
The Colliery Inn still hangs on to its paint,
but it's a backyard really, to the fresh
landscaped heart of retail you head for.

Fat where muscle reigned when this land was cleared,
the reverse somehow of a hunger strike,
this place belongs now to families, not men.
Between waddling girls and their tattooed fellas,
slow moving traffic with walking sticks shops.
Old men on the surface trying on slacks,
faces veined with years of black, delighted
now that bastard pit is gone, built over.
They dream of the roof falling above them,
wake with a cough, even the young ones.
Their grandas watch them as they pass by
and are envious, in the way angels can be,
giddily, tetchily, puzzled at themselves.
When they see a coach arrive they quicken,
run towards it, to stop it, but it's only
daytrippers from Durham. They keep feeling things

that are memories of when they were young,
blush at the innocence of their mistakes.

Hopeless shop girls buy their lunchtime coffee
from hapless scrunched up time-killed waitresses.
Old women open sun-dried tomato wraps
and flash right back to that first frothy coffee.
Their friends are dying but they do not know why.
This is a bargain of a bright morning,
there is no need to spoil it for everyone.

An angel rips off his shirt, spreads his wings
and feels the watery sun on his chest.

Trees exist, but not here, not yet.

MARK ROBINSON
How I Learned to Sing, 2013

The Easington Explosion
(lyrics)

Come listen all ye miner lads that tak the road inbye
And I will tell a tragic tale when ten times eight did die.
At Easington in Fifty One they saw the gates o' hell
But they that lived to see the sight they did not live to tell.

The day the twenty-ninth o' May a tragic trick o' fate
Found the night shift on the face and foreshift in the gate.
Explosion wrecked the Quarter seam and killed them all but one
And many a miner's humble home lost father, brother, son.

'Twas fire-damp beneath the cut coal dust fed the flame
That roared outbye till it was spent then roared inbye again
Tearing twisted road supports from their truly bed
And left behind our sorrow with the dying and the dead.

Within the hour from Houghton le' the rescue team did come
With them hope to find the blind and listen for the dumb.
But hope was killed by after-damp that gas we miners dread
Two rescue men with yellow birds were numbered with the dead.

Time has chained the widows' tears and hushed the orphans' cries,
For some the gloom will always live for some the echoes die.
She said 'God bring them comfort' her words I do recall
There's no medals made for miners but they are heroes all.

JOCK PURDON
The Easington Explosion and Other Pit Songs, 1951 |
Pitwork, Politics & Poetry: The Songs & Poems of a Durham Coalminer, 1981

[George] **Jock Purdon** (1925–1998) was a coal miner and songwriter originally from a pit village near Glasgow. He went down the pit in 1943 as one of the first conscripted 'Bevin boys', staying on in Chester-le-Street after the war. On 29 May 1951 he was working below at Harraton colliery when the message came through that 'Easington's just gone up'. The disaster at this neighbouring pit made a deep impression on him. As well as writing 'The Easington Explosion', he joined the Volunteer Mines Rescue Brigade.

Easington was one of the most modern and productive mines in Europe. The explosion was caused by picks striking yellow lustrous iron sulphide mineral, which ignited firedamp bringing down 120 yards of roof. The explosion happened between shifts, so there were 43 men relieving 38; the total death toll was 81 miners and two rescue men.

Purdon's contribution to the mining folk tradition was recognised in 2005 when a new banner was commissioned for Harraton on which Purdon is pictured with fellow singer and Harraton miner, Jack Elliot, who helped to popularise many of Purdon's songs.

The Pigeon Men

Three men are leaning on the corrugated iron,
Staring out across the fields at the china blue
Stretch of sky beyond. They are waiting for something.
'Ye couldn't buy that view,'

Kit shakes his head. His son John reaches up on tiptoe,
A little apart, on the loft roof, watching. Their backs
Are turned to the hand-stitched patchwork of crees, sheds, fences,
The secret shacks

And small doors cobbled from sleepers and iron sheeting
Hauled up from underground. It was pit-work
That made them ache to be out here in the sunshine
Among the birds.

'See yon green fields? Yonder's where Horden pit was –
The biggest pit in Europe, that. Nowt there now. Gone.'

John bites his tab, says nothing; glares into the distance.
Then he throws up his white dove like a flag: 'Come on!'

And suddenly the sky is full of pigeons.
Over Blackhills Dene and Paradise they fly –
Places that are names on the map now only:
Warren House, Whiteside,

And Clifton, Coxon, Cuba Streets – the vanished
Homes of vanished men who never dreamed
How much of themselves they nailed in the crees and gardens.
Home the birds stream,

While John, on the stock-loft roof, waves the frantic fantail.
'Come on!' he yells to the open sky: 'Howway!'
And the white wings beat at the end of his outstretched fingers,
As if he too was ready to fly away.

KATRINA PORTEOUS
Turning the Tide, 2001 | *Two Countries*, 2014

Early Morning, West Hartlepool, 1963
(from the photo with the same title by Don McCullin)

A pipe fitter's mate at the gates of dawn
Is wrenched from sleep by a sulfurous smell.
At six a.m. he'll be entering hell
With the whole damn nation following on.
He's breathed the acids that chimneys discharge,
Winced as the chemicals scoured every cell
Of his threadbare lungs, coughed up, cursed Brunel,
Whitworth and Watt for the shackles they forged.
He's walked this factory road for years, the depth
Of his soles erode with each step, the worth
Of this graft from indenture to death
Shows paltry returns for his time on Earth.
Windpipe-stripping smoke rasps his every breath.
The brass in the south. He's walking north.

EDDIE GIBBONS
The Evergreen: A New Season in the North, 2015

TEESDALE

from **Rokeby**

from CANTO FIRST

I

The Moon is in her summer glow,
But hoarse and high the breezes blow.
And, racking o'er her face, the cloud
Varies the tincture of her shroud;
On Barnard's towers, and Tees's stream.
She changes as a guilty dream.
When Conscience, with remorse and fear.
Goads sleeping Fancy's wild career.
Her light seem'd now the blush of shame,
Seem'd now fierce anger's darker flame,
Shifting that shade to come and go,
Like apprehension's hurried glow;
Then sorrow's livery dims the air.
And dies in darkness, like despair.
Such varied hues the warder sees
Reflected from the woodland Tees,
Then from old Baliol's tower looks forth,
Sees the clouds mustering in the north,
Hears, upon turret-roof and wall,
By fits the plashing rain-drop fall,
Lists to the breeze's boding sound,
And wraps his shaggy mantle round

from CANTO SECOND

I

Far in the chambers of the west,
The gale hath sighed itself to rest;
The moon was cloudless now and clear,
But pale, and soon to disappear.

The thin grey clouds waxed dimly light,
On Brusleton and Houghton height;
And the rich dale, that eastward lay,
Waited the wakening touch of day,
To give its woods and cultured plain,
And towers and spires to light again.
But, westward, Stanmore's shapeless swell,
And Lunedale wild, and Kelton-fell,
And rock-begirdled Gilmanscar,
And Arkingarth, lay dark afar;
While, as a livelier twilight falls,
Emerge proud Barnard's bannered walls.
High crowned he sits, in dawning pale,
The sovereign of the lovely vale.

II

What prospects, from his watch-tower high,
Gleam gradual on the warder's eye! –
Far sweeping to the east, he sees
Down his deep woods the course of Tees,
And tracks his wanderings by the steam
Of summer vapours from the stream;
And ere he pace his destined hour
By Brackenbury's dungeon-tower,
These silver mists shall melt away,
And dew the woods with glittering spray.
Then in broad lustre shall be shewn
That mighty trench of living stone,
And each huge trunk that, from the side,
Reclines him o'er the darksome tide,
Where Tees, full many a fathom low,
Wears with his rage no common foe;
For pebbly bank, nor sand-bed here,
Nor clay-mound, checks his fierce career,
Condemned to mine a channelled way,
O'er solid sheets of marble grey.

from III

Nor Tees alone, in dawning bright,
Shall rush upon the ravished sight;
But many a tributary stream
Each from its own dark dell shall gleam:

Staindrop, who, from her sylvan bowers,
Salutes proud Raby's battled towers;
The rural brook of Eglistone,
And Balder, named from Odin's son;
And Greta, to whose banks ere long
We lead the lovers of the song;
And silver Lune, from Stanmore wild,
And fairy Thorsgill's murmuring child,
And last and least, but loveliest still,
Romantic Deepdale's slender rill. [...]

VII

The open vale is soon past o'er,
Rokeby, though nigh, is seen no more;
Sinking mid Greta's thickets deep,
A wild and darker course they keep,
A stern and lone, yet lovely road,
As e'er the foot of Minstrel trode!
Broad shadows o'er their passage fell,
Deeper and narrower grew the dell;
It seemed some mountain, rent and riven,
A channel for the stream had given,
So high the cliffs of limestone grey
Hung beetling o'er the torrent's way,
Yielding, along their rugged base,
A flinty footpath's niggard space,
Where he, who winds 'twixt rock and wave,
May hear the headlong torrent rave,
And like a steed in frantic fit,
That flings the froth from curb and bit.
May view her chafe her waves to spray,
O'er every rock that bars her way,
Till foam-globes on her eddies ride,
Thick as the schemes of human pride,
That down life's current drive amain,
As frail, as frothy, and as vain!

VIII

The cliffs, that rear the haughty head
High o'er the river's darksome bed,
Were now all naked, wild, and grey,
Now waving all with greenwood spray;

Here trees to every crevice clung,
And o'er the dell their branches hung?
And there, all splintered and uneven,
The shivered rocks ascend to heaven;
Oft, too, the ivy swathed their breast,
And wreathed its garland round their crest,.
Or from the spires bade loosely flare
Its tendrils in the middle air.
As pennons wont to wave of old
O'er the high feast of Baron bold,
When revelled loud the feudal rout,
And the arched halls returned their shout,
Such and more wild is Greta's roar,
And such the echoes from her shore,
And so the ivied banners gleam,
Waved wildly o'er the brawling stream.

from CANTO FIFTH

I

The sultry summer day is done,
The western hills have hid the sun,
But mountain peak and village spire
Retain reflection of his fire.
Old Barnard's towers are purple still,
To those that gaze from Toller-hill;
Distant and high the tower of Bowes
Like steel upon the anvil glows;
And Stanmore's ridge, behind that lay,
Rich with the spoils of parting day,
In crimson and in gold array'd,
Streaks yet a while the closing shade,
Then slow resigns to darkening heaven
The tints which brighter hours had given.
Thus aged men full loth and slow
The vanities of life forego,
And count their youthful follies o'er,
Till Memory lends her light no more.

from **II**

The eve, that slow on upland fades,
Has darker closed on Rokeby's glades,
Where, sunk within their banks profound,
Her guardian streams to meeting wound.
The stately oaks, whose sombre frown
Of noontide made a twilight brown,
Impervious now to fainter light,
Of twilight make an early night.
Hoarse into middle air arose
The vespers of the roosting crows,
And with congenial murmurs seem
To wake the Genii of the stream;
For louder clamoured Greta's tide,
And Tees in deeper voice replied,
And fitful waked the evening wind,
Fitful in sighs its breath resigned. [...]

SIR WALTER SCOTT
Rokeby, 1813

Sir Walter Scott (1771-1832) set *Rokeby*, a book-length narrative poem in six cantos at Rokeby Park in Teesdale, home of his friend J.B.S. Morritt. His first visit to Rokeby in June 1809 had him enthusing: 'The two most beautiful and rapid rivers of the north, Greta and Tees, join current in the demesne.' Mortham Tower and Egglestone Priory made a perfect romantic setting for a poem. Scott explored the villages of Teesdale – Winston, Scargill, Gainford and Brignall, and the moors beyond. Rokeby had been forfeited by its owners for supporting the king in the English Civil War and Scott's imagination kindled as he began a new historical poem, *Rokeby*. By now, however, one may detect a certain over-casual facility in the verse.

On a second visit with his family to Rokeby three years later, Scott retired to a recess in the cliff face above the Greta and sat down to write at a rustic table with a reed surface. The scenes he described are still recognisable today. Scott had great difficulty in finishing the poem, but it was eventually published on New Year's Day 1813. It was, however, a failure, and ended Scott's career as poet. From then on, he devoted himself to the novel. However, the depiction of Teesdale in this briefly renowned work by an influential writer is said to have attracted artists to visit the area to sketch and paint the landscape. J.M.W. Turner had visited before Scott, the first in 1797, making four visits in all, the last in 1831 to produce illustrations for Scott's work.

The old ballad 'Durham Garland' provided the plot for Scott's novel *Guy Mannering* (1815). Scott's last long poem, *Harold the Dauntless* (1817), is set between the Tyne and the Wear; Stanhope, Rookhope and the Roman Wall are mentioned, while Durham Cathedral is famously apostrophised as 'Half Church of God, half castle 'gainst the Scot', which is inscribed on Prebends Bridge in Durham city. [AM]

See also note on Scott and *Marmion* on page 162.

A Jacobite's Epitaph

To my true king I offered free from stain
Courage and faith; vain faith, and courage vain.
For him I threw lands, honours, wealth, away,
And one dear hope, that was more prized than they.
For him I languished in a foreign clime,
Grey-haired with sorrow in my manhood's prime;
Heard on Lavernia Scargill's whispering trees,
And pined by Arno for my lovelier Tees;
Beheld each night my home in fevered sleep,
Each morning started from the dream to weep;
Till God, who saw me tried too sorely, gave
The resting-place I asked, an early grave.
O thou, whom chance leads to this nameless stone,
From that proud country which was once mine own,
By those white cliffs I never more must see,
By that dear language which I spake like thee,
Forget all feuds, and shed one English tear
O'er English dust. A broken heart lies here.

(1845)

THOMAS BABINGTON MACAULAY

Thomas Babington Macaulay (1800-1859) [Lord Macaulay], historian, essayist and Whig politician, was the uncle of George Otto Trevelyan of Wallington Hall, and the desk at which he wrote his famous *History of England* is in the study there. His principal volumes of poetry are *Ivry* (1824) and *The Armada* (1832), dealing with European history, and *The Lays of Ancient Rome* (1842), dramatising heroic episodes in Roman history with tragic themes, including *Horatius*, with its often quoted lines: 'Then out spake brave Horatius, / The Captain of the Gate: / "To every man upon this earth / Death cometh soon or late. / And how can man die better / Than facing fearful odds, / For the ashes of his fathers, / And the temples of his gods?"'

His much-anthologised 'A Jacobite's Epitaph', shows a fond familiarity with Teesdale, and was possibly written for the gravestone of a Jacobite friend who met an early death in exile in Italy. Macaulay himself died at the age of 59, and was buried amongst the writers whose books he loved to read, in Westminster Abbey's Poets' Corner, near to Goldsmith and Johnson. [AM/NA]

from **My Journey to Work**

With my week's wallet o'er my shoulder flung,
Down the green sloping meads I jog along
A well known path from Holwick to Bowlees,
Where Winch Bridge spans the verdant banks of Tees.
When to the roaring river drawing near,
Its rumbling sound strikes loudly on the ear, –
Foaming and dashing in its rapid course,
O'er the rough grey whin rock named Little Force,
Then flowing gently doth its way pursue,
Till by the Staple Crag 'tis hid from view. [...]

The rugged up-hill walk, and sun's hot rays,
Cause the warm sweat to trickle down the face,
Yet pushing on, the path an ascent still,
Till on the top of bleak Hardberry Hill,
Where sitting down, my wearied limbs to ease,
I, looking back, survey the Vale of Tees.
What a majestic scene can be discerned
When to the far off west the eye is turned;
Grim mountain peaks in Alpine grandeur rise,
Which in the distance seem to kiss the skies.
First in the range, from hoary mist not clear;
The outlines dim of high Cross Fell appear,
With Dun Fell, Little Fell, and Meldon too,
And nearer Mickle Fell's broad rocky brow.
A bright scene meets the eye down the vale, where
Neat whitewashed cots stand scattered here and there,
Each with its farm, reclaimed from the wild moor,
Affording comforts to the labouring poor.
No healthier dwellings in our isle are found,
Than those upon the Duke of Cleveland's ground;
Plainly are seen the rugged Cronkley rocks,
Frequented by the prowling, cunning fox.
Because its numerous lengthy caverns yield
Places for shelter, and from foes a shield.
Well may be marked the river's winding course,
Through Cauldron Snout and, nearer, the High Force;
And other interesting objects too.
Behind the hill lie hidden from the view.
Seen are the cliffs in front of Holwick Fell,

Also the deep ravine named Fairy Dell;
And Unthank bank, where once a village stood:
The craggy steeps beyond, and Park End wood.
Like a huge serpent, down the dale, is seen
The Tees, all glistening like silver sheen,
Oft curving round some hill, 'tis hidden quite,
Anon appearing in the broad sun light.
And such is life, our brightest visions fade,
Sometimes 'tis bright, anon we're in the shade;
At times we smoothly glide, at others grope
Our gloomy way, with nothing left but hope.
At yon vale foot, where Hudeshope's waters run,
Stands the small market town of Middleton,
Supported by the mines producing lead,
Where many a dalesman labours for his bread;
While others, with employment are supplied
By the whin quarries on the Yorkshire side.
Southward appears that broad and mighty swell
Of brown moor pasture land, named Arthur Fell,
And Kirk Cairn's little round plantation green,
Which almost from the ocean may be seen;
And further down, more interesting still,
The little ancient church upon the hill.
Next Mickleton appears, distinct to sight,
Beyond where moss-tinged Lune and Tees unite,
With its long street, extending east and west,
And fertile fields, in verdant beauty drest.
My face from Yorkshire for a while I'll turn,
And view that lovely scene past Egglesburn;
A vapour dense ascends on yonder hill
From the large smelting works of Blackton mill;
Long may it rise in curling wreaths on high,
And ore be raised, each furnace to supply,
To give employment to the neighbouring poor,
And keep the wolf named Want far from their door. [...]

Across the mountain ridge my way I wend,
And with brisk step into the vale descend.
On my left hand, Coldberry Mine appears;
The din of mills and jiggers strike the ears;
This sound does from the washing floors proceed,
Where from the dross the mineral is freed.
Those interested in the dressing line

Should pay a visit to this busy mine;
Three chief points gained a skilled observer sees,
These are despatch, economy, and ease. [...]

Time will not linger; leaving the brown burn,
Unto Lodge Syke old mine my face I turn.
By far the richest mine in Teesdale seen,
In fact, few in our isle have richer been;
Like ancient Carthage, it has had its run,
'Tis now wrought out, its mineral wealth is done.
Large rubbish heaps along the hill side show
The vast extent of hollow ground below.
Here toiled my father for his bairns' support,
Till poverty and toil his days cut short;
While I was but a boy of tender years.
Unconscious of his cares, his griefs, and fears,
Which like a galling burden he'd to bear,
A legacy of which I've been his heir.
Now silence reigns where clamour reigned before,
The rattling of machinery is o'er,
The anvil's ringing sound, also the noise
Of labouring men and busy washer boys;
One man alone remains extracting ore
From refuse heaps, of little worth before.
The lodging shops, where miners nightly stayed,
Are into airy cottage dwellings made.
Each with its garden plot, the peaty soil
Repaying well the cotter for his toil.
Now past the verdant patch from rubbish freed,
Where MacNomara's goat and donkey feed;
More wild and dreary grows the aspect round,
Bent and brown heather clothe the mossy ground,
Which give to nature's face a darker hue,
Home of the grouse, the plover, and curlew.
Reaching the summit of the barren hill,
'Tis a rough long descent to Manorgill;
From here is seen, far as sight can extend,
A desert vast, of which there seems no end.
One place alone, like an oasis bright,
Adds variation to the gloomy sight;
It is the well known farm of Middle End,
Near where two muddy brooks their waters blend.
Crossing the stream, and climbing up steep hill,

Keeping the path to west of Wiregill,
Where a rich prosperous mine is, which employs
A number large of men and washer boys.
The hill top gained, pleased I look round,
Knowing I've done with all the climbing ground.
Before bleak Shaftwell's dark brown hills appear,
Which form the boundary line 'twixt Tees and Wear,
And the squire's shooting box upon the hill.
Which fort-like frowns on Thornberry Gill;
And on a line extending o'er yon ridge,
The long abandoned works of old Flake Bridge.
Passing two reservoirs, built to supply
The works with water when the weather's dry,
And going down an easy gentle slope,
I reach the Rake of Little Eggleshope.
And to the shop beside the mill proceed,
Where from their load my shoulders soon are freed.
After a meal and a short rest, I find
Myself refreshed, and more for work inclined;
Then down the stony burn my footsteps wend,
And reach my cabin at my journey's end.
And now, my muse, begone, go take thy rest.
Thy inspiration suits my leisure best;
I must not be by thy vain fancies led,
'Tis here, and not by thee, I win my bread.

RICHARD WATSON
Poetical Works, 1884

Richard Watson (1833–1891) was born in Middleton-in-Teesdale, and started working for the London Lead Company at the age of ten as a washer boy when his father became seriously ill through long hours toiling in the dust, damp and darkness underground, soon to be his own working environment. His long poem 'My Journey to Work' chronicles his seven-mile walk from the village of Holwick across the Tees, passing Low Force (Little Force) to Newbiggin, then over Hardberry Hill to the mines at Little Eggleshope. Miners often lodged overnight at *lodging shops* where they slept three or four to a bed in filthy conditions, and more men were said to have died from TB than in mining accidents. The miner's *wallet* was a long bag holding food for a week's day, which might include hard cheese, bacon and a home-baked loaf of bread. Watson published a slim volume of poems in 1862 and achieved local fame as 'the Teesdale Bard'. His posthumously published *Poetical Works* (1884) includes 'Baliol's Tower and the Railway Bridge', a poetic dialogue between Barnard Castle's round tower and the Tees viaduct (since demolished) first published in the *Teesdale Mercury*, which ran an appeal to help him when he fell on hard times.

The Engine House

It was quiet in there after the crushing
Mill; the only sounds were the clacking belt,
And the steady throb of waters rushing
That told of the wild joy those waters felt
In falling. The quiet gave us room to talk:
'How many horsepower is the large turbine?'
'Seventy. The beck is dammed at Greenearth Fork –
Three hundred feet of head. The new pipe line
Will give another hundred though, at least;
The mill wants power badly.' He turned a wheel;
The flapping of the driving belt increased,
And the hum grew shriller. He wiped a steel
Rail with a lump of waste. 'And now,' he said,
I'll show you the slimes-house and the vanning shed –
This way.' He opened a small wooden door,
And the machinery leaped into a roar.

(December 1924)

W.H. AUDEN
Juvenilia: Poems 1922-1926, 1994/2003

Greenhurth Mine on the western slopes of Herdship Fell near Cow Green, upper Teesdale, closed in 1902. Greenearth is an alternative spelling. See note on pages 246-47.

In Teesdale

No, not tonight,
Not by this fading light,
Not by those high fells where the forces
Fall from the mist like the white tails of horses.

From that dark slack
Where peat-hags gape too black
I turn to where the lighted farm
Holds out through the open door a golden arm.

No, not tonight,
Tomorrow by daylight;
Tonight I fear the fabulous horses
Whose white tails flash down the steep watercourses.

(1935)

ANDREW YOUNG
Collected Poems, 1936

Priest, naturalist and topographer, **Andrew Young** (1885–1971) was born at Elgin in Scotland. He spent the years 1912–14 at the Wallace Green church in Berwick. He began his long poetic career in 1910 with *Songs of Night* and his first *Collected Poems* appeared in 1936. His lifelong interest in botany is reflected in many lyrics, and 'In Teesdale' was no doubt inspired by his time spent studying the flora of the area.

High Force to Low Force
(Upper Tees in full spate)

Under turquoise skies and an optimistic sun
the river is roller-coasting, hell-bent for the sea,
helter-skeltering over the edge, freefalling
from high; deafening in its urgency,
the water turns to smoke – billowing out
to float as crystal powder to the pool beneath.

Catching its breath, the river resumes its run,
powering its way over rocks, frothing and foaming,
spinning and spiralling, shifting silt and gravel
to tattoo its name on the cold river bed –
the magnetic impulse of the sea draws energy
from the hills in an unstoppable flood.

Rattling onwards it rushes downstream
forcing trees and shrubs to bend in its path;
skittering, somersaulting kayaks take their chance
before the lower falls where the molten river
tumbles forth to shimmer in the sunlight
as diamonds spilling from a jeweller's velvet pouch.

LINDSAY BALDERSON
Rewriting the Map, 2003 | *Stripping the Blackthorn*, 2008

Low Force

Unbearable beauty of shine
after rain's rinsed the country,
leaves bright, brittle and bronzed
hang golden medals against
fir-green and grey rock.

An air-fresh smell of leaf-rot
and water damp earth
silence lost in the river's
rush over rocks, busying
round bends, bubbles like
gaudy yellow diamonds dance
on the surface to take
some naiad's fancy......

And we three gaze
and gaze, allow the now
into our slow beings
become imbued with beauty
tread carefully down
the treacherous slope
bearing such treasure
cross the blue, one-man bridge
whilst impatient lads whoop
waiting their turn taking
energy from the swift water.

ANNE HINE
Rewriting the Map, 2003 | *Incidentals*, 2017

Cockfield Fell in Winter

Squeeze then crunch, squeak and creak
across the fell. An icy desert where white snow – drifts

and shafts open – casting miners in black pits
propped with posts.

They pick a way through the ground
to the sound of tubs and bins pushed on tracks
rattling.

Where steaming ponies pull diamonds black
mined from Fell, Edge, and Slack.

Where men and boys clothed in grime
are hot and sweating.

A monument, now white and
chilled with days gone past

and tramways picked in icy paths – freezing.

PAT MAYCROFT
Northern Grit, 2002

Whorlton Lido

Steam shimmers off walls
baked warm as loaves.
The barley grows in slabs of ochre
burning the eyes.

Panting dogs fight over discarded
junk food. River water, tawny as ale,
spews over rocks.

Pale wiry bodies swing out on ropes
in daring curves under hexagonals
of branch and sky.

Men shriek, plunging into rockpools,
a blur of red faces, muscled tattoos
and obscenities.

Rows of children bob
along currents over rocks
worn smooth as backsides.

Behind a waterfall two lovers
form a triangle of flesh –
heads touching for a chaste kiss
sluiced by miles of stinging rainbows.

At night a crimson moon
floats in a dark sea,
the sheets stick to our skin like plasters.

PAULINE PLUMMER
Romeo's Café, 1992

A Darlington rhyme

When I was a little girl, about seven years old,
I hadn't got a petticoat, to cover me from the cold;
So I went into Darlington, that pretty little town,
And there I bought a petticoat, a cloak, and a gown.
I went into the woods and built me a kirk,
And all the birds of the air, they helped me to work;
The hawk with his long claws, pulled down the stones,
The dove, with her rough bill, brought me them home:
The parrot was the clergyman, the peacock was the clerk,
The bullfinch played the organ, and we made merry work.

ANONYMOUS
The History and Antiquities of the Parish of Darlington, in the Bishoprick,
ed. W. Hylton Longstaffe, 1909

Darlington Fifty Years Ago

I stood on Bank Top when meadows were green
Where little but Cuthbert's tall spire was seen –
With far in the distance, an old-fashioned shop,
And the old Town Hall, with its cupola top,
Where magnates arraign, and condemn those who sup
To regions below, – or rather lock-up.
No North-Eastern then had its trains to annoy

The dairyman's horse, or the passive ploughboy,
He would whistle away ne'er troubling his brain
About whistles that scream from the passenger train;
Victoria Road and the streets that stand round
In his path from the plough could never be found.
No Station replete, with an Engineer's skill
Will e'er surpass that on Victoria Hill;
And the Park by the Skerne, with its walks and its ways,
Ne'er entered his mind in those slow going-days;
The Church of St John's, with sweet sounding bells,
Stands now where the guide post told to Middleton Wells,
And Eastbourne so trim, with its dwellings and land,
Was the place where the ploughboy's courtship was planned;
Yes, that was the spot for sweet meadows and trees
When soft breezes blew from the western leas,
No one then e'er dreamt of dwellings being reared,
Or that hedgerows and trees around should be cleared, –
That cowslips and violets should ever give way,
And be to the builders a spoil and a prey.
No Forge 'mid the fields, no smoke from the Hill,
Save that which arose from the old Priestgate Mill.
The serpentine Skerne rolled its waters along
By Clay Row and Parkgate, in winter so strong,
But dwellers in houses ne'er felt once the worse
As it spread over fields in its wild winter course.
For few could be seen where now crowded ones stand
By the banks of the Skerne and low lying land.
Now, tall smoking chimneys stand up everywhere,
With cloud-curling smoke high up in the air,
And the sparks from the Works, and hum from the Mills,
With pleasure and joy the workman's heart fills.
The Press, like a seed, lay slumbering and low,
Awaiting some power to give it a blow,
No *Echo* flashed out in its keen stirring way
To light up the mind in this progressive day;
No *North Star* or *Times* gave news to the North
(For light from the press had not glimmered forth).
No Central Hall, no learn'd Institute
To give to the town a Classic repute;
No Corporate Staff with a Mayor at its head,
Who by the Mace-bearer in dignity's led;
No honoured MP, with grace and renown,
Then sat in the House, from this famed southern Town.

Now, treasures of knowledge in College and School
Are everywhere found to be the grand rule;
Fair maidens are trained to enlighten this age,
And give it a lustre in history's page,
And the grand Grammar School, where learned Masters train
Aspiring youth, with rich food for the brain,
And a Library, free, where knowledge is stored
For an artizan's mind or the brain of a lord;
And places close by for true worship or prayer,
In this grand old Town are found everywhere;
'Twas here in days past, when through its lone vale,
The Passenger Coach ran first on the Rail,
A model for those in each country and clime
To traverse with speed through the boundries of time.

JOHN HORSLEY
The Sailor's Bride and Other Poems, 1889

John Horsley (1817–1893) was born in Newcastle, but lived for most of his life in Darlington, where he was 'a great worker in the cause of Temperance and a keen advocate of the Sunday School movement' as well as 'a writer of some note in his time', with volumes such as *Stray Leaves by the Banks of the Tees* (1866) apparently admired by Gladstone and Queen Victoria. His poem 'Darlington Fifty Years Ago' is included here for its portrait of the town before the coming of the Stockton and Darlington Railway, contrasted with its later industrial landscape, much of that now lost also.

Darlington

A star that sparkles in the Northern gloom.
St Cuthbert stayed here for a coffin break
en route to Durham and his splendid tomb,
before George Stephenson had chance to make
a railway town, a station to pass through.
A quiet place, a pleasant spot to wait,
Convenient and nothing much to do.

The Crescent where I live adjoins the great
Memorial Hospital. Truly fine
memorial to what? His Mam? My womb?
My husband's and my children's town, not mine.

My smokeless fire feebles in my room,
A yellow/turquoise prison of the mind.
The chains that hold me are the chains that bind.

MARILYN LONGSTAFF
Vane Women website, 2001

North Tees Epiphany

Up in the ship of warming air
I see earth roll, unroll ten miles or more
to the grey invisible sea, through terraces,
playgrounds, shops, car parks, wasted spaces.

The bridge an extinct spider, a clutch of long-cooled
towers, the low-lit clouds appalled
at the ruin of river, its nuclear cup
that must not be spilled, the whole brave balls-up.

This is where we live and if, we say if,
this airship, its skilful crew, deliver us safe
through the dream of our needful pain,
it's where we'll be glad to go home.

Always the engine's thrum as gulls weave
wind's fabric round and *Save us, save us*
their window-baffled, hardly-hoping call.
I am one ear of many, one eyeball.

Big ship's the grand, the theatrical show,
staging nativities three floors below
while this top deck sets tragicomic bones,
our breaks, distortions, fractures, agony.

Assorted healing heap, this ossuary soars
over the silenced houses, children, cars,
over the floodplain, over the ferny moor.
An hour to wait now for our visitors.

These faithful all will come, arise, adore
the newborn, the last-chancers, every floor,
will bring us frankincense and myrrh and gold
from down below, from out there's dark and cold.

GORDON HODGEON
Still Life, 2012

Teesdale, Thornaby
(FROM *The Dunno Elegies*)

To walk this wilderness you must commit
to the past, to taking of evidence
from the future. You must stand prepared
to stare down demons that draw strength from dirt,
the difficult to leave behind dirt.
Head Wrightson spilt blood here, ran it off
into the river and called it rust, or money.
These call centres exist. But they are blank
as acetates laid over a map in a museum,
blank as minds of reluctant students.
Bombs could fall and no adrenalin would flow.

George Stephenson's ghost stalks the corridors,
pulled in all directions by fear of kidnap.
Stockton chains him in, Darlington too and
the wrong side of the tracks by the Tyne.
He watches over business studies degrees
and daydreams of Timothy Hackworth
bashing metal up country, near enough forgotten.

They made things here. The she-devil walked here
clutching her handbag and nearly said sorry.
Suicides the Durham bank of the river
brought more than those souls washed up in Yorkshire.
Becoming angels left their heads bloated.
The streets are dotted with students hunting a pub.
The revolution will not be televised.
There is no song to this place, no rhythm,
it is all straight lines and ambient backwash.

Every call has an answer, an even tone
blanketing all the noise that once was here.
Recycled air turns solid after twelve hours
with hardly a calorie burnt away.

The beaters and welders and handtool-burners
gather by the river to fish and to watch.
They talk of bait and boredom, of long years
watching, of the buildings and the quiet
drawn like curtains over the banging they hear.
Sparks flew but a spark now would stand out,
bright on the soft stone and whitewash.
This place is all curves and circles, not sparks.
When this circle reaches back to its beginning,
you can feel the bombs drop. The weights
were heavy they used to move things here.

In the offices of Tees Valley Regeneration
a model appeals to the unseen gods.
It is an idea of heaven gone mad. It is innocent
boxes and balls that nothing can balance.
The angelic welders walk around us.
They are not concerned at our planning,
give permission for nothing, just spit
on the polished floors, breathless
from their sweated effort regardless.
They make no announcements about scale,
or what shape it should be, no prototypes
or macquettes can be put under glass
to start conversations in reception.
They do not know any of the answers.
They are not waiting to be shown through.
We are left with the questions, smooth
and unrewarding to the touch as iron.
There is no give here, nothing but
resistance to be found even now.

Everything is a trap for these angels.

MARK ROBINSON
How I Learned to Sing, 2013

MIDDLESBROUGH

from **Cleveland Thoughts;** *or,* **The Poetry of Toil**

   'Tis only as we look that we shall find:
The poet's mind coins beauty everywhere,
Whether the age be golden, silver, brass,
Or iron-souled, his brain mints all to forms
Of diamantine beauty, flushing back
'The light that never was on land or sea.'
   No free-will occupation can repress
The growth of beauty, for its flowers will spring
To cheer and gladden us through all our toil:
And woe betide those tyrants who dare crush
The verdure of its paths from out the soil,
Mocking the sweetest spirit of God's heaven,
Colleaguing with the sordid fiend of gain
To rob the Lord of all of His due praise.
Let Nature have her will, and beauty decks
The darkest avenues, most secret caves.
   Dost not believe with me? Come now and see
Our Cleveland workmen at their darkest toil.
The gloom of night pervades the ambient air;
The land is dark as Erebus; but, see
The chymic fires that beat back gloomy night,
With stern assertions that the living power,
Promethean, burns strong and bright within.
The fires, fierce flaming through the vaulted gloom,
Below are wrestling with the close-knit force
That stamps the rigid iron with its strength,
So powerful in its use for weal or woe.
Around the flaming furnace, bared for work,
Stand men whose swart and gleaming looks
Shine in the brilliant glow like demigods:
And are they not? What wondrous power have they
To soften and subdue with mighty art
The adamantine nature that rebels
'Gainst all save those who know its mortal part.
Titans they are – great sons of heaven and earth –
And wage a war Titanic – not a war

Of earth 'gainst heaven, but of heaven 'gainst earth.
Their fellow Titans with Briarean hands
Have mined the secret caves, where lies concealed
The destined victim of their fiery power,
With chymic force these drive him from his rest –
Inactive born, re-born a giant power.

   O mighty masters of your fellow-men,
The bay-wreath falls from off your haughty brows!
Your worship now hath passed for evermore.
Here are our heroes – here our demigods.
We worship the Creator of all work;
We honour those who work along with God.
Co-operate with Him, He lends them sight.
We have, with reverent daring, rent the veil
Of seeming facts, and seen Him as He is,
Working for good within His laboratory;
And, willing scholars, we have learned from Him
Inventions and creation's godlike powers.

   With thought-bent brows, behold the noble Watt,
Conning with care his noble schemes for man.
Obedient to his thought, up-towereth
His mighty engine, wonder of the world, –
Whose powers out-vie the fabled strength of him
Who bore the world upon his mighty neck.
How meekly plods this iron giant-slave,
Working with tireless power his work for man,
Hewing his wood, drawing his water from
The deepest depths, and thus redeeming him
From his old yoke of slavery; and brutes
Whose spirits though they tend but to the earth,
Yet have been gifts of God, may bless it too
How much then should we honour that great soul
Who tamed the giant steam, and harnessed him.
With iron harness, to the work of man!
And after Watt, a host of demigods
Have sprung to being, powerful to subdue
The earth, and make her man's. George Stephenson,
As Jason erst the fiery brazen bulls,
Has yoked his iron horse, and day and night
It bounds with lightning speed across the land,
Snorting and champing fierce its fiery bit –
In tenderest control of him who guides
Its course along the ringing iron way.

Here first the Men of Peace laid down the groove
Which guides this meteor-courser like a fate
Wherever men direct its fiery power.
Here peaceful pioneers clove quietly
The infant iron rail-path of the world.
'Annihilating time and space,' and thus
Creating time and space for nobler work
Than passing tediously from toil to toil.
To those who count their years as they have worked,
And not as they have notched their yearly mark,
It brings more years of life: nay – all the world
Lives with a stronger life-beat, quicker pulse.
And quicker circulation. Forbid, O Heaven!
That this quick coursing of the blood should prove
A fever wasting all life's energies –
That this great peace-path should be hired by Hell,
And made a war-path. Thanks be unto God!
With peaceful men it had a peaceful birth, –
Freight then its cars with peace: let all the earth
Cling closer to that principle of love,
Which adds to all our wealth, whilst it detracts
From none; and strongly scorn to aid the cause
Of war and all its hideous misery –
The principle of hate – that man from man
Should be distinct by force of chart or caste.
Do we not really form one family?
And is not God our Father, Christ our Lord?
Or is our faith a lie – a make-believe
To cheat our simpler brother, just to hold
His neck more easily beneath the yoke?
Rise up in all Thy strength, Thou Nazarene,
That died for man, but rose again in might,
Living a present Lord in every heart,
That trusteth God and all His promises –
Rise up in all Thy strength, assert Thy might:
As at Thy birth the herald-angels sang
'Glory to God in the Highest! Peace on earth!
Goodwill to men!' Now let Thy heralds shout
Christ reigneth, but by Love and Peace on earth!
Down with the War-Gods: they are Devilries!

ANGUS MACPHERSON
Cleveland Thoughts; or, The Poetry of Toil, 1872

Angus Macpherson (c. 1827-1904) was a radical poet, scientist and freemason, probably originally from Glasgow, who was behind many educational ventures in Middlesbrough from the mid to late 19th century. He was secretary of Cleveland Institute of Engineers from 1872, and secretary of the North Riding Infirmary for 32 years from 1873 until 1904; and started one of Middlesbrough's early newspapers, *The Dominie* (1875-76). His long poem in blank verse, 'Cleveland Thoughts; or, The Poetry of Toil', was published as no.11 in George Markham Tweddell's *North of England Tractates* series. Citing the examples of Burns and the 'Ettrick Shepherd' James Hogg, Macpherson argues against sentiment in poetry, and in the extract included here, further asserts that true poetry is found in the toil of men like Cleveland's iron workers and that war is incompatible with God's love and goes against the teachings of Christ.

Furnaces

   Tumult of furnaces;
Red and ominous, splashing with flame the wash of the river;
Red and seethed as a jungle dawning, transfused through the mist;
Red as the ebb-swilled flats at sunfall, glazed and a-quiver;
Red, and primordially dour, as the Hell of the Yiddish Christ.

   Tumult of furnaces;
Intoned, sacramental, the roaring that climbs from the blasts;
Eery their asthmic vomiting, baffling the sloth of the night;
While the long geyser flames tongue and leer as the darkness lasts
Staining the low-banked clouds with the bubbling crater's light.

   Tumult of furnaces;
An imminent muttering of workers, that fodder and pasture the flames,
Hunched and reticent and straining, like ogre-driven gnomes of the earth;
Yet the menace limps through their glance as they brood on their shames,
And they dream they are fuelling tall autodafés for wealth and high birth.

   Tumult of furnaces;
And where our Benarés, we fakirs, vagrant through deadlock and strife?
For the ore feasted Brahma of Ingots straddles his bulk on the track,
Rusting the plain with his belchings, and stifling the green from life,
While we Juggernaut serfs of his Progress throng for the hooves on our back.

A.E. TOMLINSON
Candour: First Poems, 1922

A.E. Tomlinson (1892–1968) studied at Middlesbrough High School and Emmanuel College, Cambridge, before enlisting as a 2nd Lieutenant in South Staffordshire Regiment in June 1915. Many of his poems draw on his experiences in the trenches. Claiming the literary middle-ground between the vision of the patrician poets and the perspective of ordinary soldiers, his work combines an awareness of social realism with an educated literary sensibility. He wrote a scathing attack on Rupert Brooke after meeting him.

Cleveland Night

Harsh cinders crunched beneath my heel
As, dipping bell, the furnace lit
With a red flame the sky of steel
And wiped out all the stars of it –
The stars whose icy points of steel,
Turning as though on brace-and-bit,
Drilled my thin skull, and through my brain
Shot screwing spasms of keen pain.

And, as I watched the ruddy flare
Of seething iron, that instantly
Dulled the cold terror of the stars,
Its fitful man-enkindled fire
Quivering to flame the frozen air
Consumed my mortal agony,
Quickening anew half-dead desire
To perishable warmth and light,
As, under shadowy crags and scars
Of mounded slag, I took my way –
Forgetful of infinity
And the menace of eventual night –
Towards the fresh hazards of the day.

WILFRID GIBSON
Coming and Going, 1938
➤ AUTHOR NOTE PAGES 232-33

Fire

I

Across the Cleveland countryside the train
Panted and jolted through the lurid night
Of monstrous slag-heaps in the leaping light
Of belching furnaces: the driving rain
Lacing the glass with gold in that red glare
That momently revealed the cinderous land
Of blasted fields, that stretched on either hand,
With livid waters gleaming here and there.

By hovels of men who labour till they die
With iron and the fire that never sleeps,
We plunged in pitchy night among huge heaps –
Then once again that red glare lit the sky,
And high above the highest hill of slag
I saw Prometheus hanging from his crag.

II

In each black tile a mimic fire's aglow,
And in the hearthlight old mahogany,
Ripe with stored sunshine that in Mexico
Poured like gold wine into the living tree
Summer on summer through a century,
Burns like a crater in the heart of night;
And all familiar things in the ingle-light
Glow with a secret strange intensity.

And I remember hidden fires that burst
Suddenly from the midnight while men slept,
Long-smouldering rages in the darkness nursed
That to an instant ravening fury leapt,
And the old terror menacing evermore
A crumbling world with fiery molten core.

WILFRID GIBSON
Chambers, 1920 | *Collected Poems 1905-1925*, 1926

Sunlight and Heat

> Imagination here has very ample scope in fancying a coming day when the bare fields we were then traversing will be covered with a busy multitude and numerous vessels crowding to these banks denote the busy Seaport.
> JOSEPH PEASE, 1828

> We have not much of a past to speak of, but we look forward to having a great future.
> MAJOR DIXON, 1887

> perhaps in another fifty years or more, this hideous mushroom town will have sunk back again into the arms of Mother Earth.
> DOUGLAS GOLDRING, 1925

> Middlesbrough, a godforsaken 'Blade Runner' kind of place.
> KATE ATKINSON, 2002

I

The Pennine rains begin their homeward course
Like Teesdale salmon swimming to the sea,
From Cross Fell, Cow Green, Cauldron Snout, High Force,

The river is impatient to be free,
A wall of water, fit to burst its sides,
A roaring tide of time and History,

Until the hills give way, the flood subsides
Past Barnard Castle, Darlington and Yarm,
Through Thornaby and Stockton, till it slides

Like strong brown ale towards this place of calm
And watery silence, land of becks and brooks,
A swamp, a treeless waste, a lonely farm,

A turnip field, a church, a world of ducks
Ignored by Celts, by Saxons and by Danes,
A 'waste' according to the Domesday Books.

But through this wild and haunted place of rains,
Peg Powler's rotten teeth, the Sockum Worm,
The cold, unpopulated Cleveland plains,

The snaking river wriggles like a sperm
To fertilise the future with desire
And restless change, to leave behind the germ

Of progress, labour, industry and fire.
For even here, where seals and salmon meet,
Necessity and History will conspire

To build an empire out of light and heat,
And burst the banks by turning muck to brass,
And on the river-floor the stones repeat

Their polished lines that say that all things pass,
And nothing is more permanent than grass.

   II

A season without rain: the Tees recedes,
Revealing its accumulated slimes –
A muddy archaeology of needs

And hopes, hard work, hard luck, hard folk, hard times,
In which we dig as if to understand
The stony economic paradigms

In which the ocean grinds the past to sand,
The river keeps its secrets as it flows
And tides will never stop at our command.

Two hundred years ago, the census shows
The population here was twenty-five;
Within a hundred years that figure rose

To *ninety thousand!* See them all arrive
From England, Ireland, Scotland, Cornwall, Wales,
A human flood, exhausted but alive;

From Durham, Staffs and Lancashire, the Dales,
Northumberland (and Germany!) they came
Force-marched by hunger, poverty and tales

Of work that lit the River Tees with flame
From iron-works, furnaces and rolling mills,
Till Stygian night was day in all but name.

Prometheus himself once taught the skills
With which they hammered Teesside iron and steel
From Durham coal and stone from Cleveland Hills,

A phoenix rising from the flame's ordeal
Obliterating rosy-fingered dawn,
Until they built a hard-edged commonweal

Within the Vulcan fires of Bolckow-Vaughan.
And so the town of Middlesbrough was born.

III

The story of this town's a neat device
For moralists who think the past must owe
The present some accounting for the price

Of Change, as if the river Tees could flow
Uphill, upstream, in order to forgive
The foolish hills for what they did not know.

This river-bank is where the present lives,
The future is an ocean which can't wait
To swallow up the past's alternatives:

A little town, the well-planned new estate
Of Joseph Pease, a dock, a railway line,
A pottery, a square – a model state;

Or else a classic study in decline,
A 1930s slum-town, workless, broke,
A failed experiment of flawed design;

A gold-rush Klondyke, breathing fire and smoke,
Ironopolis! An infant Hercules!
A commonwealth of work, a field of folk;

Or this one – post-industrial, on its knees,
Awash with crack and smack, that likes to boast
A thriving trade in women by the Tees;

A monastery, perhaps, a staging-post
Where footsore Dunelm travellers can spend
The night, midway to Whitby down the coast;

Or here, beyond the river's hairpin bend,
A wilderness of weeds and broken glass
That marks the town's beginning and its end,

A monument of burned-out cars and grass
In praise of mighty Ozymandias.

   IV

Ambition, hunger, struggle, pride and toil –
The story of this town grows by degree,
First iron and steel, then chemicals and oil.

Now they have gone who knows what we shall be?
And which comes first, the raindrop or the stream?
How long's the coal-seam hidden in the tree?

To every age the future choices seem
More urgent and compelling than the last;
We stumble through the present in a dream,

Somewhere between the future and the past,
Between the moorland rainfall and the sea,
We make the world until we have surpassed

Our former selves. In 1853
They looked the Gorgon future in the eyes
And said that by this river We Shall Be,

One Body Politic beneath the skies,
More powerful together than alone.
Such boldness and invention justifies

All those who are forgotten and unknown,
A footnote to the river's turning page,
Who made this windy river bank their own,

Who only thought to earn a common wage,
But built a town of dirt and smoke and fire
That was the very wonder of the age,

A town that spanned both past and future, via
Adventure, vision, enterprise and sweat,
A hell on earth, or else a world entire,

A story that nobody should forget,
An epic tale that isn't over yet.

V

But History is the sum of many choices,
A melody that has no single source,
The river swells with tributary voices,

A cataract that has to run its course.
From tarns collecting melting Pennine snows
On Cross Fell, down through Cauldron Snout, High Force,

The river's story's told in fluid prose:
A half-remembered tale we've heard before,
Unchanged but always changing as it flows

To meet the waves that thrash upon the shore.
As if the cold North Sea can still recall
These hills once slept beneath the ocean floor

Two hundred million years ago; a small
Time for an ocean that has sometimes felt
Volcanic islands rise, and mountains fall.

The Romans passed through here, the Dane, the Celt,
The monks, the Ironmasters – one by one
They passed away. All human empires melt

One day, just like the snow that falls upon
The distant Pennine hills. All that remains
Is this old rusty river, rolling on,

Replenished every morning by the rains;
The wind that blows the past on down the street;
Imagined futures guttering in drains;

The universal need for light and heat;
And far below the river's dirty glass
The stones that on the river-floor repeat

Their polished lines that say that all things pass,
And nothing is more permanent than grass.

ANDY CROFT
Comrade Laughter, 2004

The Cold Steel

We were surprised by the man-made beauty
Of the satsuma-coloured steelworks-sky
The night we were caught in the blackout.

When the darkness broke out suddenly around the rec,
We doorway huddled, desperate for some warmth,
Our eyes adjusting as the rippling beats of orange,

Emanating from the hell-mouth of the furnace,
Cast everything new in flickering shadows –
I swear I saw flames dance in your eyes!

Walking the same walk warm with whiskey,
Street-lamps throw different shades,
Coaxing contemplation of my unfamiliar hands.

For a moment you're back there beside me;
Though the thrill of this ghostly communion
Vanishes into vacuums, as I stare at hard starlight

Winking through a sky of squid's ink black:
In this world where the steel's stopped flowing
All is hard and separate and infinity is cold.

ANDY WILLOUGHBY
Tough, 2004

Smelter

Leaning on his shovel
On the furnace floor.
A Cargo Fleet smelter.

Sweat towel draped about his neck.
Blue bottle-glass specs
Shoved high on his forehead.

His balding head glistening.
He listens, feels, hears
The furnace song.

The loud roaring of hot blast,
The plip-plopping tinkling sound
Of steel and slag boiling.

He raises the furnace door.
Views the fiery interior.
Sees the smelt boil.

Orders the chargers in,
Trundling down the steel shop floor,
Buckets full of alloying elements.

Charge forward into the all-consuming heat.
Rotate bucket, spill contents.
Into the seething mass.

Withdraw hastily, beat a retreat
Before shaft and bucket begin to melt.
Then down the shop floor for another load.

The smelter leads his gang, starts the round,
They walk in a circle, loose limbed,
Shovels hanging on extended arms.

Knees sag, thrust forward, scoop.
Left arm as pivot, thrust down with right.
Straighten up, walk up to furnace door.

Plant feet firmly, sway of hips, swing arms,
Chuck shovel load right to the back of the furnace.
Shovel after shovel of limestone spread

Over boiling, spitting metal,
Providing a blanket of flux
To ease out impurities.

This limestone a week ago a rockface in a quarry,
in Wensleydale.
Now turned liquid, floating on top of molten metal.

Heat is energy-sapping.
He drinks a lot
To make up for the sweat oozing
From every pore of his body.

Steel has many alloys.

Chromium,
        Manganese,
                Molybdenum,
                        Mild,
                              Carbon,
                                    Tool.

All require different formulae.
All have different melting points.

He must know when
To add various elements
To increase or decrease temperature.

Add flux.
Pour. To tilt massive furnace.
Run off slag, carefully.

To leave his smelt unadulterated.
To teem it into ingots
To be later rolled into

Blooms,
      Billets,
           Joists,
                Beams,
                      Channels,
                          Piles,
                              Angles,
                                  Flats
                                        and 'T' Bars

To be
Sent to the far ends of the earth.

KEITH PORRITT
Smelter: Poetry from the Tees Valley, 2003

The Works

On your way down the wharf,
hell was on the left.

Just passing on the other side
was enough to burn your face.
Yet you crossed over,
stood on a high slab above the pit
and looked down into the inferno.
There, soot-spotted men,
stripped to the waist;
glistening dangerous as leopards,
hammered white-hot bars;
until sparks spat out like sins
into the chaotic haze.

There was no point trying to talk
above the roar and clang
of men working happily in the fire
to keep the wolf from the door.
You watched for a while
until you couldn't stand the heat,
then moved on, taking a long path
to the oil-scummed Tees.

Below the railway,
if you wanted the whole works,
it was purgatory you went through
to walk on grass,
hold a buttercup under your throat,
float on clouds of blackie-man's-oatmeal;
have a paradise of dandelions at your feet.

MAUREEN ALMOND
The Works, 2004

Dockside Road, South Bank

(FROM *The Dunno Elegies*)

Down Dockside Road things divide imperfectly,
containers block entrances to hallowed ground.
The cooling towers' pinched waists leave a smudge
of grey upon grey, cack-handed, over-looked.
Curtains cover hills that linger behind
the long back gardens of Lackenby.
In South Bank the show has not changed for years.
Parmo has left his mark in graffiti
and gravity's pull on paid-for bellies.
The betting shop is the brightest thing here.
The granddads pushing prams are whey-faced ghosts
of their granddads walking down to docks
in the bright heyday. Sculptured roundabouts,
all molten steel and welders' muscles,
cast in the downtime so we remember,
could tell you a thing or two. It's not true,
that story about the sign on one of them,
'Happy 30th Birthday, Grandma.'

Behind the last hoarding plastered with posters
lies the market stall of consolation.
There the angels fight over slim pickings,
crumbs roll into balls going back to dough,
a candy-pink dolphin-edged ashtray,
a 30 miles an hour sign from the estate,
a brochure for luxury detached living
with no garden, an artwork made of string
and nails on a black-painted board,
two daffodils, an oak leaf and an umbrella,
three lengths of cornicing and a loo seat.

The angels engage with messiness,
they say, but you can take it too far.
They are not here for the good of their health:
you will find them in the karaoke.

MARK ROBINSON
How I Learned to Sing, 2013

Teesport, Redcar
(FROM *The Dunno Elegies*)

Rolling picture of the utterly here,
land still in turmoil as markets crash,
morphing and merging in hostile arrangements
when old certainties just evaporate
like red steam leaking from pressured globes
the heart of networks of private roads.
All the power that once was here changed.
Iron made a place appear overnight,
now it is rusting the water ochre.
Ore in these dark hills, a dance in the pipe-work.
An endless mess of goods trains shuffles
through imitations of illuminations,
past stone-tongued fire-eaters and fireworks
burning messages into the heavens.
Our children wheeze, and tiny angels
keep them company in their fragile games.
This is a blank land of grey-faced fences,
barbed wire barriers and strengthened steel.
It scrubs its face raw because it is proud,
and it wants the world to be orderly.
Though the angels on the backs of trains
think it looks so shiningly chaotic
something good must come from its blissful rush,
the wind tastes bitter, chemical, beaten.
You can see its shape from Redcar beach,
nourish a warm dream of Holy Island,
so far to the North the light is different.
There is quiet there, and cleaner daylight,
permanent beside the gulls' plainsong.

But here, gates are locked, one by one
companies become simply history.
Too many to list, those that are gone.
Molten, the angels that record their names.

MARK ROBINSON
How I Learned to Sing, 2013

Peg Powler

Mothers use my name to scare their children
I don't object. I have none of my own
but understand the depth of the seduction
the way the mirrored surface draws you down.

They say I scatter trinkets to entice them
bright fairings twinkling on the banks
just close enough to deeper waters
where the fickle currents spin you till you drown.

I'm misrepresented. The mothers
need the clout of magic to colour in
what might have been an empty threat
I'd do the same. But hear me.

We do not ask for sacrifice, nor
lure tots into our waiting arms.
If they fall, we hold them gently,
rock them till the final bubble

leaves the infant mouth, floats up
and breaks the surface carrying
that last mama to ears that strain
but never hear it. Just the river rolling by.

JO COLLEY
Bones of Birds, 2015

Cook, The Bridge and The Big Man

I'm driving over the border, passed The Captain Cook
Dougy's in the back and Les Murray, fresh from clouds
Packs the rest of my small-town car, wears it like a turtle shell.
We both know he's into The Dreaming, suspect he's strayed there
Once or thrice, so we're taking him to see our Transporter
To persuade him to cross, as there are no trolls left
And Peg's just a myth to scare off truant kids.

So how do you cross that thing, in a ferry of sorts?
No man, on a flying carriage.
Where do you board?
We're already on.

I pay the ferryman's toll, Les says the crew seems amiable enough
As we set sail, suspended over the Tees cast at a low shining tide.
Riding the slow judder toward Samphire Batts we chew the fat
Of James Cook and cluck over his stroke of bad-storm luck
That left him God-fallen, cooked and eaten, first by Hawaiians,
Now by us, and the rest of his home-town.
Grimm talk, but it is Halloween.

The gates swing open to the salted sunshine of riveted places,
That would much rather drift out to sea, with privets like gunwales,
And every shop wears a security grille. I start up the engine, drive onto
Terra Firma, with Les looking back and up at the alien skeleton, saying,
Well boys, thanks for that. Got to be the weirdest bridge I ever crossed.

BOB BEAGRIE
Huginn and Muninn, 2002

Occasion for Keeping Shtum

> It's all around the town, it's all around the town
> this hard ring of iron.
> GRAEME MILES

Outside the takeaway on Parliament Road
Mill a pack of clockwork boys, full of intent
And no direction, no sense of anything existing
Beyond the tight band of hills and the boiling river.
A couple on bikes clock us coming, nudge the rest
I hold the small hand in mine a little tighter
Pull her imperceptibly closer as we pass,
Oye, Speccy Cunt! If you didn't have a kid wi' ye,
You'd be fucking dead! says one. The rest giggle
I bite my tongue, join the queue for fish and chips twice.
Deep-fried bravado and boredom, but real enough.
They know, as I do, that a pack their shape met a bloke

Roughly mine on the far side of the carriageway
Yesterday afternoon. The paper wrapping my dinner
Tells how they were arguing by the post office
Before he turned to walk on, then slipped
Spouting his thirty odd years onto the kerb
A katana turning his neck into a shish kebab.

BOB BEAGRIE
Huginn and Muninn, 2002

Acklam Rainbow

The lass with a *Frankie says* chest,
before any of us knew what it meant.
Twirling her silver baton in the street,
not once missing the beat, she throws
electric-taped broom shank to air;
catches the twist with wide hands.

I bounce a ball off the garages,
have no reason to talk here.
As girls with long socks hang round
awaiting instructions, trill glockenspiels
as her theme tune, she marches on,
never gets round to joining a jazz band.
Knees high, back straight
under pink sky and sunset street light
in her own weekly parade,
Born in the USA, here, now, in the Boro.

I listen to the nights drawing closer,
when she will not be here.
Tinned Cherry Pink and Apple Blossom
White spills its petals, leaves its stone
in the shadow of the flats.

ANGELA READMAN
Sex with Elvis, 2005

Easterside '59

It's just an ordinary place with an optimistic name.
Easterside. They send us to running water promises.
Dreams flowing when you turn the tap in your very own
indoor bathroom. House after house of plasterboard
nakedness, where we all leave the water in the tub
for the next. The excitement of planks we tiptoe across
to get to shops. Our square privets, behind which
we'll still leave our doors open, so people like us can step in.
Green gardens, schools just up the road. Easterside.
Where we'll live our lives in the promise of the name,
a spring resurrection, hope revived back to life.

We live in Easterside, hear the stamp on floorboards
over our heads in the running up and down to rooms
before we get HP carpet. And are the envy of the street
with our withdrawn curtains so that kids can smear their noses
to see John Wayne chase black and white Indians on the first TV.
We live in Easterside, do homework by streetlight,
while boys look out, do unmentionable things in their bedrooms,
in plain view of congregants gathered like birds
by the bell tower of our concrete modernist church.

ANGELA READMAN
Sex with Elvis, 2005

Easterside '89

He makes his living with his very own business,
driving the moby, everything you ever need
on wooden shelves in the back of the van.
His wife behind glass making change of plasters, potatoes,
and Bounties with wax wrapper promises of paradise.

He's done all right, since Liptons went up.
Provides the things you run out of sometimes.
Drops things into mix-ups and drives on,
before teenagers gather outside.

Cruises streets where every day is the day after the party.
The red white and blue flagstones painted for the 70s jubilee;
wallpaper tables covered in doilies and butterfly cakes peel
in chipped paint from feet, with less colour left every summer.

He drives through Easterside, pauses briefly at Darnton Drive
at the top, the sort of Hollywood Hills of the Estate.
Kids throwing his empties at the generator,
wind making them a sad steel band
against the garages teenagers attend.

He knows which street the mam and dad of the bloke
who used to be Gail's husband on Corra live on,
and the house of the girl whose name made *The Sun*.
Drives his wife's flinch away from the cries of kids
having fun playing British Bulldog, Bottle of Poison,
bottle of popcorn, bottle of piss.

ANGELA READMAN
Sex with Elvis, 2005

Boro Babe

She's got highlights in her hair and a, top knot,
Nike's in the winter and, flip-flops.
In summer she gets tanned from a, flick-top.
She's a Boro Babe.

She's got, a belly-button stud and a, ring through
her eyebrow and a tiny little, tattoo,
just to the right of her, shoulder blade.
She's a Boro Babe.

She's got, a low-cut jumper with, tassels on,
a short leather skirt that's a, tight fit
legs that go right up to her, armpits.
She's a Boro Babe.

She's got, a shiny pink bag she can, dance round,
on Fridays in Millennium, down town,
while grannie Elsie watches little, Stacey.
She's a Boro Babe.

She knows, who her friends are, how to live,
remembers where she comes from, or did,
down below the railway.
She's a Boro Babe.

MAUREEN ALMOND
The Works, 2004

Boro Girl

At the top of the steps outside the station
she's standing in her own winter zone
a cold blonde, thin as a whip.
Her faraway eyes water
while the wind makes her bones reeds
that hum like the pipes of a forgotten tribe
lost somewhere on the Mongolian plains
eternally wandering.

An invisible blizzard swirls around her.
Caught in the snow queen's spell
the crystal carried in her veins
lodges in her heart
freeze frames her future.

She holds a bunch of tulips.
Her arms bend under their weight.
They are the colour of deoxygenated blood
the colour of the burst veins
on her skin's surface
the colour of the robe worn
by a Mongolian princess
on the day of her wedding.

JO COLLEY
Weeping for the Lovely Phantoms, 2007

CLEVELAND

from **Between Stations**

From Middlesbrough to Saltburn past Coatham Marshes
as early winter comes sweeping in today from Siberia.
Restless snow flurries start to obscure looming shapes –
the final historical remains of ironworks, steel mills,
stranded black locomotives that pulled the smelt in pigs
from weary morning to never-dark childhood night,
to be converted into steel that still spans the globe.
Abandoned buildings, that still spew out smoke
in my attic-stored adolescent sketch books,
haunt the eye like shells of bombed cathedrals.
This was all marshland once; hidden slag-heaps
lie under grass-covered bumps lining the sides
of trickling inlets of the Tees with its metal cranes:
intricate insect totems poke their heads at the North Sea.
Giant deer, elk and other ancient mammal bones
dissolved into this bleak beauty by the estuary:
through whirling flakes you can see them still.
Easy too, to see the Conqueror lost in fog here
only a few feet away from Northern swords
sending Norman soldiers to their long grave
but the thick sea mist that cut him off saved his neck:
no resistance then could stop the North's razing
and now no entreaty too could save the Salamander
in the lone blast furnace: the fiery heart – last survivor
of the hundreds that lined the river banks an age ago,
making this the land of dragons with satsuma skies
welcoming the Welshmen who came to Eston mines,
recent death by neglect the final chapter of the onslaught
begun back then by the blunt-headed warrior king
they cared to name our next Prince of Wales after.

ANDY WILLOUGHBY
Between Stations, 2016

On the Gare at Night

He's carrying a piece of metal pipe
Flickering with the reflection of flames
from the steel works beyond the salt flats.

Him and his mate emerge
like an apparition
from scraggy dunes, moist with sea fret.

On one side of the spit
the sea is heaving, oily against the concrete.
It's a long way to the shore.

There's a boat with flaking paint
pitching on the waves
to TFM's top drum n bass.

Where's the tap? shouts the lad
his face in the dark moving closer
'ave yer gorr eny fags?

Beyond the lighthouse
there are fishermen whose small sons
carry the bait.

Don't smoke I say aloud
Walk briskly, I whisper to my friend.
I don't know who'll buy the steel works
or what they'll do with it.

PAULINE PLUMMER
Bint, 2011

Redcar Sands

The red flag's flying on the front today.
It's dangerous to swim, to eat the shellfish.
To expect too much from this year's holiday.

Between the surf and the clouds from British
Steel, the last cinema holds back the tide
Of change. Here only the sand can flourish.

The walk along the blackpath from Teesside
Takes years; a sunny, Brownie dream of ease,
Of bank holidays at the good seaside,

A Republic of pleasure and release.
Tommy Chilvers lived here, died in pain,
And in between was a life on the seas,

The Trades Council, the Party, Spain.
But History never works the way it's planned,
Winds blow cold and seas turn dangerous again.

The afternoon falls, the flags are furled,
And still the marram grass cuts through the sand,
Still binds the shifting dunes, this turning world.

ANDY CROFT
Nowhere Special, 1996

Potato Sellers – Cleveland

Through wasted lands, the major routes
display, in lay-by, on grass verge,
the advance guards, these far-flung ends,
of profit, enterprise, advantage.

Fifty miles north the Wall's abandoned,
poems and sheep and not a toss for Rome;
twenty miles south the squat of Fylingdales,
warning the riggs and cairns of what's to come.

And here these foot-men have to live, and now,
without a hope of proper work or pride,
a laid-on, paid-off casual regiment
that's bought and sold and taken for a ride.

Such forlorn openings, some general's joke
among the derelicts of heavy losses.
A bag's price standard, shelter plastic sheet,
killed hours to breathe in luck's exhausted gases.

Cold furnaces stand cracked, the speechless din
of radio-babble towers another day
till watch ends, lights out, nothing to report.
A kestrel beats time to its dangled prey.

GORDON HODGEON
A Hole Like That, 1994

Saltburn

Under the overhang of serrated scar,
kittiwakes brace the assassin wind for a ledge of shale.
Fault lines bleed iron ore.

Across the clifftop a green sari spread out to dry
under a fingernail moon; tankers queue for port,
lights flickering on a sullen sea.

Oystercatchers, courtly in black and white,
pick in the shallows of boiled pebbles;
waves jamming from major to minor.

Are the seagulls keening for the season
of migration? – love buried like a bulb in winter,
secretly rnultiplying under the frozen crust.

PAULINE PLUMMER
A Hole Like That, 1994

FAREWELL

from **Never Can Say Goodbye**
(with apologies to Gloria Gaynor)

Farewell to Ironopolis
And both the Hartlepoolii
And windy Ashington which is
More ultima than Thule.

Farewell O Bowes Museum
Where Woolworths meets Versailles,
And Barrow of the dank hotels
Where poets go to die,

And O farewell the nuclear coast
Whose rain resembles rain:
Spectacular diseases
Are flagging down the train.

Farewell secret Bellingham,
The capital of nowhere –
Nowhere, since it never seems
Quite possible to go there.

Adieu to cloud-capped Alston,
You boreal Andorra,
To Consett where the air is crisp
And nights are like Gomorrah.

Fair Sunderland! Your gothic
Chasm has the Wear in,
Deep enough to urinate
A conurbation's beer in.

Washington, where folks get lost
And are not even pissed!
It's taken me this long to grasp
That you do not exist.

(I shouldn't mock, since where I live
Is bookless Forest Hall,
And there, as many have remarked,
No bugger lives at all.)

Since Gateshead leaves me speechless
With its Leningradic scale,
Let's linger in the Coffin Bar
And move beyond the pale...

SEAN O'BRIEN
Ghost Train, 1995 | *Collected Poems*, 2012

Bonny at Morn

The sheep's in the meadow, the kye's in the corn
Thou's ower lang in thy bed, bonny at morn
The sheep's in the meadow, the kye's in the corn
Thou's ower lang in thy bed, bonny at morn
Canny at neet, bonny at morn
Thou's ower lang in thy bed, bonny at morn.

The bird's in the nest, the trout's in the burn
Thou hinders thy mother at many's the turn
The bird's in the nest, the trout's in the burn
Thou hinders thy mother at many's the turn
Canny at neet, bonny at morn
Thou's ower lang in thy bed, bonny at morn.

We're all laid idle, with keeping the bairn
The lad winna work, and the lass winna lairn
We're all laid idle with keeping the bairn
The lad winna work, and the lass winna lairn
Canny at neet, bonny at morn
Thou's ower lang in thy bed, bonny at morn.

TRADITIONAL
Rhymes of Northern Bards, 1812

ACKNOWLEDGEMENTS

The poems and song lyrics in this anthology are reprinted from the following books or other sources, all by permission of the publishers listed unless stated otherwise. Thanks are due to all copyright holders stated below for their kind permission.

Anna Adams: 'The Wild Life on Newcastle Town Moor' from *Open Doors: Selected Poems*, ed. John Killick (Shoestring Press, 2014). **Fleur Adcock:** 'Hotspur' and 'Street Song' from *Poems 1960-2000* (Bloodaxe Books, 2000). **Gillian Allnutt:** 'At the Friary in Alnmouth', 'About Benwell', 'After the Blaydon Races', 'Arvo Pärt in Concert, Durham Cathedral, November 1998' and 'The Singing Pylons' from *How the Bicycle Shone: New & Selected Poems* (Bloodaxe Books, 2007). **Maureen Almond:** 'The Works' and 'Boro Babe' from *The Works* (Biscuit Publishing, 2004). **Peter Armstrong:** 'Borderers' from *Risings* (Enitharmon Press, 1988); 'Among the Villages' from *The Red-funnelled Boat* (Picador, 1998) and 'Bellingham', 'Between Lord's Shaw and Pit Houses' and 'A695 Hymn' from *The Capital of Nowhere* (Picador, 2003), all by permission of Macmillan Publishers Ltd; 'Between Greenhead and Sewingshields' from *The Book of Ogham* (Shoestring Press, 2012). **W.H. Auden:** 'Roman Wall Blues', extract from *New Year Letter* and 'The Watershed' from *Collected Poems*, ed. Edward Mendelson (Faber & Faber, 1976); 'The Old Lead-mine', 'Rookhope (Weardale, Summer 1922)', 'Allendale', 'The Engine House', 'The Pumping Engine', 'Lead's the Best' from *Juvenilia: Poems 1922-1928*, ed. Katherine Bucknell (Princeton University Press, 1994; expanded paperback edition, 2003); all by permission of the publishers and Curtis Brown Ltd.

R.V. Bailey: 'Druridge Bay' and 'Whitley Bay' from *Marking Time* (Peterloo Poets, 2004), by permission of the author. **Lindsay Balderson:** 'High Force to Low Force' from *Stripping the Blackthorn* (Vane Women Press, 2008), by permission of the author. **Paul Batchelor:** 'Butterwell' from *The Sinking Road* (Bloodaxe Books, 2008). **Bob Beagrie:** 'Cook, The Bridge and the Big Man' from *Huginn and Muninn* (Biscuit Publishing, 2002) and 'Occasion for Keeping Shtum' from *Glass Characters* (Red Squirrel Press, 2011), by permission of the author. **Billy Bell:** 'Winter on the Carter Fell' and 'An Old Shepherd's Adventure at Bellingham' from *Redesdale Roadman, Border Bard*, ed. Susan Ellingham (Bellingham Heritage Centre. 2013). **Peter Bennet:** 'Hareshaw Linn' and 'Duddo Stones' from *All the Real* (Flambard Press, 1994), by permission of the author. **Michael Blackburn:** 'The North Sea at Tynemouth' from *The Prophecy of Christos* (Jackson's Arm, 1992), by permission of the author. **Robyn Bolam:** 'Hyem', 'Moving On' and 'Where Home Started' from *Hyem* (Bloodaxe Books, 2017). **Lilian Bowes Lyon:** 'The Glittering North', 'Allendale Dog' and 'A Rough Walk Home' from *Collected Poems* (Jonathan Cape, 1948), by permission of the Random House Group Ltd. **Basil Bunting:** extracts from *Briggflatts*, 'The Complaint of the Morpethshire Farmer', 'Stones trip Coquetburn…' and 'What the Chairman Told Tom' from *Complete Poems* (Bloodaxe Books, 2000).

Jake Campbell: 'A184 Hymn' (previously unpublished) and 'On Not Finding Bede' (first published in *The Fat Damsel*) by permission of the author. **Jen Campbell:** 'Treading Water', 'The Angel', 'Angel Metal' and 'Cross-hatch' from *The Hungry Ghost Festival* (The Rialto, 2012), by permission of the author. **John Challis:** 'Gift of the Gab' from from *Steps in Time* app (NCLA, 2017), by permission of the author. **George Charlton:** 'A Return to Newcastle', 'Gateshead Grammar' and 'Sea Coal' from *Nightshift Workers* (Bloodaxe Books, 1989). **Kayo Chingonyi:** 'Baltic Mill' from *Kumukanda* (Chatto & Windus, 2017), by permission of the Random House Group Ltd. **Brendan Cleary:** 'Newcastle Is Benidorm' from *goin' down slow: selected poems 1985-2010* (tall-lighthouse, 2010), by permission of the author. **Jo Colley:** 'Boro Girl' from *Weeping for the Lovely Phantom*s (Salt Publishing, 2007) and 'Peg Powler' from *Bones of Birds* (Smokestack Books, 2015), by permission of the author. **Terry Conway**: lyrics to 'Fareweel Regality' from *Songs from the North of England* by Terry Conway and Liz Law with Julie-Ann Morrison (Stonehouse Music, 2014), by permission of Liz Law. **David Constantine**: 'But with a history of ECT...' and 'The Pitman's Garden' from *Collected Poems* (Bloodaxe Books, 2004). **Andy Croft**: 'Sunlight and Heat' from *Comrade Laughter* (Flambard Press, 2004), extract from *Great North* (Iron Press, 2001) and 'Redcar Sands' from *Nowhere Special* (Flambard Press, 1996), by permission of the author. **J.S. Cunningham**: 'North' from *The Powers That Be* (Oriel Press, 1969), by permission of the author's estate.

Julia Darling: 'Satsumas', 'A Short Manifesto for My City', 'Old Jezzy' and 'Newcastle Is Lesbos' from *Incredible, Miraculous: The Collected Poems of Julia Darling*, ed. Bev Robinson (Arc Publications, 2015). **Fred D'Aguiar**: 'Sonnets from Whitley Bay' from *British Subjects* (Bloodaxe Books, 1993), by permission of the author. **Richard Dawson**: 'The Ghost of a Tree' from *The Glass Trunk* (Richie's Own Label, 2013), lyrics licensed courtesy of Domino Publishing Co. Ltd. **Christy Ducker**: 'How Mackie Did the Drowning, Plashetts', from *Skipper* (Smith|Doorstop Books, 2015).

Lauris Edmond: 'At Bywell' from *New and Selected Poems* (Bloodaxe Books/Oxford University Press, NZ, 1992), by permission of the Lauris Edmond Estate. **Alistair Elliot**: 'After Heavenfield' and 'Talking to Bede' from *My Country: Collected Poems* (Carcanet Press, 1989), by permission of the author; 'Deposition' from *Telling the Stones* (Shoestring Press, 2017), by permission of the author and publisher.

U.A. Fanthorpe: 'Tyneside in December' and 'Caedmon's song' from *New & Collected Poems* (Enitharmon Press, 2010), by permission of the estate of U.A. Fanthorpe. **Linda France**: 'Acknowledged Land' and 'The Spur in the Dish' from *The Gentleness of the Very Tall* (Bloodaxe Books, 1994), by permission of the author. **Cynthia Fuller**: 'Esh Winning' and 'Lost Landscape' from *Only a Small Boat* (Flambard Press, 2001), 'Deerness Valley' from *Background Music* (Flambard Press, 2009) and 'St Cuthbert on Inner Farne' from *Estuary* (Red Squirrel Press, 2015), by permission of the author.

Vin Garbutt: lyrics to 'John North' from *Eston California* (Topic Records, 1977) and *The Vin Garbutt Songbook, Volume One* (Home Roots Music, 2003), first recorded by the Teesside Fettlers on *Ring of Iron* (Traditional Sound Recordings, 1974), by permission of the late Vin Garbutt. **Roger Garfitt**: 'The Hooded Gods' from *Selected Poems* (Carcanet Press, 2000). **Eddie Gibbons**: 'Earl Morning, West Hartlepool, 1943', from *The Evergreen: A New Season in the North*, Vol. 2, ed. Sean Bradley & Elizabeth Elliott (Edinburgh; The Word Bank, Edinburgh, 2015), by permission of the author. **Wilfrid Gibson**: 'Devilswater', 'Dunstanborough', 'Fallowfield Fell', 'Fire', 'Hareshaw', 'Hareshaw Linn', 'Lindisfarne', 'Mother and Maid', 'Sundaysight' and 'The Cheviot' from *Collected Poems 1905-1925* (Macmillan, 1926); 'Chesterholm' and 'On Cawfields Crag' from *The Golden Room and Other Poems* (Macmillan, 1928); 'The Ponies' from *Fuel* (Macmillan, 1934); 'Cleveland Night' from *Coming and Going* (Oxford University Press, 1938); 'In Hexham Abbey' from *The Alert* (Oxford University Press, 1941); 'The Coast-Watch' from *Challenger* (Oxford University Press, 1942); and 'The Abbey Tower' and 'The Watch on the Wall' from *The Searchlights* (Oxford University Press, 1943), all by permission of Judy Greenway, trustee of the Wilfrid Gibson Estate. **J.C. Grant**: 'A Camp in Chopwell Woods', from *Plough and Coble* (Oriel Press, 1967), estate not traced. **Bill Griffiths**: The Box-Eggs' and 'The Strike' from *The Coal World: Murton Tales Reworked as Dialect Verse*, from *Collected Poems Volume 3 (1992-96)* (Reality Street, 2016).

Johnny Handle: lyrics to 'Jack Crawford' from *Down In Me Own Backyard* (2003) by permission of the author and Mawson and (Music) Ltd. **Tony Harrison**: 'Newcastle Is Peru', 'Durham', 'Divisions', 'Stately Home' and 'The Earthen Lot' from *Collected Poems* (Viking Penguin, 2007), by permission of the author. **Peter Hebden**: 'Thin Riddle' from

Steps in Time app (NCLA, 2017), by permission of the author. **W.N. Herbert**: 'Bede's World' from *Cabaret McGonagall* (Bloodaxe Books, 1996), 'The Entry of Don Quixote into Newcastle upon Tyne' and 'Song of the Longboat Boys' from *The Big Bumper Book of Troy* (Bloodaxe Books, 2002), 'The Hoppings' and 'Zamyatin in Heaton' from *Bad Shaman Blues* (Bloodaxe Books, 2006), and 'The Blazing Grater, *or*, The Olympic Torch Passes Through Tyneside' from *Omnesia: alternative text* (Bloodaxe Books, 2013). **Anne Hine**: 'Low Force' from *Incidentals* (Cinnamon Press, 2017), by permission of the author. **Gordon Hodgeon**: 'Potato Sellers – Cleveland' from *A Hole Like That*, ed. Mark Robinson (Scratch, 1994) and 'North Tees Epiphany' from *Still Life* (Smokestack Books, 2012). **Vincenza Holland**: 'The Harbourmaster's Daughter' (previously unpublished) by permission of the author. **Matthew Hollis**: 'Causeway', first published in *The Guardian* (2015), by permission of the author. **Frances Horovitz**: 'Poem found at Chester's Museum, Hadrian's Wall', 'Rain – Birdoswald', 'Vindolanda – January', 'Brigomaglos, a Christian speaks' and 'The Crooked Glen' from *Collected Poems* (Bloodaxe Books, 1985). **Alan Hull**: 'Fog on the Tyne': words and music by Alan Hull © 1971, reproduced by permission of Charisma Publishing Co. Ltd/EMI, London W1F 9LD.

Esther Jansma: 'AD 128' from *What It Is: Selected Poems*, translated from the Dutch by Francis R. Jones (Bloodaxe Books, 2008). **Joan Johnston**: 'On Falling Up Dog Leap Stairs' from *An Overtaking* (Red Squirrel Press, 2016).

Richard Kell: 'Traditions' and 'Cutty Sark Race, 1986' from *Collected Poems 1962-1993* (Lagan Press, 2001). **Tom Kelly**: 'The Time Office, 1965' and 'The Wrong Jarrow' from *The Time Office: New & Selected Poems* (Red Squirrel Press, 2012), and 'Monument' from *Spelk* (Red Squirrel Press, 2016), by permission of the author. **Kathleen Kenny**: 'Grainger Market' from *Firesprung* (Red Squirrel Press, 2008), by permission of the author. **James Kirkup**: 'View from the North East' from *The Drowned Sailor* (Grey Walls Press, 1947); 'View from the Town Hall, South Shields' from *The Submerged Village and Other Poems* (Oxford University Press, 1951); 'Tyne Ferry: Night' and 'The Harbour: Tynemouth' from *A Correct Compassion and Other Poems* (Oxford University Press, 1952); 'Spring in the Public Gardens', 'Durham Seen from the Train', 'Balloons in Sunrise', 'Penshaw Pastoral' and 'Two Haiku' from *To the Ancestral North* (Ashahi Press, 1983); 'The Town Where I Was Born' and 'Tyneside, 1936' from *Throwback: poems towards an autobiography* (Rockingham Press, 1992); 'Marsden Rock', 'The Knocker-up', 'South Shields Town Hall in Snow', 'The Old Library, Ocean Road, South Shields' and 'The Old Clothes Stall, South Shields Market' from *Home Thoughts* (Red Squirrel Press, 2011); by permission of the James Kirkup Collection at South Tyneside Libraries. **Pru Kitching**: 'Killhope' from *All Aboard the Moving Staircase* (Vane Women Press, 2004) and 'What's It Like Up There?' from *The Kraków Egg* (Arrowhead Press, 2009), by permission of the author. **Mark Knopfler**: 'Down to the Waterline' from *Dire Straits* by Dire Straits (Vertigo / Warner Bros, 1978) and 'Tunnel of Love' from *Making Movies* by Dire Straits (Vertigo / Warner Bros Records, 1980); lyrics reproduced by kind permission of Straitjacket Songs Limited and Universal Music Publishing Group, all rights reserved. **Ron Knowles**: 'Where in This Wind' from *Wearmouth 1300 Festival* (1974), author not traced.

Philip Larkin: 'Show Saturday' from *The Complete Poems of Philip Larkin* (Faber & Faber, 2012). **S.J. Litherland**: 'Durham in February' from *Composition in White* (Smokestack Books, 2017), by permission of the author. **Pippa Little**: 'The Cheviots', 'Alicia Unthank's Ark', 'The Robsons Gone' and 'Truce Day' from *Foray: Border Reiver Women* (Biscuit Publishing, 2009), by permission of the author; 'Seacoaling' from *Overwintering* (Carcanet Press/Oxford Poets, 2012). **Dorothy Long**: 'Road' from *No Random Loving* (Vane Women Press, 2013); **Michael Longley**: 'Grace Darling' from *Collected Poems* (Jonathan Cape, 2006), by permission of the Random House Group Ltd. **Marilyn Longstaff**: 'Darlington', first published on the Vane Women website in April 2001, by permission of the author.

Bernadette McAloon: 'Mistress of the Crown' from *Steps in Time* app (NCLA, 2017), by permission of the author. **Barry MacSweeney**: 'No Buses to Damascus', 'Cushy Number' and 'I Looked Down on a Child Today' from *Wolf Tongue: Selected Poems 1965-2000* (Bloodaxe Books, 2003). **William Martin**: 'A19 Hymn' from *Cracknrigg* (Taxus Press, 1983) and 'Wiramutha Helix' from *Hinny Beata* (Taxus Press, 1987) by permission of the estate of William Martin, and 'His Bright Silver', 'Song of the Cotia Lass', 'Song' and 'Durham Beatitude' from *Lammas Alanna* (Bloodaxe Books, 2000), by permission of the publisher. **Pat Maycroft**: 'Cockfield Fell in Winter' from *Northern Grit* (Vane Women Press, 2002), by permission of the author. **Peter Mortimer**: 'View' from *A Rainbow in its Throat* (Flambard Press, 1993), by permission of the author.

Jimmy Nail: lyrics to 'Big River' from *Big River* (Warner Music, 1995), by permission of the author and Imagem Music. **Norman Nicholson**: 'Caedmon' from *Collected Poems*, ed. Neil Curry (Faber & Faber, 1994), by permission of the author's estate.

Sean O'Brien: extract from 'Never Can Say Goodbye' and 'Fantasia on a Theme of James Wright' from *Collected Poems* (Picador, 2012), by permission of Macmillan Publishers Ltd.

Ellen Phethean: 'Bacchantes' and 'The West End' from *Breath* (Flambard Press, 2009; Red Squirrel Press, 2014), by permission of the author. **Tom Pickard**: 'The Devil's Destroying Angel Exploded', 'Gateshead', 'Ship 1431', 'What Maks Makems' and 'The Raw' from *hoyoot: Collected Poems and Songs* (Carcanet Press, 2014). **Pauline Plummer**: 'Whorlton Lido' from *Romeo's Café* (Paranoia Press, 1992), 'Saltburn' from *A Hole Like That*, ed. Mark Robinson (Scratch, 1994) and 'On the Gare at Night' from *Bint* (Red Squirrel Press, 2011), by permission of the author. **Keith Porritt**: 'Smelter' from *Smelter: Poetry from the Tees Valley*, ed. Cynthia Fuller & Kevin Cadwallender (Mudfog Books, 2003), by permission of the author's estate. **Katrina Porteous**: 'Charlie Douglas' and 'The Marks t' Gan By' from *The Lost Music* (Bloodaxe Books, 1996); 'This Far and No Further', 'Borderers', extract from 'Tweed', 'Holy Island Arch', 'A Short History of Bamburgh', 'Stinky', extract from 'Dunstanburgh', 'Alnmouth', 'Durham Cathedral' and 'The Pigeon Men' from *Two Countries* (Bloodaxe Books. 2014). **Jock Purdon**: lyrics to 'The Easington Explosion' from *Pitwork, Politics & Poetry: The Songs & Poems of a Durham Coalminer* (Pit Lamp Press, Chester-le-Street, 1981), estate not traced. **Rodney Pybus**: 'Routing Linn, Northumberland' and 'Bridging Loans' from *Bridging Loans* (Chatto & Windus, 1976); 'Salvaging', 'The Side', 'Passed By' and 'Down the Town' from *At the Stone Junction* (Northern House, 1978) and *Cicadas in Their Summers* (Carcanet Press, 1988), all by permission of the author; '"Our Friends in the North"' from *Darkness Inside Out* (Carcanet Press, 2012) by permission of the publisher.

Kathleen Raine: 'Northumbrian Sequence' from *The Collected Poems of Kathleen Raine* (Golgonooza Press, 2000), by permission of the literary estate of Kathleen Raine. **Angela Readman**: 'Acklam Rainbow', 'Easterside '59 and 'Easterside '89' from *Sex with Elvis* (Biscuit Publishing, 2005), by permission of the author. **Fred Reed**: 'Bamburgh Wind', 'Brazen Faces', 'Northumborland (1)', 'Northumborland (2)', 'The Pit Heap' and 'Springan' from *The Northumborman: The dialect poetry of Fred Reed* (Iron Press, 1999), by permission of the author's estate. **Gareth Reeves**: 'Stone Relief, Housesteads' from *To Hell with Paradise: New and Selected Poems* (Carcanet Press, 2012). **Michael Roberts**: 'H.M.S. Hero' and 'Temperance Festival: Town Moor, Newcastle' from *Orion Marches* (Faber & Faber, 1939), by permission of the literary estate of Michael Roberts. **Mark Robinson**: 'Angel of the North', 'Durham Cathedral', 'Dalton Park/Murton', 'Teesdale, Thornaby', 'Dockside Road, South Bank' and 'Teesport, Redcar' from *The Dunno Elegies* in *How I Learned to Sing* (Smokestack Books, 2013). **Stevie Ronnie**: 'Rebuilding the West' from *The Thing To Do When You Are Not In Love* (Red Squirrel Press, 2008), by permission of the author. **Carol Rumens**: 'Jarrow' from *Poems 1968-2004* (Bloodaxe Books, 2004), by permission of the author. **Anne Ryland**: 'Midsummer Night, Berwick' from *The*

Unmothering Class (Arrowhead Press, 2011), by permission of the author.
Francis Scarfe: 'Trawlers' and 'Miners' from *Forty Poems and Ballads* (Fortune Press (1941); 'Tyne Dock' and 'The Grotto' from *Underworlds* (William Heinemann, 1950), 'In Memoriam' from *Stand*, vol. 26 no. 3 (1985); and 'Tyne Dock Revisited' and 'The Knocker-up', previously unpublished, by permission of the literary estate of Francis Scarfe. **John Seed**: extracts from *Brandon Pithouse: Recollections of the Durham Coalfield* (Smokestack Books, 2016), by permission of the author. **Jon Silkin**: 'Killhope Wheel, 1860, County Durham', 'Strike' and 'Spade' from *Complete Poems*, ed. Jon Glover & Kathryn Jenner (Carcanet Press, 2015). **Colin Simms**: 'Out Northumberland, Out!' from *Bewcastle and Other Poems for Basil Bunting* (Vertiz, USA, 1996); five poems from *Hen Harrier Poems* (Shearsman Books, 2015) and 'High Fells April 2011' from *Goshawk Poems* (Shearsman Books, 2017) by permission of the author and publisher. **Anne Stevenson**: 'Jarrow', 'Forgotten of the Foot' and 'Salter's Gate' from *Poems 1955-2005* (Bloodaxe Books, 2005). **Sting**: lyrics to 'Island of Souls' from *The Soul Cages* (A&M Records, 1991), written and composed by Sting, © Steerpike (Overseas) Limited; 'Island of Souls', words and music by Gordon Sumner, reproduced by permission of EMI Music Publishing Limited, London W1F 9LD. **Paul Summers**: 'acknowledged land' from *Union* (Smokestack Books, 2011), by permission of the author.

A.E. Tomlinson: 'Furnaces' from *Candour: First Poems* (Elkin Mathews, 1922), estate not traced. **Helen Tookey**: 'At Tynemouth', first published in 2015 on the blogs of New Writing North (Read Regional) and Carcanet Press, by permission of the author.

Andrew Waterhouse: 'Making the Book' from 'Good News from a Small Island' from *2nd* (The Rialto, 2002) by permission of the publisher and the author's estate. **Mike Wilkin**: 'Cullercoats' from *Mugs Rite* (The Bay Press, 1996), first published as a Poetry Card (1994) by The Northern Press Gang, illustrated by Jyl Friggens, by permission of the author's estate. Andy Willoughby: 'The Cold Steel' from *Tough* (Smokestack Books, 2005) and extract from *Between Stations* (Smokestack Books, 2015). **Heidi Williamson**: 'River Wear, Durham' from *The Reader* (Winter 2016), by permission of the author. **Anna Woodford**: 'Two Up Two Down' from *Birdhouse* (Salt Publishing, 2010), by permission of the author.

Every effort has been made to trace copyright holders of the poems published in this book. The editor and publisher apologise if any material has been included without permission or without the appropriate acknowledgement, and would be glad to be told of anyone who has not been consulted.

Index of writers

n = note on or mention of a writer included in this anthology

Anna Adams 279-80
Fleur Adcock 16*n*, 33*n*, 35*n*, 121-26, 289
Mark Akenside 15*n*, 20-22*n*, 47-48, 48*n*
Gillian Allnutt 36*n*, 184, 322-23, 420-22, 454-55
Maureen Almond 37*n*, 40*n*, 503, 510-11
Anonymous 142, 192, 290, 380-81, 419-20, 483
James Armstrong 207-09, 209*n*, 227-28
Peter Armstrong 34*n*, 35*n*, 89-90, 127, 216, 226-27, 418*n*, 453, 454
Tommy Armstrong 15*n*, 432-35, 434-35*n*
Neil Astley 15-17, 33-38
W.H. Auden 15*n*, 16*n*, 45-46, 64, 64*n*, 237, 241-47, 246-47*n*, 283, 479
R.V. Bailey 184, 360-61
Lindsay Balderson 480
Paul Batchelor 187-88
Bob Beagrie 37*n*, 38*n*, 40*n*, 41*n*, 506-08
Bede 18*n*, 91-92, 92-93*n*, 95*n*, 106-10*n*, 111-12*n*, 326*n*, 359*n*
Billy Bell 205-07, 206-07*n*, 220-22
Peter Bennet 36*n*, 149, 219
Michael Blackburn 36*n*, 352
Robyn Bolam 132-34, 275-77, 309
Lilian Bowes Lyon 47, 237-38, 239-41, 241*n*
William Lisle Bowles 349
Basil Bunting 28*n*, 34*n*, 35*n*, 38-39, 52-61, 60-61*n*, 185-86, 213-14, 229-30*n*, 413*n*
Richard Caddel 16*n*, 33*n*, 34*n*
Caedmon 15*n*, 18*n*, 91-93, 93*n*, 94*n*
Jake Campbell 113, 418, 453*n*
Jen Campbell 314-15, 339-40, 379
Lewis Carroll (Charles Dodgson) 27*n*, 383-85, 385*n*
John Challis 288-89
George Charlton 35*n*, 191*n*, 275, 337-38, 460
Edward Chicken 22*n*, 317-22, 322*n*
Kayo Chingonyi 314
Brendan Cleary 36*n*, 265
John Cleveland 256-60, 259-60*n*, 260*n*
Terry Conway 234*n*, 235
Jo Colley 41*n*, 506, 511
David Constantine 16*n*, 35*n*, 429-30
Andy Croft 17*n*, 29*n*, 30-32, 37*n*, 38*n*, 40-42, 326-27, 495-99, 514
J.S. Cunningham 458-59
John Cunningham 22*n*, 271-72, 272*n*
Julia Darling 36*n*, 266-67, 277-79

Fred D'Aguiar 16*n*, 33*n*, 355-58
Richard Dawson 451-53, 453*n*
Christy Ducker 228-29
Lauris Edmond 236-37
Alistair Elliot 15*n*, 34*n*, 89, 106-10, 181-82, 191*n*
U.A. Fanthorpe 16*n*, 34*n*, 93, 359
Linda France 132, 151-58, 158*n*
Cynthia Fuller 36*n*, 38*n*, 164-65, 455-58
Vin Garbutt 14, 15*n*
Roger Garfitt 16*n*, 34*n*, 74-75
Eddie Gibbons 468
Wilfrid Gibson 27*n*, 28*n*, 66-68, 142, 162, 176, 217-18, 231-32, 232-33*n*, 233-34, 236, 349-50, 435-36, 493, 494
J.C. Grant 449-50
Dora Greenwell 446-49, 448-49*n*
Bill Griffiths 461-64
Johnny Handle 225*n*, 409-10
Tony Harrison 33*n*, 159, 191, 260-64, 284-85, 423-25
Peter Hebden 290-91
James Henry 193-95, 195*n*
W.N. Herbert 34*n*, 111-12, 268-70, 330
Anne Hine 481
Gordon Hodgeon 40*n*, 486-87, 514-15
Vincenza Holland 147-48
Matthew Hollis 164
Frances Horovitz 16*n*, 34*n*, 69-73, 73*n*
John Horsley 483-85
Alan Hull 297-98
Robert Hunter 212
Esther Jansma 76
Joan Johnston 292
Francis R. Jones 76
Ben Jonson 290*n*
Richard Kell 36*n*, 283, 328-30
Tom Kelly 114-16
Kathleen Kenny 286-88
Rudyard Kipling 65, 66*n*
James Kirkup 28*n*, 34*n*, 300-01, 341-42, 350-51, 363-64, 370-71, 371*n*, 372-79, 408-09, 425, 450
Pru Kitching 250-51
Mark Knopfler 16*n*, 294-95, 361-62
Ron Knowles 411
Philip Larkin 16*n*, 223-25, 224-25*n*
S.J. Litherland 428
Pippa Little 37*n*, 128-31, 190-91, 460*n*

523

Dorothy Long 252
Michael Longley 16*n*, 172
Marilyn Longstaff 17*n*, 40*n*, 485-86
Bernadette McAloon 295-96
Thomas Babington Macaulay 474
Angus Macpherson 15*n*, 30*n*, 31*n*, 489-92, 492*n*
Barry MacSweeney 33*n*, 253-54, 312-13, 313*n*
William Martin 34*n*, 386-408, 408*n*, 414-17, 418*n*, 422, 453*n*
Pat Maycroft 481-82
Peter Mortimer 34*n*, 353-54
Jimmy Nail 16*n*, 299-300
Norman Nicholson 94
Sean O'Brien 34*n*, 35*n*, 331, 516-17
Ellen Phethean 266, 315-16
Tom Pickard 33*n*, 38-39*n*, 209-11, 310-11, 336-37, 411-13, 413*n*
Pauline Plummer 40*n*, 41*n*, 482-83, 513, 515
Keith Porritt 500-02
Katrina Porteous 16*n*, 77-88, 134-37, 145-46, 163, 167-68, 172-75, 177-81, 181*n*, 182-83, 426, 467-68
Jock Purdon 466-67
Rodney Pybus 15*n*, 17*n*, 18-29, 149-51, 273-74, 292-94, 301-09,
Kathleen Raine 74*n*, 95-102, 95*n*, 103-04*n*
Angela Readman 37*n*, 508-10
Fred Reed 18*n*, 33*n*, 62-63, 63*n*, 138, 168, 188-90, 212-13, 286
Gareth Reeves 36*n*, 75
Geordie Ridley 323-24, 324*n*
Michael Roberts 103*n*, 280-82, 282*n*, 341
Mark Robinson 17*n*, 38*n*, 40*n*, 41*n*, 338-39, 426-27, 487-88, 504, 505

Stevie Ronnie 316-17
Robert Roxby 23-24*n*, 202-05
Carol Rumens 16*n*, 34*n*, 95*n*, 105
Anne Ryland 148
Francis Scarfe 28*n*, 342, 343, 365-70, 367*n*
Sir Walter Scott 121*n*, 159-62, 468-73, 473*n*
John Seed 436-42
Jon Silkin 33*n*, 35*n*, 247-50
Colin Simms 35*n*, 214-16, 229-30, 254-55
Joseph Skipsey 15*n*, 26-27*n*, 34*n*, 195-201, 201*n*
'Son of Reed': see Robert Roxby
Anne Stevenson 34*n*, 36*n*, 95*n*, 104-05, 443-45
Sting 16*n*, 344-45
Paul Summers 36*n*, 158
Algernon Charles Swinburne 15*n*, 27*n*, 49-50, 50-52*n*, 138-39, 139-41, 169-71, 346-48
A.E. Tomlinson 15*n*, 492-93, 493*n*
Helen Tookey 352-53
Traditional 117-21, 143, 185, 230, 296, 297, 348, 431, 517
Andrew Waterhouse 165-67
Richard Watson 15*n*, 475-78, 478*n*
William Watson 343-44
Mike Wilkin 354
Heidi Williamson 428-29
Andy Willoughby 17*n*, 41*n*, 500, 512
Joe Wilson 335-36, 336*n*
John Mackay Wilson 143-44, 144*n*
Thomas Wilson 22*n*, 24-26*n*, 332-35, 334-35*n*
Anna Woodford 464
Andrew Young 479-80, 480*n*

Index of places

in North East (or nearby) named in poems or notes

Acklam 508
Allendale 225, 234, 237-38, 246, 253-54, 313
Allenheads 225
Aln (river) 160
Alnmouth 182-83, 184, 188-90
Alnwick 122, 181, 450
Alston 246, 516
Ancroft 143
Arkengarthdale 470
Ashington 63, 187
Balder (river) 471

Bamburgh 117, 121, 160, 167-68, 171, 174, 293
Bardon Mill 241
Barmoor 143
Barnard Castle 469, 472, 478, 495
Beadnell 172-75
Belling Hill 229
Bellingham 207, 208, 214, 220-27, 246, 516
Benwell 317-23
Berrington 143
Berwick 122, 126, 143, 144, 147, 148, 150, 480

Bewcastle 230
Birdoswald 70, 74
Birtley 431
Black Heddon 209
Blackburn Common 215
Blackhall 441, 458
Blackhills Dene 468
Blackton 476
Blanchland 225, 246, 253
Blaydon 216, 260, 286, 323-26
Bloodybush Edge 232
Blyth 26, 160
Boldon Hill 401-03, 418
Bolts Law 46
Bowes 472, 516
Bowlees 475
Bowsden (Bowisdon) 143
Brancepeth Castle 348
Brandon 436-42
Brandon Walls 246
Brigflatts [sic] 60
Brignall 473
Broomlee Lough 67
Broomside Colliery 437
Brusleton 470
Buckton 143
Burdon 404
Burnhope 235, 438
Butterwell 187-88
Byker 267, 281, 282
Byrness 204, 206
Bywell 236-37
Caldwell 379
Cambo 48
Camboglanna 73, 74
Capheaton 27, 50-51
Carrawburgh 74
Carter Bar 138, 205-06, 225
Cashwell 242-43, 245
Castle Leazes 122, 126
Cauldron Snout 45, 475, 495, 499
Cawfields 66, 77, 85
Coalburn 158
Chapelgarth 407
Chatton 143
Cherry Knowle 399
Chesterholm 67
Chester-le-Street 162, 167, 451, 467
Chesters 69, 74
Cheviot(s) 129, 142, 143, 149, 159, 181, 214
Chillingham 159
Chilton 441
Chollerford 89

Choppington 201
Chopwell
Clara Vale 453
Cleadon Hills 379
Cleveland 30-32, 40-42, 489, 492-96, 512-15
Cockfield Fell 481-82
Coldberry 476
Consett 432, 445, 449, 516
Coatham Marshes 512
Corbridge 66, 225
Coquet Island 160, 184
Coquetdale 57, 135, 202-03, 212-14
Cornthwaite Park 385
Cotia (Nova Scotia Pit), *see* Harraton Colliery
Cow Green 479, 495
Cowpen 201
Crag Lough 79
Croft-on-Tees 385
Cronkley 475
Cross Fell 475, 495, 499
Cullercoats 353-54, 362
Cut Throat Dene 418
Dalton Park 465-66
Dargues Hope 215
Darlington 272, 290, 385, 483-86, 487
Deepdale 471
Deerness Valley 457-58
Derwent (river) 449-50
Devilswater 233
Dipton 433
Dipton Mill 233, 235
Dod Law 154, 214
Doddington 143, 214
Dog Leap Stairs 278, 291, 292, 294, 304
Druridge Bay 184
Duddo 149, 158
Dunstanburgh 160, 176, 177-81, 181-82
Durham 19-21, 24, 33-37, 61, 107, 162, 224, 241, 246, 247, 301, 310, 326, 355, 394, 400, 419-30, 435, 445, 448, 450, 459, 462, 465, 473, 485, 487
Durham, Co. 27, 103, 431-68, 496
Easington 422, 441, 442, 466-67
East Flass 457
East Nook 210
Easterside 509-10
Eglingham 158, 214
Egglesburn 476
Eggleshope, Little 478
Egglestone (Eglistone) 471
Eildon 135
Elemore 386

Elsdon 138, 209, 214
Elwick 143
Elswick 66, 266, 287, 303
Emmanuel Head 162
Esh Winning 386, 455-57
Eston 14, 512
Fallowfield Fell 236
Falstone 229
Farne Islands 164-65, 167, 171, 422
Fatfield 392
Felling 418
Felton 185
Ferryhill 451
Fir Tree 252
Flodden Field 162
Ford Castle 162
Forest Hall 517
Frenchman's Bay 369
Fulwell Mill 396
Gainford 473
Garrigill 246
Garsdale 54
Gateshead 25-26, 201, 314, 325, 327, 332-40, 517
Gilsland 162
Gilmanscar 470
Grainger Market 286-88, 288-89
Greenhurth (Greenearth) Mine 243, 479
Greenhead 89
Greenside 453
Greenwell Ford 448
Greta (river) 471, 472, 473
Greystead 61, 230
Grindon (Northumberland) 143
Hadrian's Wall 45, 64-90, 225, 246, 247, 269, 473
Hag House 457
Hallypike 67
Hamsterley 252
Hanging Stone 452
Hardberry Hill 475, 478
Hare Holme 457
Harehope 251
Hareshaw 207, 218
Hareshaw Linn 218, 219, 228
Harperley Banks 252
Harraton Colliery (Cotia) 389-90, 392, 406, 467
Hartlepool 468, 516
Hartley: *see* New Hartley
Harton 326, 379
Hastings Hill 394, 406
Hastings Pit 392

Haswell 440
Haughton Castle 230
Hawes 54
Hawkhope 227, 234
Haydon Bridge 216, 224-25
Heathery Hill 215
Heaton 330
Heavenfield 89
Hebburn 326, 440
Hedgehope 58, 142
Hedgeley 181
Hedley Hill 452
Hendon 407
Herdship Fell 479
Herrington 438
Hetton-le-Hole 386
Heworth 418, 440
Hexham 45, 207, 231-32, 247
Hexhamshire 61, 235
High Force 475, 480, 499
Holwick 475, 478
Holy Island of Lindisfarne 143, 159-66, 172, 233, 240, 270, 326, 420, 422, 505
Holystone 212
Homildon Hill 126
Hope House 393, 406
Horden 441, 467-68
Hough Foot 404
Houghton 470
Houghton-le-Spring 466
Housesteads 74, 75
Howick 143
Howley 399
Hudeshope 476
Hylton Castle 395, 406
Irthinghead 228
Jarrow 91, 104-16, 281, 326
Jesmond 278, 282, 303, 330
Kelloe 386
Kelton Fell 470
Kibblesworth 452
Kielder 141, 209, 215, 227-30
Killhope 247-51
Kirkwhelpington 209
Kyloe 143
Kyo Bog 452
Lambton Hetton & Joicey Colliery 386, 407
Lambton Castle 381
Lanchester 448
Langleeford 162
Langley Castle 225
Langley Park 443-45
Laygate 379

Liddesdale 135
Lindisfarne: see Holy Island
Little Harle 209
Lodge Syke 477
Longbenton 282
Longstone 50, 167, 171
Lordenshaw 154
Lord's Shaw 216
Low Fell 334-35
Low Force (Little Force) 475, 478, 480, 481
Low Newton-by-the-Sea 174, 175-76
Lowick 143
Lunedale 60, 470
Lynemouth 190-91, 460*n*
Manorgill 477
Marsden 369-71, 379
Matfen 209
Meldon 475
Melkridge 130
Mickle Fell 475
Mickleton 476
Middle Haining 399
Middlesbrough 30-32, 37, 40-41, 489-511, 516
Middleton-in-Teesdale 476, 478
Monkwearmouth 92, 159, 397, 406, 408
Morden Tower 61, 313, 413
Morpeth 48, 185, 201, 225, 234
Morpethshire 185-86
Mortham Tower 473
Mowbray Park 385, 410
Murton 461-66
Nack Fields 399
Netherton 187
Nettles Lane 399
New Hartley 193-98
Newbiggin (Teesdale) 478
Newbiggin-by-the-Sea 103, 191
Newcastle 17, 19-24, 27, 33-39, 40, 60-61, 117, 122, 126, 143, 201, 211, 224-25, 247, 256-331, 336, 450, 453
North Shields 269, 325, 363
North Tyne 61, 135, 208, 214-27
Northumberland 49, 63, 68, 122, 130, 138, 141, 142-201, 212, 229-30, 232, 234, 246, 270, 434
Oakley Colliery 434
Old Bewick 154
Otterburn 117-21, 121n, 123-26, 138, 211
Ovingham 448
Palmersville 331
Pans Bank 407
Paradise Street, Horden 468

Pennywell 395, 407
Penshaw (Pensher) 381, 392, 400, 406, 408
Percy Main 201
Peterlee 459
Pit Houses 215, 216
Pity Me 458
Plashetts 228, 229
Queen's Crag 79
Rawthey (river) 52, 53, 56, 60
Redcar 505, 514
Rede (Reed) (river) 202, 203, 207, 227, 228
Redesdale 57, 121, 135, 202-07, 218, 222
Redeswire 117, 121
Ridley Hall 241
Ridley Shiel 215
Rokeby 162, 468-73
Roker 385, 407
Rookhope 46, 242, 246, 473
Ross Sands 35
Roughting Linn 149, 155, 158
Rowley 457
Rowley Burn 235
St John's Chapel 224-25
Saltburn 512, 515
Salterfen 398
Salter's Gate 445-46
Samphire Batts 507
Satley 445
Scargill 473
Scot's Gap 246
Scotswood 60, 276, 309, 317, 324
Seaburn 385
Seaham 191, 404, 458, 460, 462
Seahouses 181
Seaton Burn 187
Seaton Delaval 160, 192
Seghill 192
Sewingshields 77-79, 83, 85-88, 89, 228
Shaftwell 478
Sharpley 404
Shotley Bridge 434
Silksworth 393, 406, 407, 408
Simonsides 60
Skerne (river) 484
Sneep, The 215
Sockburn (Sockum) 385, 495
Spittal 143
Souter Point 113
South Bank 504
South Gare 513
South Medomsley 432-33
South Shields 107, 326, 362-79
Southwick 385

527

Spanish City, 361-62
Sparty Lea 253, 313
Spennymoor 32
Spindlestone 167
Staindrop 471
Stainmore 55, 470
Stanhope 473
Stanley 435
Star Gate 453
Stockton 485, 487, 495
Stonygate 399, 400
Sundaysight 214-15
Sunderland 34, 35, 385-413, 516
Sweethope 135
Tanfield 434
Tarret (river) 215
Tarset 61, 214, 215
Team Valley 338
Tees (river) 14, 15, 45, 51, 147, 247, 255, 327, 469, 470, 473, 474, 475-78, 480, 485, 486, 496, 497, 503, 507, 512
Teesdale 469-88
Teesport 505, 513
Teesside 29, 30-32, 40-42, 496, 514
Teviotdale 57, 135, 137
Thorn Hill 391-92, 395, 398, 405-06
Thornaby 487
Thornberry Gill 478
Thornley 252, 438
Thristley Bank 399
Thornaby 487-88
Thorsgill 471
Throckley 60-61
Thurston 339
Till (river) 50, 57, 58, 139, 142, 153
Tilmouth 161
Tod Law 203
Toller Hill 472
Tow Law 452
Trimdon 225, 386, 434
Trow Rocks 379
Tunstall Hills (Maiden Paps) 392, 406, 407
Tweed (river) 57, 136, 142, 143-44, 145-46
Tweedmouth 143, 144, 349-52
Tyne (river) 14, 15, 45, 48, 50, 51, 104, 115, 133, 139, 141, 153, 218, 225, 228, 230, 232, 236, 268, 275, 277, 295-99, 301-07, 309, 314, 327, 328-30, 341, 342, 343, 353, 363, 367, 370, 473, 487,
Tyne Dock 366-68, 373, 379
Tynedale 216, 234, 311
Tynemouth 51, 106, 160, 201, 269, 325, 329, 349-53, 360, 385
Tyneside 66, 260, 267, 300, 325, 336, 346, 356, 359, 377, 453
Ushaw 449
Vindolanda 67, 71
Vinegar Hill 399
Wallington Hall 51, 132, 474
Wallsend 66, 277, 325, 330, 341, 344-45
Wansbeck (river) 48, 50, 141, 160, 207, 208
Warden Law 405, 406
Wardley 418
Wardon Law (Wardilaw) 162
Warkworth 122, 160
Warren House 468
Washington 61, 516
Wear (river) 14, 15, 45, 106, 109, 162, 247, 251, 255, 296, 327, 380-81, 412, 419, 423, 428, 455, 473, 478, 516
Weardale 225, 242, 246-52
Wearmouth: *see* Monkwearmouth
Wearside 380-418
West Hartlepool 468, 516
West Moor 331
Westoe 107, 326, 379
Whiskershiel 210
Whitburn 113, 385, 402
Whitemare Pool 418
Whiteside 468
Whitley Bay 147, 325, 355-62
Whitley Chapel 61
Whitley Mill 235
Whorlton Lido 482-83
Widdrington 160, 187
Wilds O' Wanney 207-09, 228
Winston 473
Wiregill 478
Witton-le-Wear 252
Wolsingham 252
Wooler 202-03
Wrekendyke 418
Wylam 61
Yarrow 136
Yarm 495
Yeavering Bell 154